Handicap in a Social World

Handicap in a Social World

A Reader edited by
Ann Brechin, Penny Liddiard
and John Swain
at The Open University

HODDER AND STOUGHTON

in association with
The Open University Press

British Library Cataloguing in Publication Data

Handicap in a social world.
  1. Physically handicapped
  I. Brechin, Ann   II. Liddiard, Penny
  III. Swain, John
  362.4   HV30

ISBN 0-340-27625-8

Selection and editorial material
copyright © The Open University 1981
First printed 1981. Reprinted 1983, 1986, 1988

Printed in Great Britain for Hodder and Stoughton Educational, a
division of Hodder and Stoughton Ltd, Mill Road, Dunton Green,
Sevenoaks, Kent TN132YD by Richard Clay Ltd, Bungay, Suffolk

Contents

Section 3   Professional Support

Acknowledgements

This book forms an integral part of an Open University course, *The Handicapped Person in the Community*[1]. It is one of two texts[2] that have been especially produced for the course, and therefore has drawn upon a wide variety of support and help in its initial stages. While the editors must be held responsible for the final collation and selection of material in the book many of the items were initially selected and recommended by both members of the Open University academic course team responsible for the writing of the course and the writing consultants. We gratefully acknowledge therefore, the collaboration of the following people:

Course Team

Vic Finkelstein, Mary Croxen, Ann Pointon

Consultants

Roger Blunden, Vida Carver, Brian Fraser, David Hall, Mike Oliver, Leon Polnay, Sue Reville, Andrew Sackville, Jonathon Seagrave

In the final stages of preparation we have also received valuable help, and special thanks must go to: Roger Lubbock and John Taylor, of the OU Publishing Division, Lesley Phelps and Stephanie O'Halloran for their secretarial assistance and finally Jean Robertson for her invaluable administrative support in the compilation of the final manuscript.

1 Further information about this course may be obtained by writing to the following address: Associate Student Office, The Open University, PO Box 76, Milton Keynes, MK7 6AN.
2 The second 'Look at it this way: New Perspectives in Rehabilitation' by Ann Brechin and Penny Liddiard is also published by Hodder and Stoughton. 1981.

General Introduction

The *Handicapped Person in the Community* course, which was first presented at the Open University in 1975, has recently been completely revised and rewritten in the light of the changes which have been taking place in the field of handicap. This book accompanies the new course and is designed for anyone whose personal involvement or work brings them into contact with disability. This may include social workers, teachers, therapists, doctors, nurses, health visitors, members of voluntary associations, and disabled people and their families. The general aims of this Reader and the new course are the same: to familiarise the reader/student with the radical changes that have occurred in the prospects for a better quality of life for disabled people and to relate these to the changes we can expect from professionals, voluntary workers and the general public if this potential is to be realised. In this General Introduction we hope to draw your attention to one or two of the ideas which you will find reflected and extended throughout the Reader.

Why has this change in prospects for disabled people occurred? A full historical analysis has yet to be undertaken, but a number of factors seem evident. Certainly general changes in our society have had implications for disabled people, particularly with the more recent advances in technology. For example, it has become increasingly *possible* to employ the most severely disabled people. In our welfare state, the emergence of professional groups and changes in legislation have also played a part, with the improvement of facilities, financial circumstances and services available to disabled people.

In what ways might the 'quality of life' for disabled people be changing? First, change involves a re-examination of the assumptions underlying approaches to understanding disability and helping disabled people. Perhaps the most fundamental questions challenge the assumption that the life-style and experiences of disabled people can be explained in terms of the mental and physical attributes of the individual. Essentially, alternative definitions of 'disability' focus on the restrictions that disabled people face in a particular combination of socially determined circumstances, that is in 'a social world'. Negative social attitudes and expectations can result not only in prejudice, but also in the development of disabling social systems and environments. Thus, for example, social isolation, lowered educational expectations in segregated schools, constraints on job opportunities, inaccessible public and private buildings, and financial hardship can all be seen as socially determined factors which selectively disable particular sections of the population.

Change in 'quality of life' does not lie simply in the provision of more and better services and in improved professional skills. The strongest impetus to change comes from disabled people themselves, as they increasingly organise together in the struggle for changes in society. Radical change, then, involves the rejection of the notion that disabled people are helpless and dependent and of the pattern of interaction in which one side, 'the helper', gives, and the other side, 'the helped', receives. *Choice* is crucial to improved quality of life, in the form of greater control for disabled people over the processes and decision-making which shape their lives.

To reflect our broad aims, the papers selected for this reader are drawn from a wide range of published material from both sides of the Atlantic, and a number of previously unpublished articles have been included. The book comprises four sections. In order to re-examine previously held assumptions and existing attitudes it is necessary first to understand the nature of the social world as it exists at the moment. Sections 1 and 2 together take this as their central theme and examine in detail the segregation of disabled people from an essentially able-bodied society. The general theoretical papers in Section 1 give an overview of 'The Disabled Relationship', setting disability firmly in a social and historical context. Section 2, 'Styles of Living', examines in detail the experiences of disabled individuals. The articles in this section focus upon the disabling effects of the social and physical barriers that have been created by the social world.

The third and fourth sections of the book look at ways forward and the means by which this potential for change and full integration may be realised. Section 3, 'Professional Support', looks mainly at the role professional help and services play in this process and examines how the relationship between the professional helper and the disabled individual may be changing. Section 4, 'Integrated Living', looks at different ways forward by examining large scale changes that can be made by agencies that are not necessarily professional. The role that disabled people themselves play in this process is a key concept in this closing section of the book. The papers selected for this Reader present new concepts and raise controversial issues that we hope will have a positive effect on the changing roles of disabled people in both today's and tomorrow's society.

N.B. Editorial Notes appear in square brackets [   ]

SECTION ONE
The Disabled Relationship

The articles selected for the first section of the book examine the general social and historical context of disability. The first paper (1) by Safilios-Rothschild, focuses upon the position of disabled people in modern society. Arguing that disabled people can be viewed collectively as a disadvantaged minority group (similar in some respects to 'blacks' or 'women') the author goes on to discuss the implications this has for rehabilitation in terms of the advocated 'consumer participation' model. The article by Kurtz (2) adopts a similar perspective but focuses primarily on the role of mentally handicapped as opposed to physically impaired people. Briefly, this author reviews the different ways 'mentally handicapped people' have been classified by society, usually along with 'the infirm, the illiterate and the aged'. The third article in this group turns the focus from the disabled individuals to those who professionally try to 'help' them. Here, in a slightly more complex argument, McKnight (3) examines the disabling effects of such professionalised help as it has developed within today's modern service based economies.

Disability then is seen increasingly as a socially defined problem. It seems to be society that is disabling people rather than the individual's 'condition'. The root cause of disability seems to be in the social relationships which have evolved in an able-bodied world and which take little or no account of disabled people. If this is so, it should be possible to show that other social groups can become 'disabled' too. Finkelstein, in the light-hearted article that comes next (4), does just this, and examines how the able-bodied can become disabled if we turn the world as we know it upside down. The article that follows by Farber and Royce (5) also takes us into a world of make believe and asks us to listen to an account of a futuristic experiment where the 'social and biological bases of intellectual disability have been eradicated'. The results of this experiment are disappointing and the authors of this article are forced to draw a much less optimistic conclusion than Finkelstein in his 'upside down' world. The article by Wolff (6) redresses the balance towards optimisim. With his concept of 'tools for living' and his advocacy of an updated system of provision of aids, the future for the elderly disabled looks promising.

Can a complete theory be offered in which disability is defined as a social phenomenon with its root causes in the organisation and structure of society itself? The final articles in this section attempt to do just this. The first, by Oliver (7), focuses upon family life and continues the themes of disablement by outside agencies by examining the disabling effects of certain theoretical approaches and academic disciplines. Particularly critical of psychological perspective, Oliver puts forward as an alternative a more broadly sociological approach. The second paper by Finkelstein (8) also adopts a sociological approach and traces the changing faces of disability through the course of modern social history. In this paper the author brings out the complexities and ambiguities of the disabled relationship in relation to the way western capitalist societies organise their production and reproduction. Firmly attributing 'disability' to socially caused phenomena this article brings disability firmly into the political arena – an arena to which we shall be returning, particularly in the final section of the book.

1 Disabled Persons' Self-Definitions and Their Implications for Rehabilitation

Constantina Safilios-Rothschild

The Disabled as a Minority Group

Disabled people can be conceptualized as a disadvantaged or minority group because they have a great deal in common with the old, blacks, women, the poor, and other minorities in that they are treated and reacted to as a category of people. They also share with other minority groups the fact that up to now there has been very little direct information concerning their self-definitions. The main reason for this similarity is the popular notion that disability, physical or mental (as well as old age, poverty, the female gender, or blackness of skin color), entails biological inferiority. Therefore, the disabled person is often considered to be less intelligent, less able to make the 'right' decisions, less 'realistic,' less logical, and less able to determine his own life than a nondisabled person.

There is an acknowledged paucity of direct information concerning the feelings, wishes, and self-definitions of underprivileged minority groups. Yet, without gathering sufficient direct information from their target populations, professionals assume the authority to decide the fate of underprivileged persons. Furthermore, a professional in one specific area often makes important decisions about individuals in areas in which he may have no greater legitimate knowledge and expertise (and often less) than those about whom he makes the decisions (Orzack, 1969; Haug and Sussman, 1969).

In the case of the disabled, just as is true for all other underprivileged groups, different professionals connected with rehabilitation define the self-concepts, goals, and inner motivations of disabled persons and determine their 'real' wishes and potential. They often do so either without asking the individuals about their problems, preferred solutions, and alternatives or by openly disregarding all information received from the disabled persons themselves about desirable goals and solutions (Safilios-Rothschild, 1970: 141–152 and 216–249).

When the disabled formulate innovative plans, solutions, and alternatives, such plans are usually labeled 'unrealistic' by the rehabilitation experts regardless of their degree of functionality for the disabled person, especially when the plans and alternatives do not conform to the stereotyped

This paper profited considerably from the comments of Bernard Kutner and Julius Roth.

Source: ALBRECHT, G. L. (ed.) (1976) *The Sociology of Physical Disability and Rehabilitation.* Pittsburgh: University of Pittsburgh Press, pp. 39–56 (extracts).

role of the disabled and the stereotyped sex-appropriate roles. In fact, as Julius Roth has pointed out, 'what is commonly considered realistic by professional experts is that [social] construction which helps to enhance their own rewards and their control over other people.'[1] Therefore, the goals and solutions arrived at by the experts often serve to keep the disabled within the constraints of the inferior and dependent role reserved for the disabled as a category and to discourage any significant deviations from it.

When professionals deal with individuals in this way, the disabled persons' endorsement of the official, desirable 'line,' in other words the 'acceptance' of their disability, deprives them of their most important right to self-determination and seriously reduces their options in all life sectors. [. . .].

A disabled social scientist has reacted to the restrictive disabled role as follows: 'The lingering notion [persists] that [the disableds'] range of interests and awareness is extremely limited. . . . We hear, for example, references to the "role" or the "place" of disabled persons in society, as though there were only one role for them to play, or one place for them to be' (Race, 1972a).[2]

Even in the occupational life sector in which disabled persons have been permitted and encouraged to participate actively, they are in fact allowed only a few restricted options characterized by low prestige, pay, and advancement possibilities. Only these few occupational options are officially sponsored and available to the disabled when they accept the institutional definition of themselves, despite the fact that in many, if not most, cases their disability does not objectively disqualify them from a vast array of jobs and occupations. Even in the case of the mentally retarded, many more occupations than necessary are barred (Truzzi, 1968; Orzack, 1969).

One very important and striking similarity between the rationales used to explain the restrictive nature of the feminine role and of the disabled role is the fact that, in both cases, a wide range of options are precluded 'for the sake of' the individuals in question, in order to protect them. Thus, women often are not permitted to be competitive or aggressive or to achieve successful or powerful positions because their innate sweet, 'feminine' personalities could not withstand the stress and strain that accompany high achievement and power (Safilios-Rothschild, 1974). Similarly, the disabled are cut off from most prestigious and well-paying jobs, as well as from a wide range of interpersonal relations with nondisabled persons, because they are considered to be physically fragile and mentally incapable of functioning at the appropriate level. They, too, are protected from unbearable stress and strain and unquestionable failure. Disability, like female gender, becomes all-important and all-permeating, overshadowing other abilities, talents, and characteristics. The disabled and women are judged solely on the basis of their disability or their female gender and, as a result, are automatically categorized as second-class citizens with very limited chances for self-determination (Kerr, 1970; Wolff, 1972).

There is, however, an important difference between the noncongenitally disabled on the one hand and women and blacks on the other, a difference with considerable conceptual and practical implications. Those who become disabled when they are teenagers or adults have experienced at least for some years the majority status of nondisabled persons.[3] They have been socialized into the majority status of an able-bodied person and into the prejudiced attitudes toward the disabled. Since the success of rehabilitation has been equated with the 'acceptance of the disability,' that is, with the relinquishing of majority status rights, rehabilitation entails a highly stressful resocialization process into an 'inferior' status. Only the congenitally disabled share with women and blacks the fact that they are socialized into a minority status from infancy.[4]

Minority group socialization of a large number of disabled explains the great emphasis placed on 'acceptance' of the disability, that is, on relinquishing the self-determination and choice of alternatives that are rights of the able-bodied majority. While it is very difficult to give up important majority rights, there are strong negative sanctions against deviant behaviour. The physically disabled individual is considered deviant by the 'experts' if he expresses unwillingness to give up the rights of the able-bodied. Most often, the sanction is severe and clear-cut: no access to rehabilitation facilities, at least those supported by means of societal subsidies, until the disabled role is accepted (Safilios-Rothschild, 1970). [. . .]

The Disabled as a Social Movement

Until now, the disabled, like other minorities during stages of oppression, have had low self-esteem and 'have been reticent to speak out on behalf of their own . . . cause' (Race, 1972a). This can be explained on the basis of several convergent conditions:

1. The stereotyped beliefs about the limited mental and physical capacities of the disabled and the inferior status assigned to them have had a considerably negative effect on the self-confidence and self-esteem of the disabled. This result is partly due to internalization of stereotyped beliefs by the disabled and partly due to widespread sets of social-structural barriers. The disabled, unable to generate sufficient self-esteem and self-confidence, could not effectively question, demand and protest (Race, 1972b).

2. There has been a hostile and unaccepting atmosphere for the disabled, in which their words, wishes, and plans have been scrutinized, questioned, doubted, and finally rejected as inappropriate and unrealistic. In order to stand up for their rights, needs, preferences, and potentials under these conditions, the disabled had to possess special interpersonal skills as well as a high degree of self-confidence and a clear definition of their own goals. Many, if not most, of the disabled did not possess such skills and confidence.

3. Disabled persons often have unclear, fluctuating, and occasionally contradictory self-definitions and goals, partly because of their experience of the disability. Furthermore, most disabled persons are subject to alienating conditions from the time that they incur the disabling illness or accident, especially if their disability is compensable. They are exposed to the often contradictory advice, plans, and goals imposed upon them by a variety of professionals, societal agents, as well as by family members and significant others with very different interests and motivations. Under such conflictful circumstances, some of the disabled may in fact become alienated in all senses of the term, submitting to the dictates of the most powerful expert as a function of their feelings of meaninglessness and powerlessness in the situation.

4. The very few 'token' cases of exceptionally intelligent and talented disabled persons who were allowed to succeed in the 'majority world' have had to play the 'majority game' as well as or even better than the majority group members. That is, they had to adhere, at least verbally and officially, to the stereotyped disabled role and were flattered to believe that their 'extraordinary' achievement was the result of special, unusual skills, abilities, and conditions that could not be generalized to all disabled persons. Thus, the few successful disabled people were psychologically and structurally isolated and alienated from the larger body of disabled persons so that they never became representatives and spokesmen for the disabled (Safilios-Rothschild, 1974).

During the last few years, however, disabled persons with high social status and educational attainments not only have refused the stereotyped disabled role and minority status but also have successfully set and realized their own conditions and expectations. They have verbalized and written protests against and critical analyses of the status quo of rehabilitation.[5] This development is significant because it satisfies one of the important conditions for the creation of a social movement of the disabled: the willingness of the elite members among the disabled to identify with the mass of disabled, to protest against undesirable aspects of their common experiences, and to fight along with all the disabled against discriminatory practices in order to broaden the range of options available to them. The growth of this leadership, the occurrence of public hearings on rehabilitation held by informed parties,[6] sporadic protest marches and demonstrations like the six-mile march and Capitol rally demanding 'civil rights for the handicapped' (Martin, 1972), and a two-week hunger strike by a protesting disabled woman in Paris,[7] all are promising signs of a developing social movement. [. . .]

The nature of the Self-Definitions and Their Implications for Rehabilitation

The new awareness among disabled persons, especially among the well-educated, high-status disabled, has produced some eloquent biographical statements. For example, a social scientist disabled since early adolescence has critically analyzed his experience and described his self-definition as follows:

Unfortunately, those people whose task was to rehabilitate me had also made certain assumptions about me and the world I was to inhabit after I left the home [rehabilitation facility]. The assumption about me was simple: I should be grateful for whatever existence I could scrape together. After all, there had been a time when my life itself had been forfeit and, compared to many of my peers in the ward, I was relatively functional. About the world, the assumption was equally simple— although here, perhaps, less forgivable. Society existed. Whatever it meted out to the cripple, the cripple accepted. The way of the world was not to be challenged. . . .

Once [the disabled] has accepted being pigeonholed by society, he finds that he is safe as long as he is willing to live within the boundaries of his categorization. . . . He is expected to behave in such-and-such a way; he is expected to react in the following manner to the following stimulus. . . . He reacts as he is expected to react because he does not really accept the idea that he can react in any other way. Once he accepts, however unconsciously, the images of self that his society presents to him, then the guidelines for his behavior are clearcut and consistent. (Kriegel, 1969)

The following self-definition of a disabled professional nurse also speaks quite eloquently, this time with the voice of protest:

After much thought I began to understand why I felt insulted and angry at the request to 'accept your disability.' Acceptance implies the result of a choice with the opinion to refuse. We are not injured or diseased and handicapped by choice. Why should we be made to feel obligated to accept?

Searching, learning, and trying for the new and better come through dissatisfaction with what is, not acceptance. For lack of a better word, I use cope as a more positive term. It denotes a continuous struggle with some hope of a success on a long list titled 'I can do.'

In coping, my self-set goals are often higher than those that others would set for me. I often achieve my goals because I cannot accept the restriction of those standardised and imposed ones. But it seems strange to me that, when I succeed, I am commended for 'accepting my disability so well.' Accept my disability? Never. (Jones, 1972)

What are the implications of these self-definitions for rehabilitation, that is, what changes would have to be brought about in order to satisfy the disabled persons' conditions and requirements? [. . .]

First, rehabilitation would have to be redefined from a treatment process to a teaching experience in which the rehabilitation practioners are showing the disabled ways to cope with and control their disability and to utilize available rehabilitation resources and personnel, whenever such aid is needed. This change would be significant in that it would tend to diminish the social distance between the expert and the client through the transmission of knowledge relevant to the client's condition, treatment, and exercise of control. Furthermore, it would also help alter the rehabilitation definition and focus from aiding the disabled to become as functional as possible in a rehabilitation setting to teaching the disabled to actively cope with their disability throughout life. Two assumptions underlie this new focus: (1) The peak of rehabilitation may be reached at any time in any setting, and it is largely up to the individual to bring about the greatest rehabilitation accomplishment of which he is capable. (2) A large part of rehabilitation will take place outside institutional rehabilitation settings and facilities, and the rehabilitation practitioners will be available as consultants and resources at the disabled person's home and work settings throughout life.[8]

The new rehabilitation model assumes a completely different rehabilitation practitioner-disabled client relationship in which the professional acts as a teacher and consultant rather than as an authority figure who orders and controls the disabled. Thus, disabled individuals would enjoy a much greater degree of self-determination and be free to explore different alternative solutions and styles until they could find the one that suited them best. [. . .]

This active patient involvement would facilitate a second major change in the rehabilitation process. The expert no longer would dictate but would assist the client in structuring a series of alternative goals and plans from which he could select those most suitable to his particular set of needs. This process would use the professional as a consultant rather than as the ultimate authority on goal-setting. The right of self-determination and the ability to choose among a wide range of options would be facilitated and guaranteed to the client in a rehabilitation process that did not oblige the disabled to adhere to a packaged deal concocted by the rehabilitation experts as the condition for rehabilitation.

Regardless of whether rehabilitation occurs in the home or in the institution, training the disabled would involve explanations of the disability, estimates of anticipated pain and discomfort, and adequate information about alternative types of treatment, exercises, medications and their side effects, treatment costs, and coping mechanisms. It would be essential to offer disabled persons several alternatives that specifically addressed the individual problems of low-income persons, persons with low tolerance of pain, uneducated persons, highly educated and sophisticated persons, and those extremely preoccupied with the status of their health.

This structuring of treatment alternatives for each disabled individual would be expected to stimulate bioengineers to develop new equipment and techniques to meet individual needs (Safilios-Rothschild and Yehia, 1972). Rehabilitation practitioners would have to keep up to date with the available technological innovations that could help the disabled avail themselves of more options. Requiring that all possible therapies and equipment be presented to all persons with the same type of disability might encourage and stimulate evaluation research on differential treatment effectiveness.

A third important change in the concept of rehabilitation would involve the self-definitions of disabled persons. The question raised is, How are the disabled different from the nondisabled? Many of the distinctions are based on artificial societal barriers. Breaking down these barriers would facilitate and enrich the lives of the nondisabled as well as the disabled. A striking example is the required abolition of architectural barriers from all buildings (residential, educational, recreational, and commercial), cities, and roads – from the entire environment. The institutionalization of barrier-free cities, buildings, roads, and inside and outside environments would make life easier for and many more options accessible to not only the disabled but also pregnant women, infants, persons pushing baby carriages or pulling grocery carts, old people, and individuals with broken legs (Martin and Psomopoulos, 1972). The tearing down of social and architectural barriers would, then, improve the mobility potential of considerable numbers of nondisabled people while increasing the mobility potential of the disabled themselves. [. . .]

Finally, the most crucial change in rehabilitation increasingly demanded by the disabled is not only their more active involvement in rehabilitation decision-making but their actual control of the decision-making process. This latter change would involve a significant shift of power from the hands of the professionals to the consumers themselves. This is greatly resisted by the professionals, who frequently attribute negative and dangerous revolutionary overtones to the desire for such a shift. The reluctance of the rehabilitation professionals, as of all professionals, to relinquish their extensive power and control over the lives of their clients cannot be easily broken. [. . .]

Disabled persons' noncontrolling involvement and participation in rehabilitation have been attempted by means of milieu therapy, different models of patient government, and ward advisory boards. Advisory boards made up of disabled people, the consumers, can be effective only when they have voting power on the board of directors and when the disabled representatives who vote have sufficient information and skills to understand, evaluate, and attack the issues at hand. Otherwise, powerless advisory boards and uninformed, unskilled representatives can be easily manipulated, coopted, and used as 'rubber stamps' for professionals' decisions (Thursz, 1969).

Of course, the only 'consumer participation' model that would give the disabled control over their fates would include their option to organize the rehabilitation facilities they need and to choose rehabilitation practitioners who are sensitive and attuned to disabled persons' needs, preferences, and potentials. The opportunity to organize and manage rehabilitation facilities with a great number of practitioners and consultants would not only create new, responsible, and prestigious careers for qualified disabled persons, but would also eventually greatly improve the degree of communication and understanding between practitioners and disabled (Thursz, 1969). Furthermore, the fact that the disabled would be holding the purse strings might greatly increase the practitioners' sensitivity to the needs of the disabled and thus improve the quality of rehabilitation care. [. . .]

Notes

1 From Julius Roth's initial comments on this essay.
2 One is struck with the similarity of attitudes toward the disabled and women. Witness the many conferences, discussions, speeches, and books on the 'role,' and in earlier years on the place, of women in society. Like the disabled, women have had to accept and adjust to a stereotyped role if they were to receive the approval of men and the rewards men were controlling. This 'feminine' role, like the 'disabled' role, was restrictive in that it allowed women very few options, namely only the less desirable, less prestigious, more tedious and time-consuming ones (Safilios-Rothschild, 1974).
3 The noncongenitally disabled share with the old this particular characteristic.
4 In the case of the poor, both models are possible, although socialization into the minority status from birth is the most usual process.
5 See also the articles by Wilfred B. Race, who is Director of Programme Services of the Canadian Rehabilitation Council for the Disabled.
6 In Detroit, for example, disabled college students and other high-status citizens asked for a Common Council hearing at which they presented systematic evidence of discrimination against them. (See Don Lenhausen, 'Handicapped Cite Bias,' *Detroit Free Press*, September 9, 1973.) In New York City, different groups of well-educated and militant disabled persons are becoming organized for political action. (See P. L. Montgomery, 'Five Groups of the Disabled Plan City-wide Alliance, *The New York Times*, June 19, 1972.)
7 For an account of the very recent French protest movement of the disabled, see Bernard Guetta, 'Le marché noir des handicapés,' *Le Nouvel Observateur*, no. 448 (June 9–17, 1973).
8 Bernard Kutner has discussed an ongoing experimental program in which the disabled are bused into a rehabilitation center for necessary treatment but live at home. Some programs include specific 'role therapy' for the practitioners to help them emerge from their encrusted professional roles. Through this therapy, clients are also encouraged to assume active roles in the rehabilitation process. These various treatment arrangements could help change the nature of the interaction between practitioners and disabled.

References

GUETTA, B. (1973) 'Le marché noir des handicapés.' *Le Nouvel Observateur*, No. 448, June 9–17.

HAUG, M., and SUSSMAN, M. B. (1969) 'Professional autonomy and the revolt of the client.' *Social Problems, 17,* 153–61.

JONES, J. S. (1972) 'Accept my disability? Never.' Letter published in *American Journal of Nursing, 72,* 1412–15.

KERR, N. (1970) 'Self expectations for disabled persons: Helpful or harmful?' *Rehabilitation Counseling Bulletin, 14,* 85–94.

KRIEGEL, L. (1969) 'Uncle Tom and Tiny Tim: Some reflections on the cripple as Negro.' *The American Scholar, 38,* 412–30.

LENHAUSEN, D. (1973) 'Handicapped cite bias.' *Detroit Free Press*, September 9.

MARTIN, J. (1972) 'Why not straighten out an up-and-down world?' *Washington Post,* December.

MARTIN, J., and PSOMOPOULOS, P. (1972) 'Human disability and human settlements.' Paper presented at the Twelfth World Congress of Rehabilitation International, Sydney, Australia, August 27–September 1.

MONTGOMERY, P. L. (1972) 'Five groups of the disabled plan city-wide alliance.' *The New York Times*, June 19.

ORZACK, L. H. (1969) 'Social changes, minorities, and the mentally retarded.' *Mental Retardation, 5,* 2–6.

RACE, W. B. (1972a) 'Social action.' Proceedings preview – Twelfth World Congress of Rehabilitation International, Sydney, Australia, August 27–September 1, pp. 221–3.

RACE, W. B. (1972b) 'The roles of the disabled.' Paper presented at the International Seminar on Social Planning for the Disabled, Brisbane, Australia, August 20–24.

SAFILIOS-ROTHSCHILD, C. (1970) *The Sociology and Social Psychology of Disability and Rehabilitation.* New York: Random House.

SAFILIOS-ROTHSCHILD, C. (1974) *Women and Social Policy.* Englewood Cliffs, N. J.: Prentice-Hall.

SAFILIOS-ROTHSCHILD, C., and YEHIA, M. A. (1972) 'The social implications of new bioengineering technology for the handicapped.' Proceedings preview – Twelfth World Congress of Rehabilitation International, Sydney, Australia, August 27–September 1, pp. 215–20.

THURSZ, D. (1969) *Consumer Involvement in Rehabilitation.* National Citizens Conference on Rehabilitation of the Disabled and Disadvantaged, Washington, D.C.: U.S. Department of Health, Education and Welfare, Social and Rehabilitation Service.

TRUZZI, M. (1968) 'Lilliputians' Land: The Social Role of the Dwarf.' in M. Truzzi (ed.) *Sociology of Everyday Life*, pp. 197–211. Englewood Cliffs, N. J.: Prentice-Hall.

WILLIAMS, J. I. (1971) 'Disease as illness.' *Social Science and Medicine, 5,* 219–26.

WOLFF, I. S. (1972) 'Acceptance.' *American Journal of Nursing, 72,* 1412–15.

2 The Sociological Approach to Mental Retardation

Richard A. Kurtz

[. . .]

The Retarded in Society

Social systems are composed of individuals who are incumbents of statuses and are playing roles. Some of these status-roles are specific and limited, affecting only a relatively narrow area of a person's interaction, while others are so generalized and broad that they touch virtually all the person's other social associations. Guskin (1963) observes that the mentally retarded are expected to play a generalizing and all-encompassing role [cf. Hughes' (1945) concept of a 'master status'] which emphasizes significant functional inabilities, e.g., the inability to hold a job, to take care of personal needs, to control sexual and aggressive impulses, and to behave in a usual or normal pattern. Given such generality, it would be expected that those with whom the retarded person has contact will take the retardation into account in all phases of interaction. Acting like a retarded person can become 'second nature' and can dominate behavior patterns. Recognizing the reactions of others as responses to retardation, the person may make an attempt (conscious, unconscious, or both) to play the role of a retarded individual, thus conforming to social expectations. At any given time for any given individual it may not be possible to differentiate between behavior that is a consequence of the retardation and behavior that is a consequence of behaving as one thinks the expectations of others define proper behavior. Such observations have led Guskin (1963, p. 332) to suggest that

. . . one could hypothesize nonachievement orientation, dependency behavior, and rebelliousness as patterns of behavior determined by previous and present interactions with people who have role concepts of the defective emphasizing inability, helplessness, and lack of control, respectively.

In line with this approach, Dexter (1958, 1960, 1964a, 1964b, 1967) argues that because of discrimination against low IQ in American society, the retarded are denied employment opportunities, legal rights, a fair hearing, and other opportunities which are taken for granted by others. He suggests that the discrimination takes place because the retarded have low IQs, rather than because their handicaps are actually relevant to employment, legal rights, etc. Dexter further maintains that the retarded are a creation of society, which erects barriers to those who do not fit well

---

Source: RICHARD A. KURTZ (1977) *Social Aspects of Mental Retardation*. Lexington, Mass.: Lexington Books (extracts from Chapter 1).

with the societal emphases on schooling and education. This pattern is a consequence of a changing value system in American society, which has increasingly shifted attention away from ascribed characteristics, such as family background, to achieved characteristics, such as education. With growing emphasis on schooling, education has become the key to success, and those who cannot or will not meet the requirements of the educational system are viewed as 'outsiders' who are not succeeding.

Retarded individuals who support themselves and carry on fairly normal lives despite a lack of educational accomplishment may be seen as a contradiction in a system which holds that schooling is necessary for normal achievement. This observation is consistent with the viewpoint of Sarason and Gladwin (1958) who, after reviewing a series of studies which suggest that many of the retarded actually do possess the ability to make acceptable social adjustments, indicate that the sole behavior that the retarded consistently cannot meet at an acceptable level is school performance. Furthermore (Sarason and Gladwin 1958, p. 306),

because of the hurdle of school, when we think of retardation we think of retarded *children*, and rightly so because it is only at school age that prevalence rates reach alarming proportions.

Earlier (p. 213) these same authors had stated that

. . . many children who through their final year of schooling are still labelled 'retarded' immediately thereafter merge into the 'normal' population with at least sufficient completeness no longer to be recorded statistically. The compulsory school experience may therefore be viewed for many people as in effect the most difficult intellectual hurdle which will confront them throughout their entire lives, although later in other settings they may perform tasks of substantial complexity.

Because of current emphases in this country [US], the retarded are perceived either as sick persons with medically diagnosable maladies or as individuals who have suffered from a slowdown in intellectual-personal development. These two perceptions reflect the two most important current images of the retarded: the retarded individual as a sick person and the retarded individual as a developing person. It seems fair to suggest that the first image is held by the medically oriented and the general public (Gottwald 1970; Katz 1973), while the second is held almost exclusively by educators, some psychologists, and possibly some hopeful parents.

Before the sick person and developing person perceptions became acceptable as today's brand of knowledge and belief, old wives' tales, folklore, and superstition led to a wide-ranging array of images of the mentally retarded. Previous perceptions die hard, however, and even with the growth of new understandings and more objective information about the retarded, some of the tales, folklore, and superstition still remain. However, there are many who sigh with relief when they recognize that the perceptions of several decades ago are no longer considered acceptable. Some of these can only be described as bizarre, as suggested by the image of the retarded which was presented by the superintendent of the Massachusetts State School in a speech before the Massachusetts Medical Society in 1912 (Fernald 1912, pp. 90–91):

The feeble-minded are a parasitic, predatory class, never capable of self-support or of managing their own affairs. The great majority ultimately become public charges in some form. They cause unutterable sorrow at home and are a menace and danger to the community. Feeble-minded women are almost invariably immoral, and if at large usually become carriers of venereal disease or give birth to children who are as defective as themselves.

We have only begun to understand the importance of feeble-mindedness as a factor in the causation of pauperism, crime and other social problems. Hereditary pauperism, or pauperism of two or more generations of the same family, generally means hereditary feeble-mindedness. In Massachusetts there are families who have been paupers for many generations. Some of the members were born or even conceived in the poorhouse.

Every feeble-minded person, especially the high-grade imbecile, is a potential criminal, needing only the proper environment and opportunity for the development and expression of his criminal tendencies. The unrecognized imbecile is a most dangerous element in the community.

Some Historical Perceptions and Definitions

Wolfensberger (1969) has provided a particularly helpful statement on, and discussion of, some of the more common perceptions of the past. They are of historical interest; but more than that, the reader will recognize that some of the archaic perceptions still prevail in whole or in part in contemporary society. Consistent with Wolfensberger's presentation, eight of the 'old-fashioned' images will be presented and discussed. These will be followed by a discussion of the two most significant current perceptions. Finally, an economic interpretation and the results of a literature search on non-Western societies will be presented.

The Retarded Person as a Subhuman Organism

Retarded people who have been viewed as subhuman have been described in animal-like or vegetable terms, with the implication that they lack the same type of emotional and physical needs that are assumed for normal people. Given their less-than-human condition, the retarded may be denied the full range of social resources that are implied by the term 'citizen,' which raises both philosophical (Seeley 1964) and legal (Friedman 1974) questions. Such questions tend to revolve around the denial of citizenship and human rights and privileges in such areas as guardianship, institutionalization, and education (Murdock 1972). Even granted the human condition, social and educational programs may reflect principles that are based on the behavior of lower animals, e.g., some of the current behavior modification techniques.

A question of the humanness of the retarded has become a subject of ethical, moral, and legal debate as a consequence of recent reports that in some special situations physicians have induced death by withholding treatment from severely handicapped infants (e.g., Duff and Campbell 1973). A debate has arisen, for example, on the issue of whether humanness should be defined on the basis of functioning organs or on the basis of human social behavior. Thus, Joseph Fletcher (1972) suggests that there are fifteen positive and five negative propositions which are indicators of humanness. Particularly relevant to the retarded, Fletcher states (1972, p. 1), that

any individual of the species *homo sapiens* who falls below the IQ 40-mark in a standard Stanford-Binet test, amplified if you like by other tests, is questionably a person; below the 20-mark, not a person.

The retarded are not alone as an aggregate of individuals who are perceived as subhuman. Such an image helps to explain the perceptions of teachers on an Indian reservation who are reported to have acted as if their students were without the central human invention, i.e., culture (Wax and Wax 1964); it provides a clue to some of the reasons behind attempts to change life patterns in ghetto communities without consideration being given to the desires of the inhabitants of the area (Strauss 1969); and it helps to explain the absence of health and educational resources in some of the inner cities of this country (Kurtz, Chalfant, and Kaplan 1974).

The Retarded Person as a Menace

Historically, retarded people have been considered social menaces for a variety of reasons, including a belief that unrestrained violence is a natural consequence of a strong body and a weak mind (best demonstrated by Lennie in Steinbeck's *Of Mice and Men*) and a belief that the retarded possess a remarkable potential to procreate, producing many more retarded persons. Thus, the retarded are seen as a menace in two ways: one a threat to the present society and the other a threat to future generations. Given the seriousness of such a double-menace perception, this image has led to some of the strongest historical attempts to place restraints on the retarded. An example is the several eugenic movements in the past which have called for the sterilization of all the mentally retarded (see Sarason and Doris 1969, Chapters 15 to 17). The cry for sterilization has recently been heard among professionals once again, with a call for voluntary sterilization, irrespective of whether the retardation is known to be associated with genetic factors (Reed and Reed 1965).

It should also be noted that many of the large institutions for the retarded were constructed far from centers of population during approximately the same period that the eugenic scare led to calls for sterilization. Wolfensberger (1969) ties the building of large institutions (prisonlike structures) to the image of the retarded person as a menace.

The Retarded as Objects of Pity

In this image the retarded are viewed as suffering individuals who must be pitied. As corollaries, the retarded must be sheltered against injury, and these pathetic individuals should have few demands made on them; seen as 'suffering' from their condition, the retarded are not to be held accountable for their behavior. The social response may be an attempt to bestow 'happiness' upon them, to help relieve sorrow. This perception is closely associated with several others, expecially those which define the retarded as childlike.

The Retarded Individual as an Eternal Child

An image of the retarded as eternal children suggests that they must be taken care of and must be catered to, in order to bring happiness into their lives. Consequently, adultlike demands should not be made upon them; in fact, decisions must be made for them in a planned, supervised, and simple life. Instead of expecting the retarded person to adapt to the environment, the environment must be adapted to the childlike retarded person. Such a pattern is reported among the Hutterites, who ensure an eternal-child perception by canceling the baptism of individuals found to be retarded, recognizing that they are incapable of adult behavior (Eaton and Weil 1955). In addition, according to Catholic belief, the person with a mental age of under seven is in a state of goodness and innocence, and is thus not subject to the imperfections of normal adults (Hoffman 1961). On another level, after discussing the change for eight years, in 1973 the National Association for Retarded Children changed the last word of its name to 'citizens.'

The Mentally Retarded as Burdens of Charity

Some hold the view that those who have been afflicted with such handicapping conditions as mental retardation are entitled by their humanness to the necessities of life, both instrumental and expressive. Those retarded who cannot fend for themselves and cannot take care of their basic needs are seen as entitled to societal intervention on their behalf, so they are not denied human existence.

The Retarded as Objects of Ridicule

Throughout history the retarded have been ridiculed and have been subjected to some stereotypes which portray them as comic figures. Just as the village idiot of the past was mocked, in the contemporary situation those retarded with clear physical malformations or intellectual shortcomings may be objects of ridicule. One is reminded of the hunchback of Notre Dame, whose tragedy was both physical and mental. While they sounded innocent in their time, the so-called moron jokes of a few years ago were a current rendition of this theme, and some current comedians still induce audience laughter by feigning limited intelligence.

The Retarded as Objects of Shame

In apparent shame, in some families the retarded are kept within the confines of the family residence in an attempt to hide them from outsiders. The author is familiar with one father who traced an outline of his retarded child's foot on cardboard, taking this to the store to buy a pair of shoes so that the child would not be seen in public. In some cases this perception may be a reaction to be belief that the retarded child has been 'sent' as punishment for sins.

The Retarded Person as a Holy Innocent

Occasionally, the retarded and others with handicaps have been perceived as the special children of God. Under these conditions, handicapped individuals may be judged incapable of voluntarily committing evil, and consequently they may be considered incapable of sinning (cf. Eaton and Weil 1955). In the theology of certain religious groupings, the retarded are seen as incapable of making conscious choices for evil and may, therefore, be perceived as individuals who are specially favored by God, with salvation assured (Hoffman 1961).

The Retarded Individual as a Sick Person

This seems to be the most prominent general public perception of the retarded, which is consistent with descriptions of retardation as a medical condition. There is, in fact, some evidence that this perception is becoming more and more acceptable in society. Thus, Windle (1973) reports that a 1958–1968 comparison between the designations of state residential facilities for the retarded reveals that use of the terms *schools, homes,* and *havens* has decreased while the designations *hospitals* and *centers* have increased. Especially in facilities referred to as hospitals, the administrator or superintendent is usually a medical doctor, staff members are nurses and nurse's aides, living units are referred to as wards, and the retarded are referred to as patients (e.g., MacAndrew 1973, p. 129). In such a context a hospital routine prevails, with visiting hours, admission procedures, and an emphasis on aseptic techniques.

Despite the growing importance of this designation, there are some important shortcomings in viewing the retarded as sick. Even the American Medical Association (1965) states that no specific diagnosis is possible in most cases (p. 1) and that 'cure' is not a relevant concept for the retarded (p. 64). Problems with a medical image are further demonstrated by the American Medical Association statement (p. 98) on attempts to educate physicians about mental retardation:

Any educational effort faces the built-in resistance of many physicians, both because of their pessimistic attitude toward the disease [note, however, the use of the term 'disease'] in general and because of the personal feelings of anxiety and guilt such patients may arouse.

The Retarded Individual as a Developing Person

In this perception the retarded are viewed as capable of growth, development, and learning which should be tapped. Given acceptance of such capabilities, the task becomes one of developing means by which the retarded person may be helped to utilize what has been, to this point (i.e., prior to the adoption of this perspective), wasted developmental potential. Emphasizing the modifiability of IQ test scores and the consequences of stimulation, adherents of this view have focused on manipulating the environment to make the most of the retarded person's potential for learning. There is also a corollary position that the retarded have been denied some of the rights of human beings.

Proponents often go beyond the perception per se by calling for a program of services designed to utilize untapped potential. For example, educator Kolstoe (1972, p. 208) states that

People who are mentally retarded are now being recognized as possessing the potential for leading useful, satisfying lives and contributing to the welfare of society. All that is needed to realize that potential is an intelligent program of services and training of the right kind in the right place at the right time.

Two Further Perceptions

On a much broader level, one sociologist has grouped the retarded with others in society who are also in positions of special handicap, and an anthropologist has written on the perceptions of non-Western societies. Sociologist Farber (1968) suggests that the mentally retarded have been classified by society along with the infirm, the illiterate, and the aged, all of whom lack the ability to make economic contributions to society, which makes them marginal to the workforce. Therefore, the infirm, illiterate, aged, and retarded are defined in the society as 'surplus population.' From this perspective, the retarded (p. 13)

. . . join an amorphous group that exists but has no integral role in the social organization of the society, which could easily continue to function without this surplus population. Instead, society must divert much of its energy to the maintenance of a population that is unproductive in the institutions of the economy, the family, the arts, the sciences, and the political arena.

Farber does suggest, however, that those who are surplus play some positive role since their presence contributes to society in at least three ways (p. 13):

. . . first, they generate a series of special institutions; second, they make possible the effective operation of the basic social institutions of these societies; and third, they aid in the perpetuation of the social classes.

On a broader cross-cultural level, anthropologist Edgerton (1970) has searched the literature on non-Western cultures in an attempt to identify common societal adjustments to, and perceptions of, the retarded. However, he finds it necessary to conclude his analysis with the statement (1970, p. 555) that it is necessary

. . . to call into question any notion that what is said or done about mental retardation in the world's non-Western societies is highly uniform from society to society. Quite the contrary is true. What is said and done is highly variable, so much so that, given the inadequacy of the presently available data, it is difficult to generalize about this world at all.

This statement stands in sharp contrast to the often-suggested or implied observation that nontechnologically oriented, rural, seemingly simple societies 'naturally' provide a more comfortable environment for the mentally retarded. Rather than finding any type of consistent pattern among such societies, Edgerton indicates that the environmental deterministic position, which is based upon an assumption of 'simple people for simple societies,' does not hold. [. . .]

References

AMERICAN MEDICAL ASSOCIATION. (1965) *Mental Retardation: A Handbook for the Primary Physician.* Chicago: Report of the American Medical Association Conference on Mental Retardation.

DEXTER, L. A. (1958) 'A social theory of mental deficiency.' *Am. J. Ment. Defic.,* March, *62,* 920–8.

DEXTER, L. A. (1960) 'Research on problems of mental subnormality.' *Am. J. Ment. Defic.,* March, *64,* 835–8.

DEXTER, L. A. (1964a) *The Tyranny of Schooling: An Inquiry into the Problem of 'Stupidity'.* New York: Basic Books.

DEXTER, L. A. (1964b) 'On the Politics and Sociology of Stupidity in Our Society.' In H. S. Backer (ed.) *The Other Side: Perspectives on Deviance.* Chicago: The Free Press of Glencoe.

DEXTER, L. A. (1967) 'A social structure interpretation of the history of concern about "mild" retardation.' Paper presented at the annual convention of the American Association on Mental Deficiency, Denver, Colo., May 1967.

22   *Richard Kurtz*

DUFF, R. S., and CAMPBELL, A. G. M. (1973) 'Moral and ethical dilemmas in the special-care nursery.' *New England Journal of Medicine*, 25 October, *289*, 890–4.

EATON, J., and WEIL, R. (1955) *Culture and Mental Disorders*. Chicago: The Free Press of Glencoe.

EDGERTON, R. B. (1970) 'Mental Retardation in Non-Western Societies: Toward a Cross-Cultural Perspective on Incompetence.' In H. C. Haywood (ed.) *Social-Cultural Aspects of Mental Retardation*. New York: Appleton-Century-Crofts, Inc.

FARBER, B. (1968) *Mental Retardation: Its Social Context and Social Consequence*. Boston: Houghton Mifflin Company.

FERNALD, W. E. (1912) 'The burden of feeble-mindedness.' *Journal of Psychoasthenics*, *17*, 87–111.

FLETCHER, J. (1972) 'Indicators of Humanhood: A Tentative Profile of Man.' *Hastings Center Report*, November, *2*, 1–4.

FRIEDMAN, P. (1974) *Mental Retardation and the Law: A Report on Status of Current Court Cases*. Washington: Mental Health Law Project, Office of Mental Retardation Coordination, January.

GOTTWALD, H. (1970) *Public Awareness about Mental Retardation*. Research Monograph. Reston, Va.: Council for Exceptional Children.

GUSKIN, S. (1963) 'Social Psychologies of Mental Deficiency.' In N. R. Ellis (ed.) *Handbook of Mental Deficiency*. New York: McGraw-Hill.

HOFFMAN, J. L. (1961) 'Catholicism, medicine and mental retardation.' *Practical Anthropology*, *2*, 49–53.

HUGHES, E. C. (1945) 'Dilemmas and contradictions of status.' *Am. J. Sociol.*, March, *50*, 353–9.

KATZ, E. (1973) 'The Mentally Retarded.' In D. Spiegel and P. Keith-Spiegel (eds) *Outsiders USA*. San Francisco: Rinehart Press.

KOLSTOE, O. P. (1972) *Mental Retardation: An Educational Viewpoint*. New York: Holt, Rinehart and Winston, Inc.

KURTZ, R. A., CHALFANT, H. P., and KAPLAN, K. (1974) 'Inner-city residents and health decision-makers: perceptions of health problems and solutions.' *American Journal of Public Health*, June, *64*, 612–13.

MACANDREW, C. (1973) 'The Role of "Knowledge at Hand" in the Practical Management of Institutionalised "Idiots".' In G. Tarjan, R. K. Eyman, and C. E. Meyers (eds) *Sociobehavioral Studies in Mental Retardation*. Monographs of the American Association on Mental Deficiency, No. 1, Washington, D.C.

MURDOCK, C. W. (1972) 'Civil rights of the mentally retarded: Some critical issues.' *Notre Dame Lawyer*, October, *48*, 113–90.

REED, E. W., and REED, S. C. (1965) *Mental Retardation*. Philadelphia: W. B. Saunders.

ROSS, R. T. (1972) 'Behavioral correlates of levels of intelligence.' *Am. J. Ment. Defic.*, March, *76*, 545–9.

SARASON, S. B., and DORIS, J. (1969) *Psychological Problems in Mental Deficiency*. New York: Harper & Row.

SARASON, S. B., and GLADWIN, T. (1958) 'Psychological and Cultural Problems in Mental Subnormality.' In R. L. Masland, S. B. Sarason, and T. Gladwin, *Mental Subnormality*. New York: Basic Books.

SEELEY, J. R. (1964) 'The law of the retardate and the retardation of the law.' *Mental Retardation* (The Bulletin of the Canadian Association for Retarded Children), *14*, 6–9.

STRAUSS, A. L. (1969) 'Medical organization, medical care and lower income groups.' *Social Science and Medicine*, August, 2, 143–77.

WAX, M., and WAX, R. (1964) 'Cultural deprivation as an educational ideology.' *Journal of American Indian Education*, January, 3, 15–18.

WINDLE, C. (1973) 'What's in a Name?' In G. Tarjan, R. K. Eyman, and C. E. Meyers (eds) *Sociobehavioral Studies in Mental Retardation*. Monographs of the American Association on Mental Deficiency, No. 1, Washington, D.C.

WOLFENSBERGER, W. (1969) 'The Origin and Nature of Our Institutional Models.' In *Changing Patterns in Residential Services for the Mentally Retarded*. Washington: President's Committee on Mental Retardation.

3 Professionalized Service and Disabling Help

John McKnight

The business of modern society is service. Social service in modern society is business.

This fact is reflected in the language employed. Professionals and their managers now speak of educational 'products', health 'consumers' and a legal 'industry'. Clients are defined as 'markets', and technocrats – an entirely new breed of professionals – are developing methods to 'market' services, using business accountancy systems. Computers measure and store psychological 'inputs' and family 'outputs'. There are 'units served' and 'units of service' and sophisticated economists, statisticians and planners deal with the production and consumption of social services in the same way as the production, consumption and maintenance of physical goods is accounted for. Furthermore, and this is of central importance, every modernized society, whether socialist or capitalist, is marked by the growing percentage of service in its Gross National Product, not only of services such as postal deliveries, catering, car repairs etc, but social services such as marriage guidance, birth control, counselling, education, legal arbitration, care of the young, the adult and the old in all its ramifications, and all that falls under the general heading of social help.

This stage of economic development is distinguished by its unlimited potential since service production has none of the limits imposed by goods production – limits such as natural resources, capital and land. Therefore, the social service business has endless possibilities for expansion as there seems to be no end to the needs for which services can be manufactured.

Modernized nations are therefore best defined as service economies. They are serviced societies and they are peopled with service producers and service consumers – professionals and clients.

The politics of serviced societies are gradually being clarified. Public budgets are becoming strained under the service load. Many national and local governments find themselves involved in the unprecedented politics of deciding between competing services – should we give more to education and less to medicine? Within the service sectors there are equally difficult dilemmas. Should we cut back on tax-paid abortions or should the available money be used for free 'flu vaccine?

These dilemmas are often resolved by the apolitical ideology of service. While old-fashioned politics, rooted in a goods economy, allowed a civic debate as to whether a nation needed more wheat or more steel, more automobiles or more houses, the new service politics is a debate as to whether we should have more doctors or more teachers, more lawyers or more social

---

Source: I. ILLICH *et al.* (1977) *Disabling Professions*. London: Marion Boyars.

workers. Politically the question becomes whether we should trade health for learning, or justice for family wellbeing. These choices create an impossible politics in traditional terms.

While our political traditions make it possible to decide between wheat and steel, it seems politically impossible to decide between health and education because health and education are not alternatives amenable to choices: they are services. Indeed, the allocation of services is so immune to political debate that many governments resolve the dilemma by deciding that we will have less wheat and more education, less steel and more medicine.

This is not to suggest that these choices are correct or incorrect, or even that they define appropriateness. Rather, it is to say that the apolitical nature of service is so pervasive that it is difficult for the public and policy makers to recognize that the creation and allocation of services are the central political issue in many modernized economies.

The political immunity of the services is best understood in terms of the symbolic referent of service.

Services are something one pays for.

The 'good' that is paid for is care.

Care is an act that is an expression of love. We say 'I care for her more than anyone' or 'I am taking care of my mother and father'.

Thus, *service* is to *care* which is to *love* and love is the universal, apolitical value.

Symbolically then, the apolitical nature of service depends on its association with the unlimited universality of love. Ask any servicer what is ultimately satisfying about his work and the answer will most commonly be framed in terms of wanting to care for and help people. Press on and the answer is usually that the individual 'loves people'.

Since love is not a political issue, care is not a policy question and service becomes the one business that is an unlimited, unquestionable and non-political 'good'. [. . .]

It is clear, [. . .] that the word 'care' is a potent political symbol. What is not so clear is that its use masks the political interests of servicers. This fact is further obscured by the symbolic link between care and love. The result is that the politico-economic issues of service are hidden behind the mask of love.

Behind that mask is simply the servicer, his systems, techniques and technologies – a business in need of markets, an economy seeking new growth potential, professionals in need of an income.

It is crucial that we understand that this mask of service is *not* a false face. The power of the ideology of service is demonstrated by the fact that most servicers cannot distinguish the mask from their own face. The service ideology is *not* hypocritical because hypocrisy is the false pretence of a desirable goal. The modernized servicer believes in his care and love, perhaps more than even the serviced. The mask is the face. The service ideology is *not* conspiratorial. A conspiracy is a group decision to create an exploitative result. The modernized servicer honestly joins his fellows to create a supposedly beneficial result. The masks are the faces.

In order to distinguish the mask and the face it is necessary to consider another symbol – need.

We say love is a need. Care is a need. Service is a need. Servicers meet needs. People are collections of needs. Society has needs. The economy should be organized to meet needs.

In a modernized society where the major business is service, the political reality is that the central 'need' is an adequate income for professional servicers and the economic growth they portend. The masks of love and care obscure this reality so that the public cannot recognize the professionalized interests that manufacture needs in order to rationalize a service economy. [. . .]

Removing the mask of love shows us the face of servicers who *need* income, and an economic system that *needs* growth. Within this framework, the client is less a person in need than a person who is needed. In business terms, the client is less the consumer than the raw material for the servicing system. In management terms, the client becomes both the output and the input. His essential function is to meet the needs of servicers, the servicing system and the national economy. The central political issue becomes the servicers' capacity to manufacture needs in order to expand the economy of the servicing system.

Within this analytic framework, pejoratives are inappropriate. After all, a serviced society provides an economy, a structure for social organization, and service workers motivated by the ethical values of care and love. If these service system needs are legitimate, clients can be viewed as needed, rather than in need, and we can get on with the business of researching, developing, manufacturing and marketing services without the necessity to project professional need upon citizens. We can deal in political and economic terms with the needs of servicers, freed of the apolitical mask of love.

The problem with this political resolution is political reality. Throughout modernized societies a troublesome question is being raised by the citizenry. In popular terms it is:

Why are we putting so much resource into medicine while our health is not improving?

Why are we putting so much resource into education and our children seem to be learning less?

Why are we putting so much resource into criminal justice systems and society seems less just and less secure?

Why are we putting so much more resource into mental health systems and we seem to have more mental illness?

As if these questions were not troubling enough, a new group of service system critics are asking whether we are putting more resources in and getting out the very opposite of what the system is designed to 'produce'. In medicine, this question is most clearly defined as iatrogenesis – doctor created disease. The new critics' question is not whether we get less service for more resource. Rather, it is whether we get the reverse of what the service system is supposed to 'produce'. In the terms of Ivan Illich, the question is whether the systems have become counterproductive. Do we get more sickness from more medicine? Do we get more injustice and crime with more lawyers and police? Do we get more ignorance with more teachers and schools? Do we get more family collapse with more social workers?

This is the question that is most threatening to the previously apolitical service systems because, while services defined as embodiments of care and love are a political platform; while services that are understood as being less effective than they have in the past are a political possibility; while it is even politically feasible to remove the mask of love and recognize services as systems in need of resources in order that economies may grow, it is politically *impossible* to maintain a service economy if the populace perceives that the service system hurts more than it helps – that professional service can become disabling help.

In the last few years, the progressive leaders of the service business have recognized the counterproductive threat. Their response has been to develop new strategies to deal with the counterproductivity of service systems. They have called upon the skills of another profession – the managers. Their assumption is that while professional servicers are unable to control the harm they induce, the managerial profession can become the modern reformer, controlling and directing the systems so that counter-productivity is neutralized, while at the same time protecting the political support for the growth of the service system.

The new service manager, translating his skills from the goods production sector, sees four elements to be manipulated in rationalizing the service system: budgets, personnel, organizational structure and technology. Therefore, the service manager is now busily at work instituting cost control systems, developing personnel training systems, restructuring delivery systems and introducing new technologies.

The most progressive managers have used their advanced marketing skills to develop a fifth manipulation – preparing the client. They recognize that if there is no need for service, it is possible to manufacture a need. If the popular perceptions of need do not fit the service, social service managers have developed techniques that can persuade people to fit the service through advanced marketing systems.

Will these professional management techniques stabilize the service business by eliminating counterproductive effects?

Certainly the capacities of modern management systems are impressive. Aided by the apolitical ideology of the services, one might well prophesy a collaboration between the servicers and their managers to coalesce into an irresistible force that will henceforth direct the economic policies of modernized economies.

An alternative view suggests that there may be a counterbalance – indeed an immovable object – that faces the irresistible force: a new ideology that assigns to the state the coordination of total disservice.

If such an object exists, it is found in the human necessity to act rather than be acted upon; to be citizen rather than client. It is this human imperative that suggest that even the best managed service systems will be unable to overcome popular recognition of the disabling impacts of modernized professional service.

The remainder of this essay attempts to identify the disabling effects of modernized service systems and to suggest the political consequences of the conflict between the irresistible force of client-making and the immovable object of citizen action.

Professionalized Assumptions Regarding Need

Three disabling effects grow from professionalized assumptions of need.

First is the translation of a need into a deficiency. A need could be understood as a condition, a want, a right, an obligation of another, an illusion or an unresolvable problem. Professional practice consistently defines a need as an unfortunate absence or emptiness in another.

One is reminded of the child's riddle asking someone to describe a glass that has water in its lower half. Is it half full – or half empty? The basic function of modernized professionalism is to legitimize human beings whose capacity it is to see their neighbour as half empty. Professionalized research increasingly devotes its efforts to extending the upper rim of the glass in order to ensure that it will never be filled – even by the results of 'effective service'.

In a servicing economy where the majority of the people derive their income from professionalized 'helping' and GNP is measured by services rendered, nations need an increased *supply* of personal deficiency. Thus, a society that purports to meet need defined as personal deficiency is more accurately understood as an economy in need of need. The comic distortion could be societies of neighbours whose income depends upon finding the deficiency in each other. The political consequence is neighbours unable to act as communities of competence with the capacity to perceive or act upon solvable problems.

The *second* disabling characteristic of professionalized definitions of need is the professional practice of placing the perceived deficiency *in* the client. While most modernized professionals will agree that individual problems develop in a socio-economic-political context, their common remedial practice isolates the individual from the context. The effect of this individualization leads the professional to distort even his own contextual understanding. Because his remedial tools and techniques are usually limited to individualized interaction, the interpretation of the need necessarily becomes individualized. The tool defines the problem rather than the problem defining the tool. [. . .]

The individualizing, therapeutic definition of need has met a counteracting force in some of the 'liberation' movements. The civil rights and women's liberation movements are cases in point. Their essential ideological function is to persuade minorities and women that they are human beings who are neither deficient nor dependent upon systems purporting to meet their 'needs' through individualized professional help. Instead, these movements struggle to overcome the individualized deficiency oriented 'consciousness' communicated by the professional service ideology by affirming individual competence and collective action.

The *third* disabling effect of professionalized definitions of need results from specialization – the major 'product' of advanced systems of technique and technology. We all know that this process creates highly specialized, intricately organized service systems that provide magnificent organizational problems for the new service managers. Vast human and financial resources are now devoted to the rationalization of these systems, providing politically acceptable criteria justifying economic growth through the service sector.

What is less clearly understood is that these systems impose their mirror image on the citizenry. As the systems are a set of managed parts, so the client is necessarily understood and processed as a set of manageable parts, each with its own service mechanic. These complex service systems remind one of those table mats in some restaurants that show a cow divided into parts locating the steak, the roast, the ribs and the tongue.

In like manner, professionalized service definitions increasingly translate need in terms of people in pieces. We need podiatrists for our hooves and Eye, Ear, Nose and Throat men for our snouts. Our psyche, marriage, relationship with our children, in fact our most intimate and personal activities are divided into separate bits and pieces.

Modernized professions also piece us out in time. Service professionals now assure us that we live through a set of needs defined by age. Professionals have 'found' seven life crises (formerly known as the seven ages of man) from infancy to death, each requiring its helping professional. [. . .]

While individualizing need may disable by removing people from the social context, the compartmentalization of the person removes even the potential for individual action. People are, instead, a set of pieces in need, both in time and space.

To sum up, professionalized services define need as a deficiency and at the same time individualize and compartmentalize the deficient components. The service systems communicate three propositions to the client:

> You are deficient
> You are the problem
> You have a collection of problems

In terms of the interest of service systems and their *needs*, the propositions become:

> We *need* deficiency
> The economic unit we *need* is individuals
> The productive economic unit we *need* is an individual with multiple deficiencies

The Professionalized Assumptions Regarding the Remedy of Need

These professionalized definitions of need produce a logical and necessary set of remedial assumptions, each with its own intrinsically disabling effects. The *first* of these assumptions is the mirror image of the individualized definition of need. As *you* are the problem, the assumption is that *I*, the professionalized servicer, *am the answer*. *You* are not the answer. *Your peers* are not the answer. *The political, social and economic environment* is not the answer. Nor is it possible that there is no answer. I, the professional, am the answer. The central assumption is that service is a unilateral process. I, the professional, produce. You the client, consume.

There are, of course, an impressive set of professionalized coping mechanisms that have been developed by sensitive servicers to deny the unilateral nature of professionalized service. They are described as group-orientated services, peer-orientated services, client-orientated services, and community-orientated services. Each of these rhetorical devices is a symbolic attempt to deal with the anxieties of servicers who *need* to deny the unilateral nature of their relationships.

While it is clear that many humanistic professionals seek a democratic definition for their role, it is difficult to perceive the bilateral component beyond the clients' payment, whether out of pocket or through taxation. Indeed, a basic definition of 'unprofessional conduct' is 'becoming involved with the client'. To be professional is to distance – to ensure that the relationship is defined in terms that allow the client to understand who is *really* being serviced.

In spite of the democratic pretence, the disabling function of unilateral professional help is the hidden assumption that 'You will be better because I, the professional, know better'. [. . .]

A *second* disabling characteristic of professionalized remedial assumptions is the necessity for the remedy to define the need. As professionalized service systems create more elegant techniques and magnificent tools, they create an imperative demanding their use.

The problem with these beautiful, shiny, complex, professional tools and techniques is that their 'benefits' are not easily comprehended by the public. Therefore, we see the professions developing internal logics and public marketing systems that assure use of the tools and techniques by assuming that the client doesn't understand what he needs. Therefore, if the client is to have the benefit of the professional remedy, he must also understand that the professional not only knows what he needs but also knows how the need is to be met.

Thus the complex professional remedial tools have come to justify the professional power to define the need – to decide not only the appropriate remedy but the definition of the problem itself. Increasingly, professions assume that in order to deal with deficiency, they must have the prerogative to decide what is deficient.

There is no greater power than the right to define the question. From that right flows a set of necessary answers. If the servicer can effectively assert the right to define the appropriate question, he has the power to determine the need of his neighbour rather than meeting his neighbour's need. While this power allows the professional to use his shiny new remedy, it also defines citizens as people who can't understand whether they have a problem – much less what should be done about it.

Modernized societies are now replete with need-defining research. Professionals have recently 'discovered' tool-using needs called child abuse, learning disabilities and, 'removal trauma' (the need for therapy for children who are traumatized because they are removed from their allegedly traumatic families). [. . .]

When the capacity to define the problem becomes a professional prerogative, citizens no longer exist. The prerogative removes the citizen as problem-definer, much less problem-solver. It translates political functions into technical and technological problems.

Once the service professional can define remedy and need, a *third* disabling remedial practice develops. It is the coding of the problem and the solution into languages that are incomprehensible to citizens.

While it is clearly disabling to be told you can't decide whether you have a problem and how it can be dealt with, the professional imperative compounds the dilemma by demonstrating that you couldn't understand the problem or the solution anyway. The language of modernized professional services mystifies both problem and solution so that citizen evaluation becomes impossible. The only people 'competent' to decide whether the servicing process has any merit are professional peers, each affirming the basic assumptions of the other.

While there are fascinating inter-jurisdictional disputes among servicing peers, these conflicts rarely break the rule that it is only the professional who understands the problem and the solution. The internal conflicts are power struggles over which professionals shall be dominant. A professional who breaks the rule of professional dominance will be stigmatized by all the disputants and loses his place on the rungs of the ladder to success. The politics of modernized professional power is bounded by peer review. Modern heretics are those professional practitioners who support citizen competence and convert their profession into an understandable trade under the comprehensible command of citizens.

The critical disabling effect of professional coding is its impact upon citizen capacities to deal with cause and effect. If I cannot understand the question or the answer – the need or the remedy – I exist at the sufference of expert systems. My world is not a place where I do or act with others. Rather, it is a mysterious place, a strange land beyond my comprehension or control. It is understood only by professionals who know *how* it works, *what* I need and *how* my need is met. I am the object rather than the actor. My very being is as client rather than citizen. My life and our society are technical problems rather than political systems.

As the service professions gain the power to unilaterally define remedy, need, and code the service process, a *fourth* disabling characteristic develops. It is the capacity of servicers to define the output of their service in accordance with their own satisfaction with the result. This fourth capacity develops in a service profession just as the citizen is totally and definitely transmogrified into a *critical* addict.

Increasingly, professionals are claiming the power to decide whether their 'help' is effective. The important, valued and evaluated outcome of service is the professional's assessment of his own efficacy. The client is viewed as a deficient person, unable to know whether he has been helped.

This developing professional premise is contested by the consumer movement. The movement is a valiant last stand of those disabled citizens who lay final claim to the right to evaluate the effects or 'outputs' of professionalized service.

The basic assumption of the movement is that citizens are enabled because they have become powerful consumers. In this assumption the movement is a handmaiden of the serviced society. It implicitly accepts the service ideology. Citizens *are* as they consume. Citizen welfare is defined by equitable, efficacious consumption. The service system is a given good. The citizen role is in evaluating the output. While citizens may not understand the service system, the consumer movement assumes they do know whether the system's output helps or hurts.

Professionally managed service systems are now dealing with this remnant citizen role as consumer. The result has been an increasing professional focus on manipulating consumer perceptions of outcomes. Thomas Dewar, in a paper titled *The Professionalization of the Client*, describes how the service systems are training citizens to understand that their satisfaction is derived from being effective clients rather than people whose problems are solved. [. . .]

Once effective 'clienthood' becomes a central value in society, the consumer movement as we know it now will be stifled and will wither away.

The service ideology will be consummated when citizens believe that they cannot know whether they have a need, cannot know what the remedy is, cannot understand the process that purports to meet the need or remedy and cannot even know whether the need is met unless professionals express satisfaction. The ultimate sign of a serviced society is a professional saying, 'I'm so pleased by what you've done'. The demise of citizenship is to respond, 'Thank you'.

We will have reached the apogee of the modernized service society when the professionals can say to the citizen:

> We are the solution to your problem.
> We know what problem you have.
> You can't understand the problem or the solution.
> Only we can decide whether the solution has dealt with your problem.

Inverted, in terms of the needs of professionalized service systems, these

propositions become:
> We *need* to solve your problems.
> We *need* to tell you what they are.
> We *need* to deal with them in our terms.
> We *need* to have you respect our satisfaction with our own work.

The most important research issues in modernized societies involve an understanding of the *needs* of servicers and the mechanics of their systems. These systems are obviously important. They provide incomes for a majority of the people. They support national economies. It is, of course, no secret that they are consistently failing to meet their own goals in spite of magnanimous applications of money and personnel. It is becoming more and more evident that rather than *producing* 'services' they are creating sensitive but frustrated professionals, unable to understand why their love, care and service does not re-form society, much less help individuals to function.

We should, therefore, reorient our research efforts toward the needs of servicers. After all, they are a growing majority of people employed in modernized societies and they are an increasingly sad, alienated class of people in *need* of support, respect, care and love. Modernized societies *need* to determine how we can help these professionalized servicers while limiting their power to disable the capacities of citizens to perceive and deal with issues in political terms.

And if we cannot do that we should at least understand the political impact of the disabling nature of professionalized definitions of need and remedy.

Professionalized services communicate a world view that defines our lives and our societies as a series of technical problems. This technical definition is masked by symbols of care and love that obscure the economic interests of the servicers and the disabling characteristics of their practices.

The sum of these disabling characteristics is an ideology that converts citizens to clients, communities to deficient individuals and politics to a self-serving debate by professionals over which service system should have a larger share of the Gross National Product.

The foregoing analysis is *not* an argument for the reform of professionalized service in order to remove the disabling effects. Rather, the analysis suggests that the disabling effects are intrinsic to modernized professionalized service. Whatever benefits they might provide can only be assessed after we recognize them as essentially self-interested systems with inherently disabling effects. Within this framework, the political definition of a citizen can be restored. The inherently disabling effects of professionalized services can be assessed and balanced against their possible benefits. Policies can be developed that select those service benefits that overbalance the intrinsically disabling effects.

In the meantime, the politics of modernized societies will be the conflict between the irresistible resistance of the service business and the immovable object created by citizens who have experienced the disabling help of privileged professional servicers who wear the mask of love.

4 To Deny or Not to Deny Disability

Vic Finkelstein

Disabled people have always struggled against the way they have been prevented from taking part in the normal activities of their communities. More recently, however, these struggles have taken a step forward. Disabled people have begun to organize for their emancipation and joined the growing numbers of groups struggling against social discrimination. We are taking a deeper look at ourselves, at the way we are treated and at what is meant by disability. We have noticed that it has nearly always been others who have researched, written, analysed, examined our history, and proposed their knowing solutions for us. More and more disabled people have had experience of 'disability experts' and increasingly we have come to recognize the humiliation this relationship may take for granted. Can it be that having others research on the lives of disabled people (rather than us expressing our own experience) has something to do with the very nature of disability? What, then, is disability?

To many of us, the single factor that unites us together in our struggles is that it is our society that discriminates against us. Our society disables people with different physical impairments. The cause, then, of disability is the social relationships which take no or little account of people who have physical impairments. If this definition is correct, then it should be possible to prove that other social groups can become disabled, in an imaginary society which took no account of their physical status. In such an imaginary society it would be possible for physically impaired people to be the able-bodied!

Let us see whether we can turn the world upside-down and show that disability is a socially caused problem. An upside-down world where the 'able' become the 'disabled' and the 'disabled' become the 'able-bodied' and where we show, too, that far from adjusting and accepting disability perhaps, just perhaps, it is healthier to deny and struggle to eliminate disability?

Let us suppose that those who believe in segregation could really have their way. We will imagine a thousand or more disabled people, all wheelchair-users, collected together and settled in their own village where they had full management and democratic rights. We will suppose able-bodied people do not often visit the village and that the wheelchair-users control all aspects of their lives. They make the goods that they sell in their shops with special aids, they work the machines that clean the street, run their own educational colleges, banks, post offices, and transport system of the village, and so on. In fact, for the villager, being in a wheelchair is like

Source: *Magic Carpet*, New Year 1975, xxvii, No. 1, pp. 31–8.

everyone else in their world of people that she or he meets in daily life. They see wheelchair-users on television and hear them on radio. Able-bodied people, however, are only rarely seen and little understood.

In the course of the life of the village the wheelchair-users plan their lives according to their needs. They design their own buildings to suit their physical situation. One thing the wheelchair-user architects quickly discover in this village is that because everyone is always in wheelchairs there is no need to have ceilings at 9′ 6″ or door heights at 7′ 2″. Soon it becomes standard practice to build doors to a height of 5′ and ceiling or rooms to a height of 7′ 4″. Naturally the building codes set out in the regulations made these heights standard. Now everyone is happy in the village; all the physical difficulties have been overcome and this little society has changed according to the physical character of its members. At last the buildings and environment are truly in tune with their needs.

Let us say that when all the adjustments had been made and became fixed, in this wheelchair-user society, a few able-bodied had, through no choice of their own, to come and settle in this village. Naturally, one of the first things they noticed was the heights of the doors and ceilings. They noticed this directly, by constantly knocking their heads on the door lintels. Soon all the able-bodied members of the village were also marked by the dark bruises they carried on their foreheads. Of course, they went to see the village doctors, who were, naturally, also wheelchair-users. Soon the wheelchair-user doctors, wheelchair-user psychiatrists, wheelchair-user social workers, etc., were involved in the problems of the able-bodied villagers. The doctors produced learned reports about the aches and pains of the able-bodied in society. They saw how the bruises and painful backs (from walking bent double so frequently) were *caused* by their physical condition. The wheelchair-user doctors analysed the problems and wrote their definitions. They said these able-bodied people suffered a 'loss or reduction of functional ability' which resulted in a handicap. This handicap caused a 'disadvantage or restriction of activity' which made them disabled in this society.

Soon special aids were designed by the wheelchair-user doctors and associated professions for the able-bodied disabled members of the village. All the able-bodied were given special toughened helmets (provided free by the village) to wear at all times. Special braces were designed which gave support while keeping the able-bodied wearer bent at a height similar to their fellow wheelchair-user villagers. Some doctors went so far as to suggest that there was no hope for these poor sufferers unless they too used wheelchairs, and one person even went so far as to suggest amputation to bring the able-bodied down to the right height! The able-bodied disabled caused many problems. When they sought jobs no one would employ them. Special experts had to be trained to understand these problems and new professions created for their care. When one able-bodied disabled person applied for a job as a television interviewer, a special medical examination had to be arranged to see whether he was fit for this work. In the end it was decided that he was not suitable. It was felt, the wheelchair-user doctor pointed out in the case file, that a television interviewer wearing a helmet all the time would not be acceptable. Since the cameras would only show the top of his head (because the able-bodied were always bent double by the harnesses they had to wear) he would not be suitable for interviewing. It is well known, the wheelchair-user doctor wrote, how difficult it is to communicate with the able-bodied because it is not easy to see their facial expressions and meet eye-to-eye while they are bent double.

In time special provision had to be made in the village to provide a means of obtaining money for these able-bodied disabled to live. Voluntary societies were created to collect charity and many shops and pubs had an upturned helmet placed on the counters for customers to leave their small change. Painted on the helmets were the words 'Help the able-bodied disabled'. Sometimes a little plaster-cast model would stand in the corner of a shop – the figure bent double, in their characteristic pose, with a slotted box on the figure's back for small coins.

But one day, when the able-bodied were sitting together and discussing their problems they realised that they were never consulted by the wheelchair-users about this in the little society. In fact they realized that there may be solutions to their problems which had never occurred to the wheelchair users simply because they never looked at these in the same way as those who had them. It occurred to these able-bodied disabled people that perhaps the *cause* of their problems had a social solution – they suggested that the door and ceiling heights be changed! They formed a union to fight segregation. Of course some of the wheelchair-users thought the able-bodied disabled were failing to accept and adjust to their disabilities, and they had chips on their shoulders because they argued so strongly for social change and a change in attitudes by the wheelchair-users. The able-bodied disabled even argued that perhaps, just perhaps, their disabilities could be overcome (and disappear!) with changes in society.

5 The Mentally Retarded – Valuable Individuals or Superfluous Population?

B. Farber

E. Royce

Department of Sociology, Arizona State University

The aim of research on mental retardation is the eventual elimination of those biological and social conditions that lead to social incompetence and intellectual disablement. It would seem that cognitive and social inadequacies often block the mentally retarded from filling useful social positions and from fully integrating themselves into society. Along with several ethnic minorities, the aged poor, and the severely physically handicapped, the retarded are superfluous insofar as the major institutions of the society are concerned (Farber, 1968). But, bit by bit, the genetic components of mental retardation are being uncovered, prenatal diagnosis perfected, and medical techniques of remediation discovered. Simultaneously, household attributes detrimental to child development are being discerned, distortions in early mother-child interaction detected, and the cultural influences on maladaptive behavior located. Presumably, in some distant future, we will be able to apply these findings and to engineer lives so that 'mental retardation' will be wiped out.

It is possible, however, that many problems that we associate with mental retardation have little to do with personal defects or with remedial pathologies in the social system. They may instead inhere in the very conditions of social order, or at least in the social order as it is presently established. In order to gain insight into the nature of these problems, I would like to present the results of a mental experiment, a technique applied by sociologists in order to undertake functional analysis (Merton, 1957; Johnson, 1960). I shall describe a world in which all biological and social conditions leading to intellectual impairment have been identified and are capable of control. What then follows from this ability to control intelligence? I shall present the results of my analysis to you as if I were speaking to a scientific assembly five hundred years from now. Suppose that the year is 2476, and I am addressing members of the Congress of Human Engineering.

Fellow human engineers: This year, we are celebrating the 400th anniversary of the invention of the Savant computer implant, which has revolutionized modern society. In pre-Savant days, five centuries ago, history records that people actually had to

Source: P. Mittler (ed) (1977) *Research to Practice in Mental Retardation, 1*. Baltimore: University Park Press, pp. 45–51.

congregate in schools to relearn each generation even such simple mechanics as reading and number manipulation. The cultivation of talent through time-consuming, expensive, and often unsatisfactory education was the only way to equip personnel for highly technical tasks. Today, however, with basic knowledge – in languages and mathematics – being phased into the implantee directly, and with the capability of transplanting Savants from one generation to the next, society is assured of an abundance of highly trained and proficient personnel and of progress through successive memory gains from generation to generation.[1] Compared with the intellectual capacity made possible by the Savant, 'natural' brains are, to use those ancient terms, feebleminded or even imbecilic. Certainly, the Savant has been a source of tremendous benefit. At the same time, this glorious demon continues to precipitate crises in the social order. Perhaps the most effective way to illuminate our present predicament is to review the history of the Savant.

The Savant was made possible by a series of engineering feats beginning with the development of microscopic computer components and sophisticated surgical techniques.[2] By the twenty-second century, engineers had already produced highly complex brain supplements for skull implantation. But in these early experimental stages, research was still oriented toward overcoming and/or supplementing cognitive deficiencies in an effort to eliminate mental retardation. The first Savant computer implants were crude, and the early implantees could only slightly improve upon their previous intellectual capacities. With improvements in memory activation, feedback mechanisms, and brain-computer interface, further experimentation produced highly promising results: chimpanzees who were chess wizards and children with Down's syndrome solving differential equations.[3] It was at this point that scientists, now clearly perceiving the potentialities of the Savant, directed their research toward augmenting normal intellectual functioning.

History records the competition among nations over the development of Savant components and the subsequent race for brain-power supremacy. The international scene was calmed somewhat when the Savant-producing nations agreed to share their technology with other countries. Global strife, however, soon gave way to the domestic unrest that persists to this day. Regretfully, technological improvement often brings forth more moral and legal issues than it solves. Technically, it was possible three centuries ago for virtually all members of society to have full Savant capabilities, which at that time was a Cattell ratio of 24,000, using the old Stanford-Binet norm of 100 as a base. With a complete distribution of full-capacity Savants, though, it was feared that the social order would break down.

To avoid chaos, the Congress of Political Processes, utilizing the concept of creative scarcity, devised our present-day system of social stratification based upon a differential distribution of Savant implants. The status A class, comprising leaders in scientific, humanistic, political, and industrial fields, receives full-power Savant

---

[1] Because the Savant makes possible successive memory gains over generations, early myths about the genetic inheritance of acquired characteristics and the existence of group memories – the racial unconscious – have become a scientific reality. (See Lisa Watson and Jacqueline Crick, *Savantism and Lamarckianism* (New York, 2402).)

[2] A definitive history of the origins of the Savant is of course Michael Richard Toynbee's *The Savant Transformation* (Cambridge, 2353).

[3] The immediate impact of these experiments on society was for industry to demand mass production of chimpanzee Savants (CHIMSAV) and for organized labor to call for an end to Savant experimentation and the destruction of all existing Savants. In the end, the government invoked the principle of creative scarcity and restricted Savant implanting to humans.

implants in all areas of intellectual functioning. The status B class, consisting of industrial and governmental specialists and middle-range intellectuals, receives Savant implants with full-capacity Cattell ratios for only those particular abilities needed for occupational and cultural specialties.[4] The status C class, technicians and skilled workers, receives Savants commensurate with their job requirements. Status D class, which holds the unskilled laborers and the consumers of popular culture, provides the basic pool of people and their children who are eligible for Savant implants. Finally, there is the Status E class, the ineligibles who for one reason or another have lost their right to a Savant implant.

A major step in the stabilization of the social order came in 2154 when the Congress of Justice ruled that the individual implantee is the legal owner of his or her implant, and Savant inheritance laws were passed to enable parents to transmit their implants to their children.[5] The inheritance of Savants staved off many problems during the past three centuries. But now we are facing a difficulty that has haunted societies through the ages: A demand for the reallocation of personal property, and of course the Savant is our most treasured possession.

Major demographic shifts and social developments, begun as early as the twentieth century, may provide us with an insight into our current problems concerning the Savant and its distribution. The twentieth century laid the groundwork for intensive-energy technologies – nuclear and solar – and brought profound changes in occupational and social structure in our society. Particularly in the United States, the great migrations at the end of the nineteenth century helped to create an urban society. These surges in urban population accompanied vast industrial expansion. As the twentieth century wore on, the core institutions – the economy, government, and education – increased in complexity manyfold and required much more technical training and social sophistication for effective operation than ever before. To meet this need, the proportion of the work force in professional, administrative, and technical occupations rose enormously.

This modification in occupational structure was accompanied by dramatic demographic shifts. One was the drastic decline in foreign immigration – since industry's need for unskilled workers languished. Another was the decline of the agricultural population. Advances in agricultural technology and the virtual extinction of the small farmer made possible the influx of rural and small-town populations to the cities. Then, when these resources were virtually exhausted, there came an increased reliance upon women and other persons who traditionally had been marginal to highly-trained segments of the labor force. It became acceptable (and even desirable) to be highly mobile, to reduce the impediments of having children, and to subordinate domestic loyalties to work commitment.

These demographic transformations produced transformations in socialization. The participation of new groups in a set of institutions requires their learning appropriate social norms. Just as in the United States the theme of the nineteenth century had been the Americanization of immigrants, the major movements of the twentieth century focused upon the normalization of groups formerly considered to be superfluous or marginal to the core of the public culture – the educational,

---

[4] At this time, howver, the spillover effects of specialized Savants upon general mental functioning are still not fully understood. (See Benjamin Axelrod, 'How Specialized Are Status B Savants?' *International Journal of Experimental Savant Psychology*, 2475, 327, pp. 596–602.)

[5] This landmark decision was enunciated in a brilliant opinion by Justice Daniel Alan Brandeis and has been reprinted in *The Savant and the Law* (New York, 2178), edited by Tanya B. Rashi and Julia Mae Rambam.

political, and economic institutions (Farber, 1968). Normalization took various forms – Civil Rights movement in the case of ethnic minorities, the Women's Liberation Movement, the Mainstreaming Movement among the handicapped, the Advocacy Movement, and so on. These movements were based on the assumption that social inequality is rooted in factors over which individuals have no control, most of all ascribed status; that is, the idea that one's birth is a major determinant of personal destiny. Normalization was intended to eliminate ascribed status and personal misfortune as elements in governing schooling, occupation, marital choice – all summed up by the concept 'life chances.'

What was the result of these twentieth century movements? First, of course, they did bring many people who previously had been marginal or superfluous into the economy, and in doing so, they inflated the educated labor pool. Yet, declining birthrates, declining immigration, and declining foreign markets, together with other complex factors, capped off industrial expansion and created a surplus of potential bureaucratic, technical, and professional workers. With this surplus, unemployment rates increased, and wages and salaries were depressed.

This situation occurred, we must remember, as the general educational level of the population rose. The intended elimination of ascribed status as a basis for personal destiny meant that people had rising expectations of economic and occupational achievement because of their higher educational qualifications. But as early as the twentieth century, social scientists had found that as educational levels in a society rose, they rose for people at all levels. Consequently, those groups previously at the bottom in education remained at the bottom. Overall, education as a resource merely underwent inflation (Boudon, 1973).

But problems occurred not merely for those who remained in their previous position of relative deprivation; with the expansion of the educated work force, they occurred also at higher educational levels. The twentieth century is not unique in generating problems of unmet rising expectations because of a general rise in educational level. Historians tell us that even around 1820:

> Just because France had created an excellent educational system, the educated youth . . . , whose supply exceeded the demand, faced what they considered a bleak future. The France of the Restoration abounded with doctors without patients, lawyers without clients, and young men spending their time in waiting rooms of the high and mighty. Not really being in demand, these young men suffered not only from material discontent but also from a deep seated spiritual malaise (Coser, 1971).

In the twentieth century, marginal groups – ethnic minorities, the poor, the physically handicapped, the mentally retarded – were treated in ways that led to exaggerated hopes for upward social mobility on the principle of equality of opportunity. As one disillusioned, retarded man told an interviewer in a research project, 'I have had a hard life. I tell you. If I had to live it over, I wouldn't do it' (Henshel, 1971). Objectively, this young man's living conditions were on the whole better than most of his retarded contemporaries. But the idea that literally all ascribed attributes should be wiped away in determining social rewards produced disappointment – disappointment resulting from the discrepancy between, on the one hand, generated hopes and expectations and, on the other hand, actual conditions and realizable goals.[6] At the same time, this idea of equality of

---

[6] Compare with Komarovsky (1964) for the effects of disappointment over the failure to be upwardly socially mobile on self-esteem and marital relationships in working class families.

opportunity engendered fear in a majority of the population that their lot in life was insecure; they were faced with a threat of status loss – a decline in their hold on resources. Their reaction to this threat, as has occurred in other times and other places, was to ensure the inoperativeness of the principle of equality of opportunity (Hofstadter, 1963).

Realizing the potential destructiveness wrought by unmet heightened expectations, present-day Savant society has had to make certain assumptions about social life. First, it has had to accept the axiom that 'some envy appears for any degree of inequality, and that envy is proportional to inequality' (Boudon, 1976). Second, it has introduced the assumption that upward social mobility – the heightening of expectations and meeting those heightened expectations – should be determined by the principle of randomized opportunity.

Let me explain the principle of randomized opportunity. It is opposed both to the principle of equal opportunity and to the principle of allocating careers according to talent. The principle of equal opportunity involves the neutralization of effects of ascribed status and personal misfortune in fostering upward mobility. It is the equivalent of giving everyone a Savant and thereby raising everyone's expectations for preferential treatment in occupation and allocation of resources – just as educational inflation had done earlier in history. Given the scarcity of preferred occupations and resources, this principle would inevitably create disappointment and resentment for large segments of the population. Consequently, Savant society has had to abandon the principle of equal opportunity as unworkable.

The principle of allocating careers according to talent has other deficiencies. If upward social mobility is based only on talent, then the person who lacks talent (or fails to pursue a career consonant with his other talent) feels much guilt, frustration, and envy, while the person with talent is in constant anxiety over the stability of his position – his continued access to resources. Twentieth-century studies show that this principle, too, is highly destructive to personal integrity and social order.[7] Besides, as a matter of practical concern, with Savant implantation the exact degree of 'natural' competence is of little interest.

This leaves us with the principle of randomized opportunity. According to this principle, all Status D persons (as well as those who have served their punishment time in Status E) have an equal opportunity to move into a Savant status by random selection. Social science findings from the twentieth century have indicated that the poor and working class of that time regarded social mobility as a matter of 'fate' or 'luck' (Cohen and Hodges, 1963); what Savant society has done is to formalize this conception into a method for actually determining upward social mobility. The number of implantations at any time is sufficient to maintain hope of receiving one. This hope of social mobility has somewhat mitigated the amount of envy generated by inequality. True, the envy is there and is often expressed openly. But it is this fine balance between envy and hope that motivates Status D and E people to live within the Savant scheme of things.

And now to our present danger! There is a growing black market in Status A Savant implants. This black market is so widespread that it is bringing unrealistically high expectations to buyers, expectations that cannot be met by our social order; and corresponding fears of possible status loss are emerging among those who now occupy Status A positions. Fellow human engineers, what should be done? We could salve our guilt by arbitrarily deciding that we can indeed have a whole society of Savants

---

[7] See the mental experiment by Michael Young (1958) describing the events of 2033.

and then try to work out difficulties afterwards. But I am fearful that the problems generated by the mass distribution of intellectual competence are inherent in our social structure: While we recognize the right of each individual to be intellectually competent in principle, we must maintain individual differences – indeed, even group differences – to sustain our social order and to ensure the continued fulfilment of expectations for each Savant class. In fact, the only times we were able to establish a goal of a Status A Savant for everyone were in the early years when this was impossible. At this time, we must end the black market sales of Savants and eliminate its illegal possession: We must destroy illegal intelligence before the Savant inflation destroys our social order!

This ends the mental experiment. What are my conclusions? To begin with, no matter what controls I placed on the allocation of Savants, the end result was similar: The successful remediation of mental retardation led eventually to a general inflation of intelligence in the society, with the least intelligent persons still in a position of relative deprivation. What began as a strategy for remediation, ironically, ended as the very means for sustaining the condition it was intended to correct. But the possibility of a constantly escalating level of intelligence leads to still another question: Is there an upper limit to the intellectual resources that a society can manage? But this question requires my return to Savant society for yet another mental experiment. At any rate, the study of social conditions relevant to mental retardation should lead ultimately to more general questions about social order and its contradictions.

Summary

A futurist mental experiment is performed that assumes that contemporary social and biological bases of intellectual disability have been eradicated. The results suggest that social order requires the persistence of mental retardation and eventually tends to turn remedial strategies into means for perpetuating those very phenomena they were designed to eliminate.

Acknowledgment

We are grateful to Rosanna Farber for her valuable suggestions and comments – no superfluous person is she!

References

BOUDON, R. (1973) *Education, Opportunity, and Social Inequality.* New York: Wiley-Interscience.

BOUDON, R. (1976) 'Review essay of John Rawls, A Theory of Justice.' *Contemp. Sociol. 5,* 104.

COHEN, A. K., and HODGES, H. M. (1963) 'Characteristic of the lower-blue-collar class.' *Soc. Probl. 10,* 303.

COSER, L. A. (1971) *Masters of Sociological Thought*, p. 32. New York: Harcourt Brace & Co.

FARBER, B. (1968) *Mental Retardation: Its Social Context and Social Consequences*, pp. 3–22 and 103–18. Boston: Houghton Mifflin Company.

HENSHEL, A. (1971) *The Forgotten Ones: Case Studies of Chicano and Anglo Retardates*, p. 153. Austin: Rehabilitation Research and Training Center in Mental Retardation, University of Texas.

HOFSTADTER, R. (1963) 'The pseudo-conservative revolt.' In D. Bell (ed.) *The Radical Right*, pp. 75–95. New York: Anchor Books.

JOHNSON, H. M. (1960) *Sociology, A Systematic Introduction*, p. 75. New York: Harcourt Brace & Co.

KOMAROVSKY, M. (1964) *Blue Collar Marriage*, pp. 285–93. New York: Random House.

MERTON, R. K. (1957) *Social Theory and Social Structure*. pp. 56–60. New York: Free Press.

YOUNG, M. D. (1958) *The Rise of the Meritocracy, 1870–2033*. New York: Random House.

6 Tools for Living: a Blueprint for a Major New Industry

H. S. Wolff

Clinical Research Centre, Harrow

[. . .]

But in order to look into the future, let us first go back into the past, say 20,000, 30,000, or 50,000 years in human existence and consider the concept of wild man. In the same way that there are wild animals, there must at one time have been wild man, who was probably evolutionarily adapted quite well to the environment in which he lived. Like all wild animals, wild man almost certainly did not have a geriatric problem. Once he became inefficient, once he could no longer catch his food or survive the winter, he was eaten by a sabre-toothed tiger – so the problem of the old did not exist.

It was only when man began to produce a surplus, as it were, that he began to become caring man, in the sense that he was prepared to devote some of the surplus for the care of the elderly, and for the care of those members of the family or tribe who, for some reason or another, were unable to live independently. [. . .]

Time now rolls on for 20,000, 30,000, or 50,000 years to modern man. Modern man finds himself under two pressures. The first pressure is that just because of his success in his ability to change the environment very fast he has now constructed for himself a set of stresses for which evolution has no remedy – whether these are environmental pollution, living in cities, or eating too much. In consequence, he suffers from a whole series of diseases which are induced by his very success.

The second pressure from which modern man suffers is the fact that he has been able to extend the life of old people very considerably. Therefore, the proportion of the population which is beyond the independence of either stage of wild man is now appreciable, and makes up about one-sixth of the population of most Western European countries.

If we come now within, say, 100 years of today, we find that there has been a further change. In his transition from the intelligent animal to becoming human, man coped with the care of those people who were unable to live independently by inventing the family. It was very largely the family – the extended family – which took on the duties of caring for that part of the population which was not independent.

Until a relatively short time ago it was not uncommon for two, three, or

Source: BRAY, J. and WRIGHT, S. (eds) (1980) *The Use of Technology in the Care of the Elderly and the Disabled*. London: Frances Pinter.

four generations of a family to live in the same village or, in an urban situation, to live in the same town, and to provide care services for one another. In the United Kingdom, in a Victorian family, which means less than 100 years ago, it was not uncommon for the youngest daughter not to marry and leave home until she had finished looking after her parents. There was a strong sense of obligation within the family to provide the social services, which at that time were not provided by the State, from within the resources of the extended family.

We have now added a third problem of modern man, in that because we are producing smaller families, and because of the increased mobility of individuals, this extended family form of care has largely disappeared – for example, the son who might have looked after his parents has become a computer programmer at the EEC in Brussels, leaving them behind. [. . .]

This brings us to the present day when we are faced in a country like the United Kingdom of 56 million people, with about $2\frac{1}{2}$ million people who require, for age reasons alone, some form of external care. If we compare these numbers with the numbers of people who require an artificial kidney, or some dramatic form of surgery or other costly medical treatment, they are very large indeed, larger perhaps by two orders of magnitude. As such, their importance in terms of population statistics, and perhaps in terms of the total amount of benefit which a care service can provide to a population, has to some extent been neglected in the past. It has been neglected particularly in the provision of technological aids. [. . .]

There are therefore three new factors we need to consider when looking into the future.

First, we have a greater survival to old age, which means increased numbers.

Second, there has been a decrease in the protection which the extended family conveys, because of smaller families, greater mobility and a decreased sense of obligation amongst members of a family to accept the responsibility of long-term care for a grandmother, or even a great-grandmother.

Third, I believe that we, the next generation of old people, will have a higher expectation of what old age should be like. I do not think we will be satisfied with the fairly rapid decline for many people of mobility, of excitement in life, or comfort, which the previous generation of old people has been prepared to accept. We shall be a much more demanding elderly population. [. . .]

Here I would like to introduce the concept of 'tools for living'. Because I believe that this new form of consumer, the 50 million elderly people in the European Community, will require what are essentially consumer products to compensate for their failing physical, sensory and perhaps even mental powers. They will want to be more like the people they were 20 years earlier, in terms of their performance. These consumer products will range in type from near standard domestic and other consumer goods, like washing machines, to specialist aids which will have much in common with those produced for the severely handicapped. These special products will include special communication products, special mobility and personal hygiene products – all of which will compensate for the failing physical and sensory powers, to make people more independent and, in a sense, to do what evolution has failed to do, which is to adapt us to becoming old.

If all my forecasts for the future are going to come true what must we do? There are four things which we have to do and these, in a sense, have to happen in parallel.

First, we will need people with sufficient imagination to develop the concepts of the sort of devices which are likely to be required. There has to be a degree of anticipation in this. Unfortunately, we cannot simply talk to people and ask them what they want and what they need, because of the inevitable delay of translating the concept into a product. This calls for a degree of imagination and speculation, as indeed is necessary in any form of innovation. There has to be research, but this research ought to be co-ordinated, so that there are not 15 laboratories within the EEC all inventing the same piece of equipment. Here, already, is one function for the Community to perform: that is to promote a very much better exchange of information in this field.

Second, a concept has to be developed for a method of distribution of these technological aids – these tools for living. This is not just a question of having the traditional relationship of a production centre and a shop in which the products are finally sold. These products are not like motor cars or washing machines, because the customers themselves may not be the best judges of what products they need. It is not like buying a pair of shoes, trying them on and finding out whether they hurt – and, if they hurt, not buying that pair of shoes. Whatever form the marketing organization takes it will have to embody within itself a means of providing informed and objective advice to consumers – which is not just a hard sell. It must do so, however, without at the same time prejudicing the free market.

I believe very firmly that in order to make these tools for living more readily available to the ultimate customers, and to establish a viable industry, the barriers will have to go which exist at present in many countries towards obtaining these things – because they are distributed by governments only after examination, form-filling and a considerable administrative procedure.

Some time ago I did a television programme in the United Kingdom during which I canvassed the idea of having what I called 'Granny-care' shops. The reason for choosing that phrase was because in the United Kingdom, France, and Canada, there is a very successful chain of shops, called Mothercare, where anything can be bought for the mother and young child. Based on that idea, I suggested that there should be a chain of shops where everything could be bought for grandmother, from a flannel nightdress, which is unfashionable and difficult to buy elsewhere, to quite complex technological devices, but where advice would also be available. [. . .]

I am sure that we have to simplify the provision of these tools for living so that obtaining them is more like going into a shop and buying them, rather than having a product which costs perhaps £2 having to be prescribed at a cost of perhaps £70. I am afraid that this is one of the problems which exists in a number of countries.

Having organized the method of distribution, the third, and perhaps the most important thing that needs to be done, is to prepare the market by raising the cultural expectations of the people concerned. For example, it is almost impossible and quite pointless to go to a grandmother of 75 years old and to try to get her to change the habits of a lifetime. It is no good telling her that she cannot go on making tea or coffee like she does now, using a kettle, because one day she could pour all the hot water over her feet, but that instead she should use a special device designed to help old people to make tea safely. This is because, unless she is an exception, she is at the least flexible part of her life and to get her to change her lifetime habits is very difficult.

This need to educate people to accept technological help when they become older is very important. [. . .]

To summarize, the world which I see in 10 or 15 years' time is a world in which the 60- to 80-year-olds will represent a new kind of consumer. These consumers will have spending power, they are very likely to have an industry created to mop up this spending power, and the products which they will require will range in kind from modified domestic items to items which are indistinguishable from the most sophisticated aids for the handicapped. It is here that there will be great benefits for the young, severely handicapped market, who will in this way form part of an industry which, because it is an appreciable industry, can well afford the research, development, and special production techniques necessary to make the rather more special products which the severely handicapped person requires.

It will, moreover, be a world in which the majority of employed people will work in service industries, and where an important part of the service industries will be the care industry. In the same way as the individual will have tools in his own hand to help himself, the worker in the service industry will also need rather different tools in his or her hand in order to help others. This is another market of tools for living.

It will be a world in which we hope that preparing people for their old age will be part of the cultural education of every person – that, in the same way that people are now prepared for retirement, they will be prepared for the compensatory devices which they will need when they become less able to look after themselves.

Lastly, methods of sale will have to be developed by which these tools for living can be introduced into the population, methods which are ethical in the sense that good advice is given to consumers, but which at the same time are still commercially viable.

Perhaps I should say in parenthesis that I believe that governments, one after the other, will find it both economically and politically attractive to provide support for the elderly and handicapped, not in terms of manpower or issuing hardware, but by issuing monetary support, leaving the deployment of such support to the consumer. By providing money in this way the market will be further stimulated but it will be even more necessary to build in the extra part of ethical objective advice, so as to ensure a correct matching of the product and the individual who will use it. [. . .]

7 Disability, Adjustment and Family Life–Some Theoretical Considerations

Michael Oliver

(a) Introduction

This paper will compare and contrast two theoretical approaches to the problem of adjustment to disability. It will argue that the psychological approach has so far dominated to the comparative neglect of the impact of disability upon family life and upon non-disabled members of a disabled person's family. An alternative sociological approach will be advanced and it will be suggested that such an approach must be much more broadly based and take into account social situations as well as individual experiences.

The concentration on theory and the polarisation of two alternative frameworks considerably simplifies both the scope of personal experiences and the complexities of theoretical frameworks. However, it is the belief of the author that what follows may be simplified, but it is essentially accurate.

(b) The Psychological Approach

A number of psychological theories have been utilised in studying how individuals cope with the onset of disability, albeit as the result of sudden trauma or progressive and ongoing debility. Personality theories[1], body-image theories[2], motivation theories[3] and interpersonal theories[4] have all provided that starting point for a variety of empirical studies. All of these theories have one thing in common – they assume that the onset of disability does not just bring about physical changes, but also changes of mental function. The mind has to adjust to these bodily changes. Hence an individual's personality must alter to come into line with his changed status or role, or he must come to terms with a changed or defiled body-image, or he may make greater or lesser efforts to achieve his goals in spite of or because of his disability, or he will have to adjust to the different way he is treated in interpersonal relations with others.

Starting from this assumption that something happens to the mind as well as to the body, a number of psychological mechanisms of adjustment have been identified, or more appropriately borrowed from other areas such as death and dying. Disabled individuals are assumed to have undergone a significant loss and as a result depression may set in. In order to come to

Source: Paper presented at the Second European Conference of Rehabilitation International, September 18–21, 1978. Sevenoaks: Naidex Conventions.

terms with this loss, a process of grieving or mourning will have to be worked through, in similar manner to those who must mourn or grieve for the loss of loved ones. Only when such processes have been worked through can individuals cope with death or disability.

Some writers have seen these mechanisms as a series of stages or steps which have to be worked through. A recent study[5] in New York University Hospital identified a four-stage process by which newly disabled paraplegics come to terms with their disability.

Stage 1 – Shock – the immediate reaction to the physical and psychic assault of spinal cord injury often characterised by weeping, hysteria, and occasionally psychosis with hallucinations.
Stage 2 – Denial – a refusal to accept that complete recovery will not take place.
Stage 3 – Anger – often projected towards those physically active around them, who serve as constant reminders of what has been lost.
Stage 4 – Depression – a realistic and most appropriate response to a condition of severe and permanent disability and a necessary stage if adjustment, rehabilitation and integration are to be achieved.

Albrecht[6] characterises this and various other schemes as developmental models and argues that they all, at least partially, assume that:

1 an individual must move sequentially through all of these stages to become fully socialised;
2 there is but one path through the stages;
3 an individual can be placed clearly in one stage by operational criteria;
4 there is an acceptable time frame for each stage and the entire process;
5 movement through the system is one way, that is, the system is recursive.

There are a number of general criticisms that can be levelled at those theories or explanations. Firstly, the model of man which these theories implicitly draw upon is one where man is determined by the things that happen to him – the adjustment to disability can only be achieved by experiencing a number of these psychological mechanisms or by working through a number of fixed stages. Secondly, adjustment is seen as largely an individual phenomenon, a problem for the disabled person, and as a consequence, the family context and the wider social situation are neglected. Finally, such explanations fail to accord with the personal reality of many disabled people, particularly those with traumatic spinal cord injury, who may not grieve or mourn or pass through a series of adjustment stages.

Despite these criticisms, it would be true to say that these theories have been the dominant mode of explanation and this needs to be explained. A major factor in this is that these theories are in accord with 'the psychological imagination' in that theorists have imagined what it would be like to become disabled, assumed that it would be a tragedy and hence decided that such an occurrence would require difficult psychological mechanisms of adjustment. However, the psychological imagination may not be an appropriate starting point for such theorising or research – it is surely a value judgment to assume that disability is a tragedy and scientific research should be objective and value free. Another factor is that these explanations are individualistic and thereby politically convenient. When a disabled person fails to internalise the rehabilitation goals set by the professionals or persistently pesters his local Social Services Department, he can be characterised as having problems in adjusting to his disability. This conveniently leaves the existing social world unchallenged; the goals of the rehabilitator remain unquestioned and the failure of the welfare department to provide the right assistance can be ignored.

While these and other factors may explain the adherence to these psychological theories, they do not explain why these theories have been empirically validated by a number of studies. I want to suggest that these theories become self-fulfilling in at least two ways. At a methodological level, having conditioned research in the sense that they posit adjustment to disability as a problem, researchers then ask questions relevant to that problem and get answers which are then presented as findings, valid social facts. To my knowledge, there have been no studies which started out with the assumption that disability was not a problem. The following quote[7] nicely illustrates the point:

Reflection on the many problems to which the cord injured person must make an adjustment impresses one with the gravity of the psychological processes which occur following cord injury.

Such an individual is confronted with grieving over his loss, coping with pain and phantom sensations, alterations in sexual functioning, loss of bladder and bowel control, the frustrations of immobilisation, loss of vocational goals and earning capacity, feelings of uselessness, role reversals in the family and the attendant loss of self-esteem and the social stigma of being 'different' in the public eye. *It is an amazing tribute to the flexibility and magnificence of the human spirit that so many people whose lives are thus devastated survive and function at the level of physical and social independence which most cord injured people achieve.* (My italics)

As so many paraplegics are able to function at a reasonable level, it is surely more logical to assume that this is a normal everyday reaction and need not be described in such glowing terms. To put the matter simply, adjustment may be normal and not a problem at all.

There is a second way in which these theories may become self-fulfilling in that they may actually create the reality they purport to explain. In the case of mental illness it has been shown[8] that psychiatrists impose their definitions of the reality of particular problems upon their patients. Similarly in the study of criminal behaviour it has been shown that criminals will often verbalise theoretical explanations as excuses for their behaviour even in compulsive crimes like pyromania, kleptomania and child molesting[9]. With regard to disability, many disabled people will have contact with the theories described above not through meeting academic psychologists or participating in research projects, but through the everyday contact with professional workers who are also internalising these theories. Professional journals are beginning to disseminate these theories widely. An article in *Occupational Therapy*[10] argues not only that individuals must experience the following phases of shock, denial, turbulent aggression and working through, but also that there are a number of adaptions that patients must make including adaptions in body-image, adaption in role-image, loss of security and loss of self-esteem.[. . .] What is being argued is that the psychological mechanisms and processes that research has identified and described are themselves the product of that research activity both as a result of its methodological predispositions and the spread of this knowledge to professionals who are then able to impose this definition of reality upon their clients. Indeed, these psychological theories have taken on the attributes of what one writer[11] has called a 'paradigm' – that is, a body of knowledge to which all those working in the field adhere. However, the same writer has shown that paradigms are sometimes replaced or overthrown by 'revolution' and this revolutionary process is often sparked by one or two critiques of the existing paradigm.

Thus far, a critique of the existing paradigm has been attempted; what follows will be a preliminary attempt to map out an alternative theoretical framework.

(c) The Sociological Approach

The alternative theoretical scheme to be advanced is based on a sociological theory known as 'symbolic interactionism' drawn largely upon the work of an American social psychologist, G. H. Mead, and some of his students[12]. The two essential components of this theory are 'process' and 'meaning' – the experiences which individuals have, the things that happen to them are not fixed or stable, but rather take the form of a process through which individuals can negotiate their own passages. Further, these negotiated passages are not determined by the events that occur (like paralysis as the result of accident) but only by the meanings that individuals attach to these occurrences. These meanings are not themselves solely the product of individual consciousness, but are arrived at as the result of interactions with other people, close relatives and friends and the public at large; to use the language of symbolic interactionism, significant and generalised others.

The crucial question then is: what kind of explanatory framework does this scheme provide for those who become disabled as a result of injury to the spinal cord? Firstly, it sees the individual as a free agent in his own destiny – not in the sense that he can choose whether to be paralysed or not, but in the way he regards his paralysis. He does not have to experience certain psychological mechanisms nor follow any set of fixed stages – his adjustment will depend solely on the meaning he attaches to his social situation. He may experience some or all of these feelings identified by the psychological explanation, but he does not have to – he can regard his paralysis as a disaster or a triumph, but there are no basic processes which he *must* work through. Additionally, he may become depressed or grieve or mourn many years after he becomes disabled and not immediately after trauma. His feelings will be related to his particular social situation rather than his physical condition. Secondly, the meaning that disability has for particular individuals will be created in interaction with both significant and generalised others. Within symbolic interactionism, the term significant other[13] refers to those individuals or groups who can have an influential effect on what meanings an individual may attach to his particular situation. On the other hand, the term generalised other[14] can be taken to mean society, the general public or public and social attitudes. What needs to be considered then are the effects that both significant and generalised others may have upon the meaning of disability for individual paraplegics.

With regard to significant others, there are two kinds who may be influential. To begin with there are those professionals, doctors, nurses, physio- and occupational therapists, whom the paraplegic will encounter during his stay in a spinal unit. They will generally put forward a positive view of the nature of paraplegia and stress such factors as personal independence, the ability to work, drive, compete in sport and so on. Hence psychological adjustment is not usually regarded as a problem in spinal units and few, if any, special arrangements such as the provision of skilled counselling or psychiatric assistance, are usually made.

Then there are others like husbands, wives, close relatives and friends, children and so on, who may not have such a positive view of the nature of paraplegia and issues like the management of incontinence, the problem of sores, the adequacy of finance, inaccessibility and immobility may provide the crucial meanings of paraplegia.

In relation to the creation of meaning in interaction with the generalised other, the way society treats disabled people is the crucial factor. At the level of social consciousness it would be possible to argue that the meanings associated with paraplegia are positive. However, at the level of individual interaction where meanings are created, these positive attitudes are not carried through. High rates of unemployment[15], a mean and stigmatising benefits system, a collapsing medical service and poor social service provision provide an everyday reality very different from that which might be suggested at the level of social consciousness.

Thus, within this theoretical framework, the meaning that disability has for individual paraplegics is created and negotiated in interaction with both significant and generalised others. In these interactions and negotiations positive and negative meanings may exist side by side, conflict and change temporally. The individual may exhibit many of the mechanisms identified within the psychological paradigm, however, not as a direct result of his disability nor in a necessarily ordered sequence, but as the result of his changing social circumstances and situations and the variety of positive and negative meanings that this gives rise to.

In line with the title of this paper, our central concern is with the family and the effect that sudden disability may have upon interfamilial processes. Certainly in the field of handicap generally, the disruption of normal family processes and functioning has been recognised, particularly with regard to handicapped children[16] and the mentally handicapped[17]. Further, in the case of the parents of handicapped children, a variety of parental responses to disability in their children have been identified including shock, anger, guilt, grief and embarrassment[18]. However, an argument similar to the one advanced earlier in the paper has been readvanced regarding the responses by the parents of handicapped children; there is a similar myth to the one concerning the psychological adjustment to disability and that is the myth concerning parental feelings of guilt, shame, etc., about their handicapped children[19].

Unfortunately, there has been little direct concern with the effect that disability might have upon a person's family, when that person becomes disabled suddenly and in adulthood. Specifically, with regard to spinal cord injury, the authors referred to earlier who put forward the developmental framework for adjustment to paraplegia[5] consider the effects that sudden disability can have upon a family[20]. Nonetheless, their consideration is solely geared to how a family can help the disabled person through the developmental stages of adjustment identified in this previous paper. Certainly there is no consideration of the fact that non-disabled family members (as significant others) can be actively involved in creating the meaning that disability will have not only for the disabled person, but for the whole family.

While psychology has provided the theoretical framework for consideration of individual adjustment to disability, the major framework for consideration of the effects of disability upon family life has been derived from functionalist sociology, typified by Parsons and Fox[21] in their consideration of the effects of illness upon the urban American family. However, much of their argument is now out of date for they argue that the extra-familial care of the sick and disabled is functional to family life and stability since it removes potentially disruptive elements from the family situation. However, this argument was advanced before the ideological attachment and practical commitment to community care had taken hold in the 1960's and 1970's[22].

Interactionists have, by and large, not attempted to provide an alternative theoretical framework, but simply studied family processes at first hand. Thus a number of studies have discussed the role of other family members in creating, defining and treating behaviour that eventually comes to be recognised as mental illness[23]. So, too, with physical illnesses, it has been shown that the meaning symptoms have for both sick individuals and other family members play a crucial part in determining when sick people eventually go to the doctor for a diagnosis[24]. A recent study of patients presenting at a hospital for cataract surgery has shown that the crucial factor in the decision to operate was not the objective measurement of peripheral vision, but the perception of defective sight as a problem in living by the patient and his family[25]. Within this tradition, a much neglected study of the wives of alcoholics has shown that their response was crucial in determining what subsequently happened to the family[26].

With regard to spinal cord injury (and perhaps disability generally) what is being suggested here is that adjustment to sudden traumatic disability is often harder for non-disabled members of a family than for the disabled person himself. A recent letter to the problems' page of a woman's magazine poignantly illustrates this point[27]:

My wife and I badly need help. Our only son has become paralysed and we simply cannot cope with this mentally although every practical help is being given to us. We thought of going to a marriage counsellor-but there is no marital problem as such. Far from it. We're devoted but very unhappy and unable to help each other.

It has already been suggested that one reason for this may be that the newly disabled paraplegic may be exposed to positive meanings associated with his disability whereas the rest of the family may not. Another reason may be that allowances are made and sympathy extended to the disabled person whereas other family members may simply be told to 'buck up as its not them that are paralysed'. Finally, in line with the psychological paradigm, most if not all of the support services will be concentrated on the disabled individual, his problems and needs, to the consequent neglect of other family members.

However, the point of this paper is not to provide an alternative interesting explanation, but to provide a theoretical framework which may serve as a guide to further research. Hopefully, this framework may challenge and ultimately replace the psychological paradigm which has dominated research so far.

It certainly suggests that adjustment to sudden, traumatic disability must be conceptualised as more than just a problem of individual adaptation.

(d) Conclusion

Recently there has been revised political interest in the family as a social group. This paper has provided both a critique of the individualistic approach to disability and a theoretical framework which emphasises the importance of the family. The implications of this at a practical, policy level are that state and voluntary provision should be much more broadly based. It is not enough to aim at adjusting the individual to a virtually unchanged social environment, but rather that the meaning of disability must be changed, not just for the disabled individual, but for society as a whole including non-disabled researchers, professional workers and other family members.

References

1 ADLER, A. (1927) *The Practice and Theory of Individual Psychology.* New York: Harcourt Brace & Co.

2 SCHILDER, P. (1950) *The Image and Appearance of the Human Body.* New York: Internation Universities Press.

3 MASLOW, A. H. (1954) *Motivation and Personality.* New York: Harper.

4 WRIGHT, B. A. (1960) *Physical Disability – A Psychological Approach.* New York: Harper and Row.

5 WELLER, D. J., and MILLER, P. M. (1977) 'Emotional reactions of patient, family and staff in acute care period of spinal cord injury.' Part One. *Social Work in Health Care, 2*(4).

6 ALBRECHT, G. L. (ed.) (1976) *The Sociology of Physical Disability and Rehabilitation.* Pittsburgh: University of Pittsburgh Press.

7 HOHMANN, G. W. (1977) 'Psychological aspects of treatment and rehabilitation of the spinal cord injured person.' *Paraplegia Life,* May–June.

8 SCHEFF, T. (1968) 'Negotiating reality: notes on power in the assessment of responsibility.' *Social Problems, 16,* 3–17.

9 CRESSEY, D. R. (1962) 'Role Theory, Differential Association and Compulsive Crimes.' In A. Rose (ed.) *Human Behaviour and Social Processes.* London: Routledge and Kegan Paul.

   TAYLOR, L. (1976) 'The Significance and Interpretation of Replies to Motivational Questions: The Case of Sex Offenders.' In P. Wiles (ed.) *The Sociology of Crime and Delinquency.* London: Martin Robertson.

10 IBBOTSON, J. (1975) 'Psychological effects of physical disability.' *Occupational Therapy,* January.

11 KUHN, T. (1962) *The Structure of Scientific Revolutions.* Chicago: University of Chicago Press.

12 MEAD, G. H. (1934) *Mind, Self and Society.* Chicago: University of Chicago Press.

13 SHIBUTANI, T. (1962) 'Reference Groups and Social Control.' In A. Rose, *op. cit.*

14 MEAD, G. H. *op. cit.*

15 MARSHALL, T., and OLIVER, M. (1978) *Work and Disability: an Employment Survey of Paraplegics and Tetraplegics.* Spinal Injuries Association.

16 HEWETT, S. (1970) *The Family and the Handicapped Child.* London: George Allen and Unwin.

17 TIZARD, J., and GRAD, J. C. (1961) *The Mentally Handicapped and their Families.* Oxford: Oxford University Press.

18 MACKEITH, R. (1973) 'The feelings and behaviour of parents of handicapped children.' *Developmental Medicine and Child Neurology, 15,* 524–7.

19 ROITH, A. I. (1963) 'The myth of parental attitudes.' *Journal of Mental Subnormality, 9,* 51–4.

20 WELLER, D. J., and MILLER, P. M. (1977) 'Emotional reactions of patient, family and staff in acute care period of spinal cord injury.' Part Two. *Social Work in Health Care. 3,* 7–17.

21 PARSONS, T., and FOX, R. (1952) 'Illness, therapy and the modern urban American family.' *J. Social Issues, 8*(4), 31–44.

22 SCULL, A. T. (1977) *Decarceration: Community Treatment and the Deviant –* a Radical View. New Jersey: Prentice Hall.

23 SAMPSON, H., MESSINGER, S. L., and TOWNE, R. D. (1952) 'Family processes and becoming a mental patient.' *Am. J. Sociol., 68,* 88–96.

24 STIMSON, G., and WEBB, B. (1975) *Going to See the Doctor*. London: Routledge & Kegan Paul.
25 HILBOURNE, J. (1976) 'Some problems of adjustment of elderly patients undergoing cataract surgery.' Paper delivered at University of Kent (unpublished).
26 JACKSON, J. K. (1954) 'The adjustment of the family to the crisis of alcoholism.' *Q. Jl. Stud Alcohol, 15,* 564–86.
27 Letter in *Woman's Own*, 10 December, 1977, p. 65.

8 Disability and the Helper/Helped Relationship. An Historical View

Vic Finkelstein

In this short essay attempts have been made to draw attention to a long neglected area of study: the historical origins of the relationship between disabled people and those, professional or lay, who may work with them in a helping role. For convenience the discussion is centred around the disablement of those who have physical impairments (excluding those with partial sight or deafness, as well as mentally handicapped and mentally ill people). However, it is maintained that the general social theory of disability, which underpins this essay, can be fruitfully applied to each specific group. Space only allows a sketch of the salient features of what can be called the 'helper/helped relationship in disability'. Future research will be necessary to unravel the complex details of this relationship which has matured over the past 300 years. It is hoped that this essay will seed such research as well as encourage practitioners to take a more positive attitude towards supporting physically impaired people when they try to bring a new helper/helped relationship to life.

There can be no doubt that over the past two decades there has been a radical improvement in the situation of disabled people in the United Kingdom. Twenty years ago few disabled people were to be seen in public. Although the numbers are still relatively very small there has been a significant increase. Reserved parking spaces for cars, ramped entrances to buildings, adapted toilets, captioned television news broadcasts, 'bleeping' pedestrian crossings, are all material examples of special facilities now available for disabled people within the larger community. Non-disabled people, therefore, not only are more likely to come within sight of disabled people, but have increasingly to adapt to sharing an environment which is also designed for others. Disabled people are becoming part of the community and entering into its social relations.

Paradoxically, probably the most significant measure of this changing and *improving* situation is the greater number of physically impaired people who have come forward to express their views and describe their *problems*. The sudden spurt in 'consumer' groups, too, reflects the growing confidence of disabled people that they should be active in championing their own cause. While this activity has, in the first place, taken the form of protest against social discrimination and inadequate help, it also shows that disabled people are moving from passive social relations to active ones. It is this trend that is particularly significant in the history of disability and in the relationship between helpers and helped.

Source: Previously unpublished Paper written for this Reader.

Traditionally, disabled people have been viewed as passive, unable to cope with normal social relations and dependent upon others. The professions came into being with this assumption as the key to the relationship that developed over the centuries between the active able-bodied helper and passive disabled object of attention. The refinement of professional education and training programmes over the years has not only entailed acquisition of specilised skills in 'treatment' but formalised ways of behaving towards patients and clients. This aspect of 'professionalism', how to dress for work, how to talk to patients, professional ethics, and so on, represents the accumulation of traditional practices which serve to maintain distance between active helpers and passive helped. 'Disabled people cannot do certain things', goes the idea, 'and therefore we intervene to help. In order to help it is necessary to be clear about what is the problem and who has it. We must, therefore, separate ourselves from our patients so that our actions are aimed at the ones needing help'. Central to this view is the notion that disabled people possess the 'problems'.

Now as disabled people have become more active in defining the 'problem' the traditional helper/helped relationship has come under strain. The suggestion is that in addition to their physical problems disabled people are placed in an oppressive relation to able-bodied people. This is particularly so when as a result of physical impairment they are assumed to be socially passive, inadequate and helpless. Since some of these assumptions underlie the evolution of the professions, the point of irritation between helpers and helped, in the modern era, can be easily recognised. For the momentum towards integration to gain pace it has become imperative that traditional restrictive professional practices give way to a new helper/ helped relationship. To do this it is necessary to take another look at the assumptions handed down to us by history and, until recently, only interpreted through the eyes of active able-bodied helpers.

Phase 1

It is convenient to take our starting point with the emergence of the British capitalist system. In its earliest period, prior to the Industrial Revolution, the population was overwhelmingly rural and production essentially agricul-tural with limited craft production but growing merchant trade. The importance of the market in the life of the community had become established and trade increasingly dominated the economy and social relations. Food, clothing and other goods were produced for sale in the market and one's ability to survive became determined by the ability to produce something for sale, reselling commodities bought from others, offering a service such as transporting goods to markets, or owning land. In these conditions 'cripples' can be assumed to have lived not very differently to the cripples under feudalism. In the small communities of early capitalism everyone knew each other and had a relatively fixed social status with its attendant family and social obligations (the inheritance of feudal rights and duties). Those who survived severe physical impairment, either at birth or through injury, would have lived as cripples within their communities. It is this proximity between able-bodied and crippled people which explains the ease with which writers could include crippled characters in the literature when writing about the common people. Conditions of life were extremely harsh for cripples, but in a context where life was harsh for all the common people, the circumstances of cripples would not have seemed significantly worse.

Apart from performing domestic duties for their families, such as cooking, making clothes and looking after the young children when possible, cripples unable to perform agricultural work could have supplemented the family income by spinning and weaving. Small and portable, the early machines could have been easily adapted to suit individual physiques. The work was carried out in their homes and cripples had no need to seek employment beyond the family. However, the rural population was being increasingly pressed by the new capitalist market forces and when families could no longer cope the crippled members would have been most vulnerable and liable to turn to begging and church protection in special poor houses. Market forces soon favoured machinery which was more efficient and able to produce cheaper more plentiful woven material. Those working larger looms would more likely survive and cripples would have had greater difficulty working such equipment. The tendency of capitalism to sift out the infirm from the able-bodied started with manufacture for sale in the market and from the earliest days being a cripple implied more than just having a physical impairment. When a group of people are sifted out of the general population by a manufacturing process this reflects the relationship between people and the way society produces and reproduces itself. The physically impaired people living in early capitalism were just as crippled by capitalist production using increasingly efficient machinery, as they were by the physical condition of their bodies. The cripples of early capitalist society started parting company with the cripples of feudal society and the social impediment to integrated community living became a small component together with the physical impairment component that went into making the new cripple. It took the Industrial Revolution to give the machinery of production the decisive push which removed crippled people from social intercourse and transformed them into disabled people.

Phase 2

Manufacture, largely based upon spinning and weaving, gradually spread in the rural areas until a large proportion of the population was engaged in these home industries. Several inventions increased the efficiency and power of these machines. Water power was harnessed in the drive for faster and more productive equipment. By the late eighteenth century highly complex mechanical devices were in use and the advent of the steam engine finally paved the way for very large machines attended by several workers. The size of the equipment necessitated special buildings and the increasing need for workers to travel to their place of employment. At this time the manufacture of machinery, which was for the production of commodities, became an important economic development. Spinning machines, for example, designed in this way were for use by average human beings and had to be usable by any worker freely employed on the labour market. Such a worker could not have any impairment which would prevent him or her from operating the machine. It was, therefore, the economic necessity of producing efficient machines for large scale production that established able-bodiedness as the norm for productive (i.e. socially integrated) living. For physically impaired people the machine determined their social status, rather than people determining the social significance of machinery – production for profit undermined the position of physically impaired people within the family and the community.

The Industrial Revolution also led to the growth of new industries – in particular the metal and coal mining industries. In both these areas disabled people could expect no salvation. Indeed, the conditions of work were such that new physical impairments were being created in the form of industrial injuries. Capitalist farming methods were also increasingly introduced and the steam engine played its part in encouraging the migration from country to town. Unemployed workers mingled with unemployable disabled people in the growing towns. The need to control population mobility became necessary as well as the need to control civil discontent amongst those out of work. So it was that the next step was taken and civil authorities began building special secure places for disabled people, and others who had no permanent home or source of income, and staffed these places with wardens and attendants.

By the 1850's conditions in industrial Britain were ready for large numbers of people to be uprooted and thrown into the new industrial factories. Beggars, thieves, vagabonds, unemployed workers and cripples were an endless source of concern to the authorities. At the same time industrial workers began organising with greater efficiency, demanding safer working conditions and compensation for industrial injury. Efforts were made to improve working conditions, and the sanitation in the cities, while the medical profession became increasingly involved both with illness and physical impairment. In a climate of great productive activity those who did not work were regarded with abhorrence and held to be responsible for their poverty and afflictions. But the work ethic made it necessary to distinguish between those who were able-bodied but did not work and those who were physically impaired. The latter were to be accepted as rightful recipients of charity and the former as indolent wasters to be hounded and punished for their sins. Thus the final segregative process occurred which set disabled people apart from all others. Even in unemployability physically impaired people were to be removed from their fellow citizens.

In presenting the process whereby cripples were transformed into disabled people it is not implied that there were no positive aspects. It is clear that to be given charity rather than being punished for not working has its advantages. But the advantage was gained by their ultimate removal from the social community – firstly from the working class family and then from the unemployed bottom layer of society. By the end of the 1800's and into the twentieth century it had come to be accepted that disabled people ought to be 'protected' by being placed in large institutions or, when families refused to abandon their members, to be hidden out of sight. The only source of income for the disabled population was charity.

Having a captive population of disabled people made it possible to study some of the underlying physical conditions more carefully and systematically and this went hand in hand with the general advance made by the medical profession at the turn of the century. Of particular importance, too, was the process whereby labour shed in efficient industries moved into the services. This meant that more labour became available for use in institutions. The First World War brought women into industry under conditions where they could assert some control over the way they were employed. Such experiences led to greater independence and acceptability as employees in services for disabled people. Nursing became a recognised profession for women. The transition from domestic work where they might well have had to care for an elderly disabled relative to paid employment looking after sick and disabled people was not too difficult a change. By the time the Second World War had started disabled people had been removed from their community roots for so long that the increasing numbers of people working with them could accept the historical assumptions about the intrinsic causes of their social isolation without a second thought.

The Second World War gave a tremendous impetus to the development of specialisms within the professions working with disabled and physically impaired people. Medical practices were improved so that more severely disabled people survived and physical treatments were developed which helped disabled people manage in activities where they were incapable before. Of particular importance was the availability of domestic appliances which could be operated with the minimum of physical energy and skill. Teaching a physically impaired person how to go to a well, fetch a pail of water, collect firewood and light a fire to make a pot of tea may have been impossible last century, but teaching a similarly impaired person to fill an electric kettle with water, switch on a button, etc. to make a pot of tea today is well within the accepted aims of modern rehabilitation practice. In this respect the growth of wealth in Britain has been the basis for those helping disabled people reach increasingly complex goals in activities of daily living.

The increased wealth of the nation, large numbers of workers in service industries (especially the post Second World War health and welfare services), and an isolated disabled population available for intensive treatments paved the ground for the next development in disability. At the turn of the century non religious charitable organisations played an increasingly significant role in the care of disabled people and disabled children and began to organise on a massive scale (e.g. the Spastics Society) to agitate for state intervention and better forms of treatment. They were particularly concerned about the education of their children and set about creating such a service.

There have always been a few physically impaired people who managed to avoid the disabling pressures of the social system and find a place within the society where they have achieved recognition as fellow human beings. The past two decades, however, have seen increasing numbers of disabled people using the skills learnt from professionals as a step towards social reintegration. The movement of this group into the community, however, has confronted them with the experience of disability as a form of social discrimination and oppression. The successful disabled integrators have found that society, uncontaminated by their presence for centuries, has designed a world which does not recognise their existence. Such people have been forced to protest, at first individually and then collectively about their social situation. This protest has not been confined to the material world of buildings and streets but includes a rejection of the now well established view that disability means passivity in organising and managing one's own life. Like the parents' organisations these new self help groups started providing their own services.

Centuries of isolation have been followed by help to counteract this segregation and disabled people have begun articulating their own interpretations of their social situation as well as redefining the roles and limitations of the helping professional and lay workers. It is clear that professional practice which grew up on the basis of the social exclusion of physically impaired people led professionals into a set of practices which have now become a barrier to further development of their client group. What should be clear from the above historical sketch is that it is not professional practice, as such, which impedes the increased flow of disabled people back into the community but that aspect of their relationship which places them in an active controlling role over a passive patient or client.

Phase 3

It will be clear that we have only started entering the new phase whereby the helper/helped relationship will become reformed into one of equality. Exactly what the requirements are lies in the future but it is clear that any future relationship between physically impaired people and those who help them will have to encourage the utmost activity of the client in the decision making process and access to all records, plans and planning meetings will be necessary. If disability was a social imposition on physically impaired people, the reintegration of disabled people will not only remove their disabilities but introduce a new era of cooperative work between helpers and helped.

SECTION TWO
Styles of Living

This section is closely linked to the previous one in that it also sets out to examine the social world. It differs from the first part in that it looks more specifically at the disabling effects of society on the *individual's* experiences and relationships. If the central theme of the first section was 'disabling relationships', the central theme of the second is 'social barriers'.

The articles in this section set out to illustrate, largely by personal account and case history, the social barriers to integration that are created by society. The first article in the section (9) is taken from the discussion by a group of 'experts' (both able-bodied and disabled) of the principal social barriers that face disabled people and presents a fair summary of the major areas of concern. This sets the scene for most of the readings that follow: it highlights the fact that social barriers occur in all facets of our life and our day to day relationships with people, and by doing so introduces the concepts of prejudice and discrimination. Many of the themes of this opening article are picked up in the second by Davidson (10). Here, adolescents with cerebral palsy discuss with their ex-teacher the problems they face and the barriers they feel society unjustly creates.

Turning to the barriers that are created in personal relationships the next three articles present insight into and informative accounts of the experiences of disabled people. The first of these, by Hicks (11), examines specific problems faced by people with visual impairments in forming meaningful relationships. Written by an academic mainly for professional workers, it is a sensitive and thought provoking account of the factors involved. The article by Wills (12), again focusing on the problems of visual impairment, looks specifically at the developing parent-child relationship when the child is disabled. Placing a welcome stress on the positive factors in mothering (all too often ignored by professional workers) this article examines the relationship that can develop between the 'ordinary devoted mother' and her blind baby. The article by O'Neil (13) gives a light hearted and lively account of his own experiences of another sensory impairment, that of deafness. In what is essentially a very personal account, O'Neil aptly shows the illogicality of the aid supply system as it often appears to the disabled consumer.

This theme of fighting the barriers of illogicality and inconsistency of the service system is continued in the next reading (14). Written by the parents of Kim, a mentally handicapped child, this extract from their book gives an eye-opening account of their experiences as parents. It highlights the problems they faced in trying to ascertain the facts about their daughter's disability and their fight for her rights.

From the social barriers that can be created in personal relationships we turn in our next article (15) to a brief examination of the restrictions faced by disabled people in the field of employment. The short extract from the Snowdon report illustrates the prejudice of the employers – note how the case histories contrast with the actual recommendations of the Committee. Perhaps one of the greatest physical barriers that disabled people face is an architecturally structured society built to able-bodied norms and specifications. The article by Gormley and Walters (16) summarises the findings of a social survey on mobility needs. Reporting on the pattern of mobility and the use of mobility aids by disabled people this article represents a very useful summary of the major areas of concern.

Finally, we have chosen to close this section with a brief extract from Oswin's account of a typical day in a children's long stay hospital ward (17) – an alarming example of the extent to which social barriers can degrade and dehumanise.

9 Social Barriers to the Integration of Disabled Persons into Community Life

Identification of the Principal Social Barriers

[The following report is based on discussions which took place at a meeting of a group of international experts in Geneva in 1976, from 28 June to 5 July. The group consisted of representatives from many different nations and membership was as follows: six experts appointed directly by the UN Secretary General; six experts appointed by the Council of World Organisations interested in the handicapped; and various representatives of the following organisations: International Labour Office, World Health Organisation, Rehabilitation International and the Council of World Organisations.]

[. . .] On the basis of the background documentation and the general exchange of views on the subject, the Group proceeded to identify the principal social barriers to the integration of disabled persons into community life. Several different models were suggested in an effort to illustrate the complexity of the problems and to establish a pattern for the most pragmatic approach to the task assigned to the Group. After an extensive exchange of views, the Group agreed to use in its further deliberations the formula shown in the figure below.

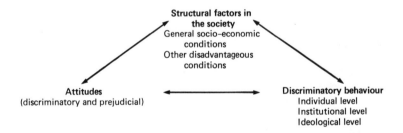

The Group agreed that for the purposes of its discussions the phrase 'social barriers' would denote the attitudinal, institutional and societal factors functioning in the economy, culture and organization of community life which impede disabled persons from fulfilling the normal social roles of members of the community and from participating in the normal economic, political and cultural activities of their society on a par with the able-bodied. [. . .]

Source: United Nations Department of Economic and Social Affairs (1977) *Social Barriers to the Integration of Disabled Persons into Community Life*. New York: United Nations Publishing Service.

Prejudicial Attitudes

For the purpose of its discussions, the Group agreed to use the term 'attitudes' in a broad sense, not differentiating between beliefs and values. In this context, 'attitudes' refers to an individual's predisposed thoughts, feelings and actions towards others. A 'prejudiced attitude' towards the disabled predisposes a person to respond primarily to the disability rather than to the sum of personal characteristics.

It was recognized that prejudices about disabilities have existed throughout history and that for centuries disabled persons have been considered impure, inferior and despicable and have, therefore, been kept apart from the rest of the community, if not outside it. Many theories of attitude formation have been advanced. These theories differentiate between the factors generally present in society and the factors specifically related to the disability condition. Each individual's attitudes are formed on the basis of a wide range of variables such as economic, social and cultural factors, family attitudes, religious beliefs, his past experiences and, of course, his specific personality traits. In addition, there are specific disability-related elements which may affect the process of attitude formation. These elements may include the origin of the disability (whether it was caused by a war injury or an industrial accident, was a congenital defect or a self-inflicted condition), the person's age at the onset of the disability, the prognosis of the disability, the visibility of the disorder and its cosmetic quality.

Attitudes can be conceived of as having many facets or components so that different aspects may create different problems and have different origins. Thus, one may, for instance, accept disabled persons as co-workers and neighbours but have negative feelings about intimate relations with them. Therefore, one may manifest certain behaviours in one context and quite different ones in other contexts. Also, attitudes that assume a person with a particular disability is functionally inferior may be held not just with regard to that disability condition but may be generalized to other types of disability as well.

It has often, and correctly, been observed that people with disabilities may share the prejudices about disabilities held by the larger community. Research data suggest that this can lead in the disabled to feelings of self-rejection, shame and an exaggerated sense of rejection by others. This, in turn, may stimulate such self-imposed behaviour as segregation or aggressive behaviour and lower levels of expectation.

While the examples cited above may have referred to various types of physical disability, it is obvious that the same concepts and complex elements of attitudes are applicable to a fuller range of individual differences, including mental, emotional and social conditions. Thus, uneasiness in interacting with someone 'different' is common in response to aging, mental illness and mental retardation, as well as certain other conditions.

Discriminatory Behaviour

Discriminatory behaviour may take place either because a person is prejudiced or because prejudices have been built into the laws, regulations and customary norms and requirements of different social structures and institutions. However, a distinction has to be made between individual, institutional and ideological discrimination.

Individual Discrimination

Direct individual discrimination was considered to refer to the discriminatory manner in which an individual may behave, regardless of the existing rules, norms and requirements. This may take the form of either avoiding contact with the disabled or, when in contact, of manifesting superficial acceptance or straightforward rejection. In fact, discriminatory behaviour may often become graver in degree from less intimate to more intimate contact. In general, the more there is at stake in an interaction or a situation, the graver is the discriminatory behaviour.

In indirect individual discrimination, an individual may avoid or reject the disabled person not directly because of his physical impairment but rather because the impairment negatively affects the disabled person's physical attractiveness and/or is believed to affect the level of his competence or intellectual functioning.

In covert individual discrimination, the individual concerned is not aware of his or her discriminatory behaviour.

Institutional Discrimination

Direct institutional discrimination may occur through legislation when, for instance, disabled persons with specified impairments are excluded from some types of employment or are forbidden to marry, have access to or use of such community services as education, health or transportation, enter public places or own property. It may also be the result of protective legislation which grants some, but only some, groups of disabled people specific advantages or benefits justified on the basis of their disability.

Another type of direct institutional discrimination takes place through institutional segregation of the disabled from the non-disabled. Thus, the creation of a segregated world for the disabled, although necessary in some specific circumstances, may often become direct discriminatory behaviour. This may be the case with the development of special educational programmes, occupations designed for the disabled only and segregated occupational settings, such as certain sheltered workshops.

Indirect institutional discrimination may take place when social structures and institutions are designed with certain specific models and norms in mind. For example, the occupational structure for certain types of occupations may be designed according to the physical norms for non-disabled young males and, therefore, may be entirely inappropriate for some disabled persons. By accepting those norms, employers can discriminate against the disabled without direct reference to disability and, consequently, can justify the exclusion of the disabled from these types of employment in terms of the 'nature' of the occupation or of the occupational setting. Indirect institutional discrimination may also occur when, for example, some types of occupations and jobs are specified as requiring the lifting of a certain minimum weight, kneeling, climbing or standing at a machine or bench; many disabled persons are thus excluded from employment, although such obstacles could, in many instances, be overcome by relatively simple and inexpensive job adaptations.

Another form of institutional discrimination can take place without direct reference to the disabled status of people because direct discrimination has taken place elsewhere. For example, when disabled people do not have access to certain types of training or to transportation, they may be excluded from some jobs not because they are disabled but because they do not possess the required type of training or simply because they cannot get to the place of employment.

Ideological Discrimination

The type of social philosophy prevailing in society and the extent to which society accepts responsibility for the individual may create discriminatory behaviour. For example, whenever a philosophy of survival of the fittest prevails in a society, discrimination towards the disabled takes place without even being considered discriminatory. It is only when societal responsibility for the individual becomes accepted that even the notion of discrimination towards the disabled becomes relevant and meaningful. The extent to which egalitarian ideologies prevail in a society influences the behaviour of its members. If these ideologies do not prevail, there is little concern about equalizing the chances of different groups in society, including the disabled. As long as 'normality' and, more specifically, what constitutes the 'normal' image of man in society are understood in a very narrow sense, the disabled will continue to face important social barriers to their integration into all aspects of life. The more the disabled can organize themselves and create a social movement that could lead to the redefinition of the concept of 'normality', the less will be the tendency for overt and direct discrimination.

Societal Factors

In discussing areas or situations in which, or in connexion with which, barriers are created to the integration of disabled persons into society, the

Group identified the following societal factors that might create or affect the creation of such barriers:

(a) The state of development of a country (its economic situation and the standard of such social services as education, health, welfare and housing);

(b) The political and economic system and ideology;

(c) Legislation;

(d) Values and norms and the impact of the communications media on them;

(e) Culture (arts, science, literature and others).

Individual attitudes and prejudices that result in discriminatory behaviour often have a direct relationship to these broad social areas. The state of development of a country has a straightforward linkage with services, their coverage and also possible imbalances. Political systems reflect the philosophy of and approach to social behaviour, while legislation provides the norms for it. Where the political system consciously seeks changes in society, it also provides an opportunity to reassess the social attitudes towards the disabled. The prevailing economic system has a direct relationship to employment policies, conditions and opportunities. The system of values and norms has a direct bearing on discriminatory social behaviour. The Group, therefore, felt that a review of social barriers to integration should take these factors into account.

The Standardization of Society as a Cause of Social Barriers

Society and most of its functions have been developed to meet the requirements of normal or average or standard situations, a tendency which seems to become more pronounced in more developed societies. This development, as such, was considered acceptable and necessary in many respects, to the extent that it serves effectively a large majority of people. As a matter of principle, disabled persons are not in a position different from that of other citizens in relation to this development. On the contrary, it has an equally positive significance for them as long as their needs correspond to those of 'normal' people. However, while people are usually able to satisfy all or most of their needs by the standard production and procedures, individuals in exceptional situations or with special needs, such as disabled persons, may experience difficulties. Disabled persons are in a different situation because their handicaps may substantially limit the possibility of their making choices and it may create special individual needs which cannot, perhaps, be fully met within a structure designed for 'normal' persons.

There is a tendency in modern society to categorize and classify people, particularly with respect to the provision of its services. This is needed for many practical purposes and can be useful from the point of view of the society as a whole. However, if a classification based on one feature only, e.g., a physical disability, spreads out to label the whole personality, it may have a segregative effect. Such features can be identified in social services, for instance. There seems to be a general trend of development away from selective services, which are usually more effective but also more expensive, complicated and time-consuming, to more universal social services, which are less expensive, simple and more efficient administratively. But, there may be a certain danger that, if a movement from selective and special social services to universal and standard services alone dominates the development, some of the special needs of disabled persons may remain unmet, thus creating situations where social barriers to integration become evident.

The Inaccessibility of Social Services as a Factor in Creating Barriers to Integration

The existence of adequate rehabilitative and other social services is a precondition for the successful integration of disabled persons. But even where such services exist, their limited availability and accessibility, geographically and/or physically, may create obstacles to their use. Usually, some special arrangements are necessary to enable the disabled to use these services. This can be done by means of better dissemination of information on the availability of services, individual counselling of clients, training staff to cope with the general and specific needs of the disabled and making it economically possible for the disabled to take part in rehabilitation activities.

The Structure of Society as a Cause of Social Barriers

By not always being able to provide for a comprehensive approach, the division of labour may, at times, have adverse effects, because it may result in dividing the social services from other activities required to meet human needs in different sectors. The unsatisfactory level of co-operation and co-ordination as well as the undefined division of responsibility, including gaps and overlapping, may result in insecurity and complicated procedures for the disabled person who has to address himself to a number of agencies, each of which may take care of only one part of his needs. There are, however, some notable examples in many countries of a trend towards a new model in which all social services for an individual or a family are concentrated in one local centre.[. . .]

10 'Them and Us'

M. B. Davidson

[The following extracts represent a teacher's report on a series of discussions held between herself and her pupils, all of whom had cerebral palsy.]

'People Like You'

'People like you shouldn't be allowed to live.'
'Have you heard anyone really say that?'
'Of course! She said it to me!'
'What did you do?'
'I was so surprised, I laughed; and then I was so angry I just went away, as quickly as I could, in case I was rude.'
'We were looking out of the window the other day, my neighbour and I, and a child with artificial legs passed. "People like that shouldn't be allowed to live," she said. "Why not?" I asked. So she drew back and said, "Oh, I didn't mean people like you. You can get around and do things for yourself." I was stunned! Surely everyone has a purpose?'
'I was shopping one Saturday and it was quite busy and I know I am slow and my sticks get in the way, though I am as careful as I can be. But a woman turned round and snapped at me, "Why can't you do your shopping on other days and not get in the way? People like you don't need to shop on busy days". She never seemed to think that I've got a job too. I'm out of the house soon after eight o'clock and not home till after six in the evening.'
'Some people seem to think you shouldn't even want to work, if you have any kind of handicap. I got an interview quite easily, but, when he saw me, it was like a knife coming down. "People like you shouldn't apply for jobs," he said. Thank goodness my mother was with me.'
'People like you' is what hurts so much. It implies that a great gulf is fixed and cannot be bridged – the differences are too great. The disabled feel that this is not so, that the important things are those which are in common, the places where we are all the same.
'It's because we are in a minority,' it was said in discussion.
'Coloured people get this kind of disdainful treatment too; so do women sometimes; so did the Jews at various times in history. The majority will not believe you are the same as they are and that you feel, in all essentials, as they do. You can't get them to understand it – it's like Shylock saying, "If you scratch us, do we not bleed?".'
What is even more painful is the realisation that people seem to think a disabled person will be devoid of normal intelligence.
'I notice, in my office, that people tend to tell me the same thing over and

---

Source: M. B. DAVIDSON (ed.) (1977) *You Tell Me*. Edinburgh: Scottish Council for Spastics.

over again, as if I couldn't understand what they are saying. It often happens. I'm not sure whether they mean to help, or if they think I am mentally handicapped too! But it's very irritating.'

'I think people are shy of us sometimes. I have a good friend now who says she had never met a disabled person before she knew me. It does mean we usually have to make the first approach – we have to break down barriers of fear or embarrassment – a shyness. It means a constant effort, but we have to do it.'

'In these days, when so much is said about integrating people, there are still some who make you feel inferior. When I was out recently, in my chair, I met a lady I know with a friend of hers. I don't speak very well, but I said, "Hello, how are you?". She made no effort to answer me or to speak to me directly. She just said to her friend, "Oh, look how excited she is to see me", as if I were deaf or without any understanding, though she knows me. If she had had any decency, she might have waited to talk about me until I'd gone away. I do find my speech problem harder and harder to bear. I know, from experience, how difficult it is to listen to someone whose speech is worse than one's own, but I always try to understand because I know how much depends on the attitude of the listener.'

'Who's Seeing to You?'

'A good deal of lip service is paid to your intelligence and ability nowadays, but when it comes to relating this to practical matters it becomes a question of "Who's in charge of you?" "Who's seeing to you?" You have to adjust to these social occasions and take things as they come. If you say something to a stranger and he doesn't understand, it's important to change the verbal form. For example, you say, "Can I have a ticket to X?" and they don't get it. So you say, "A ticket please", and they say, "Where to?" and you say "X". This is good if people are pushed for time, as they are at stations. You need to be as quick and efficient as you can, and that inspires confidence in others. If you just stand (or sit in a chair, like me!) and gaze around and wave your arms, they just say "Next please"!'

'When I meet people for the first time, it's not that I want to be assertive, I just want to show that I can manage. I had to go for a College interview, so I just signed on in the usual way and wandered in, in my wheelchair. I was met with considerable warmth – there hadn't been any "Oh, that handicapped chap's coming today" stuff. And I was ready with my answers and information on the spot – that helps. They didn't know me at all – they just accepted me. People, in the initial stages, have varied expectations of those in wheelchairs – they can't help wondering how you'll speak and move.'

'I find people, on the whole, friendly – there's always the odd one, of course, who can't stand you. But a great many do try to help, like resettlement officers. Amongst those, the young ones are best, those nearest your own age – they understand; they'll bend over backwards to help you.

Some of the older ones don't bother; I think they feel there isn't much they can do. I do think, too, that there are those who quite definitely dislike physically disabled people so that they don't want to be with them, or to employ them. It's a minority, I think, but you have to accept it.'

'We Go Out by Different Doors'

'What I hate most is condescension – the way some people, who probably feel sympathetic, throw a favour at you. I told you about the man in the pub who noticed me there and flung some money on the counter saying, "Here, get yourself a drink!" Why couldn't he say something like, "Hello; cold night, let's have a drink!" I'd have accepted cheerfully. That's no way to show sympathy.'

'I don't think people should show us sympathy, or, at least, not pity. You can sympathise with anyone about anything – like having a cold or missing a bus; but that's not pity. Pity is a thing we do not want – it's degrading. We just want ordinary friendly interest and encouragement.'

'I think that what we really need most are friends who accept us as friends and ask us to do things with them, just as they do with other friends. I recently made a very pleasant friend and, one night when I had tickets for a concert I asked if she would like to come. She did and we enjoyed it greatly; it was lovely to be out with her on my own and not with a crowd – otherwise one loses the point of going out.'

'The students I have met, since I started going to evening classes, have been great. It isn't only that they are helpful about transport, it's that they invite me to come and have coffee and meet the others and join the talk. I can't say how much I enjoy it; and they seem to accept me completely.'

'I suppose it's true that one of the main obstacles with which spastic people have to contend is their physical appearance, which can look awkward and so attract attention. But it's surely just as true that the more the public sees of these "awkward" people, the less conspicuous they will seem; and it will come to be understood that the degree of physical disability is not an indication of mental or intellectual abilities. Does it matter if a man needs two hands to steady his cup of tea? Surely this need not have an adverse effect on his relationships with those with whom he is in company?'

'To my mind, the greatest difficulty does not lie with the handicapped person, but with the community. There should be no question of his feeling he has to "enter" the community; he is naturally and of right an integral part of it. The public lack confidence in dealing with handicapped people, but if they can understand that the mentality of the disabled is on an equal level with the "normal" person, there should be relatively little difficulty. The public must come to feel that a handicap, in the majority of cases, does not ostracise a person and should not keep him from his rightful place in society.'

'The public needs to be educated; they should mix more with handicapped people and then they would understand. I think Disabled Week should be wiped out altogether because it exploits disablement. "Right," they say, "you're disabled so we'll raise money for you. We'll give a concert." Or else *we* give the concert and they come as the audience – but we go out by different doors! Concerts and so on may raise money, but they don't get to the root of the matter. Society likes to keep you together, you see, and to regulate your working and your living. This generation must bring about changes.'

'I speak slowly and with some difficulty but, over the years, I have found that talking to strangers has given me complete confidence and has helped my speech. I just made myself do it. I would ask them the time, or make easy remarks like, "It's a fine day". Sometimes, I was not understood, but I kept on trying and, through time, I found that most people could understand me. Some people do seem to think that a person in a wheelchair is apart or different in some way. I do dislike the person who pats me on the head (at my age!!) and asks me my name. I have travelled quite a bit on my own and found most people helpful but there are others who treat us like Martians or Men from the Moon! When I travel by train, I have to go in the guard's van and, on one occasion upon arrival I heard the guard say to the porter, "Look, there's a cripple in the van!" I felt as if I were a wild beast, ready to bare my fangs and spring! You need a sense of humour – everyone does. I was having a drink with some friends at a hotel and a man leaned forward and asked my friend, "How do you know when he's had enough?" My friend left it to me to answer, so I bent forward and whispered, "When I get out of this chair and walk to the door, you'll know I've had enough!" '

'Our Way'

'Perhaps we are partly to blame ourselves. I think we are often shy, too, and because we are self-conscious we project a bad image of ourselves. I think spastic people do this because they are often clumsy – people with other handicaps are not necessarily clumsy, so it makes us feel rather stupid. I know it's difficult but, if you can, I think you should be as open as possible; if people want to know what's wrong with your hands or your feet, tell them. The trouble is that they often don't like to ask or even give you a chance to explain – they feel it's tactless to notice.'

'It would be easier for us, I think, if we could accept the fact that a lot of people have handicaps. They may seem fairly slight to us, like people not seeing very well, or suffering from headache or hay fever, or having a bad temper or a bad skin, but they are real handicaps to the people who have them – they do disable them somewhat. It's just that our disabilities are so much more noticeable, even when they are not very heavy, and we feel embarrassed and that makes others feel embarrassed too. I know it's hard, but I think if you can you should accept your situation and go on from there – that could be our contribution to the "Them and Us" attitude.'

'Well, "acceptance" of disability is a fairly bitter verbal pill to swallow, though I suppose it can become enriching in a sense. No, I don't think I can accept the total inability of my handicap – if I did, I'd just sit back and "take it"; that's how heavy it is. All the same, I don't spend my time kicking against the pricks. After all, if you've a river to cross and you can't swim, you've got to find some means to get to the other side. So you use your mind – I've noticed how oddly my mind can work to minimise frustration and the expenditure of energy; it's making the most of what you have. And somehow, the more one does, the less one realises the handicap; after all, your nose isn't only there to blow – you can turn pages with it, I watch my wife as she approaches a problem – she's less handicapped so she uses the more traditional ways – and, if it seems difficult I say, "Why not try it my way?" This can be regarded either as a surrender or a conquest – you are finding a way to do a thing skilfully, even gracefully. It seems odd to speak of an ugly thing like one's body being graceful – spilling one's tea around is hardly graceful. Still – just bend down and go "slurp, slurp" – one manages. One must learn to manage!'

'If acceptance means coming to think of oneself in a certain way through the efforts of counsellors and so on, I can't take that; it's not enough. You must learn to do it for yourself. Of course, you can listen to advice and accept it or reject it, but you must move on from that to find what you are capable of doing and it must be more than they expect – or, at least it may be. It's always up to you, in the end.'

'I do kick against the pricks. The thing is that great mental effort is required to cope with physical handicap and this produces psychological difficulty and often deep depression. I doubt if other people really understand how bad this can be. The result is that I find I am fighting all the time – I can't relax. I just don't know how to manage life in a relaxed way because I've had to fight all the way. And it's so tiring – even a very ordinary day's work leaves me with little or no energy for social life. In spite of this, it's worth fighting on – I remember a point at which I realised that the people I was working with weren't thinking of me any longer with sympathy but with affection; that was good. Sometimes, though, I feel the most important things are those you don't fight for – the "happy accidents"; in fact, we need a spot of serendipity from time to time!'

'Doling Out Smarties'

'There is, of course, another side to this – I mean the people who praise you too easily and without understanding. No doubt it's kindly meant, but if the praise is given without discrimination or if it's not as between equals, it has a hollow ring.'

'I feel dreadfully embarrassed when people pass comments on me in my hearing, like saying, "Oh, there's courage for you!" Perhaps I'm too sensitive about it, but I think everyone must feel it. People mean to praise you for what they feel is your success, but the success isn't really there – you know that yourself. You may have achieved something, but there are large areas of life where you are deeply unhappy and they never see this.'

'People often praise you if you've 'got on' in some way. I don't think that's very fair. I don't go to FP [Former Pupil] days or things like that because all the attention seems to go on people who have made the grade – or so I feel, anyway. I think it doesn't really matter whether one has become a doctor or just remained at home, so long as one is doing one's best. I like to go to places where we all feel in it together.'

'Of course, I appreciate people who are kind and friendly. You need companionship – I get quite desperate with loneliness sometimes. You need someone of your own, your own sort of age and style, with whom you can be quite open. Everyone needs that – not just a disabled person, but we may find it harder to get. And I think that some of us, at any rate, need someone who is known to be ready to act as a counsellor or a sort of social consultant – not a social worker, that's too professional, and not a parent – that's quite a different relationship. But it must be someone who doesn't diminish your dignity.'

'Dignity is important. I don't want to be treated as a "success story", or to be praised in an off-hand sort of way, like someone doling out smarties. People who have known you when you were young, brought you up or taught you, are pleased when you do well and make the grade. They feel it to be self-rewarding in some measure. But they remain quite unaware of all you know you haven't done or haven't yet achieved.'

But what about 'Them'? What are the attitudes of the community? These are as varied as the people who make up the community, a mixture of concern and carelessness, sympathy and irritation. The young people can accept this – they only want to be a part of it; and it seems certain that such integration would benefit the able-bodied public as much as the disabled. In a recent newspaper article, Michael Hare Duke wrote:

In a whole variety of ways, a community which overcomes the temptation to segregate people for specialist attention and takes the risk of integration is in the process of discovering its own resources. It may seem easier to discuss people as 'problems' and remove them to a safe distance. In fact, by such a process, a community is refusing to accept the truth that everybody has a 'shadow' side, which needs to be acknowledged. They are emphasising the split between health and sickness which makes illness a threat, something which we pretend happens to THEM but not to US.

11   Relationship and Sexual Problems of the Visually Handicapped

Susan Hicks

[*Mrs Hicks Le Poidevin (née Hicks) is completing a doctorate at Corpus Christi College, Oxford, for which she was sponsored by the Regional Association for the Blind, on the provision of services for the visually handicapped in England. She was formerly Research and Mobility Officer.*]

Introduction

Because of the inabilities to acquire information through sight and to make eye contact with other people, the visually handicapped, and particularly the functionally blind, may encounter relationship and sexual problems which are not common to other disabilities. These problems differ for those whose visual impairment is congenital (from birth or infancy) or adventitious (occurring after visual concepts have been formed). They apply to initial encounters, to the range of potential partners, to sexual relationships, and they have clear implications for education and counselling and for professional relationships with the client.

This article is intended for counsellors in sexual and relationship problems without specialist knowledge of visual impairment, for educators and administrators in schools and institutions for the visually handicapped, and for social workers and rehabilitation staff working with the visually handicapped.

The Committee on Sexual Problems of the Disabled, despite approaches to organisations for the blind, are lacking in counsellors who are competent to deal with the sexual problems of the visually handicapped (Stewart, 1977), and these aspects are not included in the training of specialist rehabilitation staff with the visually handicapped. Therefore, there is a need for interchange of information, so that those with experience in sexual and relationship counselling can obtain working knowledge of visual handicap, and vice versa.

Non-Verbal Communication and Personal Relationships

A complete psychological model of man must take account of man's interpersonal nature . . . Relations with others are the most important part of human life. Most of the essential human characteristics cannot be manifested by a person in isolation . . . Interaction is conducted by the two channels of vision and hearing with the verbal and non-verbal closely co-ordinated . . . Social behaviour is

Source: *Regional Review*, Spring 1979, No. 65.

produced as a stream of closely integrated responses, subject to continuous correction as a result of feedback, controlled by more or less conscious plans and subject to partly verbalized rules derived from the culture . . . The self-image is largely constructed out of the reactions of others and leads to self-presentation behaviour to create appropriate response in later social situations. (Argyle, 1972)

The relevance of Argyle's work is applicable to the congenitally blind child from the moment of birth. It has been established (Stern, 1977) that for the sighted infant, earliest relationships (particularly that with the primary care-giver which is usually the mother) profoundly affect the pattern for future relationships. In fact, patterns of social interaction are well formed within the first six months of life. What bearing does this have on the relationship between a sighted mother and her blind child? If her reactions to him are not warm and positive because she is suffering from the shock, guilt and grief of having produced a blind baby, the child's self-image and ability to relate to others will suffer.

Furthermore, in a sighted child, mutual gaze is a prime element in creating the bond with the mother. (Stern, 1976). This normally happens instinctively, but the mother of a blind child must be made aware that she and the child are being deprived of this first channel of communication so that she can begin to find ways of compensating for this lack. It is therefore essential that she and the family should be given appropriate help and support from the moment the child's visual handicap is discovered. The handicapped child brought up in an accepting and caring family atmosphere can develop the normal ability to relate positively to others.

In the course of normal interaction, both during childhood and adult life, non-verbal signals give people vital feedback as to how they are reacting to one another, and behaviour is continually modified in response. Thus for the sighted person, the non-verbal channel of communication is vitally important. Morris (1978) cites seventy-two different means of non-verbal communication and body language. In fact, where there is a conflict between the verbal and the non-verbal aspects of communication, it is the latter which takes precedence. (Argyle, 1972)

Anyone, therefore, who is so visually handicapped as to be unable to make use of this non-verbal channel of communication is at a severe disadvantage. Compensating for this lack of visual communication is a *social skill* that both the visually handicapped and sighted have to learn. The sighted person must be made aware that the visually handicapped person will receive no non-verbal signals from gesture, facial expression or eye contact. The visually handicapped person must bear in mind that he may be receiving incomplete information from tone and language, that sighted people expect to receive these signals – if only unconsciously – and that he may not be sending out the non-verbal signals that sighted people expect. In one case where this adjustment was not made, a husband and his newly blinded wife ceased to be able to converse naturally at a deep level until her sight was restored by an operation.

Just as a visually handicapped person is unable either to give or to receive the appropriate non-verbal signals to the same extent as a sighted person, so he may find himself unwittingly giving meaningless, inappropriate or anti-social signals. There is a category of mannerisms sometimes called 'blindisms' which congenitally totally blind children in particular develop and which persist if unchecked. These include rocking the body backwards and forwards, eye poking, swinging the head or body around and twiddling the fingers. The causes of these mannerisms are not certainly known. It is likely that they are associated with deprivation of stimulation and inability to release energy because of restricted mobility in the blind child. A further, deeper cause may lie in what is collectively termed 'maternal deprivation' (Bowlby, 1951, 1973; Rutter, 1972).[1] The significance of these mannerisms for purposes of this discussion is, first, that they may be generally bizarre in appearance and off-putting and, second, that on occasion a sighted person may interpret them as having a meaning which was not, in fact, intended. Rocking, for example, might be taken to indicate agreement. The counsellor's task in pointing out their social disadvantages is straightforward, but breaking these ingrained habits may be extremely difficult. Finding alternative forms of stimulation and activity might be helpful, and considerable will-power is often necessary to consciously break the habit.

There are other forms of socially unacceptable behaviour (occasionally extreme) which the visually handicapped may exhibit. It would probably never occur to a sighted person that anyone needed telling that it was undesirable to indulge in heavy petting (or, though rarely, masturbation) in public. Furthermore, the totally blind have the additional disadvantage of being unsure of what is socially unacceptable in a given situation, such as knowing at a party what other people are doing or wearing, or when it is private enough to kiss someone.[2]

Problems in Initial Encounters

There are some problems which are common to anyone with a severe visual impairment. At a social gathering, for example, the visually handicapped person cannot look around to see who might be of interest: one has the problem of finding out about the existence and proximity of an interesting person. One must either be told by a third party, wait for the other to make the first move, or initiate conversation with who ever is proximate. A related problem, having found out about the existence of someone with whom one would like to converse, is that of mobility – of making one's way over to her or him independently, at the risk of making a fool of oneself, or stumbling over or colliding into anything that comes between, or wait for her or him to come over and make the introduction. This is particularly difficult for the man who is visually handicapped in societies where the male is expected to make the initial overture. It is little wonder that shy people just do not bother. Mobility can be equally problematic in trying to make an escape.

Problems resulting from lack of eye contact particularly affect initial overtures – the subtle messages and expressions of interest in another person which sighted people, even though disabled, transmit to indicate willingness to get to know each other better. Of course, the visual qualities which make a person physically attractive to a sighted person do not affect a blind person in the same way, for whom personality is undoubtedly more important.

A sighted person usually starts a conversation by catching the other person's eye, and because there is no eye contact, one often feels unsure of whether or how to approach a blind person to start a conversation. The techniques for normal social interaction which he has learned and takes for granted are inadequate for the new situation. Thus the ability to take the initiative and to put a sighted stranger at ease is an important social skill for visually handicapped people to cultivate, particularly if they have reserved dispositions. This applies equally, though in different ways, to the newly blind and to those emerging into the sighted world after long residence in institutions for the visually handicapped.

Thus, making initial contact and expressing interest is a much more conscious and deliberate operation for the visually handicapped than for sighted people.

The Congenitally Blind

The congenitally blind – who have never had vision – present the counsellor with quite a different problem.

Unlike the sighted child who naturally observes distinguishing physical features of people and animals, the totally blind child will not see how the body of the male and female differ, or how it changes with puberty, in pregnancy and old age, nor will he have the opportunity to observe reproduction in nature. It may well happen also, that he will remain ignorant far longer than a sighted child of the facts of intercourse, foetal development and birth. Moreover, the congenitally, totally blind may fail to form accurate basic concepts, have inadequate anatomical understanding and a poor body image of himself and others. (Vogel and Muxen, 1976)

Such basic mental conceptual inadequacy may exist even though a reasonably accurate definition may be given. A remark which illustrates this is the actual comment made by an adolescent boy blind from birth:

'I think I know *what* a girl's breasts are, but I'm not sure I know *where* they are!' (Dickman, 1975)

Again, one adolescent was perfectly able to define correctly the technical process of intercourse, but believed that the vagina was located under a woman's right breast. (Foulke and Uhde, 1975)

Another difficulty is that the congenitally blind often find it hard to arrive at general concepts; when presented with a particular model of a real-life object, they may accept it literally, unaware that it may be totally inaccurate as regards size, texture and proportion. Thus, it is important when using models for instruction to indicate in what ways the model differs from the real object being depicted. Also, when examining a tactile diagram, the congenitally blind may totally fail to grasp how a two-dimensional representation relates to a three-dimensional real-life object. In view of this, those concerned with the use of plastic life-size models of male and female anatomy for the totally blind criticize the models as being inadequate. (Vogel, 1976; Choate, 1972) The use of live models, therefore, has been advocated to facilitate more realistic concept generalizations in skin texture, size and consistency.

Implications for Education and Rehabilitation in Relationships and Sexuality

Now that we have considered the problems encountered by the visually handicapped, the implications for education and counselling in sexuality and relationships in schools for the visually handicapped and in rehabilitation counselling will be discussed next.

There is an urgent need to devise planned programmes concerned with the physical, psychological, social and moral aspects of human relationships. Short term remedial programmes are required for the visually handicapped young adults of today, because in the present educational system many of them suffer from not having had the benefit of such instruction at the proper time in their lives, and consequently have developed antisocial and other problems and misconceptions. If and when the deficiencies in education of the past in this respect are corrected, such remedial treatment should remain necessary only in exceptional cases. Long term programmes required for education to avoid the perpetuation of these deficiencies should be developmentally phased from infant school through adolescent assessment centres. Such programmes might include the following aspects:

(1) *Physical aspects:* sexual physiology, anatomy, reproduction, fertility, birth control, and sexually transmitted diseases;

(2) *Psychological aspects:* adolescent adjustment, emotional repercussions, marriage prospects including genetic counselling, the problem of stigma and sighted people's attitudes;

(3) *Social skills:* the importance of personal appearance and behaviour, dating, personal relationships, putting sighted people at ease, non-verbal communication, independence and self-sufficiency skills;

(4) *Moral and ethical issues:* values, individual responsibility to regard the welfare of others in sexual conduct.

Detailed suggestions on curriculum, equipment and instructional aids and resources on tape, and in Braille or large print are available in the American literature on the subject. (Neff, 1975; Berquist, 1968)

However, in England, there is little if any general access to books on sexuality in Braille, large print or on tape. A lack of accessibility of visual information in general is a major restriction caused by blindness. But society imposes further restrictions on the blind from obtaining information on sexuality through their only two alternative means of acquiring this information – hearing and touch. The visually handicapped should have the same right of access to information given by the printed word as the sighted for whom it is readily available. The choice should be theirs to accept or reject. An authoritative modern sex manual, such as *The Joy of Sex* (Comfort, 1976) should be available on cassette, in large print and Braille.

Moreover, the English are not a particularly tactile race and it is socially unacceptable to explore another person's face or body to find out what he or she is like. These social restrictions on touching may have to be explained to blind children and to immigrants from more tactile countries. There is a lack of socially acceptable alternatives to this tactile satisfaction of one's curiosity about what another person is like, but with one another, blind people do often become more tactile.

Adequate preparation and training of parents, teachers in schools and rehabilitation counsellors is vital for the success and quality of a programme on sexuality and human relationships. Counselling should be available for the visually handicapped, both individually and in group seminars or classes, given by sensitive, responsible and enlightened speakers who can present material in a competent and professional manner and put the visually handicapped at their ease. A climate of accessibility of information creates an improvement in the overall knowledge and attitude of the visually handicapped person which is far more essential than the incidental accumulation of biological facts.

Ideally, sex instruction should take place in the home. Parents should be encouraged to recognize the child's needs and discuss the subject freely, and where this is appropriate, acquire specialized knowledge and materials. Where this does not happen, children can acquire misinformation, and become frightened and confused.

Most visually handicapped children attend residential schools which then take on, to some extent, the parents responsibilities. Young people in single-sex residential institutions often emerge socially immature and with unrealistic notions about relationships with the opposite sex due to their isolation from them, whilst those in co-residential establishments often find there is little opportunity to form close relationships within the institution. There is a big difference between sensitive supervision and undue restrictions preserved for their own sake, and not thought out afresh, in light of what will best prepare the students for the outside world.

Problems in Professional Relationships in Rehabilitation

I will now consider several implications for rehabilitation.

The social or rehabilitation worker may feel inhibited in initiating discussion about the sexual relationship of the individual or couple. If a couple are sexually incompatible and are unable to talk to each other about it, it may be particularly difficult or demoralizing to discuss this with a third party. One might ask *what right has anyone to intrude* upon the utmost privacy of a couple or individual by enquiring about the quality of their sex life and whether it has been affected by visual loss.

This is a valid objection in the case of a social encounter. But the professional is aware that visual handicap is likely to demand adjustments in sexual relationships and that this may cause difficulties. In that respect, *the couple have a right to be informed that help is available* which would give them the opportunity to discuss and attempt to resolve their problems with a competent third party if they so wish. What is important is that the couple or individual understand the relevance of the intrusion into their privacy, and while able to refuse it, are not deprived of the opportunity to eradicate the negative effects of visual handicap on their sexual relationship. At best, their previous sex life may actually be improved by bringing problems into the open and attempting to find solutions to them. All the counsellor need do is to include the topic of sexuality when enquiring into the problems that visual handicap has created.

A second, separate problem in professional relationships may occur between a female rehabilitation worker and a male visually handicapped client (or, indeed vice versa) who attempts to fondle her or who becomes aroused. This is particularly likely to occur with males who have little or no sexual outlet and where a close rapport has developed with the female rehabilitation worker, who may be one of the client's few female acquaintances, through perhaps daily interaction. The worker should be prepared for this so that the situation is avoided if possible or is handled with diplomacy. It illustrates the difficulty of demarcating the professional relationship; the worker must remain an agent of the social services, however personally sympathetic he or she may feel to the individual's frustrations.

Finally, workers should remember the need to compensate for the lack of the visual channel of communication in giving feedback. They can do this by providing a sense of contact through expressive tone of voice, nearness to the other person, or a squeeze of the hand which can equal sympathetic gaze.

Extending the Range of Potential Partners

All types of handicap restrict one's range of potential partners. There is a good deal of intermarriage between visually handicapped people. This is perhaps because their opportunities for making contact with sighted partners are more restricted in that they have been educated or lived exclusively in the blind world, or because the stigma of visual handicap may put off sighted people from forming meaningful relationships with the visually handicapped.

The professional worker may need to think of ways to extend the visually handicapped client's range of social contacts. Someone may need to act as a 'matchmaker' in initiating the first encounter between the visually handicapped person and a potential partner (or, indeed, to a whole group of sighted people). London *Floodlight*, for example, is a booklet on evening classes and activities, and lists seven organisations for people to meet others with similar interests. But it is in integrating with such groups and breaking down the initial barriers that the young visually handicapped person may need help. This must be given imaginatively and informally in order to enable the sighted and visually handicapped to be natural and at ease with one another. In fact, it is a matter of acquiring the social skills discussed earlier.

Conclusion

I would like to conclude with two quotations:

Sex is a part of life – only a part but one not to be denied. The power of sex for good and for evil is so great that we must make every effort to see that it is exercised responsibly. To act responsibly, a person needs all the relevant knowledge he can understand. Mistakes are made, not because of too much knowledge, but because of too little. (Johnson, 1974)

Problems related to sexuality can rarely be separated from emotional growth and personal capacities and the inter-relationship of the people concerned. (5.4) There is more to human sexuality than its physical expression. Sexuality is a function of the whole personality – physical, mental, emotional. It therefore affects and is affected not only by the development of the individual on all these inter-related fronts, but also by the individual's capacity for care, concern and affection within a relationship. (Home Office Working Party on Marriage Guidance, 1979, Paras. 5.4, 5.3)

Notes

1 The body of research on maternal deprivation may be of profound relevance to the understanding of personality problems, difficulty in forming meaningful relationships, and chronic depression in adult life, particularly for children separated from their parents from a very early (critical or sensitive) age, and raised in residential institutions. This topic, however, is beyond the scope of this paper.
2 These specific examples were mentioned to the author at a meeting of the National Federation of the Blind in February, 1979.

References

ARGYLE, M. (1972) *The Psychology of Interpersonal Behaviour*. Harmondsworth: Penguin Books.
BERQUIST, L. (1968) 'A Guide to Family Living and Sex Education at the Oregon State School for the Blind.' (Unpublished.)

BOWLBY, J. (1951) *Maternal Care and Mental Health.* Geneva: World Health Organisation.

BOWLBY, J. (1973) *Attachment and Loss, Volume 2: Separation.* London: Hogarth Press.

CHOATE, R. (1972) 'Sex and the handicapped: a report from Sweden.' *Times Educational Supplement,* March 19, 1972.

COMFORT, A. (1976) *The Joy of Sex.* London: Quartet Books.

DICKMAN, I. (1975) *Sex Education and Family Life for Visually Handicapped Children and Youth: A Resource Guide.* New York: American Foundation for the Blind.

FITZGERALD, R. (1970) 'Reactions to blindness: an exploratory study of adults with recent loss of sight.' *Archs gen. Psychiat.,* April, *22,* 370.

FOULKE, E., and UHOE, T. (1975) *Do Blind Children Need Sex Education?* p. 11. Sex Education for the Visually Handicapped in Schools and Agencies: Selected Papers. New York: American Foundation for the Blind.

GREENGROSS, W. (1976) *Entitled to Love, The Sexual and Emotional Needs of the Handicapped.* Rugby: National Marriage Guidance Council.

JOHNSON, E. (1974) *Love and Sex in Plain Language.* Philadelphia: Lippincott.

MORRIS, D. (1978) *Manwatching.* Frogmore, St. Albans: Triad/Panther Books.

NEFF, J. (1975) *Behaviour Objectives and Learning Activities in Sex Education for the Visually Handicapped: Suggestions for a Curriculum,* pp. 50–76. Sex Education for the Visually Handicapped in Schools and Agencies: Selected Papers. New York: American Foundation for the Blind.

RUTTER, M. (1972) *Maternal Deprivation Reassessed.* Harmondsworth: Penguin Books.

STERN, D. (1977) *The First Relationship: Infant and Mother.* London: Fontana/Open Books Publishing.

STEWART, W. (1977) 'Relationships, love and the young visually handicapped.' A Paper presented at the conference 'The Visually Handicapped Young Adult' which was sponsored by the Southern and Western Regional Association for the Blind.

VOGEL, D., and MUXEN, M. (1976) 'A sex education programme for long-blind adults in a rehabilitation centre setting.' *New Outlook for the Blind, 70,* (3), 104.

12 'The Ordinary Devoted Mother' and her Blind Baby

D. M. Wills

'The Ordinary Devoted Mother and her Baby' was the title of a series of talks broadcast in 1949, by D. W. Winnicott. Its implication, that ordinary mothers *are*, for the most part, devoted placed a welcome stress on the positive factors in mothering at a time when professional workers, in their attempts to understand early handling problems, had perhaps become too preoccupied with the negative factors. However, when the baby is blind, 'ordinary devotion' in the mother is often not assumed to be probable or perhaps even possible, and the mother is frequently blamed for things that go wrong with the child's development. Yet, the majority of mothers of blind children also become devoted, especially when they are given some degree of support and insight during the vicissitudes of the child's development. For the mothers of sighted children, such support and insight are more easily available.

This paper is based on work with the mothers of blind children, mainly under 3 years of age, during visits to and observations in the home. [. . .]

[. . .] This paper does not concern itself with the classification of parental reactions to blindness; these have been described, e.g., by Lairy and Harrison-Covello (1973). Instead, it attempts to focus attention on the need for immediate support for parents of these children, and on the importance of providing them with relevant information about development. [. . .]

That a parent reacts with grief, anger, and depression, and perhaps with some revulsion to the birth of a blind baby, is of course natural.[1] But it is too simplistic to assume that the grief, anger, guilt, and depression will *necessarily* lead to withdrawal and understimulation of the baby, resulting sometimes in his rejection on the one hand, or his excessive protection on the other. A mother will respond to the catastrophe in terms of her psychological makeup, with its strengths and weaknesses, and will be influenced by the help that is given by the family and others.

[. . .] Fortunately, as Mac Keith (1973) points out, any revulsion is usually accompanied by a wish to protect the helpless baby. Mac Keith

The work with blind children is part of the Educational Unit of the Hampstead Child-Therapy Course and Clinic and as such was maintained by the Great Foundation. Inc., New York. The research work with the blind was assisted further by the National Institute of Mental Health, Bethesda, Maryland.

The research has been directed since its inception by Dorothy Burlingham. I am deeply indebted to her for ongoing help with the work on which this paper is based, and my thanks are also due for many helpful comments on the paper itself to A. Curson and A.-M. Sandler.

Source: *The Psychoanalytic Study of the Child*, 1979, *34*, pp. 31–49.

makes the interesting point that parents 'fall in love' with a normal baby so that the child is felt as part of them whatever happens to him; but if a handicap is evident at birth, there is no time for this to happen. In my experience, most parents do 'fall in love' with their blind babies to a greater or lesser extent, but it may take them longer to do so. Of course, the degree to which the handicap affects the baby's appearance will influence the parents', and particularly the mother's, reaction. When the baby's eyes look more or less normal, a loving relationship is facilitated; when they are absent and only sunken eyelids meet her gaze until artificial eyes can be fitted, it will be impeded. (The blind children discussed in this paper had no additional major handicaps. All were within or above the average range of intelligence by 5 years.) [. . .]

Since vision plays the main role in organizing experience in the sighted, how does the blind infant circumvent this deficiency? Perhaps we handicap ourselves by concentrating on children whose late development appears deviant, and would be wise to pay equal, if not greater, attention to the well-developing blind child, to the way the mother of such a child manages to follow his interests and needs and so make up to some extent for the constant lack of visual feedback. Rather than expecting the lines of development in blind children to progress like those of sighted children (even if they lag a little), we should expect greater unevenness between the lines. For instance, in assessing a blind child of 3 years, I would look for: his ability to relate to, and discriminate between, people; the growth of his curiosity about the world around him; and his ability to move and communicate. I would not be unduly concerned with everyday skills at this stage. Desirable as these are, they are useless without the former accomplishments. [. . .]

Parents, feeling perhaps that they know so little about a blind child's development, may want immediate information about education so as to see the way ahead for their child. They are often angry, at this stage and later, with various members of the 'establishment': doctors, local authority visitors, and the worker herself. They are often angry about the paucity of nursery school and school provision. Some of this anger may be warranted, since services for the preschool and school-age blind are in a state of flux; but some, no doubt, is a very natural way of avoiding sadness. However, after the early stages, most mothers want to report and demonstrate all the child's latest achievements, however small. Some mothers like to hear of similar experiences in the development of other blind children; others simply prefer to talk of their own children. Some mothers wish to meet others who are in a similar situation, others do not. But if the worker can offer support and help in whatever area the need is felt and, if necessary, even accompany mother and child to the hospital, it will do something to relieve the inevitable and continuous stress on the family.

A mother's love, whatever its admixtures, for her sighted baby develops and is cemented by the pleasurable interaction between herself and the child, a process in which visual interchange plays a very great part. The mother can understand the child on the basis of her own sensory experience and so is soon responding to him meaningfully; this gives her not only pleasure in the relationship but a feeling of value as a mother. The mother of the blind child, however, at a time when she is sad and disappointed, is confronted by a passive baby whose responses to her overtures are by no means obvious. For example, he may become still and silent when she comes to pick him up in order to *listen* to her approach. He does not smile and coo like a sighted infant who can *see* her approach (Burlingham, 1964):

Sarah was blind because of retinitis pigmentosa. During her first 6 months she became silent not only at her mother's approach, but also when her mother left the room, even if she were crying at the time.

A mother is relieved and interested when she is alerted to the reason for this behavior. She cannot understand the child easily on the basis of her own experience, and it will be a little time before she learns to interpret the small cues the baby offers, and so to respond to him in a way which furthers an enjoyable interaction between them.

The situation is often made worse by relatives and friends who pity and thereby further depress the mother, nor is it helped by the advice, still given to some mothers, that the child will have to be taken away and 'trained' at 3 years. This advice not only may sap the mother's self-confidence but also may make her avoid too deep an involvement with the child because of the prospect of losing him to a nursery boarding school at 3 years.

During this early period the worker must help the mother onto the blind child's wavelength by stressing the need to make up for the child's loss of vision by close contact in other ways, and by pointing out the degree to which the child's cathexis of the world around will be mediated by her:

On my first visit to Cynthia (blind from retinitis pigmentosa) at 9 months she sat in her mother's arms with her hands held up and fisted like a younger child. I commented on this late fisting of the hands and suggested the mother should play with them. A fortnight later, on my second visit, Cynthia was beginning to open her hands as she held them in the air, at times touching her mother, who said all this had started after my last visit.

The worker can also help the mother by asking questions about the meaning of their joint observations. This gives more background and insight to both. The worker can suggest other goals toward which the mother can aim during the first year. The benefit from such a contact is by no means onesided. As the mother comes to understand her child, the worker is also learning from her, building a picture of the early natural history of these children, about which all too little is known with certainty. The mother can be told this, and that she is helping the worker with insights that can be recorded and used by other mothers. Once alerted to a general point, for example, that a blind child takes an important step when he first reaches for an object on a sound cue alone, a mother may be able to think of some clever way of interesting her child in carrying out the activity:

Cynthia in her second year loved playing with mother's hands as she sat on her lap. The mother used this to get her to reach on a sound cue. She faced the child toward her on her knee. She clapped her hands in various positions around the child, encouraging Cynthia to reach out for them.

Again, Sheila (blind from retrolental fibroplasia), a backward blind girl, at 3 years had regressed from walking freely. When the mother was alerted to the need for Sheila to explore her environment, she took to carrying her around the sitting room, always clockwise, always entering by the same door (out of 3), meanwhile naming objects to Sheila as she reached them.

This kind of incident does something to restore the mother's confidence in herself and furthers her pleasure in handling the child. It also is a useful learning experience for the worker.

At the beginning of the first year the worker can tell the mother that the baby will smile about the normal age, but in response to her voice, since he cannot see the mother's face. But voice will not regularly elicit the smile, the most reliable stimulus being 'gross tactile or kinaesthetic stimulation' (Fraiberg, 1971b, p. 115). Mothers work very hard to obtain these early smiles which make them feel in better contact with their baby. Indeed, the main task in the first year is for the mother to establish a strong relationship between herself and her blind baby, so that the child begins to make the move from preoccupation with himself and his own body (his most available source of pleasure) to interest in his mother and her body and so to the objects with which she supplies him:

When Boris[2] was very small, his mother tied noise-making toys on each side of his carry-cot, and by 6 weeks said she knew which he preferred. By 2½ months the mother was taking Boris along in his carry-cot as she moved about the flat working; when she had to leave the room, she would kiss him on coming back. In spite of his having been born without eyes, she established a very positive relationship with him. One day when he was 11 months old, he was rocking with great pleasure on his little horse and his mother tickled his ear from behind. He stopped rocking and turned, smiled, and put out his hand to catch hers. The fact that Boris turned from rocking himself to touching his mother showed that he had made the first move from interest in himself and his own body to his mother. This meant that she could continually widen his experience.

Fraiberg (1971a), who intensively studied a small number of intact blind infants, suggests that parents be alerted to the various little indications of attachment which the blind infant shows. She points out that the early smiling is already selective, and is given in response to the *parents'* voices, not the worker's; that around 5 months the blind infant shows a preference for the mother's arms, but squirms when the worker picks him up; and that between 8 and 12 months stranger anxiety begins to develop, thus indicating an important step in the child's attachment to the mother.

As for motor development in the first and the early part of the second year, the *postural* achievements of the blind child are essentially similar to those of the sighted. Sitting, stepping movements with hands held, and standing unsupported may all be expected to appear around the usual time. But *self-initiated* mobility is delayed. Attempts to lift himself by his arms when prone, to raise himself to a sitting posture, to pull himself up to a standing position, and to walk by himself – all these achievements will require motivation supplied by the mother (Adelson and Fraiberg, 1974).[3]

There are few standardized norms of development available for young blind children, but the worker can turn to the Maxfield and Buchholz Social Maturity Scale for Blind Pre-School Children (1957), and to the Norris et al. (1957) breakdown of a very similar scale, the Maxfield-Fjeld.[4] Despite the obvious significance of the mother-child relationship, however, these scales do not adequately cover it; instead they concentrate on the child-*toy* interaction, which well beyond the first year is of lesser significance. It is probably unwise to link any behavior too closely with age levels, because blind children who ultimately do well often show, at earlier stages, developmental lags in one area or another.

Mother and Child in the Second and Third Years

Most mothers look forward to the time when the blind child will be able to walk a few steps alone, realizing how important it is for him to explore the environment he cannot see. But since this is a self-initiated activity, it is delayed in many blind children. Norris et al. (1957) report it at 21 months; Adelson and Fraiberg (1974) report it at $15\frac{1}{4}$ months. It has to be borne in mind that, without sight, standing upright considerably diminishes the child's contact with the environment since contact by touch with his surroundings is suddenly reduced to the soles of his feet. Some children panic in this position, and refuse to relinquish support from the mother's finger or from a pushcart. Others may suddenly give up the few free steps they have learned to take because of some upsetting experience in another area of their lives.

If the first year has gone reasonably well, and the child is starting to move about by crawling or hitching, the mother usually anticipates that now in the second year he will begin to play with toys or household objects. Here she may suffer a further disappointment if she expects him to enjoy the constructive and manipulative type of play typical of the sighted child. The blind child remains centered on people. His interest moves only very slowly from people, who are to him so much more meaningful in terms of sound, touch, smell, and movement, than the inanimate world around him (Burlingham, 1967). Moreover, it is difficult to find toys and activities that are suitable for a blind child.

Sarah, at 15 months, certainly enjoyed handling combs and other everyday objects. The mother was in despair about her inability to find suitable toys. Sarah tended to sit and throw all her playthings—a plastic telephone, dolls, ring towers, rattles, cotton reels—over her shoulder. She was not yet able to imitate the noises mother made with pots and pans. We therefore discussed letting her do some of the 'naughty' things children love at this age, and 2 months later she was, for instance, tearing up at least one newspaper a day. Such an activity allows the child gross hand movements; moreover, she gets a satisfying feedback, the rustle of the paper and the effect she has had on it since it is now in bits!

Sometimes the play of blind children looks repetitive and meaningless, but they need more time than the sighted to build on the basis of cumulative experiences.

Edward (blind from unknown causes) was 2 years when his mother said that he played with toys for only some 10 minutes each day. Mostly he walked around in the room where his mother was or went with her as she did her work: downstairs for the ironing, upstairs to 'help' with the beds. He was allowed to open certain drawers, to fling the contents out, describing each as he did so (his speech was advanced). He and his younger brother played a little with the contents before his mother put them back. While this gives the mother little respite, the child is all the time learning to understand what goes on in his world.

The mother now waits hopefully for speech to develop, but here again the expectation of speech is somewhat different at this age for the blind child. The Vineland, a scale standardized on sighted children, places the item 'Uses names of familiar objects' in the second year (Doll, 1947), while the Maxfield and Buchholz Scale (1957), standardized on blind children, places this item a year later, a placement which Norris et al.'s study (1957) supports.[5] Since this is a norm, some children are in advance of it; but some, who eventually develop normal speech, lag far behind and continue to echo what the mother says or to name the object only when it is present. It therefore is essential for parents to support the child's understanding by keeping their language simple and meaningful, by playing little body games with him where he can respond to simple instructions, and by showing him, through their own responses, that words can *get* him things. Moreover, parents need to provide ongoing mouth pleasure through such activities as blowing bubbles or 'raspberries.' They need to make language fun, and not to let it become an issue between them and the child.

Some blind children vocalize very little in the first year, even though they are well-mothered. Other children, also well-mothered, may show a speech delay which is part of a general backwardness, and which may be linked with damage other than blindness. The extent of this may be difficult to assess until 3 or 4 years. In both cases the parents not only have to suffer disappointment at this lag in development, but at times may even be blamed for it. All too often the assumption is made that the child has not been adequately stimulated. In fact, many concepts used by the sighted are at first difficult to grasp for the congenitally blind child. For instance, he is presented with a variety of sensory cues concerning an object such as a 'table' when only sight or long experience can bind these into a whole. Again, while sighted people frequently speak of what they are *seeing*, the blind child's main experience may be of what he is *hearing*, to which, often, they make no reference. Older children may give us insights into this:

Sam (blind from retinitis pigmentosa) was 5½ years when I heard a taped record of one of my sessions with him and realized that his bringing birds into his play was linked with the birds singing and twittering in the garden outside. I was habituated to this and so had ignored it. We all still have much to learn about how the blind organize and make sense of their world.

In the second year, there may be problems in the feeding area. For example, many blind children cling to the bottle. This seems to be due to a tie to the familiar rather than an arrest in development. The children cannot see others eat normally and lack encouragement from this experience in terms of rivalry or a wish to imitate. The mother may have to exercise considerable ingenuity if she is to help the child through this phase without a head-on collision or without winning compliance at the price of a reaction in some other area of development.

Many normally developing blind children suffer from a prolonged period of separation anxiety (Fraiberg, 1968). This may partly be due to their unavoidable dependence on the mother who has to act not only as a love object but also as an auxiliary ego in supporting their activities. These children probably take longer to achieve a stable idea of the mother's continuing existence and to be sure of her ultimate return whenever she is absent, since they are without a *visual* image to assist their recall of her. The anxiety reaction is often not easily understood:

Cynthia (2 years) became clinging and uncooperative after visits to the Welfare Centre accompanied by her mother. She showed the same response after being taken by her mother and left to stay the night with the very familiar grandmother. The mother thought that this was a reaction to a change in routine since Cynthia did not immediately come to her when she came to collect her. I suggested that Cynthia was reacting to the separation. The mother concurred in this after the next joint visit to the grandmother when she observed that Cynthia was unwilling to leave the room where the mother was in order to play in the garden. Following a day spent alone with her grandmother, Cynthia continued to stay close to her mother for some time.

A blind child who cannot glance at the mother on her arrival to collect him or her probably misleads the mother (and later on his teachers) more easily than does the sighted child, whose reactions are easier to observe and interpret. The following anxiety reactions show some protraction:

Edward (2.1 years) was taken to visit a local nursery by his parents, and, with his agreement, was left in a large group in the care of an adult who played with him for 10 minutes. On his return home, about 11 A.M., he demanded a bottle and to be put to bed, where he stayed for $\frac{3}{4}$ hour. That night, an hour after he had been put to sleep, he screamed nonstop for 5 minutes. The mother understood this behavior as reactive to the brief separation. He showed a similar but more intense reaction a month later to a further separation from his mother.

Here we see the blind child's overcompliance, his subsequent response, withdrawal, and belated expression of the affect in anxiety and rage. Helped by his advanced speech, the mother was in very good contact with this child and so understood the reactions, which could well have been missed in a less verbal child since they did not occur in the context of the event itself. Such a belated reaction can sometimes be avoided by reminding the child *before* the next separation that he did not like his mother leaving him last time. This intervention enabled Edward to cope better on subsequent occasions. Even if such a comment provokes an outburst, this is better for the child's development.

The Step to Day Nursery School in the Third Year

When the child is about 3 years old, the mother may look for a small day nursery school group to relieve her of the constant task of supporting the child's understanding and of widening his experiences and contacts. Since there are so few blind children, she is unlikely to have a specialized school in her locality and may try a sighted group where the teacher is sympathetic. Some teachers do not want the mother to stay with the child until he is able to let her go, and the child not only has to undergo sudden separation, but, if there are many children, the noise will confuse him and he may well become overwhelmed by the new experience. However, the mother may be fortunate in finding a smaller and more suitable group and the transition may go more easily.

We were able to make arrangements of this kind for Cassie:

When she was 20 months old, Cassie lost her sight (due to retinoblastoma) and her mother brought her to our nursery school every week for some months in order to watch the teacher's handling of other blind children. As the journey was some distance, the teacher continued the contact by visiting once a fortnight. At 3 years (the usual age for intake) Cassie asked to come to the school again. She came twice with her mother and then came with the escort only, telling her mother to stay at home.

Some home visits by the teacher before the child starts probably are the ideal arrangement in that the child gets to know her, and the teacher gets a better picture of the child and his or her background. Some schools do manage to arrange this and find other suitable ways of introducing the child to school, and of appropriately handling the child's separation anxiety before it becomes acute.

When it is difficult to find the right nursery group, the mother, and sometimes the worker, may be tempted to make arrangements for the child to attend two different groups during the week. For the blind child in particular this is not a good idea. Since without sight it is so much more difficult to make sense of his surroundings, the blind child needs to be in *one small* group where he can gradually learn to relate to known adults and a few children.

As we come to understand better what the blind child is facing when he starts in a day nursery group, we may be able to make more adequate provisions for his first experiences away from home. Quite apart from the mother's need for some relief from providing the constant support that the blind child must have, his tie to his mother must slowly be loosened as it must be with the sighted child. Both blind and sighted children do not develop well without a strong relationship with the mother or her substitute; but both need to make some move toward a measure of independence. The child without sight, which does so much to make the world attractive, is less strongly motivated than the sighted. However, it is crucial for his further development how his strong tie is loosened when he starts in a day nursery group, especially if his speech is not well developed. If the separation is sudden, it is liable to be traumatic, and while some children may make a spurt in some areas of development in order to master the situation, others become confused and regress.

It is outside the scope of this paper to discuss the traumatic impact of placement, whether gradual or sudden, in weekly boarding school at 5 years (and sometimes younger), but here again the children frequently regress in such a way that teachers find it difficult to believe when mothers tell them that the child performs better at home. While these schools offer many benefits, including teaching geared to the child's somewhat different and delayed understanding of the world, they cannot but be disorientating for a blind child. In Britain greater variety of provision is badly needed (Vernon et al., 1972).

Conclusion

In this paper I have attempted to highlight the difficulties the mother may have to contend with in bringing up a blind child, in order to demonstrate that it may not be her ability in mothering which is at fault, but rather that too little support and knowledge are made available to her. If her blind child develops well, we can probably assume that she is a *more* than ordinarily devoted mother.

Workers offering such support need training in child development of both sighted and blind, and a willingness to follow and get to know the children in their homes. I did not regard my task as psychotherapeutic in the strict sense; rather, I worked with the mother in an attempt to support her and to understand the child with her help.

Why, when there is such a wealth of careful research on school-age blind children, has so little attention been paid to the pre-school years, especially since it is known that by the time they are 5 many children show deviant development? The first reason is probably a practical one. Since there are very few blind children in Western cultures where workers are available, they are geographically very scattered, and keeping regular contact weekly or fortnightly requires much traveling. A second reason may be that such children distress us, perhaps more than those with any other handicap. All of this may have led to the wish to equate the blind with the sighted. As a result, even when careful work *is* done, certain basic questions are not asked. There is a tendency to describe the blind child as a sighted child lacking only one sensory modality, and while this tendency certainly lays stress on his need for normal childhood experiences, it can be used to deflect attention from his somewhat different course of development, and from a proper understanding of the ways he can use to circumvent his lack of vision.

We still have much to learn from blind children themselves. The range of sensory input on which they must rely is in all the rest of us largely dominated and organized by vision. They show very little facial expression, which hinders our observations. For these reasons we have to make a very special effort to empathize with their experience of their inner and outer world.

Notes

1 This is sometimes considered a good reason for delaying the diagnosis of blindness. Late diagnosis, however, also has its dangers since the blind infant needs more handling and contact of all kinds to compensate for the loss of visual interaction.
2 Fraiberg's group had the advantage of her and her colleague's support.
3 This paper was written prior to the publication of Fraiberg's book (1977) in which she slightly modified some of the median ages she gave in her earlier papers.
4 Dr. Joan Reynell at the Wolfson Clinic, London, is in the process of publishing a Developmental Scale for Blind Children which should prove very useful (Reynell, 1978). [Reynell-Zinkin Scales for Young Visually Handicapped Children (1980). Windsor: NFER.]
5 Fraiberg's recent book (1977) places 'uses words to make wants known' in the second year for her advantaged group (p. 225).
6 Fraiberg (1968) describes a somewhat similar case of a younger child, Jack, who reacted with long screaming fits after a longer separation from his mother.

Bibliography

ADELSON, E., and FRAIBERG, S. (1974) 'Gross motor development in infants blind from birth.' *Child Dev.*, *45*, 114–26.
BURLINGHAM, D. (1964) 'Hearing and Its role in the development of the blind.' *This Annual*, *19*, 121–45.
BURLINGHAM, D. (1967) 'Developmental considerations in the occupations of the blind.' *This Annual*, *22*, 187–98.
COLONNA, A. B. (1968) 'A blind child goes to the hospital.' *This Annual*, *23*, 391–422.
DOLL, E. A. (1947) *Vineland Social Maturity Scale.* Minneapolis: Educational Test Bureau.
FRAIBERG, S. (1954) 'Counselling for the parents of the very young child.' *Soc. Casewk*, *35*, 47–57.
FRAIBERG, S. (1968) 'Parallel and divergent patterns in blind and sighted infants.' *This Annual*, *23*, 264–300.
FRAIBERG, S. (1971a) 'Intervention in infancy.' *J. child Psychiat.*, *10*, 381–405.
FRAIBERG, S. (1971b) 'Smiling and Stranger Reaction in Blind Infants.' In J. Hellmuth (ed.) *The Exceptional Infant*, pp. 110–27. London: Butterworths.
FRAIBERG, S. (1977) *Insights from the Blind.* New York: Basic Books.
FRAIBERG, S., and FREEDMAN, D. A. (1964) 'Studies in the ego development of the congenitally blind child.' *This Annual*, *19*, 113–69.
FREEDMAN, D. G. (1964) 'Smiling in blind infants and the issue of innate vs. acquired.' *J. child Psychol. Psychiat.*, *5*, 171–84.
HEWITT, S. (1970) *The Family and the Handicapped Child.* London: Allen & Unwin.
LAIRY, G. C., and HARRISON-COVELLO, A. (1973) 'The blind child and his parents.' *Res. Bull. Amer. Foundation for the Blind*, *25*, 1–24.

MAC KEITH, R. (1973) 'Feelings and behaviour of parents of handicapped children.' *Develpm. Med. Child Neurol.*, *15*, 524–7.

MAXFIELD, K. E., and BUCHHOLZ, S. (1957) *A Social Maturity Scale for Blind Pre-School Children*. New York: American Foundation for the Blind.

NORRIS, M., SPAULDING, P., and BRODIE, F. (1957) *Blindness in Children*. Chicago: University of Chicago Press.

REYNELL, J. (1978) 'Developmental patterns of visually handicapped children.' *Child: Care, Hlth & Develpm.* (Oxford), *4*, 291–303.

SANDLER, A. -M. (1963) 'Aspects of passivity and ego development in the blind infant.' *This Annual*, *18*, 343–60.

SANDLER, A.-M., and WILLS, D. M. (1965) 'Preliminary notes on play and mastery in the blind child.' *J. child Psychother.*, *1*, 7–19.

SHERIDAN, M. D. (1960) *The Developmental Progress of Infants and Young Children*. London: HMSO.

VERNON, M. et al. (1972) *The Report of the Vernon Committee on the Education of the Visually Handicapped*. London: HMSO.

WILLS, D. M. (1968) Problems of Play and Mastery in the Blind Child. *Brit. J. med. Psychol.*, *41*, 213–22. Also in E. P. Trapp and P. Himelstein (eds) *Readings on the Exceptional Child*, pp. 335–49. New York: Meredith Corporation, 1972.

WILLS, D. M. (1970) 'Vulnerable periods in the early development of blind children.' *This Annaul*, *25*, 461–79.

WILLS, D. M. (1978) 'Entry into Boarding School and After.' In P. F. Portwood and R. T. Williams (eds) *Readings on the Visually Handicapped Child*. Leicester: British Psychological Society, *2*(2). 39–44.

WINNICOTT, D. W. (1949) *The Ordinary Devoted Mother and Her Baby*. London: Tavistock.

13   Using Two Aids

Peter O'Neil

Hindsight can be a marvellous thing. It allows a clear view of past events in their proper perspective. For instance, my mother was forever telling people that I was 'as deaf as a door nail'. The problem was that I suffered badly from sinusitis and catarrh as a child, and this affected my hearing. I can remember often finding myself out of step with my classmates when reciting arithmetical tables. Yet I was not aware as such that I was hard of hearing – it never entered my mind as a serious possibility.

At one stage an operation on my mastoid processes was considered – but thankfully came to nothing. Swimming was disallowed because of the influx of water through perforated ear drums. At an early age, before perforations were evident, I learned a trick of holding my nose and blowing to equalise pressure in my ears. On a gliding course in the open countryside, I was accused of being deaf, and at grammar school I often had trouble hearing the teachers. But still, although these things were irksome, I didn't think that I had a fundamental hearing problem. Even when training at university. Until one day when I came across sphygmomanometers and stethoscopes. Then I became concerned and visited my GP, who syringed my ears and pronounced me cured.

Then, nearly three years ago, it's fair to say my life style changed dramatically, as it often does with many people following an accident. One Sunday morning I took a bath, and afterwards whilst cleaning my ears with cotton buds, I fell over my bathrobe, against the wall and was painfully aware of the stick perforating my left eardrum. To cut a long story short, I saw my GP (a different one – we had moved) who sent me to a local hospital where after $2\frac{1}{2}$ hours waiting in the evening, and repeated enquiries, nothing was done. By this time there was no more bleeding but considerable discomfort and slight deafness in the affected ear.

No one seemed perturbed, so I decided to leave it to heal, but a few days later I could feel a pulse in my left ear. My doctor saw nothing to worry about but sent me to the ENT Department at another hospital, at my prompting. By the time I was seen I had developed a sore throat and a slight hearing loss was evident in both ears. Hearing tests were made, and after examination, the doctor at the hospital diagnosed pulsatile abscesses, which he later drained without anaesthetic. An unforgettable experience, the pain was indescribable, and I nearly lost consciousness. Impressions of my fingerprints will still be apparent in the rubber pad on the bed, I'm sure. The infection cleared up with antibiotics, but I was a little worried and often embarrassed (at work especially) by a gradually increasing inability to understand what was being said to me. An acquaintance who wore a

Source: *Hearing*, 1979, *34*, No. 2, pp. 56–60.

hearing aid suggested that I seek further help, and that perhaps an aid would be of use to me. The idea horrified me.

The situation worsened. I was not coping at work. I began to consider that, whether I liked it or not, I probably needed a hearing aid. I began avoiding social engagements; dinner parties etc, were difficult, embarrassing affairs. I returned to the hospital, and was told my ears seemed to be healing well, and when I eventually brought myself to broach the subject, was airily told that I didn't want to wear a hearing aid – did I? I didn't – did I?

One day, feeling acutely embarrassed for some reason, I walked into the premises of a hearing aid dispenser. I was listened to with sympathy and after a hearing test, was advised that a hearing aid would be of considerable help to me. Then began a desperately frustrating and unhappy period during which I tried several aids, and suffered severe disappointment. I was learning the hard way that using an aid is a little more difficult than it would seem! Badly fitting earmoulds causing soreness. Booming voices and whistling seemed to be my lot along with noise and yet more noise. I began to feel very nervous and irritable. I was unsure of my voice when speaking, so tended to listen rather than take part in conversation – an attitude which was invariably misunderstood by others. I was ill at ease socially, but in the quieter surroundings at work I could cope with an aid and so the strain was eased a little there. I also realised at this time that these little instruments were quite expensive.

At my wife's prompting, I returned to the hospital, where I was given a hearing test and quick examination. The audiologist commented on my hearing loss and told me that I would benefit from using a hearing aid. I was referred to an Audiology Clinic for the fitting of such.

I was in fact fitted with a BE12 and a temporary mould which I could not use at all. I was given no guidance and still felt out of my depth. I was depressed and anxious. Before my individual earmould was ready (which took over two months), I returned to the clinic and was advised to try the OL56 instead for a while. That was worse, and in a state of despair I went back again. This time one of the technicians devoted a considerable amount of time to me and gave me a good deal of advice and a couple of booklets to read. This helped a great deal – so did the cold cure acrylic ear mould which she made whilst I was there. Some months later I was coping with my aid, but was still finding it difficult and wearing it only occasionally. I was getting used to being unable to hear clearly and tending to ignore anything that did not interest me because of the effort involved. It seemed that my hearing loss was a lot worse now.

I wore the BE12 with my new individual earmould. It was good but I had to deal with wind noise, uni-directionality of sound, and soreness in my ear from the mould. However, I gained confidence with it to the extent that I thought I ought to try the OL56 again. It sounds incredible now, and it must have been irritating to the technicians at the clinic to have me chopping and changing – but they were always helpful and patient. I bought a commercially made earmould and found in fact that the OL56 was now more comfortable, the sound was better, and there was no wind noise. I could hear better with it after a little practice and the position of the speaker was not critical. But there was always 'clothes noise'. At this time I noticed that the tinnitus I had experienced since the beginning had decreased markedly.

At about this time, I was also introduced to the use of binaural NHS aids. Without doubt this system has had a profound effect on my life. More about this later.

Surgery to relieve my problem was not advised from the start. Later enquiries and discussion with other deafened adults has dissuaded me further from considering it. (At one point, with regard to the BAHOH, I did join the Association to meet other people in a similar position to myself, but in fact I found it difficult to identify with its members, the majority of whom were profoundly deaf, not hard of hearing. I had enough difficulty communicating with hearing people without having to cope with finger-spelling etc.) The RNID were always very helpful when I contacted them, and I subscribe now to this magazine [*Hearing*].

At some point it became clear to me that a major obstacle to coping with my aid was the apparent poor fit of my earmoulds. It took far too long to obtain these through the NHS, and then they usually did not fit. Similarly, several commercially made moulds did not fit – and they can become expensive. The solution then lay in making my own, which I did, using several types of impression materials, and utilising cold and heat-cured acrylics, silicone inserts etc. Early efforts were poor, but later results have proved most satisfactory. [. . .]

Looking back it is difficult to say which was my 'first' proper aid. I remember dreading having to use my first NHS aid – purely because I was vain. When I did wear it I soon found that advice plus booklets are all very well, but your aid is a very personal thing which ultimately only the subject can learn to cope with. The OL56 is bulky and noisy when touched, the volume setting is critical. You adjust it so that you can hear conversation comfortably; but the same setting whilst washing dishes could make your ear drums meet in the middle of your head. And when your first battery runs down, it's surprising how long it takes for the penny to drop.

Initially I was very conscious of wearing an aid, and assumed that everyone else was too. It colours your attitude to social contact. On the other hand, hearing people are often embarrassed and don't know how to react or behave when they see that you wear an aid. They either ignore you, or alternatively the phrase 'deaf treated as daft' applies. Only a few carry on as normal and accept your explanation if difficulties occur in communication. It's an understandable thing, because even today deafness is not socially as 'acceptable' or as sympathetically viewed as other afflictions. I hated having my opinions and preferences sought via my wife whilst I stood ignored at her side. I soon put an end to that.

There is one other thing I found peculiarly difficult to adapt to. I love music, and soon found to my despair that sound through an aid is definitely 'different'. I still enjoy music but my favourite pieces are enjoyed very much from memory, as I don't hear some of it – but I know it's there, even though I have a 'flat' audiogram. The difference in the timbre and quality of sound from an aid can give you the impression that you're not hearing at all well with your aid – but in fact a little practice shows that you are hearing well enough, given the limitations of electronically produced sound.

If I were to use only one aid, I would prefer a bodyworn aid. This may seem odd to many people, but to me it's now a simple choice. The object is to hear as well as possible. To achieve this, I would wear the bodyworn type in my left ear, with my right ear free to use the telephone; this allows me to hear well with fewer directional problems. I find difficulty with one postaural aid if it is on the side opposite to the speaker, and I have learned to ignore noise from clothes etc. Using the telephone presents a minor problem. If the line is clear I can hear well with my unaided right ear; I have not yet managed to use a postaural aid with the phone because of distortion and oscillation.

If you are lucky enough to have two postaural aids with a hearing loss like mine, you're in clover. I hear very well indeed with two postaurals – in fact I often think the hearing of my friends may be suspect! It's not all that easy of course, and again practice and adaptation feature strongly; but with two aids I do not often need to face the speaker and I can more easily distinguish the sounds I want to hear from background noise. I can deal much more easily with noisy surroundings, and can use less amplification on each aid – although initially the difference in loss between the ears is noticeable. It is important to fit each ear with an aid of sufficient power to help relieve the specific loss in that ear.

Ear inserts in postaurals seem to me to 'block' frequently and need adjusting with a finger. This is something which doesn't occur with button type earmoulds, and it's not, in my case at least, due to condensation within the plastic tubing – this can be cured using relief channels with 'sinter' inserts. I wear glasses and find that even now the side arms push postaural aid 'elbows' outwards: enough to cause discomfort and soreness sometimes. This might appear a minor problem, but believe me it can be quite a nuisance. I do find that resonance in the lower frequencies when driving, and on foot in the city streets, is irritating and distracting. And wind noise can be diabolical.

Experimentation has shown me that when shopping in the city, or in similar circumstances, I get best results wearing a body aid in my left ear and a postaural in the right. Sometimes I remove the postaural because the noise level is such that my unaided right ear can understand speech.

I have to be careful in choosing the clothes I wear – not because I'm particularly fashion-conscious, but simply to avoid distracting noises when wearing either a bodyworn aid or a postaural. For instance a postaural with a forward facing microphone is noisy when scratching the hair or adjusting glasses; one with a rear-facing microphone picks up noise from collars.

These days my hearing loss normally presents only minor inconveniences, and thankfully I can continue practising my profession without hindrance. Very few, if any, of my more recent new patients are aware of my hearing loss. Generally speaking if I can't understand the patient, neither can my nurse. Those patients who know of my hearing loss are by and large extremely helpful and understanding, although initially many were taken aback and bemused by their 'deaf dentist'. It's quite amazing how many patients and friends suffer themselves from a hearing loss, and/or have relatives or acquaintances who are similarly handicapped. So why is deafness still regarded as fair game for comedians?

Dental equipment has an amazing range of sounds: high pitched air turbines, reverberating amalgameters, 'white noise' from aspirators etc. Initially I found them almost unbearable for extended periods through a hearing aid, but now, no problem.

I am now very dependent on my aids and would be lost without them. I have not found lipreading easy or of much practical value despite attending many classes. This is probably because I rely on my ability to hear well with aids; but if this were not the case I don't feel that lipreading would be of much value to me. This may come as a shock to some of you and may be dismissed as ignorant comment – but the importance of lipreading and the role it plays for hard of hearing persons should perhaps be reconsidered. I have met adults who were born profoundly deaf, who lipread with amazing facility, but never hearing impaired adults.

In conclusion I would like to acknowledge my debt to all those people within and without the NHS involved in my case for their help and guidance and for providing me with the means to minimise my handicap. I cannot stress this too much.

The NHS, as we all know, is overstretched and short of funds. Yet in so many fields it continues to provide good patient care, thanks to the ability and professionalism of its staff. With this in mind, and realising that Audiology is only one aspect of the whole, I hesitate to criticise. However, although the treatment received by patients must vary, I cannot help having qualms about the circumstances and depth of treatment that I experienced in the early stages. Furthermore, being deaf, especially if the onset is sudden, is not miraculously cured and dismissed by the fitting of a hearing aid *per se*. It's a very disturbing and distressing thing. I'm not saying anything new here, I know, but it's easy to become 'hardened' to situations one meets constantly, and difficult to respond to individuals. I put it to you that despite the extremely high standards I have observed in individuals overall, the NHS is 'case hardened' with regard to hearing impairment. The problem, I suspect, lies at the top, not the bottom of the ladder. If you feel that I have been grossly unjust in my statements and I remain ignorant of the true state of affairs, please forgive me – I'm only saying what I feel from experience.

Changes are being made with regard to types of hearing aids available to patients under the NHS. As regards the binaural system I can attest to its real value – after all we were meant to hear with two ears – and I hope that it will be possible someday to provide this facility, amongst others, for all those who could benefit from it.

Notes

1 Peter O'Neil is a pseudonym, for professional reasons.
2 This article is based on an address given to the North of England Branch of the British Society of Audiology, on 16th February 1979.
3 Authority for the issue of two hearing aids for simultaneous use by individual patients is contained in DHSS/Welsh Office Circular C 260, dated July 1977, paragraph two:

Two hearing aids (bodyworn or postaural) may be issued to patients only if they are prescribed as clinically necessary by an otologist or audiological physician and are intended for simultaneous use.

14 Kim

M. and D. Collins

I could feel all of them looking at me, and Kim and I stared at each other across the broken eggs. I remembered the reassuring words I had spoken to a parent over the 'phone only a few days before on the difficulties of shopping with a handicapped child, and how one simply had to develop some kind of tough veneer to deal with it. But as I looked down at the spreading mass of egg yolks, I once again felt the familiar rising panic. If it had been my son, I could have dealt with it, but Kim was another matter. Any incident concerning her touched on emotional strings so deep that they vibrated at the slightest touch.

The assistant was very hostile.

'I'm sorry, I'm afraid she is a bit clumsy, she is mentally handicapped.' The woman stood there silently as I bent to retrieve at least some of the eggs, and I felt a sympathy for her embarrassment. If you really wanted to analyse it, I suppose you could say that by stating Kim's handicap so baldly, I was actually using it as a weapon, making my protest against a system that went to such great lengths to isolate both of us from society. I wanted her to know what it was really like for us.

The fact that I could say at all that I had a mentally handicapped child was in fact the end of a very long road of gradual acceptance. In Kith and Kids, our group of parents, each with a handicapped child in the family, examples of encounters as painful as this one are brought out, for the sheer relief of sharing them, whenever we meet and talk together. There was the neighbour of a deaf boy who sent a note to the mother instructing her coldly, 'please do not send your child to play with my son'; the passer-by who walked up to the mother of an autistic boy in the street and said 'if I had a child like that, I'd get myself sterilized'; and the onlooker observing a screaming autistic two-year-old, who at that time cried constantly and wore out both his parents, who remarked 'you don't deserve to have children – fancy leaving him outside a shop crying like that'. People are very quick to condemn – and who can blame them, for what can 'normal' people know about what it feels like to be the mother of one very severely mentally handicapped girl in our group, for instance, who copes all day with a spastic, highly hyperactive child who never is still for a moment, tears off the wallpaper, pulls down the curtains and pulls her paper nappies to shreds, strewing the debris around the room, and has continuous fits? This child is still surrounded by a united family and warmly contained within her own home, but the short-term care they desperately need in the holidays is still not forthcoming: we are told that there is a lack of facilities, lack of social workers, and in general we note a lack of social conscience. What the eye

Source: M. and D. COLLINS (1976) *Kith and Kids*. London: Souvenir Press (extracts from Chapter 1).

does not see, the heart does not grieve over. But a handicapped child can be born to any family, to any person in any circumstance. Handicap is not confined to any class or colour. And when it does happen, what do you do, where do you go?

Kim was our first child and I had no measure to guide me in her development. I just became uneasily aware that in comparison with my neighbour's child of the same age, Kim fell far behind. My visits to the clinic were not very helpful. She was a big bouncy sort of baby and she ate continuously.

'How is baby getting on?'

'Well, she never seems to stop eating, she will take the whole bottle and more and I never seem to know if she has had enough.'

'Well, when she has had enough, she will stop, don't worry.'

'But she doesn't.'

The nurse was a doddery woman, she had obviously dedicated her life to mothers and babies, and she was a Miss. In the end I gave up. This first difficulty, that Kim had apparently no appetite stopping-point, seemed to register some interest years later when I was questioned about Kim's early development, but at that time no one took any notice at all.

When she was two, she was still not talking so we had her hearing tested. We were becoming vaguely worried about this slowness in speech, though physically, she blossomed. [. . .] Our anxiety increased, and in June 1965 we went to see Dr Simon Yudkin, the fine paediatrician who died tragically young.

He sat Kim on his knee and asked her to draw a circle, showing her what he wanted her to do. I knew that she was not capable of doing any kind of drawing or colouring, even though she was nearly four years old. We could see from his face that he was pessimistic. On the other hand she was extraordinarily good at doing jig-saw puzzles so that some of the other simple tests she managed to complete very well. He advised us to have her IQ tested and this was done at the Nuffield Centre. Again, although verbally Kim's competence was behind her age, on all the tests involving puzzles she pulled up. When we returned to Dr Yudkin, however, he told us that he could not agree with the Nuffield assessment of a low 90, and that in his opinion there was something wrong.

Parents are only human and tend to hear what they want to believe, so we walked out of his rooms in Harley Street feeling that the great doctor was only being pessimistic and 'didn't really know what he was talking about!' Unfortunately, he was only too right. He advised us in any case to get Kim into a good nursery school to develop her speech, and this we set about doing. My doctor, on the other hand, was convinced that her slowness in talking had a great deal to do with her tonsils. She had had a continuous round of very high temperatures and sore throats when she was a baby – now I often wonder in the small hours whether one such time, when the temperature was particularly high and I could not reach my doctor, had anything to do with her brain damage. . . . I remember asking him one day:

'Do you think she is backward? I would rather know if you think there is any possibility.'

He looked at Kim doing a puzzle – she was about three and it was one of these big-piece ones with buttons to pull them out. He asked her to hand him the various shapes, naming each one to her, and watched her complete it. Then he said:

'Well, I think that if she can do this sort of thing, there isn't much to worry about.'

So Kim went into the children's hospital in Great Ormond Street to have her tonsils out. We debated what to say to the Staff nurse about her: I knew it was going to be difficult to explain. Sometimes Kim simply did not seem to grasp situations about her. Yet I had had no 'official' confirmation that something was wrong, I had no experience of my own to rely on – how could I expect the nurse to understand? In the end, I explained tentatively about Kim's lack of speech and that she was likely to be difficult. On our next visit, we were told that the only thing wrong with Kim was us, her parents. So I was left with the feeling that I must have an overactive imagination, be stupid, or neurotic – yet instinct told me that I was *not* worrying unduly, that there was something fundamentally wrong. [. . .]

Needless to say, having Kim's tonsils removed made absolutely no difference at all. [. . .]

By then, Kim was attending a very good nursery school, run by Mrs Tudor Hart, but was still somehow 'different'. The nursery school staff did their best to help Kim socialize with the other children. However, after a particularly difficult day when Kim had messed herself and spread the dirt all over the place, the principal asked me to have a chat with her. She felt that we should 'do something' about 'seeing someone' about Kim's behaviour, which she seemed to think was rather 'spastic'. I remember she seemed very matter-of-fact about it, but I staggered out of there absolutely blinded by tears. I wandered along the road thinking only of the word 'spastic', and all that that conjured up in my mind. I felt I could not go home, my mother was staying with us for a few days and I could not bear to explain to her why I was so upset, so I 'phoned a friend who collected me in her car without a word, and I stayed with her most of that morning.

So – we decided to go to the Spastics Society. She had an IQ test and again it came out at a low 90. The psychologist felt she certainly was not spastic but sent us back to Great Ormond Street to see a neurologist. His child, it turned out, happened to be at the same nursery as Kim, which seemed important to me at the time because his general attitude to us as parents was rather dismissive, suggesting that we were over-anxious without actually saying so. I told him that it was this same nursery that had suggested that we should investigate, and I pointed out her very clumsy running and walking, that she could not jump with two feet together, could not pedal a bike. He tested her reflexes with the hammers they use on these occasions and asked her to walk up and down and run. He looked at us and said:

'Would it make you feel better if I said she was spastic?'

To this day I can remember the room, the consultant with the spectacles, the surrounding white coats of the students, and the absolute shock at those words. If this remark had been made to me today, now that I have gone through the training course that all parents with handicapped children have forced upon them by professionals who treat parents as if they are without any kind of intelligence, I would not have been so meek and mild about it. [. . .]

I remember passing the local child guidance clinic one day when Kim was about four-and-a-half and suddenly deciding, more on impulse than anything else, to go in. After all, I reasoned with myself, that was what I needed, guidance! Something must have gone wrong with the system that day, for, as I discovered much later, I should have had a doctor's letter before making an appointment, but no one said anything to me about that and I just made a date to see the educational psychologist. We were becoming dab hands at this by now, Maurice and I, so we went along prepared for the usual questions and the inevitable test. But we were very aware that this particular interview was going to be important, as Kim's whole future education could rest on the decision our local education authority might make about her schooling, and this was our first attempt to bring our daughter to the attention of the education authorities.

So we were very diplomatic. What was patently obvious was Kim's lack of speech. At this age, the number of words she used was less than a hundred, and she could not string sentences together in any coherent form, although she was able to understand most commands. We went through yet another IQ test, and again because these tests before the age of five are mainly based on non-verbal puzzles, the result was the same 90 – 'too high', said the child guidance centre, for an ESN school (special school for the 'educationally subnormal'). However, she had to have a label and because of her non-ability to verbalize this psychologist decided she was 'aphasic'. But there is no school for aphasic children in London: in fact there are only two in the country, although the Education Act states that this is one of the categories that demands special facilities.

It was decided to try Kim at the local infants school, and in retrospect I think this was a good move, as the teacher was a dedicated and involved person, and in the two years that she attended, Kim made tremendous progress – she was reading five- to six-year-old standard Ladybird books, and the family group system on which the school was based allowed her to operate at her own level. So every morning I walked round the corner, saw Kim into her school, and worried about how she was going to manage. There were a few traumas. Then one day Kim just wandered out of school at lunchtime and disappeared. Eventually, she was found by the police picking flowers in the park at Alexandra Palace, totally unaware of the chaos she had caused. The following morning the headmistress told me that she could no longer keep Kim in the school. I asked her where she suggested she should go, since I had been assured that she was not ESN. 'She would come under the term maladjusted,' she replied. The whole thing was ridiculous.

Maladjusted she certainly was not, so began our first minor scuffle with authority. Maurice 'phoned the education officer for the borough, demanding a place in a special school for aphasic children locally, knowing full well that none existed. The officer said that no decision to move Kim could be taken without the school doctor assessing the situation, and that he would write to the doctor in due course about it. Maurice offered to come to the Town Hall himself and take the letter direct to the doctor, which offer threw the man into a state of verbal confusion and extracted a faithful promise that the letter would be posted. We said that we would 'phone the doctor in the morning to check that the letter had arrived.

The first lesson – authority does act when faced with firmness and determination.

It was also that devastating encounter with the primary school headmistress that led to the first real help for Kim. I was walking down the school path afterwards, lost in my worry about Kim, and badly thrown by that word 'maladjusted' – instinctively, I knew that this was just not the case.

'I don't know if it will be of any use to you, but I know of someone who might be able to help you.'

I turned round to find a tall grey-haired woman trying to attract my attention. She had obviously followed me out of the cloakroom but I had been so distracted that I had simply not noticed. She then went on to explain that she herself had a son with a learning problem and had taken him to a woman called Mrs Dane who had devised some kind of intensive exercises. Apparently, she ran a sort of 'clinic' but was not recognized by the medical profession and her treatment was private. My first reaction was, I admit, very sceptical. 'Some kind of quack,' I thought. But subsequently, while we were struggling to establish our right to keep Kim at the primary school, Maurice and I discussed Mrs Dane further and looked up her name in the 'phone book. We were very desperate for some kind of practical help, and if there was any way at all to help Kim towards speech, or towards some more general awareness, we were anxious to explore it. We decided that in any case there was no harm in finding out, so we made an appointment to see her.

Mrs Astrid Dane held her clinic in a building attached to a Convent. [. . .] Everywhere, there was a deep sense of religion, not just because of the Convent School on the other side of her path and the glimpses of nuns as they passed the windows, but also because of the pictures hanging on the walls in what I took to be her office. At first it seemed a bit unreal, and removed from our way of things, but the questions she asked were very down to earth. Was Kim blue at birth? Did she wet the bed? Could she ride a bike? Catch a ball? It suddenly dawned on me that she was asking the right questions! Mrs Dane explained that she expected any child she treated to attend her clinic for up to fifteen minutes a time maximum, three times a week, and the charge would be £1.50 for each session. She insisted on the three times a week. To me, that sounded an incredible hurdle. There was school to consider – how would I explain her absences to the headmistress? There was the distance: I could not drive at that time and it was quite a complicated journey by public transport. And there was the cost.

And what did she do anyway? Her apparatus consisted of wall bars, a large padded table, trapeze hanging from the ceiling rather like a circus, two ropes, a see-saw and something that looked like a huge mound of tiny wooden steps. Her idea, it seemed, was to make the child concentrate and to increase her co-ordination. Climbing the little steps, not missing out a single one, for instance, took a lot of thinking about. By building up the child's confidence with more and more concentrated physical exercises, general concentration in other areas of learning could be increased. I looked at the room and at Mrs Dane and wondered how this seemingly frail old lady was going to cope with a heavy child like Kim. How on earth was she going to get her on the ropes in the first place, or even into the room itself? But her frailty as it turned out belied a will of iron, and discipline was uncompromising. Mrs Dane stood no nonsense, the exercises were done to a strict routine which did not vary, and the children soon found this out.

The idea of something physical appealed to the commonsense – Kim had great problems with co-ordination, she was very clumsy when she ran so we decided to try it. How we would do it, I just did not know. But we did in the end work out a plan of action, and the school went along with it. Kim was to attend at 9.00 a.m. three days a week, Maurice arranged to take her twice a week and a great friend came to collect me in her car for the third morning, for a whole year until I eventually passed my driving test. I shall always be very grateful to her for her generosity during that time. [. . .]

For the first time, we felt that Kim was receiving some kind of practical help. Even the headmistress confirmed that she was more controlled at school, and her teacher said 'Whatever it is you are doing, it seems to be having a good effect.' We continued with Mrs Dane for three years, until Kim went from the local primary school to the Gatehouse school. When this change took place, we decided that the long journey she would have to make would be quite enough for her to cope with.

When Kim was seven, we knew that the era of the infant school was at an end. The transition to junior school was looming up, and we decided that any idea of keeping her another year in the infant section to 'wait and see' was simply postponing the issue – we wanted to find somewhere where Kim's problems would be recognized and not just tolerated.

We had already been back to the Nuffield Centre to have her retested by the same psychologist we had seen with Dr Yudkin, and again the result came out a low 90. The tests once more did not show anything concrete, except that she was slow. They again did simple hearing tests which involved whispering etc., because we had never managed to get an accurate reading on more complex tests since Kim would never co-operate. We were interviewed by the head of the department. He asked the usual questions, like was she difficult to feed as a baby (a question that throws me into a fury whenever I think about it, and remember how my continual questions at the clinic were brushed aside). After a few more details, he leant back in his chair and said something like:

'You know, you are obviously educated, your home environment is cultured and so your child seems slow to you, you are impatient about her progress and cannot accept the fact that you have a dull child. After all, if you were a working-class family, her development would not seem so different at all – you must just accept the fact that she is not very bright.'

If you, the reader, find it difficult to believe that this kind of thing happens, I do not blame you. But I am not inventing anything, and hundreds of other parents of handicapped children can tell stories to match mine. No one suggested Kim was mentally handicapped, no one suggested an EEG, no one suggested that the sum of all of her difficulties (not pedalling, not speaking, not jumping, not knowing when to stop eating) could possibly add up to a serious disability. No one, in short, suggested she was not a normal child. Up to this time we had been ready to continue our life, trying to accept Kim's difficult behaviour and to explain it away as 'Well, she doesn't talk very well and is a bit slow'. But now she was seven and we decided that we had to try something more constructive.

But trying to find an alternative to our local primary school put us in a real dilemma. Kim had by now had six IQ tests, and in all of them her rating was too high for an ESN placement, although it seemed generally agreed that the normal school framework was not suitable for her. What alternatives were there? Then one day we were listening to a radio programme and heard mention of a Montessori school that takes one handicapped child into every class – the children including mongol, blind, deaf, autistic, backward, the whole range of handicap. The school was the Gatehouse School, and it sounded as if it would be just the place for Kim. Sometimes, things go for you. On this occasion, the stars were in the right place.

Mrs Wallbank, the headmistress, is an exceptional lady. Her office in the school, which at that time was based in the City, was small, very ancient-looking and always filled with the body of a very large dog that guarded her, the room and everyone else in a friendly but overpowering way. She had agreed to see us because she was opening a small unit for handicapped children, who she planned would eventually be integrated into the ordinary classes. There would be six children and one teacher.

We had not as yet admitted openly that we had a handicapped child. But we explained our feelings about keeping Kim in the infant section of her present school for another year, and said that we knew she needed some special help that she couldn't get where she was. Mrs Wallbank spoke to Kim and listened to everything we had to say, showed us around and told us some of the experiences she had had with other children who had passed through her hands. She then laid it straight on the line, and she was the first person we had met who was prepared to commit herself. She told us to accept the fact that Kim was indeed handicapped and backward. It could happen that if other parts of her brain started working overtime, she could pick up a lot; but we were not to be too optimistic, and must fight tooth and nail to see that her time for learning was not wasted, for these early years were vitally important and it was useless just to wait and see.

We have always been grateful to her for that interview, and after a week of utter depression and desolation, we came through knowing that we had to accept the fact that we had a handicapped daughter, and that life had changed.

Our interview at the local primary school took place some time later. The child guidance clinic had agreed to our accepting the place offered to Kim by Mrs Wallbank, if the local Medical Officer of Health agreed too. She came round to the house to see Kim in her home environment, and said she would endorse the placement, but that we were lucky to get it as there were lots of children who couldn't write and do other things well in school! When I asked her if she didn't feel that Kim seemed different from other children, she shrugged it off, saying 'not so different'. To me, who watched Kim alongside other children every day, waiting in vain for any sign of her catching up with them just in social development, let alone in academic progress, this seemed incredible. [. . .]

Mrs Wallbank's new unit was housed on the ground floor of a large private house in St Johns Wood. There was even an indoor swimming pool, a great amenity for children with real problems of motor co-ordination. The teacher was excellent, Kim settled down very well, and altogether we felt relieved that she was now receiving some definite help in a small framework. The other children had varied problems, but all came under the general category of 'brain-damage'.

After she had been in this unit for a year, Kim finally went into the big school. She had a programme worked out for her and things were going well. However, at the back of our minds nagged the knowledge that we had never had an official assessment of her: she was attending the school under a label – 'aphasic' – that had been attached to her almost by chance. [. . .]

The Wolfson Centre is a low building, modern with a receptionist and armchairs, tastefully decorated in the subtle colours that are supposed to make you feel at ease. We were offered a cup of tea. Kim had her photograph taken, which I disliked very much: seeing the face to fit the number in a file makes one feel even more 'your life in their hands', somehow. One of the Centre's psychologists took her for an IQ test in another room and we had our first and last interview with a social worker (Kim is at the time of writing thirteen and I have yet to see another). She talked mainly about contraception. The assessment is termed a 'day assessment', but except for her IQ session Kim was not observed in any other way, although we did this time have several physiological tests, including an EEG which showed nothing unusual. It was all very pleasant.

We had made the approach for this assessment, not the authorities. But what we were yet to discover was that even so, a report goes automatically to the local authority-and that parents do not see it at all. They can only get a verbal explanation from their own doctor – supposing of course that they have a sympathetic doctor. If we had known this before that interview, I wonder if we would have gone? We discovered also that the Centre could not help with any decisions on schools, since this is decided by the local authority. The Centre can only suggest. The IQ this time was definitely low, and our murmurs querying how it was that all the previous six IQ tests could have been so wrong were brushed aside with the remark that this psychologist was 'very eminent in her field' (since the other places we had visited were not exactly in the wilds of Siberia, we found this comment very strange). To the Centre's credit, it did send staff members to visit Kim at the Gatehouse, who were very impressed with the way she was being handled. We warned them that we did not want this arrangement altered as we were very happy with her there.

As Kim was reaching puberty at ten, however, and the gap between her and the other children was becoming wider and wider, we decided that it would be better for her to get into an ESN school, if possible, near home. We hoped also for some kind of social contact locally for her (something which to this day we have not been able to find). Since her label was not ESN I went to see the doctor who decides these things for the Borough, at the local clinic. The contrast with Wolfson could not have been greater. We were in and out of there in just over fifteen minutes. We got what we wanted – again we were in command of the change. But what, I couldn't help wondering, of the parent who had not yet come to terms with the fact of the child's handicap; who was inarticulate, or shy; or who was simply unaccustomed to dealing with authority . . . waiting to see this man on whom the child's whole future might depend? The perfunctoriness, the coldness of the occasion was both callous and offensive. A family with a handicapped child has a hard time enough coping from day to day in any case, without having to find the energy to fight for rights, to take on the experts and the officials of local government as well!

15 Extracts from Evidence to the Snowdon Working Party

[The extracts printed here relate solely to the problems of employment. The Snowdon Report also addresses itself to a much wider range of problems that disabled people face (for example, housing, education, transport, mobility). Readers interested in these areas are advised to consult the full report.]

Recommendations of the Snowdon Report

[. . .]

Employment

20 The premise on which our Sub-Committee's philosophy is based is that employment itself is crucial to the integration of disabled persons of employable age within the life of the community, and that such employment should, so far as is practicable, be as similar as possible to that of able-bodied people in respect of conditions of work, status and pay.

21 At the present time there is evidence of considerable unemployment, mis-employment and under-employment of disabled people and a clear indication that existing legislation and provisions for the disabled are inadequate.

22 A National plan for the full employment of handicapped people should seek wherever possible to make work available for the handicapped alongside able-bodied workers.

23 Segregated arrangements should only be made where these are shown to be absolutely necessary.

24 To achieve such integrated employment, however, it is necessary for special support for the disabled to be provided.

25 The Aids to Employment Scheme requires extension and development – not least in regard to human assistance.

26 We support the principle of a Quota System, whereby employers of 20 or more persons are obliged to recruit a percentage of their work force from a Register of Disabled Persons, but the present system needs strengthening and reform.

27 We advocate a differential weighting for quota purposes in relation to the severity of handicap.

28 Further, the employer's view as to the suitability of a disabled person for a particular job should no longer be conclusive. The Disablement Resettlement Officer should be able to refer disputed cases to one of the

Source: INTEGRATING THE DISABLED (1980) Evidence to the Snowdon Working Party, Vol. 2. London: The National Fund for Research into Crippling Diseases.

District Advisory Committees, with power to grant or withhold an exemption certificate.

29 Government departments and local authorities should be covered in the Quota System.

30 Our most radical suggestion however and the one which we believe could do most to further the integration of disabled persons in employment is our recommendation of a Disablement Employment Tax, to be levied on all employers and paid into a Disablement Employment Fund, to which the Government would also contribute. From this Fund employers would be compensated for expenditure incurred on registered disabled employees and would also be relieved of the Tax in respect of any registered person employed.

31 Social Security Benefits can in certain instances operate as disincentives to the employment of the disabled, and we make the point that disabled persons should never be worse off financially by working.

32 We propose that the Secretary of State's power to reserve certain occupations for disabled persons be discontinued.

33 We urge that research and publicity be undertaken to open up new avenues of employment to disabled people.

34 We also advocate the provision of a spectrum of job opportunities ranging from fully open to fully sheltered conditions, based on the principles of supported integration.

35 We outline the requirements for improved careers guidance, training and rehabilitation of the handicapped.

36 We welcome the steps being taken to upgrade Resettlement Officers, who should have power to evaluate employers' reasons for refusing to employ a disabled person.

37 There is need to improve the access to places of work for disabled people. In some instances the provision of hostel accommodation is advocated – in others financial assistance to make it easier for the disabled to move nearer to their place of work.

38 We have not made special recommendations for the mentally handicapped or the educationally subnormal. Their needs vary widely according to the nature of their disability. In general, however, we believe our recommendations are as applicable to their needs as to those with other forms of disability.

39 Finally, we stress the desirability of employing disabled people themselves in administrative and managerial positions, including the senior positions in the system of sheltered workshops, and also involving them as much as possible in the implementation of policy affecting their employment.

[. . .]

General Letters from Individuals

[. . .]

I am a disabled person, I suffer from Amnesia and Epilepsy. I find it very hard to find work. I think it is true that employers let each other know about us people. The number of firms I have gone to look for work, filled in an application form and it always asks if you are a registered disabled person, or if you suffer from epilepsy. I have been out of work for over a year, I am 31 years old. I do get really annoyed when I go back to a firm after filling in an application form and the person says 'sorry we can't give you a job because we know you are a registered disabled person'. Firms are supposed to employ a disabled person if they employ too many people, and the larger the firm the more disabled people it employs. I have been told that rather than take the risk of employing someone who suffers from epilepsy, they would take some person on who is in a wheelchair.

Hull is supposed to be the best city in this country for looking after people like me. I was told by the manager of the last firm I worked at to give my notice in because he had found out I had a green card. He said he had never sacked anybody from that firm, if I didn't give my notice in he would find me the worst jobs. The men advised me to, so I gave my notice in. I couldn't draw any unemployment benefit for six weeks. I couldn't claim a penny on social security because I live with my parents, so what could I do? [. . .]

The real secret behind a disabled person living a happy and useful life, is simply to work; – but if possible, not with other disabled people. There are snags of course, but they are not unsurmountable. Employers need to change their attitudes towards disabled people and regretfully, I feel that some disabled people ought to adopt a different approach to employers. It is no good trading on a disability; – master it and ignore it – harsh words. I know, but it's the only solution.

From 30 years experience I have proved that however efficient a D/P is at his/her work, she is denied the same prospects as her able-bodied colleagues. It is a mystery to me why this should be so, and I suspect that it is due to a fair amount of mistrust on the part of the employer.

I am a Civil Servant and lost a leg over 30 years ago. To date I have given 22 years service and during that time I have seen some of my colleagues give second-rate service and yet, receive promotion. Evidently, Government Departments prefer second-rate able-bodied workers to disabled people who are efficient! To be blunt I don't think employers really like employing D/P's. They think we are all 'passengers' consequently, they pre-judge and mistrust us.

Believe me, Government Departments are the worst offenders when it comes to being unfair to disabled people. I have had to fight the Civil Service every inch of the way, and the only promotion I ever gained was earned by passing an Exam. It seems odd to me that a Government legislates to protect disabled people at work, yet does nothing to enforce the laws they make! [. . .]

I am a paraplegic by nature of my disability and as such am confined to a wheelchair. I have worked continuously from a chair for the past 14 years doing various unskilled jobs evolving around assembly and inspection in a factory. Around three years ago, after being made redundant I attended a government training course in Electronic wiring, after which I found myself a vacancy in this new trade. After two successful years with my present Company I have now been promoted to Prototype and Development, which leads me to say that, not only my present Employer, but past ones as well, have only had to make very minor provisions to the work and other areas that I have frequented. These being namely a lowering of a workbench some 3 inches (although this is not absolutely necessary), a reserved parking space, again not absolutely necessary, and the provision of a small wooden ramp if any steps are encountered. In my present firm, one step is present at the entrance to the canteen, which has been ramped. One firm I worked for actually knocked two toilet cubicles into one to provide toilet facilities for the four wheelchair workers that they employed. So on the face of it, it would seem that factory employers could very easily, and successfully employ at least a couple of wheelchair workers, as they would find that many jobs could be done by such workers with little or no alterations needed to the premises. But not so in practice, as you would be surprised at the prejudices that one meets when applying for a suitable vacancy. I have been fortunate, and as such always employed fully, but I do not have the freedom to change jobs and thereby gain valuable experience, although the area I reside in is thickly populated with Electronic type firms.

One of the main stumbling blocks I have come across seems to be the holding of a green card. That is the Disabled registration employment green card. I have a Card, and so it appears does half the population of Great Britain. People with hearts in poor condition can have one, asthma sufferers can have one, bad backs, heads, eyes, hearing, limps and even ingrowing toenails sufferers can obtain one, in fact if half the green card holders in my firm stood in a line, nobody would be able to pick out the so called disabled from the physically fit. So what chance has a more severe disabled man or women got when applying for a job and is told by the management that they already employ their official quota (4% or thereabouts) of disabled (Green card workers) people and they do not want any more. When one makes enquiries, it is found that the so called disabled workers are made up of rather ridiculous ailments when compared with say wheelchair users. I do not say that all employers adopt this attitude, but it is fairly widespread, and is used as an excuse for their prejudices towards more severely disabled.

My idea towards a solution is fairly simple, it would involve a system whereby two or more categories of disabled persons would be established and a small percentage of each could be employed by an organisation. The system could be flexible as some premises are more suitable than others. It is true to say that any scheme involving legislation especially where the disabled are concerned needs the goodwill of all concerned, but we have to start somewhere. [. . .]

I have suffered from myasthenia gravis for fiteen years. Although this is by no means a disabling disease, I have found it inhibiting, particularly in employment.

I was able to obtain a professional qualification and at 29, I hold a senior position in a large company. This position was not easy to obtain, and was almost lost. When I attended the interview, I saw no reason to mention my disability until I knew I was on the short list. I would at this stage mention that this disease in no way affects my work, nor does anyone know I suffer from it until told. When my prospective employer was told, he asked various questions, but subsequently wrote and declined to employ me. There had been some delay in receiving this letter, and prior to its receipt I had managed to find out that myasthenia gravis was the sole reason for the company not wishing to employ me. After I received this letter I discussed the matter with the company and they said they would be happy to employ me if my consultant could give them certain guarantees about my health. These were given, and the position offered, which I still hold. This is not the first time this has happened, and probably it will not be the last.

I have probably been able to overcome these difficulties as I am reasonably articulate, but had I not been, perhaps I would have found obtaining employment difficult.

On the whole, I have not found, neither do I believe, employers intolerant, but were ignorant of the disabled's abilities and difficulties. Employers need education and the best way is to bring pressure to bear to employ disabled and see just how well they fit in. [. . .]

16 Mobility Needs of Disabled People in the UK. A Formal Sample Survey

Richard Gormley (Lucas CAV)

Larry Walters (Lucas Research Centre)

[. . .]
1 Objectives

This survey of disabled people was designed to obtain information about the mobility problems of disabled people.

Specifically, we compared the responses of three matched groups of disabled individuals to 87 questions covering:

(1) patterns of mobility – to and from work, trips outside the home, common activities in the home, leisure time activities
(2) usage of mobility aids, particularly electric wheel chairs
(3) sources of information on mobility aids – printed sources and people who gave advice and information
(4) satisfactions and dissatisfactions about mobility aids, wheelchairs and components, particularly the joy stick controller
(5) financial conditions affecting supply of mobility aids
(6) social factors affecting the use of mobility aids such as electric wheelchairs

The three groups were disabled people who currently use electric wheelchairs, disabled people who have never used electric wheelchairs and disabled people who have used electric wheelchairs in the past, but do not now use them.

2 Summary of Conclusions

1. Disabled people go out infrequently, for short periods, and the types of trip they do make are largely restricted to essential shopping, and visiting friends and relatives. Indoor mobility patterns are also severely limited in comparison with the general public. Many disabled are unable to carry out simple activities within the home such as 'making the beds,' 'washing clothes' or 'cooking/preparing meals.' There is a serious need for continuing development of all devices and methods for improving the mobility of disabled people, both in the home and outside it. Those devices should make full use of all relevant modern technology.

Source: Paper presented at the Second European Conference of Rehabilitation International, September 18–21, 1978. Sevenoaks: Naidex Conventions.

2. Information resources in the UK are poorly developed. Many disabled people who have to look for facts about mobility aids are not sure exactly what information they need, or where it can reliably be obtained. The sources most frequently found to be useful by disabled individuals are friends and relatives, and their own disablement organisations. Government funded sources such as DHSS brochures and booklets, health visitors, social workers and family doctors are effective in an alarmingly small proportion of cases. There is an increasing need for a national, disinterested organisation to speak with one voice in detail to *all* disabled people about *all* types of mobility aids, not just those favoured by Government.

That requirement for the whole of the country cannot be met by existing organisations with the present facilities and financial resources. There is an urgent need for more Aid Centres and for an organisation which has a function comparable to that fulfilled by the Consumers' Association for the general public.

3. Disabled peoples' incomes are still on average, low. Total weekly income from all sources to complete households containing disabled individuals are roughly equivalent to the weekly average pay of one member of the national workforce. Insufficient extra resources are available to disabled people to meet added costs of mobility and other needs essential to normal life. For example, 45 % of disabled people have spent money which did not come from government, charities or any other 'free' source on mobility aids. The ability to lead an independent life, and spend moderate sums on personal interests, which usually involve moving around, is still not possible for many disabled people. This picture of continuing financial difficulty was confirmed recently by the impressive EIU survey.*

4. There is a favourable balance of opinion about the technical performance of modern devices to aid mobility, such as electric wheelchairs. For example, of those who had seen joystick controllers on electric wheelchairs 72 % gave positive comments and 34 % were able to identify disadvantages.

5. Very few disabled people made any reference to the 1970 Chronically Sick and Disabled Persons Act. However, considerable evidence of improved relations between disabled people and the general public was uncovered by this study. Detailed statistics indicate there is both increasing contact between the two groups, and an improved level of mutual acceptance.

3 Method Outline

[. . .]
(a) Sampling

Contacts established during the preliminary programme of interviews with experts were approached with a view to listing names and addresses of

* See Appendix: 'References and Organisations'.

disabled individuals to meet the target sampling frame of 600 completed interviews. Those approached were enthusiastic and co-operative. In general however, release of names and addresses is not consistent with the tradition of organisations concerned with the disabled, without the individuals' prior consent. Accordingly, we supplied reply paid Screener Cards to the thirteen organisations listed in the Appendix, and in total 6,950 Screeners were mailed out. Administrative and postage costs were met by Lucas CAV, and donations were also made as appropriate. The Screener operation provided over 1,500 legible names and addresses of disabled individuals which we could then contact directly. The 21 % response is low. Reasons include screeners which, due to administrative delays were not received by the disabled individuals themselves, or were received too late, inaccurate/out of date primary lists*, reluctance of disabled individuals to take part in the survey and membership of disabled individuals amongst two or more participating organisations.

There was a substantial proportion in favour of the self-completion interview method. Of those who replied to the Screener, 1200 were mailed the Main Questionnaire. Although the latter was an eight page document requiring several hours to complete, the response rate we now achieved was very satisfactory. Of the approximately 900 Main Questionnaires which were returned 608 were selected to complete the sampling frame for computer analysis.

The authors do not contend that this study is based on a strict probability sample. Most sophisticated statistical tests are therefore inappropriate. There is an element of self selection in the sample, and individuals who are generally unreceptive to taking part in surveys or are physically restricted from doing so are probably under-represented. However the final sample of 608 individuals conforms to the original sampling frame, and all relevant groups in terms of age, sex, income and type of main disability are included. It is therefore possible to make reasonable generalisations to the total UK disabled population.

(b) Analysis

The majority of questions are open-ended. They were coded by reviewing a verbatim listing of answers for each question, and constructing categories to account for as much of the verbatim material as possible. Close-ended questions were pre-coded on the questionnaire. Over 130 headed computer tables were produced. This paper is based on those tables and further hand analysis.

---

* i.e. membership lists, etc. held by participating organisations.

4 Results

(a) Restricted patterns of Mobility

One in three of the total sample, and one in four of current electric wheelchair users leave their homes to go to work. In terms of other types of trip, over half the total sample mentioned 'shopping' or 'visiting friends/ relatives' first when asked what types of trip they make most often outside their homes. The next most frequently mentioned types of trip were 'theatres/other public places' (17 % of the total sample), and 'clubs/centres for the disabled' (13 %). Table A below also shows that 17 % of our sample didn't know what trip they take most frequently. It is likely a large proportion of those respondents do not make trips outside the home. The distribution shown in the table is different from that for the general public, and indicates a lower level of mobility.

Table A: Types of trip made most often – first mention

Base	No.	%	Base	No.	%
	608			608	
Shopping	333	55	Swimming/walking	34	6
Visiting friends/			Car Outings	34	6
relatives	311	51	Adult education	30	5
Theatres/other public			Watching sports	14	2
places	106	17	Hairdressers	12	2
Club/centres for the			Library	11	2
disabled	82	13	Outings/trips with		
Club/centres (other)	66	11	children	8	1
Church	57	9	Other	97	16
Doctor/hospital/clinic	57	9	Don't know/no answer	3	1
Teaching/voluntary work	47	8			

The restrictions on trips outside the home suffered by disabled people are put into even sharper focus by Table B, opposite, which shows whatever type of trip is made most often, it is made infrequently and is of short duration relative to the general public. Again, including those who seldom if ever go out, about half the total sample take their 'most often' trip once a week or less often. For 54 % of the total sample the 'most often' trip lasts thirty minutes or less.

Table C shows a different pattern of moving around inside the home from that obtaining for the UK general public. For example, only 20 % of our sample go up or down stairs, while the comparable figure from a general

Table B: Number of trips and length of time

Frequency of 'Most Often' Trip			Average Length of 'Most Often' Trip		
Base		608	*Base*		608
	No.	%		*No.*	%
Less than 1/week	25	4	0–10 minutes	86	14
1/week	253	42	11–20 minutes	149	25
2/week	126	21	21–30 minutes	93	15
3/week	59	10	31–45 minutes	54	9
4–5/week	41	7	46–60 minutes	62	10
6/week or more			61 minutes or more	80	12

Table C: Activities in a typical day spent at home

	Base	*Yes* %	*Not Able* %	*Not Applicable* %	*Do not know/ No Answer* %
Leave one room to go to another	608	93	4	1	2
Go up or down stairs	608	20	41	28	12
Cook/prepare meals	608	30	38	20	11
Make the bed(s)	608	18	51	19	12
Wash clothes	608	20	45	23	12
Dust/clean house flat	608	17	47	25	11
Go into the garden	608	61	22	10	8

public survey is 94%. Of those disabled people who do not go up and down stairs, over half are unable to do so. This restricted pattern of activity spans a large range in terms of age, income and degree of disability.

(b) Poor Use of Information Resources

Regular publications of voluntary organisations formed by the disabled themselves appear to be more important than institutional sources of information about mobility aids.

At least 80% of our total sample mentioned 'news letters' of the disablement organisations, and nearly three quarters of those respondents said that source was the most useful. In comparison 7% of the total sample said 'DHSS brochures and booklets' were most useful in obtaining information about mobility requirements.

In terms of people who give information on mobility aids, disabled people rely more heavily on friends, relatives, manufacturers and the ALAC's than they do on health visitors, social workers, physiotherapists or even their family doctor. Disabled individuals are unsure what information they need. For example, nearly half our sample replied 'don't know' or gave uncoded (vague) answers when asked what they would need to know before obtaining an electric wheelchair. Less than 10% mentioned information such as ability to climb kerbs, ability to cope with slopes, speed, or the need for a home trial. In terms of where they expected to get information, nearly 70% mentioned manufacturers. The next most frequently mentioned expected sources were 'Aids Centres' (56% of the total sample) and 'DHSS/ALAC' (54%). Only 15% mentioned their doctor or GP and only 24% 'hospital or clinic'.

(c) Extra Financial Burden

In spite of well publicised intentions to help the UK disabled population to obtain aids needed for improving mobility, over half our sample had used their own financial resources to buy mobility aids. For 87 respondents the aids obtained by those methods had cost £500 or more. Table D below also shows where these extra expenses which fall on disabled people are met. The proportion who used their 'own income/savings' approaches half. [. . .]

Table D: Where personal funds spent on mobility aids obtained

BASE: THOSE ANSWERING	312 No.	%
Own income/savings	134	43
Family	59	19
Charity disablement organisation	43	14
Spouse	11	4
Pension	10	3
Friends	6	2
Other	31	10
Don't know	18	13

Lack of funds was also indicated by answers to a hypothetical question which asked our sample to imagine they had substantial extra discretionary income. Almost all respondents had definite ideas on which items to aid mobility the extra money would be spent. Nearly half of the total sample said it would be spent on running a private car and a further 26% mentioned purchase of an electric wheelchair. Other items mentioned were 'taxis' (12 % of the total sample), 'other special aids' (2 %) and 'public transport' (1 %). The answers to another question in the area of finance indicate 75 % of the total sample reject outright purchase of aids such as electric wheelchairs (in comparison with other purchase methods) because they cannot afford that method.

(d) Acceptability of Modern Mobility Aids

In terms of the performance and the technical features of mobility aids experienced by our sample of disabled people, the level of criticism was surprisingly low. Although most aids were covered, from walking frames to the government's invalid car or 'trike,' from shoulder crutches to DHSS attendant controlled electric wheelchairs, the focus of our study was on self-drive electric wheelchairs. Answers in that area showed a favourable balance between positive and negative experiences and opinion. For example, Table E, shows 27 % of those who have/had an electric wheelchair mentioned 'increased mobility,' and 16 % said their most recent chair has

Table E: Advantages and disadvantages of most recently acquired electric wheelchair

Base: Those who have/had an electric wheelchair			*Base: Those who have/had an electric wheel chair*		
	331			*331*	
Advantages	No.	%	Disadvantages	No.	%
Increased mobility	89	27	Problem with batteries	48	15
Manoeuverability	53	16	Too large/clumsy indoors	47	14
Easy to control	46	14	Cannot climb kerbs	43	13
Folds up/easily transported	42	13	Battery life not sufficient	39	12
Independence	40	12	Heavy/difficult to fold/		
Comfort	38	11	transport	35	11
Good over slopes/rough			Slow	32	10
ground	33	11	Uncomfortable	29	9
Speed/gears/good drive			Difficult to control	22	7
system	28	8	Unreliable	21	6
Easy to get into/use	24	7	Problems with repairs/		
Reliable/robust	18	5	servicing	12	4
Good range/batteries	13	4	Movement too jerky	12	4
Smooth ride/stable	8	2	No brakes for parking	6	2
Attractive/smart	7	2	Expensive	6	2
No advantages	8	2	Needs battery charge		
Don't know/no answer	38	11	indicator	8	2
			Limited range	8	2
			Cannot disengage motor	6	2
			Other	2	1
			Don't know/no answer	50	15

the advantage of high 'manoeuverability.' Many other advantages were mentioned such as 'easy to control,' 'folding/transportation' and increased 'independence'.

Based on the total sample of 608 disabled people, nine miles was given as the average distance an electric wheelchair should be expected to travel on one battery charge. Again manufacturers' current products conform to that requirement (although there are technical reasons why batteries should not be run until fully discharged). [. . .]

The preponderance of disadvantages (mentioned by relatively small numbers of respondents) concerned the vulnerability of joystick controllers to operator error and the general difficulty of imprecise, unpredictable movement. The second area of criticism is the positioning of the joystick controller. A small number of respondents felt they were not placed in the best position on the chair and that they can catch in clothing.

(e) Improved Public Attitudes

Answers to several questions indicated directly or indirectly that, largely due to the efforts of disabled people themselves, there has been a substantial shift of public attitude favouring disabled people. For example, 88 % of the total sample agreed that the public attitude towards disabled people has improved over the past few years. Table F, below, indicates the predominant

Table F: Reasons for improved attitudes towards the disabled

BASE	533 %
Publicity/public knowledge	33
People see/mix more	31
Public more aware	29
Growing tolerance/understanding	6
Accepted as human/not mentally sick	6
More buildings/facilities	8
Independence of disabled/fighting for rights	13
Mention of 1970 Act	3
Other	15

reason is to do with greater publicity for the problems of disabled people, and contact between disabled people and the general public. The second most frequently mentioned reason concerns recent work by disabled people to obtain greater degrees of independence and human rights. Interestingly, the 1970 Act was mentioned in this context by only 3 % of the total sample.

Appendix: References and Organisations

A. Sources Used as Background Study

1 HARRIS, A. M. *et al.* (1971) 'Handicapped and Impaired in Great Britain.' London: Office of Population Censuses and Surveys, HMSO.
2 BROWN, M., THOMAS, N. M., and SMITH, A. (1972) 'Report on the Survey of Chronically Sick and Disabled Resident on the Isle of Wight.' Institute of Local Government Studies/Department of Social Administrators, University of Birmingham.
3 ROYCROFT, B. (1972) 'Report on the Survey of Chronically Sick and Disabled People Resident in Newcastle-Upon-Tyne.' Newcastle Department of Social Services.
4 FRYERS, T., BANNING, B., and NEWTON, P. (1974) 'The Chronic Sick and Handicapped in Salford.' Department of Community Medicine, University of Manchester and Salford Department of Social Services.
5 'Report of the Working Party on Mobility Allowance' (1976). Central Council for the Disabled (now the Royal Association for Disability and Rehabilitation).
6 'Poverty and Low Incomes Amongst Disabled People' (1977). A submission to the Royal Commission on Distribution of Income and Wealth – Low Incomes Reference. The Disability Alliance.
7 FENWICK, D. (1977) *Wheelchairs and Their Users.* A survey among users of National Health Service Wheelchairs in England and Wales, to establish their characteristics and attitudes to their wheelchairs and to the operation of the wheelchair service. London: Office of Population Censuses and Surveys for the Department of Health and Social Security.
8 SIMKINS, J., and TICKNER, V. (1978) *Whose Benefit?* An examination of the existing system of cash benefits and related provisions for handicapped adults and their families. This study was undertaken by, and published by, the Economist Intelligence Unit Ltd. The Disablement Income Group was deeply involved in preparing the information.

B. Organisations Which Helped Mail Out Preliminary 'Screener' Questionnaire

1 Arthritis and Rheumatism Council.
2 Association of Disabled Professionals.
3 Department of Health and Social Security, Blackpool.
4 Disabled Motorists' Federation.
5 Disablement Income Group.
6 Disability Alliance.
7 Liverpool Association for the Disabled.
8 Multiple Sclerosis Action Group.
9 North Wales Community Action.
10 Royal Association for Disability and Rehabilitation.
11 South Lakeland Council for the Disabled.
12 Spastic Society.
13 Spinal Injuries Association.

17 Scenes in Ward 7

M. Oswin

Ward 7 accommodated 21 multiply handicapped children aged from three to 14 years. Eighteen of the children were receiving permanent long-term care, two were weekly boarders, and one was in for short-term care. Nine of the 18 long-term children had been admitted for permanent care before the age of five years.

Thirteen of the 21 children were non-ambulant, 19 were incontinent, four were known to be blind, 19 were speechless, 20 did not wash or dress themselves and seven did not feed themselves. All had the ability to grasp objects in their hands.

All the problems which have been discussed in this report were found to be incorporated in Ward 7, and this appendix describes some typical scenes in the ward. The overriding impression of the ward was the intense aloneness of the children who lived in it.

A Typical Evening

At 4 pm

Two of the 21 children had been taken home for the night, and one was out with his foster-mother. Nursing Assistant Jones, and State Enrolled Nurse Smith were on duty for the remaining 18 children. There was a new little girl in the ward today: six-year-old Mary. She was ambulant, and had been admitted to the 'sick' ward a week ago for short-term care, and had just been transferred to Ward 7. She stood in the middle of the day-room, cuddling a soft toy hippo which she had brought from home, and looking timidly about her.

The day-room contained a battered settee, a large air-bed, and some wooden boxes with holes in and square boxes arranged as three steps. Ambulant children were walking about; the non-ambulant children were lying on the floor. A few children sat under the radiators and held the warm pipes with their hands, others rested their bare feet on the pipes. There was a sense of poverty in the room, and it was slightly cold.

A narrow corridor led from the day-room, on each side of which were linen cupboards, store-rooms, a bathroom, washroom and lavatories. The corridor led into the bedroom, which was so small that the beds were in rows across the centre of the room as well as all around the sides. The children's clothes were kept in two large cupboards just inside the bedroom. There was

Source: M. OSWIN (1978) *Children Living in Long-stay Hospitals*. London: Spastics International Medical Publications with Heinemann Medical; Philadelphia: Lippincott.

no room for individual lockers. The day-room had a newly-built extension to it, known as 'the sun-lounge'. At one end of this sun-lounge there was a colour television, a plastic settee, three plastic armchairs and a strip of carpet. At the other end there was a sideboard minus its doors, four tables, and kitchen-type chairs; this was where the children ate their meals.

At 4.15

Supper started. There was a shortage of clean bibs, so soiled ones were reused. These dirty bibs were lying in a damp heap in the broken-doored sideboard, and as the staff lifted them out a sour smell of stale food arose, and lumps of cold porridge, potato and sponge-pudding fell from them. They were shaken and then tied around the children's necks. There was also a shortage of bowls and spoons, which caused a major inconvenience during supper because the two staff had to keep leaving the children and running to the kitchen to rinse bowls and spoons. When they did this, some of the more able children went to the trolley and ate scraps from the scrap bowl, or grabbed food from the plates of the less able children. As it was so inconvenient to keep going to the kitchen to wash dishes in the middle of feeding the children, the staff eventually gave some of the children their puddings in unwashed bowls which had been used by other children.

Fourteen of the children could feed themselves, which was said to be due to the psychologists of the hospital directing the ward staff in the principles of behaviour modification. The ability to feed themselves appeared to be an isolated skill, for only two of the 14 children were also reliable about the lavatory, and only one of them could wash and dress himself.

The children were given their meals in two sittings, so that they could be individually supervised. Those who could manage without help were encouraged by praise, and the others were encouraged to lift their spoons to their mouths on their own after being helped to load them. Thus while actually sitting at the table with a plate of food in front of them and spoons in their hands, the children received attention. However, immediately a child finished eating he ceased to receive attention. Some of the non-ambulant children were then carried silently back into the day-room and placed, still sticky, onto bean-bags. Others remained sitting at the tables; their faces were covered with food and they sucked at their food-covered hands. A few of the children got off their chairs as they finished eating and went under the tables, where they used their hands to shovel up spilt food into their mouths. Some of the ambulant and crawling children went to the waste-bowl on the trolley and picked at the slimy mess of everybody else's leavings, and poked into the bowl containing the dirty cutlery to suck off the food which had been left on other children's spoons. Then they went to the slower eaters and tried to take food from them.

At 4.55

The staff cleared the tables, went into the kitchen and remained there to have a cup of tea. Nursing Assistant Hartley arrived at 5 pm. She would be on duty until 8 pm. She joined the other two staff in the kitchen.

The 18 children were left without supervision. Eight-year-old Monty (two years in hospital) and 14-year-old Douglas (11 years in hospital), both ambulant, began to tip over the chairs in the sun-lounge, and leant on the window-sills and opened and slammed the windows. They were high-spirited and healthy, and this was their usual behaviour after meals. Seven-year-old James (five years in hospital) was sitting in a baby-buggy at the end of the sun-lounge. His buggy got tipped over during the rompings of Monty and Douglas. He was unharmed but very startled. Monty began to loudly slam the low gate between the lounge and the day-room.

Nine-year-old Shirley remained sitting at the table where she had eaten her supper. She was a weekly boarder, and spent most of her time between Monday and Friday sitting at a table in the sun-lounge, in a state of silent, abject misery. She had a frail appearance, and wore a caliper on one leg. She had had a stressful time towards the end of supper today, because her plate had been snatched first by 13-year-old Elizabeth and then by Douglas (who had proceeded to eat her supper with his fingers). Shirley always ate very slowly, and she often had her food stolen by the more able children.

Three-year-old Tom, ambulant, but with very little sight, wandered about the two rooms. Sometimes he sat down on the floor. He had been admitted to the hospital only a few days before, and was in for long-term care. Mary, the new little girl, stood looking through the day-room doors into the corridor. Her toy hippo appeared to be lost. She held her hands limply at her sides.

At 5.30

The children's drugs were given out. This was the first staff involvement with the children since 4.55. The SEN stood in the corridor beside the drug trolley. The two Nursing Assistants stood by her with dessert spoons in their hands. The SEN put the appropriate drug for each child into one of the spoons held by the NAs, who had meanwhile filled the spoons with jam from a pot standing on the drug-trolley. The NA then opened the day-room door, found the right child for the drug, and pushed the spoonful of jam and the capsule into his mouth. (This was the usual procedure for giving drugs in Ward 7: it was done hurriedly and without conversation with the child.) Because so much jam had been put into their mouths the children became very sticky: they continued to sit about with sticky faces and with jam trickling down their chins onto the front of their clothes. Little streaks of dried jam, long there and hardened now, were stuck on the radiator in the day-room because the children on numerous previous drug-giving occasions had wiped their sticky mouths along the radiator by which they had been sitting when given their drugs. There were also streaks of fluff-covered jam down the sides of the wheelchairs.

SEN Smith went off duty at 5.35. NA Hartley and NA Jones would be in charge of the ward for the rest of the evening, and would have to get the 18 children ready for bed, and their clothing sorted out by 8pm. Neither had had any training in looking after handicapped children, or in residential care work. NA Jones was middle-aged and had started working in the hospital 18 months earlier. She said that on her first day she had been given the choice of spending a week looking around the hospital at the various wards, or starting work straight away as an NA on Ward 7. She had decided to begin as a nurse immediately, but had been very upset for a few days because of the children's grave handicaps. She had not attended any lectures or been given any guidance. She said that she 'just picked up what to do' from the other staff. She was kind to the children, and with different leadership would have made an excellent houseparent. NA Hartley was in her late twenties and had been working in the hospital for seven months. She said that she had applied to the hospital for domestic work but had been offered a job as a nursing assistant.

5.40 to 7.25

NA Hartley and NA Jones had to be in the bathroom, washroom and bedroom during this period, and a number of children were left un-supervised in the day-room. Non-ambulant children who were waiting their turn to be bathed or washed, or who had already had their turn, were lying on the floor by the radiator or sitting in wheelchairs or baby-buggies. The ambulant children wandered about the day-room and sun-lounge. Douglas and Monty continued to rampage about in the sun-lounge, shoving at the tipped-over chairs. Nine-year-old Dermod (four years in hospital), cerebral-palsied but able to crawl, remained in the corner where he always put himself after meals. He rested his bare feet on the warm pipes.

Shirley still sat alone at the bare table in the sun-lounge, where she had been sitting since finishing her supper at 4.55. She had shrunk into herself as Douglas's romps with the chairs continued unabated around her, and, completely still, she stared blankly at the untidy, comfortless scene in front of her.

Mary began to strip little pieces of wallpaper off the day-room wall. She dropped the paper on the floor. Six-year-old Jill, who had been admitted to the hospital the year before, bottom-shuffled along behind Mary, picked up the bits of wallpaper and ate them.

NA Jones was working in the small bathroom, undressing and washing one child at a time on a large table. NA Hartley was with a group of children in the wash-room/lavatory area. She was following the usual wash-room routine of sitting four or five children on the lavatories and then partially or fully undressing them as they sat there. After sitting on the lavatories for about 10 minutes, each child was taken across to the wash-basins to be washed. If he was non-ambulant, he was lifted onto a large table in front of the lavatories and washed as he lay there.

The children in the washroom were being washed with one shared flannel. There appeared to be a shortage of bathroom commodities; nappies were being used as towels, and there were only two hairbrushes for all the children. All underwear and nightclothes were communal, including the standard issue dressing-gown made of towelling.

Twelve-year-old Brian (in hospital for nine years) had dried mucus caked on his face because his nose had not been wiped for him for many hours. The mucus could not be removed, even after being soaked with the flannel. NA Hartley decided to leave it on in case his face was made sore by too much rubbing. Brian was a very big boy, and it was difficult to find pyjamas to fit him. The jacket eventually put on him was too tight and came high up his back.

Some of the children were returned to the day-room after being put into nightclothes. They were not wearing slippers, and their feet were cold.

Although the two NAs were almost overwhelmed by their chores, they were very kind to the children during the getting-to-bed routines. NA Jones called me into the bathroom to see a child smiling as she washed him, and she took me to see children whom she had put to bed. She went to each bed and peeped at the children. She said: 'It makes you wonder, doesn't it? I wish there was more time to spend with them and play with them as we would our own'.

At 7pm the washing and changing of children was all finished. Eight children were in bed; 10 were back in the day-room, dressed in their nightclothes. It had taken the two NAs 1 hour 20 minutes to attend to the 18 children. The NAs began to tidy up the bathroom and washroom, and pack up the dirty clothes. The 10 children in the day-room were in the following positions:

10-year-old June sat in a wheelchair, sucking her hands;
nine-year-old Dermod was in the corner where he was always to be found; he was stripping off his nightwear;
six-year-old Jill was shuffling around the room on her bottom;
13-year-old Elizabeth sat beside Brian on the air-bed, on which eight-year-old Monty lay asleep;
six-year-old Mary walked wearily up and down the room;
13-year-old Charles, blind, stood holding the radiator;
14-year-old Douglas was kneeling in the middle of the day-room floor;
three-year-old Tom stood holding the radiator.

At 7.25

The two NAs had just finished packing the laundry. They walked through the day-room into the sun-lounge, turned on the colour television and put

Jill in front of it. Then they went into the kitchen, where they sat smoking and drinking coffee. While it seemed wrong that the children were left alone so much, these two women must have been very hot and tired because they had washed and changed 18 children since 5.40pm and had tidied up the bathroom and packed up all the dirty laundry.

At 7.30 the positions of the children were:

June was in her wheelchair, as before.

Dermod was still in his corner, now stripped, and he lay on his back playing with a wheelchair tray that had been on the floor near him. He held it onto his face and twiddled with the rods and screws.

Jill was crouched in front of the television in the sun-lounge.

Elizabeth, Brian and Monty were still on the air-bed.

Mary stood in the middle of the room, now sucking her hands.

Charles had sat down on the floor, his back against the radiator, and his hands and arms stretched out each side of the warm pipes. He looked very cold.

Douglas was still kneeling in the middle of the floor.

Tom still stood by the radiator.

At 8pm the staff were still in the kitchen and the 10 children were in the same positions as before. [. . .]

Whose Responsibility?

Which professionals could be held responsible for the deprived conditions in Ward 7, and the appalling loneliness of these children?

There were no therapists working in the hospital; social workers never visited the ward; the doctors gave no guidance at ward level, apparently because they were engrossed with committee work and with out-patients; the nurses appeared to be fighting a losing battle because of shortages of staff, and their goodwill and kindness was being dissipated by the poor conditions and lack of support.

Fourteen of the children could feed themselves because psychologists had instructed the ward staff in the principles of behaviour modification (see p. 137). It cannot be denied that it is valuable for ward staff to understand the principles of behaviour modification, because they can then appreciate how a child learns and how he may systematically be taught acceptable skills. However, it seems that although much patience had gone into training the children in the physical skill of feeding themselves, the psychologists took no further part in improving the children's environment. It was disquieting to realise that the children's ability to feed themselves was a social skill made almost meaningless because it had no carry-over into the rest of their lives. It was merely a physical performance, and even a misleading one insofar as it was likely to convince people who did not recognise the children's deprivation that the hospital was providing good care – because the children had been taught to feed themselves.

In this same context, one might well ask what use it was to have taught a child to load his spoon with food and lift it to his mouth if he later crawled under the table and licked up other children's dribblings because there were too few staff to give him constant attention. The psychologists could be said to have created a false situation in teaching children a social skill without at the same time taking action about the deprivation which is inherent in under-staffed institutions, and which denies the children the mothering they need and eventually distorts their development. Perhaps the first priority for the psychologists should have been to effect changes in institutional care rather than to teach children how to manage their spoons.

How much responsibility did the hospital school-teachers take for the care of the children in Ward 7? The teachers said that they were well aware of the poor child-care in the ward, but felt unable to do anything about it in case they spoilt the good relationship which existed between the school staff and the hospital staff. Their lack of action prompts the questions of how much will professionals shut their eyes to in the interests of preserving 'good relationships', and when do professional responsibilities towards the children have to take priority over good relationships?'

SECTION THREE
Professional Support

In this section we shall be looking at what the professionals have to offer. The first two sections have been discussing disability in society in a broad framework, and considering the relationship between the circumstances of individuals and the society in which they live. Within our Western society there has been an increasing tendency for one aspect of that social relationship to become predominant, namely the helper/helped relationship. Not only has it become predominant, to the extent that disabled people are thought of as essentially dependent beings, but it has also become crystallised by the professionalisation of support services for individuals with impairments. John McKnight's paper in Section 1 (3) draws out clearly the implications of such developments.

In this part of the book we will explore this professional support in more detail, drawing on a selection of papers which reflect a common concern with the day to day services offered and received. We have tried to select papers which do more than simply describe a cross-section of professional activities, and, with the help of a number of specially commissioned papers, have tried to present an impression of the changing face of professional work. It was our intention that the papers selected should illustrate issues by drawing on practical and specific examples, which can then be seen as having relevance for professional support in general. In reading them we would ask that you consider the issues raised in a broader context cutting across conventional discipline boundaries.

The first paper, by Blaxter (18), provides a valuable scene-setting introduction to the section. She raises fundamental questions about the structure and delivery of services and goes beyond the more obvious task of examining the intrinsic inefficiencies of a complex and overlapping system, to explore the implications of the consumer's interpretations of the service rationale. Within such a system, professionals are struggling to improve efficiency and effectiveness, and experimenting with new approaches. The following three papers illustrate this: the first by Lamont and Langford (19) in relation to physiotherapists working in the community; the second by Haig and Hope (20) describing an approach to speech therapy with young children; and the third by Jay (21) considering the evolving roles of occupational therapists. Newson, in her paper (22), is also concerned with developing more effective ways of working. She concentrates here on assessment and with great clarity conveys the crucial importance of the 'shared assessment'.

Also on this topic, Ainscow and Tweddle (23), in a discussion of educational problems, raise some important issues about the focus of assessment. They argue the importance of identifying those features of a situation which may be amenable to change, and of not becoming involved in theorising about factors which are beyond control. In a very concrete way this kind of approach has been influential in making professionals far more useful to clients in solving immediate problems. At the same time, it seems to us a somewhat narrow approach which, taken in isolation, could well distract professionals' attention from more long term, and, at first sight, unattainable changes. Taking up this issue of where the focus should be, Brechin's paper (24) discusses the practice and implications of behaviourism as a technique of intervention. Does it tend to divert attention from external, apparently fixed and long term features of a situation, however unacceptable they may be, by focusing on the 'abnormality' of the individual's behaviour?

Stubbins (25), too, is concerned about the need for a balanced approach and focuses here on the part played by Disablement Resettlement Officers. In particular he questions the relationship between the training schemes offered and the job requirements, suggesting in this case that perhaps too little is understood of individual clients' potential for change.

Feeney and Galer (26) introduce us to the world of ergonomics, stressing that designing for disabled people is the same as designing for anyone else: the same principles apply, and careful planning and feedback are paramount. In a very different sphere, Rubissow's article (27) presents the same argument. The comprehensive paediatric service she describes has been developed gradually to provide for handicapped children and their families. Only careful planning and feedback has enabled the emergence of a suitably individualised and flexible service.

The move towards a more open style of professionalism is reflected in many of the papers in this section. Durrant's overview (28) of personal social work provides a valuable summary of some of the critical changes taking place, and leads us to our final paper. Here, Bannister (29) in his commissioned article draws on construct theory to provide a framework for understanding some of the difficulties inherent in any professional approach. The construct theory provides a useful basis for drawing together many of the difficulties which have been recognised repeatedly in previous papers.

18 Power and Inanity

Mildred Blaxter

[. . .]
This study addresses the questions 'What are the principles on which this welfare system is constructed? What are its main components, and how are they articulated together?' After a brief glance at the official, 'authorised' version of the structure as it is written into legislation, two levels of analysis are then set side by side: on the one hand the modified version of the 'official' structure which represents its functional shape, based on what the administrators of the particular local services see themselves as doing, and on the other the varied impressions of the structure which are held by the potential clients. These are not competitive versions of 'the way it really is', but simply alternative modes of providing a comprehensible account – from different viewpoints – of a reality which is continually developing. [. . .]

The starting-point of this study is a wide and loosely-defined group of *clients*: those who may require some formally-provided service, in any area of life, because of social needs arising from illness or disability. The system examined is the total network of professionals and officials offering such services in one place, a Scottish city, at one time, 1972/73. The potential clients were 240 men and women aged 16–64 (thus excluding services exclusively for children and the old) who had an illness or accident sufficiently serious to be likely to lead to long-term or permanent impairment. They represented a wide variety of types and degrees of impairment, and may be regarded for the present purpose as a random sample of the physically impaired. They were a selected group in that they had all had recent contact with a hospital, but they were not necessarily newly impaired. [. . .]

The 'Given' Structure

The definition of an 'agency' is necessarily arbitrary. The formal system was defined as all those organisations whose legislative backing, or written-down mandate, or official statement of their aims, included services in the community for the assistance or welfare of the sick and disabled. These were all society's agents in a wide sense, providing things which the taxpayer, the ratepayer, or the charitable man had tacitly agreed that it was good and proper to provide. All organisations with distinct administrations, normally

Source: A. DAVIS (ed.) (1978) *Relationships Between Doctors and Patients*. Farnborough: Saxon House in association with the Institute of Medical Sociology, University of Aberdeen.

located in different places, and with different workers, were counted as separate and a total of fifty-nine was reached. [. . .]

Obviously, such a system must be very complex, and too large to represent diagrammatically in all its detail. From 'above', how may a simplified model be portrayed? One method might be to begin with the legislative basis for the provision of each service (which means that there will be clear divisions between that which is statutorily provided and that which is voluntary) and depict the administrative chain of responsibility. [. . .] The usefulness of such a picture to explain how a particular client obtains a particular service is, however, severely limited, in part because it does not show the interrelations between agencies, and in part because it imposes a spurious tidiness. [. . .]

A more functional model, representing the 'working' system as it would be agreed to be, in principle, by administrators might place the client in the centre. Around him would be arranged the major departments of central or local government or other organisations, grouped according to the area of life involved – money support, welfare goods and services, employment. Between the client and the agencies would appear a circle of key workers who were the major referral agents from one part of the system to the other, expected to cooperate in assessing and providing for the needs, in the community, of the individual client – the social workers, nurses, Health Visitors, Disablement Resettlement Officers, and so on. Such a model is shown in Figure 1, and this is the general arrangement that will be repeated, for purposes of comparison, in further diagrams illustrating specific parts of the system.

Looked at in detail (even though the examination is still confined to the 'formal' system, without yet taking into account the clients' perceptions) the system must be expected to be very much more complex than this simple model. As an example, a small part of it – a selected group of practical goods and services provided for the assistance, in the community, of impaired people – is 'expanded' in Figure 2. Duplication and inconsistency are immediately evident, for which explanations may be offered in terms of historical circumstances or of local, national, or professional politics. [. . .]

An added complication and interest in this particular case of services for the physically impaired arises from the fact that the area has always been one in which it has been accepted that voluntary or charitable effort should be prominent. Thus, for instance, though certain services for the blind are a statutory duty of the local authority, at this place and time a voluntary society continued to carry them out as it had done since 1843. There were many other examples of services still provided by voluntary bodies – sometimes in duplication of official services, sometimes by formal delegation, sometimes to fill gaps left formally empty. Some of these (the provision of aids, transport, recreation) can be seen in Figure 2.

Other anomalies may be the result of policy decisions or professional politics. That the most expensive 'goods' – adapted motor cars, or complex electronic equipment – are left firmly in the hands of high-status medical

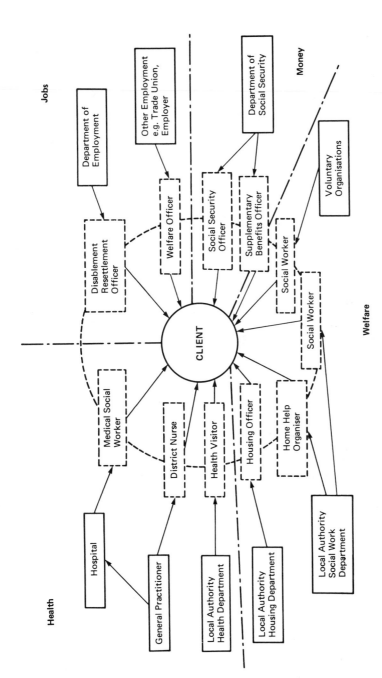

Jobs

Money

Welfare

Health

Department of Employment

Other Employment e.g. Trade Union, Employer

Department of Social Security

Voluntary Organisations

Disablement Resettlement Officer

Welfare Officer

Social Security Officer

Supplementary Benefits Officer

Social Worker

Social Worker

CLIENT

Medical Social Worker

District Nurse

Health Visitor

Housing Officer

Home Help Organiser

Hospital

General Practitioner

Local Authority Health Department

Local Authority Housing Department

Local Authority Social Work Department

Fig. 1 'Functional' model of health and welfare services for this group of clients (at one place and time) showing the organisation responsible and the key referral agents.

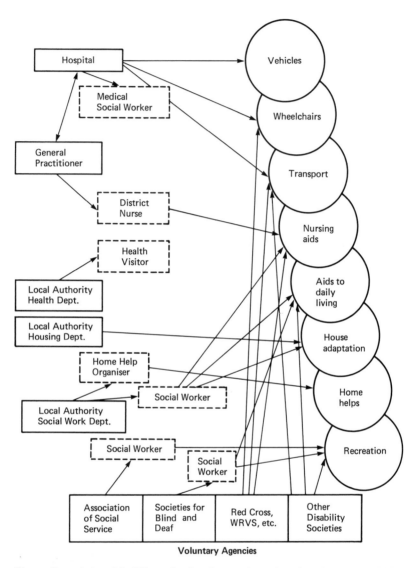

Fig. 2 Expanded model of Fig. 1 showing the agencies and workers throughout which a selected group of practical goods and services could be obtained, according to the formal system.

professionals, to be 'prescribed' according to the exercise of professional judgement, is certainly a method of restricting demand and minimising critical complaint about allocation. Reasons for the fact that services which, in this particular field, may be thought to be very similar are still carried out by a number of workers each under a different administration – local authority social workers, medical social workers, health visitors, social workers employed by voluntary organisations – may be sought in the history of the organisations concerned, rather than in any rational assessment of 'needs'.

Another small part of the system which may be used in example is shown in 'expanded' form in Figure 3: this is the provision of rehabilitation, retraining, and employment, which can be seen to be equally illogical and equally redolent of social history. It would be rational to provide an easy progression through physical rehabilitation and occupational centres to sheltered work or retraining and assisted employment in open industry. Administratively, however, this progression is interrupted by discontinuities at every point. 'Occupation' is a welfare service provided, statutorily, by the local authority, or a health service provided in hospital therapy units. The local sheltered workshops, Remploy and the Workshop for the Blind,

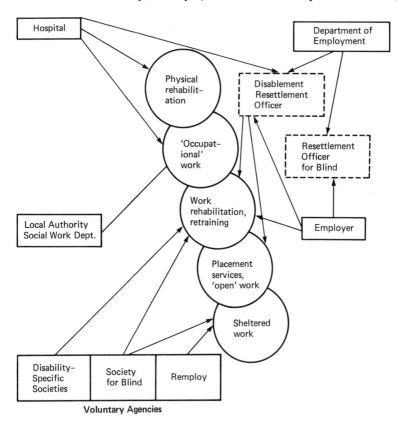

Fig. 3 Expanded model of another part of Fig. 1, showing the agencies and workers involved in the provision of rehabilitation and assistance with employment.

represent older and separate strands of social history: on the one hand the official concern for (originally) ex-servicemen, and on the other humanitarian and charitable provision for the blind. Disabled 'workers' – those who are capable of gainful employment – are provided for under the immediately post-war Disabled Persons (Employment) Acts, but the long history and power of the voluntary agencies representing the blind has ensured that this group of 'the disabled' is still statutorily a group apart, with a separate branch of the Department of Employment's resettlement service.

Only two examples have been given, but every part of the simple model of services of Figure 1 can be shown to be equally complex in detail – and this still only at the level of formal administration, of asking 'Who is responsible for this service, and what does their official remit state that they do?'. It is not surprising that the client's perception of the system was found to be a little confused.

The Client's View

The survey subjects were not, it must be made clear, asked to perform the difficult task of analysing the structure as they saw it. The following is an attempt to form models based on what these 240 people actually did and the way in which they explained their actions. Of course, they could hold several models simultaneously, and there was no necessity for these to be compatible.

One may start, as in the previous section, with very simple models. These are the organising devices required for everyday purposes by people whose actual contact with the system was not great. The commonest appeared to be logical and straightforward systems based on geography – In what building is the service based? – and on history – Whose business has this area of life always been?

On the first, geographical basis, the system is shown in Figure 4. These are the 'official' agencies which may be supplemented, by individuals, with other welfare agencies (church, employers, charitable societies) which they may happen to know. The evidence for this model is the way in which the survey subjects spoke: 'I went to Tower Street but they sent me down to Heather Street'. 'I saw the man at Abbey House, and he said don't worry about them at Harbour Street, I'll fix them', 'At the Town House they said I'd need a note from the Hospital'. Very often the names of the departments located in these buildings were not known, and interviewers for this survey soon learned that, for the majority of subjects, 'Have you been to Heather Street about this?' was a much more efficient question than 'Have you been to the Supplementary Benefits Office?'

The use of this model created some problems. The agencies of Figure 4 were seen as official, though in administrative fact a few (the Blindie, Tower Street) were independent voluntary bodies. 'Tower Street', the offices of the local association of voluntary social services, was older-established and in

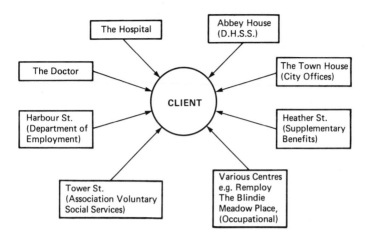

Fig. 4   Clients' geographical model of the available services.

general better-known than the local authority social service department at 'The Town House', and this caused great confusion since few people were able to distinguish between social workers from the two sources. Some people, being sent from Tower Street to the Town House, mistakenly blamed 'government bureaucracy' or 'there are so many different departments of the social security' for 'being pushed from pillar to post'.

In the second, historical, model the system was firmly divided into functional sections: the Health Service, the Insurance or Security, the Welfare, the City, and the Employment. Figure 5 shows this model, with some of the assumed functions of each division; that it articulated rather badly with the geographical model added to confusion. Some of the categories were, to the clients, straightforward: 'Health' was self-explanatory, and 'the City' was in charge of long-established services such as housing or home helps which everyone knew had always been its function. The difference between 'National Insurance', 'the Security' and 'the Welfare' was more problematic. 'Welfare' was, to most of the subjects, goods and services supplied to the poor. People with little experience of social services might use the term rather vaguely: 'A lady came from the welfare after I got home from the hospital, to see how I was doing'. 'Welfare' was a service with a long history, which had altered gradually over the years without changing radically; in talking about a current interaction with various sorts of worker in social welfare people often reminisced about 'welfare ladies' of times long past. [. . .]

A few older people used the word 'welfare' to mean discretionary money benefits, but for most people it was 'national insurance' or 'security' (dating firmly, with the Health Service, from 'after the war') which were concerned

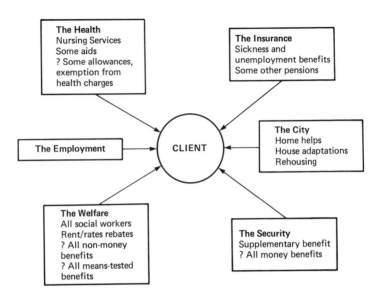

Fig. 5   Clients' historical model of services with examples of some of the assumed functions of the agencies.

with money. 'Insurance' was the preferred term of younger people, who used it for routine benefits, reserving 'security' for means-tested or discretionary benefits. 'Security' was used for all money benefits by those who were in fact less secure, who either had extensive contact with social welfare agencies or else felt themselves to be in danger of dropping into the class of people who did. To use the term 'social security' for all benefits, whether insurance-based or not, seemed to be helpful to these people in blurring the distinction: since it was all one system, to slip from one branch to another implied no stigma.

To those whose contact with the system was minimal, however, 'security' was to be avoided: 'Our family's never had anything to do with the security, I wouldn't want to start now' (wife, 50 explaining why she was refusing to apply for an 'attendance allowance' for her stroke-victim husband); 'I wouldn't ask for aught, everyone says they make you feel degraded. You have to tolerate an invasion of your private and personal matters, if you go to the security' (welder, 47, who had been advised to go to the Supplementary Benefits Office. [. . .]

Negative attitudes to a group of agencies may, of course, arise out of the clients' perceptions of the way in which they are treated by the agencies. In fact, however, those with a great deal of contact with 'security' were less likely to be critical. The attitudes illustrated were more typical of those with little contemporary contact, and seemed to derive largely from historical stereotypes. [. . .]

Patterns of Usage

These simple models will not be adequate for extensive forays into the system, or where some good or service is required which does not fit these models. People might have some idea, for instance, that a disabled person's vehicle might be available, but from whom? Is this health, or welfare? Or perhaps social security, or even the department that deals with licensing of motor cars? In fact, the correct department was the Limb and Appliance Centre of the hospital.

What picture of the system can be derived from the clients' actual usage of it? The pathways of enquiry and referral observed in individual cases were labyrinthine, and serve principally as illustration of clients' (and agents') perplexities. [. . .] In the case of Mr Ritchie, for instance, permanently bedfast and with a wife who was also disabled this was bedboards and nursing equipment recommended by a consultant on a domiciliary visit. 'I didn't like to ask him to get them and Dr. X (general practitioner) didn't seem to know', he said, and decided that the specialist's clinic at the hospital would be the best place to telephone for advice. There, he was told to consult his GP but since he was in more frequent contact with a district nurse he explained the problem to her. His account was that she said, 'We can't supply them, but I'll try the hospital stores'. Some days later, Mr Ritchie's local authority social worker, on a regular fortnightly visit, said that she had been informed about the bedboards and would be obtaining them. 'She said, you should have got in touch with us about that, that's our business to supply them, but how was I to know?' [. . .]

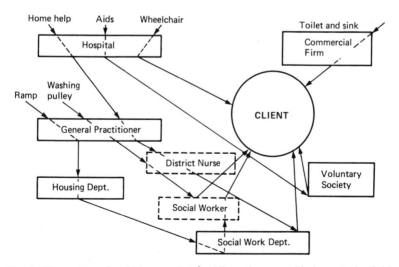

Fig. 6   The pathways by which one patient [middle aged woman with rheumatoid arthritis, wife of an office manager] obtained a number of different aids and services in the home.

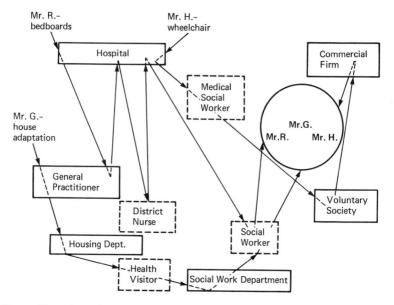

Fig. 7   The pathways by which Mr. R., Mr. G. and Mr. H. obtained equipment for use in the home. (Figs 6 and 7 may be compared with Fig. 1 [and with each other])

The effects of these defining processes upon help-seeking and referral are shown, in very simplified form, in Figure 8. Here the actual pathways of referral for the selected group of services of Figure 2 are depicted, for this particular sample of potential clients. (Not all 240 required *any* service, of course. The diagram simply illustrates the nature and relative volume of the traffic flow: nothing is being said about the relationship of supply, demand and need). Conspicuously, people chose to enter the system through agencies of health rather than welfare. 'Key-workers' were by-passed, in part because they were in general overworked and too few in number and in part because the referring agents first approached (usually, for these services, doctors) were unsure of the 'correct' pathways anyway, and saw themselves as 'cutting out red tape' by attempting to deal with things themselves.

The Effect Upon the System

Of course, definition of need depends on perception of provision. If there were few referrals for, for instance, telephones, this was because few people realised that they might be provided; it implies nothing about the need for telephones. The ways in which service-provision affects service-use are well-

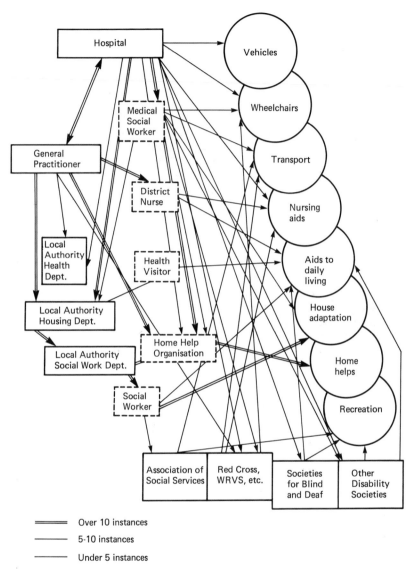

Fig. 8 The actual weight of referrals, in this sample, for the group of goods and services shown in Fig. 2.

documented, and need not be illustrated. The question which is being asked is rather: do the clients' perceptions then, in turn, affect the structure of agencies?

Clients have stereotypes of agencies, as agencies do of clients, and clients' stereotypes can be reinforcing, just as agencies' can. Thus, their patterns of usage may force patterns of behaviour upon the agencies. This was the explanation for some of the patterns shown in Figure 8. If the majority of patients saw medical social workers as being concerned primarily with money, and perhaps the organisation of residential after-care for the elderly, then the social workers necessarily found themselves spending a great deal of time on these activities, with less opportunity to define their own functions. If the patients insist on using their doctor for services which the system has defined as 'social' (and if the system does not provide him with a clear and efficient formal pathway to a central social agency) then his attempts to do his best for his patients will inevitably mean a fragmented structure.

It is often demonstrated that agencies can stigmatise clients. Clients may stigmatise agencies, too, perhaps in reaction, so that the process is a circular and reinforcing one. The clearest illustration of the process was perhaps the clients' use of the Register of disabled workers. To be on the register was very firmly seen – rightly or wrongly – as being stigmatising. Sometimes this attitude was based on the worker's perception of his own experience, but more often it was simply 'what everyone knows'. [. . .]

The result was a self-selection of clients which reinforced the stereotypes. Those who became registered were likely to be the particularly disadvantaged – older, unskilled, and unemployed for a long time. [. . .] The reaction, at the national level, to these characteristics of the clientele was the suggestion that the category of 'disabled' should be replaced by another including 'all those people with distinct social or personal problems – the socially handicapped'[1]. So the process becomes circular.

In other fields besides the area of employment similar current movements of social policy were towards the integration of services, and in particular the closer association of health and social welfare. Influential contemporary ideologies stressed the integration of 'the disabled' with society, the substitution of functional assessment for rigid clinical categorisations, and the provision of services for 'need' per se, without distinction as to the cause of that need. Organisational manifestations of these policy movements included the assumption of welfare functions towards the disabled by social work departments, the transfer of provision from disability-specific voluntary societies to local authorities (this, however, had barely reached the area under consideration at the time) as well as the suggestions being made by the Department of Employment that the services for the disabled should become subsumed under wider services for all the 'difficult to place' in employment.

Pressures from the behaviour of the group of clients observed, however, ran counter to these movements. In part, this was due to inertia in the system: the common stock of knowledge about 'how things work' could not be quickly changed. In part, it was due to the fact that people know individuals – Dr Brown and Nurse Black and Miss Green – rather than 'agencies', and for most of the clients under consideration the only individual with whom they had a familiar relationship was their general practitioner. Thus, though in the formal system the GP is a professional exercising specialised functions and delegating more general 'welfare' work to others, in the system as perceived by the client he may be the only person to whom access is easy and familiar. The client's queries and requests may therefore tend to be channelled through him, a situation he may or may not enjoy depending upon his view of a general practitioner's function: 'The doctor said, oh, no, you're the sixth today and it's nothing to do with medicine, is it. I felt really bad – it wasn't the sixth for *me*, it was the first time ever – and who else could I go to? I thought it was his business'.

In any case the clients did not necessarily share the 'official' view that integration was a desirable principle. They did perceive, by direct experience of its time-wasting frustrations, that a fragmented system was inefficient. On the other hand, there were broad categories of life which they preferred to keep separate.

They were perfectly well aware that the way in which they were perceived by agencies would differ from agency to agency, according to the agency's function. They found this perfectly acceptable and indeed sometimes advantageous and resented any transfer of categorisations between agencies. They reserved the right to play different roles to different audiences. [. . .]

An example of the different perceptions of various agencies, and the functional nature of this variation as seen by the client, was the situation of one man in the sample who was caring single-handed for his five children. To hospital consultants, who could find no serious disease despite his many symptoms, he was a malingerer who had wasted their time and they summarily dismissed him: nevertheless the fact that he had been intensively investigated in hospital gave him some legitimation for a presentation of himself as being a complex medical case which had baffled the experts. To his general practitioner, on the other hand, who was generous with 'sick' certificates, he was obviously a man who did have symptoms and certainly *was* frequently ill. To the Department of Employment, he was workshy and in need of rehabilitation. To social workers, who did not necessarily share the orientation towards the importance of gainful employment, the central feature of the situation was the motherless children. Without any access to his medical records, they believed him to be considerably disabled and had great sympathy for him. The agency of the DHSS providing his income had some sympathy but found him a difficult client because of his inability to remember to fill in forms. In the interstices of all these overlapping definitions, Mr Stephen managed to retain his own individuality and independence, and existed quite happily.

In particular, clients expressed by their actions a clear desire to keep separate the areas of 'health' and 'welfare'. In part this was a product of their historical model, and in part an expression of their perception of the financial bases of the services. Health services, to which everyone had an unquestioned right, and for which most people paid in their 'insurance stamp', were one thing: welfare services supplied on a discretionary basis were another. Aids or appliances brought by nurses or obtained through the hospital were accepted gladly by people who were horrified that they might ask 'the welfare' for anything. [. . .]

People who appeared to be entitled to discretionary additions to supplementary benefit were more likely to have applied, *and* more likely to have had their application granted, if the money was for things clearly connected with a medical condition (e.g. diet) rather than for things which anyone in poverty might need (e.g. heating). A medically-prescribed diet came clearly within the sector of 'health', but money for extra heating was historically associated with 'welfare', even though the grounds for the need might equally be ill health. Doctors, the legitimators of this need, were more aware of the provisions concerning diet than heating, and the clients knew that their claim was more likely to be accepted. Thus, their help-seeking behaviour reinforced their image of the helping agency.

Conclusion

The case of Mr Stephen, defined differently by many different agencies, is a reminder that this analysis of a system is very incomplete. It has compared the perception of the clients with the formal system, and shown some of the ways in which the client's view may actually create what it perceives. It has, however, largely ignored the perception of the individual workers within the agencies, and the ways in which they create their own roles and functions. [. . .]

A completely adequate analysis would have to take into account the relative importance of an event for agent and client, and the relative 'weights' of the infrequent crucial encounter and the mass of frequent trivialities. This study would, however, suggest that such an analysis would necessarily take an evolutionary view of complex structures, showing that they are created and changed in stages through critical feed-back processes. [. . .]

Reference

1 DEPARTMENT OF EMPLOYMENT (1973) *Resettlement Policy and Services for Disabled People*. London: HMSO.

19 Community Physiotherapy in a Rural Area

Pat Lamont

Ros Langford

Senior Physiotherapists, Community Physiotherapy Team, Telford, Salop

Telford is a new town, embracing new estates with transient populations, gradually becoming more stable and developing a sense of community; and several old established areas. [. . .]

Referrals

Between us we now cover referrals from 11 medical practices. Where our territories meet, a new referral is added to the case load of the one with time available.

We are based at the Wrekin Hospital in Wellington, Telford, and new referrals are usually made there by telephone. The majority are from general practitioners, consultants, the physiotherapy department and latterly the day hospital which was opened at the Wrekin Hospital earlier this year [1979]. In practice, as we have come to know the other members of the community health team, we find referrals coming from district nurses, health visitors, social workers, tenants' welfare officers and speech therapists. In these cases we check with the GP concerned before making the initial visit.

Some doctors use the service much more than others, probably because they are more pro-physiotherapy than others, and because some appreciate more readily the cases where physiotherapy is useful. This is largely a matter for education, in other words we need to make doctors more aware of the nature of our service.

We usually collect new referrals and messages at midday in the department, and we appreciate the benefit of working from a hospital department base. Of necessity, we work in isolation – the decisions, and the mistakes, are ours alone. The chance to talk over difficult cases with colleagues of one's own profession, the access to records and X-rays, the chance to visit patients who have been admitted, the general interchange of ideas and opinions, including the opportunity to have a good laugh, can and do make all the difference to a job which carries a fairly heavy burden of responsibility.

Source: *Physiotherapy*, January 1980, *66*, No. 1.

During the lunch hour, most of our clerical work is done – telephoning to make appointments with patients, or to discuss patients with other community staff, writing letters recommending house alterations, and so on. We have a secretary to help with clerical work, but this is the only time during our peripatetic day when we are available on the end of a telephone, so lunch tends to be sandwiches and coffee between 'phone calls.

Walking aids, collars, and so on, can be picked up at this time, and we carry in our cars infra-red lamps, faradic batteries, weights, dressings, leaflets, record cards, and similar items. We share an ultrasonic machine.

Liaison

Have you ever wondered, when working in hospital, what really happened to patients when they were discharged home, probably still far from 100 % fit, perhaps with a permanent disability, often incapable of doing their own shopping, cooking and daily chores? [. . .] Much more thought needs to be given by hospital staff to early planning for discharge. It is no good leaving arrangements for meals on wheels, home help, wheelchairs, alterations to the toilet so the 70-year-old bi-lateral above-knee amputee can use it, until the day of discharge. [. . .]

Liaison is, however, the responsibility of each of us; it is up to us to try to keep other members of the team informed, and to make them aware of what we need to know. This is often far from easy from the purely practical point of view. There may be many people involved with one patient and they may be very difficult to contact when you need them. This is especially true of community work when most of us are rarely at the end of a telephone.

When we started in the community, we made a conscious effort to meet as many people as possible, both the professionals and members of the various voluntary organisations in Telford. A list of these was available from the library. This initiative has proved invaluable; it is usually easier to get what you want if you know someone personally, than if you are just a voice at the end of a telephone. [. . .]

Physiotherapy in any community is the same as physiotherapy in hospital in that the principles of treatment we employ are identical; the difference is one of relationship. In hospital, the patient is entering our world, voluntarily placing himself in our hands to be made better. We are seen as figures of authority, in charge of strange looking machines and busily directing the activities of other patients, in an institutional atmosphere that, however, friendly and welcoming, is alien to him.

As community physiotherapists, we are admitted to his world, usually gladly, but we are the strangers at the gates. The onus is on us to prove our worth in his environment, rather than on him to be a 'good' patient in ours. There is a one-to-one relationship and inevitably we are more aware of him as a member of his family and his neighbourhood.

Indications for Home Treatment

When the service was first conceived, the original purpose was to give advice to the patient and his family and to give a course of treatment in the home only if this was particularly indicated. This advice and assessment is still an important part of the service, but the following situations are those where domiciliary physiotherapy is particularly valuable.

1 *Where a journey to hospital is too exhausting* and counter-balances the benefit of treatment.
2 *Where a family needs advice* on how to cope with a patient and his problems.

Frequently, this needs to be continuing advice and support over a period, during which the family can come to trust and feel at ease with someone with medical knowledge. When, for instance, a stroke patient is discharged from hospital the family has often not been given any real insight into the nature of spasticity, and on days and in situations when spasticity is more pronounced, they may interpret this as the patient being awkward. There are many problems in management and other aspects of the condition which relatives need to discuss in detail to gain confidence. Families of patients with terminal diseases welcome advice on how to move the patient around and how much activity should be encouraged. Advice to families of patients with severe mobility problems, on transfers, toileting and rearrangements of furniture, can make all the difference between the family coping or not coping with the situation.

Seeing patients in their own homes gives a very different insight into their problems – they may walk beautifully with a walking frame in the department, on the level wide open spaces, but this may not prepare them for a house which is cluttered with furniture and where there are steps, uneven floors and loose mats. Occasionally, however, a house-proud wife or an elderly person may be very reluctant to make any alterations in this respect.

Observing family relationships may give the clue as to why a patient makes rapid, little, or no progress. Return to health and fitness is dependent on emotional factors as much as on physical factors. Particularly in severely disabling conditions, it needs considerable confidence within a marital relationship for a patient to regain a really active role unless he sees himself making a 100% recovery. [. . .] Development of confidence within the new relationship pattern so that the patient can move out of a position of dependency to a more active, functional role, often takes place very slowly regardless of his physical capabilities. This process may be encouraged by support and frankness in the discussion of problems and the prognosis, to help the patient and his family to see the situation as realistically as possible. The advantage taken of functional capabilities is ultimately up to the patient, but perhaps care should be taken not to push him too hard if emotionally he seems unready to accept new responsibilities, as this can only lead to a sense of failure.

On starting work in the community, however, it is amazing to find how well severely ill and disabled patients are cared for by loving families and this may surpass hospital care. For example, with hemiplegics, a family who has been instructed in transfer, mobilisation and posturing techniques can give the attention to these points that can rarely be achieved in a busy ward. The patient, especially if he is elderly, is likely to be less confused in his own home, and the family knowing his special interests can provide stimulation towards goals that are related to his normal activities.

3 *Where the acute nature of the condition is better treated at home* – for example, many chest patients, acutely painful back and neck conditions, and severe exacerbations of arthritic or rheumatoid conditions.
4 *Where mothers with young children need treatment for post-natal incontinence,* home treatment may be the alternative to going without altogether, because of their busy daily schedule.
5 *Most of the physically handicapped children* in this area are treated by the physiotherapy staff in the special schools, but for the pre-school age child and for the child with occasional chest troubles, post fracture problems, and so on, home treatment is preferable as it is less frightening; often advice to the parents and an occasional check is all that is required.
6 *Where patients need daily treatment,* for example, the early CVA* or amputee, sometimes treatment is given partly in the hospital department and partly at home, to avoid the fatigue of a daily journey and to ensure the benefits of treatment in both places. A patient may begin with domiciliary physiotherapy and later attend for treatment in the department or vice-versa.

Contraindications to Home Care

There are cases where severely ill and disabled patients may be too heavy a burden to be reasonably cared for in their particular family circumstances. With the pressure on hospital beds and the aspirations of the health services to nurse as many patients as possible in the community, one does find sometimes quite intolerable situations where a spouse, without the support of an extended family, is caring for an incontinent partner with grossly limited mobility and perhaps mental deterioration. It may be impossible to leave the patient even for shopping and if the patient is unfit to travel for day care, or there are no such facilities on a permanent basis, the situation may become a living hell for both partners. Patients with such disability should not, in our opinion, be sent home unless adequate means can be provided for giving the partner regular and continuing relief from the strains and responsibilities of such a situation.

Over the last year it has become apparent that there is a need for

[*   Cerebrovascular Accident (Stroke)]

treatment sessions in several health centres. Accordingly we now provide a service to four of the group practices. [. . .]

The great majority of GPs in Telford do not have direct right of referral to the hospital department and were referring to us the whole spectrum of patients in need of physiotherapy, many of whom were waiting several months for a consultant referral before they could receive treatment. These patients are now assessed by us at the health centre. [. . .]

If any of the patients we see at the health centres are assessed as needing a lengthy course of treatment, and the specialised facilities of the department, or can travel easily to the hospital, our colleagues there will take these patients from us as we are happy to undertake home visits for their patients when necessary after discharge from the department or from the wards.

This two-way traffic is essential to the rational working of a comprehensive rehabilitation service where patients are treated in the most appropriate place for their particular needs.

The scope of possibilities available has increased over the past year with the opening of a day hospital at the Wrekin Hospital, which has proved a particular boon for the patient who needs constant encouragement, correction and activation throughout the day. We can advise referral to the consultant in charge, by the GP concerned, and again close communication and co-operation between us and the physiotherapy staff of the day hospital can only be beneficial to the patient. [. . .]

The role of a community physiotherapist in any area depends very much on the local geography of that area, on transport, communications and ease of access to medical services in terms of distance from hospitals and health centres. It depends also on the professional and voluntary services existing and the personalities of the people in those services, the quality of working relationships and the degree of communication.

Successful rehabilitation of a patient depends not only on his physical disability and our skill in treating that disability, but on the quality of his relationships with his wife, his family and his community, and as community physiotherapists it is our responsibility to treat him in this context.

20 The Role of a 'Family Group' Nursery in the Therapeutic Programme of Four Speech and Language Delayed Children

Helen M. Haig, Senior Speech Therapist

Rosemary J. Hope, Senior Nursery Nurse, Department of Paediatrics, Charing Cross Hospital

[. . .]
Young Speech and Language Delayed Children

The therapeutic value of groups for young speech and language delayed children has been recognised for some time as an important supplement to individual treatment. Group treatment usually takes the form of perhaps four to six children with similar problems having a session together at regular intervals to stimulate their speech and language development. The aim of such a group would be to promote an interest in language activities through a desire to participate in the group, without focussing attention on speech in any individual child, and to improve general sociability.

These groups are often very successful, but they have many limitations. Their duration is often very short so that the organisation of the group tends to be artificial, rather than one involving real-life situations. This can lead to an over-intensive approach which may not be really conducive to the general aims of the group, particularly as nursery children are not developmentally ready for highly organised activity.

Secondly, the only competent language model for the children to copy is that of the adult, which however simplified is in some ways less interesting and attractive to a child than the different language levels of the different age groups in a normal nursery setting. Children with speech and language delay frequently display associated behaviour problems, so that another problem in forming such a group is that their behaviour problems may be compounded by bringing them together!

A child with communication difficulties is often quite overwhelmed by the competence and independence of other children in a large unstructured nursery with minimum adult supervision, so a compromise between excluding the child from the normal group altogether, for the reasons given, and exposing him to it without special provision had to be found.

A different policy from the usual one for integrating speech delayed children into groups was therefore evolved in the Child Development

Source: *Early Childhood*, November 1980, *1*, No. 2

Centre at Charing Cross Hospital. This happened quite naturally as a result of the structure of the nursery, and of general principles of treatment adopted within the Centre.

The Child Development Centre

The Child Development Centre is a unit which is part of the Paediatric Department where children, mostly pre-school, with handicaps of many kinds are assessed by an inter-disciplinary team. Situated within the building, and an integral part of the unit, is its 'normal nursery'. The nursery provides nursery facilities for the children of employees in the hospital as well as caring for handicapped children. It is organised on a family group basis with one nursery nurse in charge of a 'family' of four or five normal children plus one or two handicapped children. There is thus a very high ratio of staff to children.

Handicapped children referred to the Child Development Centre for assessment attend the centre on a daily basis for a period lasting two to three weeks. During this time they are attached to one of the family groups in the nursery, making a close relationship with their nursery nurse, and join in the normal nursery routine. Meanwhile they are also assessed by other members of the team both individually and in the nursery. At the case conference at the end of the assessment the findings of the team are reported, and recommendations made for the child's management. When it has been felt that a child has particularly benefited from the nursery environment, it is recommended that the child should continue to attend the nursery full-time if he can be accommodated, or for specified periods each week.

Daily Routine

The nursery has a daily routine which allows for both structured and free activity. For an hour and a quarter each morning there is a period of structured play. Four activity groups are set up with one nursery nurse in charge of each. One group does an art activity sitting together round a table rather than painting alone at an easel; different materials of all sorts of textures and colours are used. The second group is for construction work and puzzles; the third is for sand and water play, and the fourth is a story corner with the nursery nurse in charge reading or telling stories. Special interest activities are set up from week to week as the staff are inspired!

Each nursery nurse makes sure that every child in her family group and any handicapped child attached to it spends some time at each activity. The children are thus moving freely to activities which interest them, but are also given help and encouragement to try new things and to complete the tasks they undertake.

A child with poor verbal skills is often greatly lacking in independence, clings to his mother, does not explore his environment and is afraid to initiate any self-directed play or activity. While a child remains lacking in general independence, he is unlikely to improve his ability to communicate. Within this structure of supported activity groups, a child can gain considerably in confidence as he is helped to move around the nursery to the different activities.

At the end of the morning, the nursery have a group activity all together. This usually consists of listening to records, or singing songs and participating in action rhymes. The children eat lunch in the dining-room sitting in their family groups. Both at lunch and at tea, the same children are always together with their own nursery nurse. A child with speech and language problems is naturally afraid to relate to adults and children outside his own immediate family circle, since they may be unable to understand him – and he them. A meal with a familiar group that does not change is the first step that such a child might dare to make into the outside world, and in learning to communicate with it.

Four children having individual speech therapy can be described who were felt by the speech therapist to need group treatment, but not necessarily in a 'language group'.

David

David, at three years, presented as a rather disturbed little boy from a broken home. He had been attending a nursery with only one adult in charge of twenty-four children, and where a radio blared constantly. Prior to his assessment, at the Child Development Centre, he had been excluded from the nursery for disruptive, aggressive behaviour. Comprehension of language was found to be normal, but speech consisted only of monosyllables so that he was unable to express himself usefully at all.

It is likely that much of his aggressive behaviour could be explained in his inability to communicate in any other way than by fighting. No-one had the time or skill to interpret his quite elaborate use of gesture, which suggested a higher language competence. He had a mild conductive hearing loss, which was not sufficient to account for his extreme lack of concentration and severely delayed speech. He benefited greatly from the one-to-one relationship in the individual speech therapy sessions that were introduced, but needed to learn to socialise in more varied social situations. He was integrated full-time into one of the nursery family groups for over a year. Meal-times in the nursery were the first occasions when David began to learn attentive and co-operative behaviour. He learned to sit still, wait his turn to be served, and gradually to ask to get down from the table progressing from 'down', to 'get down', to 'can I get down please?'. Regular meal-times were regular times for sitting down and listening, as well as for eating!

The adult in charge of the group of children needed to talk aloud, to organise the group so that David heard a daily accompaniment of, 'he likes jam – he doesn't like marmite – pass him the jam. Who is ready for more milk? There isn't any left in the jug. Who is going to get more?' At the same time, there were children in his group at varying stages in speech development. He had a two year old and a four and a half year old pattern of speech to copy, as well as that of the familiar adult.

During nursery rhymes and songs, David had to sit and listen too, and soon felt out of place if he was the only child in the group who was not sitting still when the records were being played. In some songs it was necessary to do an action when he heard his name called so he had to concentrate carefully in case he missed his name, and his opportunity to perform – which he enjoyed. As David's general listening and concentration improved and his ability to attend to an adult – so it was easier to work at an individual level with specific sounds and words, and to help him to progress eventually to normal speech.

David's learning to be sociable and attentive was a long process and could not have been achieved in brief group sessions. There were many emotional attitudes to adults which had to be gradually unlearnt. He had to find out that it could be rewarding and safe to co-operate with adults and to fit into a group with others. This could only be achieved in a 'real-life' group.

Shaun

Shaun at eighteen months was a cheerful looking child, of professional parents, with verbal comprehension well above his age level, but with very little sign of any expressive speech developing. He did not attempt to make any speech sounds at all except 'Mum' occasionally, while his favourite sound was merely 'ugh!' Muscle tone was low, and he was very overweight. There were no abnormal patterns of movement – but he needed a great deal of encouragement from an adult to move at all. His only method of independent movement was bottom-shuffling. He pointed imperiously to everything he wanted without moving and said 'ugh' and would produce a storm of disapproval if his desires were not instantly met! His mother despaired of him ever talking.

Shaun was relying totally on his mother to be both his arms and legs and his 'mouthpiece'. With a little guidance from a physiotherapist Shaun laboriously developed more variety of movement, and when he was away from his mother began to make some attempt at copying speech sounds in individual play sessions with the speech therapist. Once he had learnt that sounds could be meaningful and that he obtained approval for them and the reward of being understood, single words began to come fairly quickly, but he was still greatly lacking in independence.

When his mother came into the room at the end of the therapy session, he would often become quite speechless again, and literally envelop himself in her skirts. She would not discourage him. It was then felt that Shaun needed to develop independence in a group with other children as he was still only confident enough to speak at home – or with the speech therapist when no-one else was present. He joined a nursery family group and formed a strong attachment with his nursery nurse. He was very bewildered at first by the nursery, and solidly did any activity put in front of him without taking any notice of the other children.

It eventually began to be possible to 'join him up' with other children a little, and although he remained very adult orientated, he began to be independent enough to move around the nursery and to initiate activities himself and to join in group activities without any direct adult contact. Language developed to a normal level for his age, and he was finally able to transfer to a local nursery even though articulation of speech was a little immature, and movement was weak. Shaun had thus become quite verbal with a little individual help and some parental counselling but he needed the larger environment of the nursery to develop social skills and independence more fully. A small language group would not have been sufficiently challenging for him.

Jagjit

Jagjit was an Indian girl of three years. She had no movement in her left arm (due to a brachial plexus lesion) following a road accident at one year ten months, and speech had regressed for a while. The family were Punjabi speaking. Jagjit attended the Centre for individual speech therapy since, although her Punjabi was recovering, she was not learning English as well as the rest of the family. Initially she also attended a language group for immigrant children in the mornings and a nursery in the afternoons.

Jagjit responded well to individual speech therapy sessions, and obviously enjoyed them immensely. She took great pride in a 'speech book' she was given, and learnt everything in it – but she did not seem to be able to generalise this learning to the nursery she attended. Her behaviour was poor there, and she did not join in group activities. She therefore joined the nursery at the Child Development Centre full-time where she had daily speech therapy. The nursery nurse in her family group knew the words and phrases Jagjit was currently learning in speech therapy sessions, and insisted that she used them. Jagjit's learning of new words needed more specific reinforcement than afforded at a large normal nursery. Jagjit continued to learn new language, very slowly, but her general behaviour and integration into the nursery routine improved considerably. When the family moved away from the area, she was able to attend a normal school where there were special remedial facilities for second language learning.

Kelly

Kelly was first assessed at the Child Development Centre at the age of two years five months. She was the youngest of a family of three sisters and the second to have a severe expressive language problem. The eldest sister's language was normal and a fourth sister, born when Kelly was three and a half also appeared to be developing language normally. Although Kelly was too unsure of herself to co-operate with formal testing, verbal comprehension appeared to be within normal limits. The only word she ever used was 'dada' occasionally, and she had only started babbling three weeks before the assessment. Speech development was like that of a nine month old baby.

Kelly was able to copy speech sounds which she did with great enjoyment, but, like her sister, could not retain these sounds and use them in a meaningful way. She had no physical problem in copying sounds – although she showed some clumsiness in fine motor movements with her hands. She was generally too frightened to move around much, although she was well able to walk. If ever her mother disappeared from sight, Kelly became very distressed, and could not function in any way at all. Kelly eventually learnt to separate from her mother for short periods for speech therapy sessions – although she was so frightened initially that it was not possible to attempt any specific work on speech. She would stiffly co-operate with doll play, however, which interested her very much – and gradually unthawed so that she would join in with any activity providing it was sedentary.

It began to be apparent that Kelly just would not move from her chair, and she became quite panic-stricken if there was any suggestion that she should. It was not actually essential to treatment that Kelly should move around, but her general lack of confidence impeded her overall progress it seemed. It was too time-consuming in individual sessions to coax Kelly to move off her chair, and it was an aspect of therapy that could best be tackled in an environment where there was a lot of movement and larger apparatus.

Kelly joined a family group in the nursery for one morning per week where the nursery nurse for that group was able to shelter her to begin with from what no doubt appeared to be a bewildering and frightening scene. She did not attempt to join in with any of the activities at first, but just sat on her nursery nurse's lap. Eventually she was persuaded to ride slowly around the playgroup on a little three wheeler bike – which she obviously found half terrifying and half immensely enjoyable.

She did not interact with any of the children, but watched them constantly with great interest. She gradually learnt to join in group music and in songs involving actions with her hands which were within her capabilities. Kelly still has severe expressive language problems for which she continues to receive regular speech therapy, but she now attends a normal play-group twice weekly, which alleviates the considerable pressure on her mother. Through learning to socialise in a normal group despite her severe language problem Kelly was able to make the move to a normal nursery.

Sociability and Independence

There are certainly some advantages of 'language groups' if the children are sufficiently well matched, since the work can be paced as fast or as slowly as

21   The Role of the Occupational Therapist

Peggy Jay

Occupational therapy is a much misunderstood profession. There are many reasons for this. Probably the main one is that their training equips occupational therapists (OTs) to work in so many different areas that the various jobs individual therapists are doing seem to bear little resemblance to each other. It is therefore difficult for other people to get a clear picture of just what is occupational therapy. One OT may work with physically handicapped children, using play as the medium of treatment, while another may spend most of the time making hand splints and other orthotic devices for orthopaedic patients of all ages. One may be working as part of a team using behaviour modification to treat people with agrophobia, alcoholism or mental handicap, while another uses activities of daily living, such as cooking, to help long term psychotic patients re-learn basic skills so that they can return to live in the community. One OT may be driving round the countryside visiting handicapped people in their homes while another is running a Day Centre for geriatrics in the middle of a town.

Another reason for the misunderstanding is that occupational therapy has evolved over the years to meet the changing needs of the disabled population and to help implement the provisions that government is making for them. Yet the name 'occupational therapy' has stayed the same, largely because there is no clearly better alternative. Consequently, many people still think of occupational therapy as a way of occupying or diverting ill people, usually with basketry, when this aspect of treatment almost disappeared from the work that OTs do many years ago. Craft work can be valuable for exercising stiff joints or weak limbs, particularly in the hands and arms. It can also be a useful medicine for helping people relate to others in a group or to get the satisfaction of achievement in learning a new skill. When it is used as a diversion, a way of killing time, without any therapeutic intent, and when it is supervised by a craft teacher, or someone other than an OT, it is quite erroneous to refer to it as occupational therapy.

Yet another reason for the misunderstanding is that many OTs work under different names, Rehabilitation Officer, Advisor to the Disabled, Disabled Living Advisor, Occupations Officer and so on. And yet the job that they are doing calls for the skills of an occupational therapist. This mainly occurs in Social Services departments, and one of the reasons is that it offers a way of paying OTs on a different salary scale from the nationally negotiated Whitley rates which apply to NHS employees.

There is a very considerable shortage of OTs available to fill the vacant jobs. This means that many people working in the field of disability have never seen their work and so have not had the opportunity to appreciate

Source: Previously unpublished Paper written for this Reader.

their role. At the same time as the demand for OTs has increased, other professions have become more involved in helping disabled people cope with the everyday activities that they find difficult. Physiotherapists now include Activities of Daily Living [ADL] in their basic training, social workers may supply aids, and nurses working in the community are dealing more with the practical problems arising from disability. Yet OTs were the first professionals to consider the need to help people cope with activities of daily living over 30 years ago. From this work has stemmed the Disabled Living Foundation, mainly staffed by OTs; and the Aids Centres around the country and the travelling Aids exhibitions. These make it possible for disabled people to try out a variety of aids and to get advice from the OT in charge. Fifteen to twenty years ago OTs and OT technicians spent a proportion of their time making aids such as bath seats and stocking aids. Now there is a whole industry, with manufacturers often consulting OTs about what is needed, and a twice yearly National Aids for the Disabled Exhibition (NAIDEX). There are quite a number of books on the subject, many of them written by OTs. It is good that other professionals are becoming involved in this field, because this increases the likelihood of handicapped people getting the help they need. But it is not so good when other professionals begin to feel that this is now their role, even when there is an OT available, because the OT is more likely to know whether an aid is necessary or whether an alternative technique would be preferable. The OT is also more likely to know more about a wider range of aids, and will have a selection of these in the occupational therapy department together with facilities for trying them out and learning to use them.

This leads on to another problem for OTs. They are not usually the first professionals to be involved in helping the disabled person. The doctor, the nurse, the physiotherapist are all needed in the earlier stages of illness and the skills of the OT come later. In the community the social worker may be the first person to be in contact with the disabled person. So the OT is very often dependent upon other colleagues for referrals and if these people are uncertain of the OTs' role, or if they think that they have already provided all that is necessary, the disabled person may be denied further help that is needed. As far as social services are concerned the understanding of the OTs' role depends very much upon the structure of the department and where the OTs fit in the hierarchy. If the OTs are the acknowledged specialists in disability, and disabled people seeking help from social services are automatically referred to them, then the OTs' role is clear.

What do OTs have to offer? They have a knowledge of all types of physical disability, how to treat these disorders and hence an idea of prognosis. This is particularly important when working in the community. It is necessary to know what a disabled person can achieve in order to set realistic goals. There is no point in arranging comprehensive services for someone bed bound after a stroke when with treatment that person could be taught to dress, wash and carry out most household tasks independently.

OTs have also learned about psychological and psychiatric processes, and have an understanding of the various methods of treatment when these become problems. This is also important when helping people with physical disability. Disability is a disaster that has similarities with any other life crisis, such as the breakdown of a marriage or unemployment. The individual's reaction to such a crisis usually depends more on his or her characteristics, personality, background and so on than on the type of disability. The lives of two people with identical physical impairments can have quite different outcomes, one living an independent life and the other totally dependent. Goble and Nichols (1971) identified many of the factors involved and these need to be understood in order to help in giving disabled people the opportunity for maximum independence. Physical disability is seldom just a physical problem.

OTs have practical skills. In hospitals they run workshops using woodwork and other technical activities. This means that when they have to go out into people's homes they either know or have little difficulty finding out what is possible in the way of adaptations to make a home more convenient for a disabled person. OTs also have managerial and administrative skills. In order to run a hospital department, providing a service for doctors in different parts of the hospital, and ordering and accounting for the turnover of stock used in the treatment of patients, they have to learn about organisation of staff, reporting and book-keeping. They will use similar skills in running a Day Centre or organising the provision of aids and adaptations by a local authority.

Because OTs are always working alongside other professionals, preferably as part of a team, they are very well aware of the role and the contribution that others can make in helping a disabled person. This is not always reciprocated. A small informal survey in a leading psychiatric hospital found that while the OTs were well aware of what the psychologists were doing, the psychologists had little idea of what was the OTs' role.

As handicapped people become more aware of what should be available to help them, so they are quite rightly demanding a greater say in what they are given. Because occupational therapy in hospitals requires that the patient is actively doing things, rather than passively accepting treatment, OTs are used to co-operating with disabled people and their families to assess priorities, identify the felt needs, set realistic goals and make contacts at appropriate stages of rehabilitation. This means that OTs find it easier than some of the other professionals to work with, rather than dictate to, the disabled person.

What should OTs be doing? At the moment there are too few of them so that some of the work they have pioneered is being taken over by other disciplines. At the same time they are moving into new areas of work such as schools. This means that there are fewer and fewer OTs available to staff the hospitals. Perhaps there should be a re-examination of the areas in which OTs can make the most impact in helping people to overcome the problems of disability. The areas outlined below have been selected because they are particularly relevant to the handicapped in the community. There are

many other areas of development in hospital treatment, such as helping
people overcome the problems of perceptual dysfunction, that are just as
important.

Hospital patients are discharged far more quickly than they used to be. In
some hospitals, where there is good co-operation between all the staff, the
patient does not get discharged until the OTs have assessed that he or she is
able to cope at home. Often there will have been a home visit to check the
situation and to assess what local support services will be necessary. But this
does not happen everywhere. In some hospitals, by the time the patients are
fit enough to come down from the ward to the OT department they are
being sent home instead. The ambulance service has become so erratic in
most places that to come back for treatment as an outpatient requires real
dedication and stamina. There is the wait at home for the ambulance to
arrive, the roundabout journey to the hospital, the probable arrival at the
wrong time for an appointment with consequent further waiting time, and
then the wait for an ambulance again for the return home. Some patients
need a day or two to rest at home after such an ordeal.

Treating people in their own home is one way of dealing with this
problem. Physiotherapists are beginning to do this and are enthusiastic
about their results. OTs have been working in the community for many
years now, increasing dramatically in number since the passing of the
Chronically Sick and Disabled Persons Act in 1970, which coincided with
the Seebohm Report and the demise of the Welfare Officers. A proportion of
community OTs are health based like the physiotherapists, but the majority
of them work in Social Services or Social Work departments. There are
advantages and disadvantages to both systems. The Social Services
department has a duty under the Act to make certain provisions for disabled
people. Having an OT attached to each social work team will mean that
there is a specialist available to assess the disabled person's needs and to
make recommendations about what should be done. But Social Services
departments tend just to deal with crisis situations. When a problem has
been solved the case is closed. Yet some disabilities are progressive, like
multiple sclerosis, and even so called stable conditions, such as anteria
poliomyelitis, become more of a problem with increasing age. OTs would
prefer to keep a case load of disabled people making perhaps half yearly
visits so that help can be given before deterioration produces further
problems. Also, OTs do not want just to give out suitable aids with
instructions for their use. Experience has shown that a great deal of
reinforcement is needed to enable people to take advantage of such help,
and frequent return visits may be necessary before the disabled person is able
to use aids and adaptations with confidence and achieve maximum
independence. There is not always time for this within a Social Services
organisation, which is not primarily intended to provide treatment, and the
OTs are in a position where they are not able to exercise all their skills to
help the disabled person. If additional community OTs were health based,
would they be able to give a course of treatment, in a similar way to

physiotherapists, enabling the disabled person to achieve maximum independence? There are already a few OTs working closely with General Practitioners, and this may be a trend for the future.

One area of work in the community that should continue to develop is the collaboration between architects and OTs. So many of the problems faced by disabled people stem more from inappropriate housing than from disability. Architects know little about disability, and if left without help tend to think all disabled people are wheelchair bound and to plan accordingly. Nor are they in a position to understand the psychological needs of the different age groups, such as the need for privacy among younger disabled people and the need to be able to sit and watch the world go by in older people. It is not only in adapting existing housing that this co-operation is needed, but in planning new council housing, that will in the future service the needs of the increasing elderly and disabled population, without later expensive adaptations.

Hospital based OTs, and particularly those in Rehabilitation Centres, have been very much involved in assessing disabled people for work (Jay and Jones, 1977). This has included liaising with the Disablement Resettlement Officer, visiting firms to look at likely work situations or to discuss the disabled person's abilities with the personnel officers and simulating possible jobs in the OT department. OTs running Day Centres help their clients get used to a modified work situation which may lead to open employment later. An OT has been involved in a feasibility study on the setting up of an information bank of aids used by disabled people to enable them to be employed. An OT is now working in a local authority with the task of assessing the employment needs of local disabled people. A pilot scheme is underway in a large firm in the City of London where an OT is employed to look at the various jobs available within the organisation with the task of assessing their suitability for disabled people. Integrating disabled people into work in a period of recession is an area where OTs are particularly well qualified to help and where they should be asked to make a much larger contribution.

Some disabled people may never get back to work and can benefit by being given help to develop an interest in appropriate leisure activities. OTs working with people with psychiatric disorders are increasingly concentrating on this aspect of treatment. So are OTs in the community, who are running various forms of Day Care to help people who cannot work, not just to get out of the house but to find stimulation by taking part in a range of interesting activities.

Due to changing attitudes in education, and the publication of the Warnock report [1978], more handicapped children are being accepted into normal schools. This raises all sorts of problems, not only problems of access, which can be formidable, but also of attitude. Children can be very unkind to anyone who is different and teachers may have difficulties when faced with a child whose disability is outside their experience and whose potential is hard to assess. OTs working with children are beginning to go into schools to help with the transition period (Burr 1980). Children going to special schools are also often in need of help. Too often they are under achievers and their teachers need help to encourage them to develop their maximum potential. If OTs can contribute towards helping handicapped children get a better education they may well have less problems to face as handicapped adults.

How can OTs become more effective in helping disabled people? The first step is probably to raise the status of the profession and the calibre of people entering it by having degree courses. There is already one degree course for physiotherapists in Belfast and others will inevitably follow for both professions. This does not mean that there should not still be a diploma course. It does mean that some of the school leavers, who have the potential to make good OTs but who at present are recommended to fulfil their academic ability by going to a university, would join the profession. As OTs move into new areas of work, where they will inevitably be working in comparative isolation, they will need to become more autonomous. In the United States and Australia, where OTs already have degrees, there is already at least one Professor of Occupational Therapy and OTs take administrative posts such as the director of a Rehabilitation Centre. Degree courses will not necessarily produce more clinically competent OTs, indeed one of the dangers of a university training is that it is possible to produce therapists who are too academic and lack practical skills. But such training should produce therapists who have the confidence to take a more decisive role and to co-operate on a more equal footing with other professionals. Doctors have taken very little interest in recent years in developing Rehabilitation Services and there is a declining number of specialists in Rehabilitation medicine. If disabled people are to get the treatment they deserve then therapists must play a more dynamic role. Already this is happening in several ways. District therapists have been appointed with full managerial responsibility for all the services provided by OTs within a health service District. This includes recruitment and appointment of staff and managing the budget allocation. Another example, doctors know little about prescribing wheelchairs or completing DPIs, the form used by Disablement Resettlement Officers. Often OTs fill in these forms, or in the case of wheelchairs sometimes physiotherapists, and the doctor signs them. With more highly trained therapists, this could become one of their responsibilities.

With recent increases in pay, more men are coming into the profession. But occupational therapy is still not a career often recommended to boys leaving school. With a degree course and better career prospects (there is already one deputy director of Social Services who is an OT) more men should come into the profession, which would give it more stability. The tendency for occupational therapy to be viewed as a stereotyped women's career unfortunately means that there is a high job turnover among young therapists. The average work span after qualification is about five years although more and more therapists are returning to full or part time work after raising a family.

One final area where occupational therapy must expand is research. For too long the techniques and methods used by all the remedial professions have been largely traditional and their value has not been proven. There is now a Society for Research in Rehabilitation, a multi-disciplinary professional Society, which has provided a forum for papers on work in both hospitals and Social Services departments. More research projects are being funded and more therapists are being trained in research methodology. It is essential for OTs to evaluate what they are doing, from treatment techniques to ways of supplying aids more efficiently.

It is only when OTs know what they do best, and what they can discard as being of little value, that they can finally decide the areas in which they should be working so that their role has most impact in giving disabled people the help that they deserve.

References

GOBLE, R. E. A., and NICHOLS., P. J. R. (1971) *Evaluation of a Disabled Living Unit*, Part 1 of *Rehabilitation of the Severely Disabled*, London: Butterworths.

JAY., P., and JONES, M. S. (1977) *An Approach to Occupational Therapy*, 3rd edition. London: Butterworths.

BURR., L. A. (1980) 'Supporting the handicapped child in normal school.' *The British Journal of Occupational Therapy*, *43*(6).

22 Parents as a Resource in Diagnosis and Assessment

Elizabeth Newson

Child Development Research Unit, Department of Psychology, University of Nottingham

[. . .]
Using parents as a resource has had a long and fruitful history so far as our research unit is concerned. It was in 1958 that we initiated our longitudinal study of child-rearing attitudes and practices in 700 Nottingham families[1], later to be extended to the families of children with specific handicaps[2]; and from the beginning we were sustained by Allport's then unfashionable suggestion that if one wanted to know what people were thinking, feeling and doing, one might do worse than just ask them.[. . .] Once we had had the experience of being forced, within a research framework, to devise a 'facilitating environment' in which parents would find themselves able to impart complicated information, the next step into the clinical field seemed a natural one to take[3].

We start from the basic assumption, that parents in fact have information to impart: that parents are experts on their own children. This is not to say that what they know of their children is in any systematic or integrated form: one cannot ask the parent to bring along to the clinic an ordered case-history of the child. Nor can we assume that their knowledge of the child is effective in making them 'good' parents; often they are bewildered by the child, believe themselves to be very inadequate parents, and feel guilty about much of what they do. Nonetheless, they know more about the child, on a very intimate level, than anyone else does; the fact that their knowledge may be diffuse and unstructured does not matter, so long as it is available. It is the professional's job to make it available: structuring can come later.

I find it extraordinary that the resource of parents as an information store is so often neglected: as a clinician I would not dare manage without it. So often, parents are not asked the questions which would supply otherwise unobtainable information; their potential contribution as members of the team is not considered; they are *ignored in their expert role*. A major resource for the people who are trying to find out about their children is wantonly wasted. What is still more extraordinary, and indeed humbling, is that when someone does start using parents as a resource they are so grateful. I am embarrassed for my profession every time a parent says to me 'Thank you so

---

Source: T. E. OPPÉ and F. P. WOODFORD (eds) (1977) *Early Management of Handicapping Disorders*. Amsterdam: Associated Scientific Publishers.

much for listening': why do they not *expect* professionals to listen? Sometimes I feel that I should say to them 'Thank you so much for all you have told me and how you have helped me' – and yet this is still not right, for thanks are not quite appropriate from one member of a team to another. Teamwork between parents and professionals, with the common aim of meeting the needs of the child, is what we should be trying to achieve. [. . .]

The Assessment Clinic

In choosing to focus on assessment in this paper, I am conscious of making a very artificial and reluctant division between assessment and remediation; and of course parents are an equally valuable resource in the remediation of their children, and are beginning to be recognized as such. But to me there is no purpose in making an assessment at all unless remediation is kept firmly in mind: how are our findings to be *used* in setting out guidelines for future developments? Sometimes one has the uneasy feeling that an assessment has been done in order to pin on an appropriate label as an end in itself: to tidy the child away, put him on the right shelf and forget about him, because he's now neat enough to be forgotten. If we are to be of use to the child, assessment must be a continuous process, which moves into remediation and continues through remediation, and therefore of necessity cannot be divided from it. Ideally the first assessment will establish a framework, a set of guidelines, for initiating specific kinds of remediation: which will in turn feed back comments on the validity of some of the assessment findings and suggest new ways of making further assessments: which will indicate subsequent remediative techniques and goals. To serve the child, assessment must be positive (by which I do not mean unrealistically hopeful), dynamic and progressive.

Perhaps I can most usefully discuss parents' potential contribution to the assessment by describing what happens in my own clinic. The children I see tend to be between 3 and 6 years old (though they might be either younger or older), and they are likely to have fairly complicated problems. Most of them show developmental delay of an anomalous rather than a general kind; many have speech and language problems; many have impaired social relationships. Often there has been some feature in the history (such as epilepsy) which has caused the child to receive a 'tidying label' and prevented more significant problems (such as autism or aphasia) from being investigated or even recognized. Many of the children have attentional difficulties, are very withdrawn, are hyperkinetic, are obsessional and ritualistic, and so on – problems which make it extremely difficult to carry out a formal test, or even to get the child to sit at a table for more than a minute or two; indeed, these children often come to us with the reputation of being 'untestable'. Fortunately, we rarely wish to carry out traditional tests with these children, certainly not during the first assessment session. The children may be referred by any professional who wishes to do so –

paediatricians, psychologists, social workers, family doctors, teachers, speech therapists and so on – or they may be referred by parents themselves.

The team, apart from the parents, consists of four psychologists, three of whom happen to be trainees; obviously this happens to be idiosyncratic to my clinic, because it is a training ground for psychologists – elsewhere, different disciplines might well collaborate. The child is seen in a large playroom, where one of the trainees works with him. The playroom is a rich environment with opportunities for many different kinds of play: the toys one might hope to find in a well-stocked nursery, plus a large climbing frame, a sink, a dried-pea tray (instead of a sand tray) and two very big squashy armchairs. It is a room full of distractions, and this in itself can tell us a great deal about how far a child is willing or able to attend to one thing at a time, and for how long. A bare room may be appropriate for a formal test or for specific kinds of remedial work, but does not suit our purpose here.

I never know how to describe the person who works with the child in the playroom – 'psychologist' does not differentiate from the other professionals, 'assessor' seems too formal and 'therapist' is premature. It really comes nearest to his or her function to use the word 'discoverer' – in the sense that his/her role is to 'discover' the child to the rest of the team, who are watching from the observation room. The 'discoverer', then, will work with the child in whatever ways seem appropriate[4] with the aim of drawing from him as detailed a picture as possible of the things he can do – cognitively, linguistically, imaginatively, manipulatively, socially, and in all the ways these categories overlap – what conditions he needs in order to do them (does he need pressure, or withdrawal of adults' attention, or extrinsic rewards, for example?), and what things he cannot do in this setting, however great the rewards. Although the 'discoverer' will have some idea of the *kinds* of things he or she will be trying out during the session, there will also be a strong element of responsiveness to the child's own behaviour; so that if the child begins to show a particularly high potential in one kind of play, this may be followed through in more detail than was originally envisaged, while suggestions from the parents may also become incorporated in unforeseen ways. The session in the playroom is likely to last between $1\frac{1}{2}$ and 2 hours, according to what the child can tolerate; it is usual for him to tolerate a much longer period than would normally be expected of him, and often he resists going home at the end.

One long wall of the playroom is entirely made up of one-way mirror, so that the whole of the playroom is comfortably visible to people sitting in the observation room; a microphone ensures that the observers can hear what goes on, but they cannot be heard by the child. The two trainees are responsible for keeping a record of everything that takes place, though they are aided by a tape-recorder in the playroom. [. . .] The 'discoverer' is not asked to take notes at all during the session, but to give all his or her attention to the child; a contribution to the report is, however, made later in terms of what the child 'felt like' to work with – subtle reactions to physical contact; eye contact and referential looking; lability of mood and how great an effort was needed to avoid tantrums or withdrawal – all features which may be of considerable importance, yet which might not be adequately observed from the far side of the screen.

The other members of the team are myself and the parents or other caretakers, occasionally joined by other professionals involved, if the parents wish this. Our main role is not to observe the child, although we do so; but to establish a picture of him as he has been in the past and as he now is, using the child as we see him today as a visual aid. Thus something the child does may remind the parents of something else that we might want to know about; or the parent might say 'Now . . . you see what he's doing now . . . well *that's* what I meant when I said . . .'. Or I might ask 'This little gesture he's making now – is that something he often does? When does he mostly do that?' or 'How does he compare today with how he usually is? Does he usually flit around about as fast as this, or is he more or less active than usual? When does he seem to flit most?', and so on.

I believe it is essential that the observation of the child and the interviewing of the parents be done *in conjunction* in this way, because it is only by dovetailing the two that they can contribute so valuably to each other: both interview and observational session have seemed impoverished by comparison on the rare occasions that we have had to separate them. Often a parent's comment upon a child's action will put this into better perspective for us in terms of the child's whole behaviour pattern. By being taken seriously as an information resource, the parent also becomes enough at ease to comment on the actions of the 'discoverer'. 'I don't think *I'd* let her get away with that' said one mother, when the psychologist, tentative with a child he did not know well enough yet, was 'kid-gloving' to avoid a tantrum. 'Show us how you would handle it' was the reply, and with a rapid switching of roles the mother proceeded to do so, teaching us in the process a good deal more about what her daughter could do with a little pressure. Similarly, specific behaviour mentioned by the parent can often be demonstrated there and then in the child. For instance, a remarkable phenomenon of self-hypnosis in a 3-year-old autistic child, which could be triggered off by offering the child a dishcloth, was first described and subsequently elicited: it had not been witnessed by a professional previously, for who in a clinic would ever think of giving a 3-year-old a dishcloth?

The assumption is often made by clinicians that professional observations in a clinic are somehow more valid in the assessment of the child than the parents' report. Considering that clinicians usually make their observations in this one context, to which the child himself comes as a stranger, while parents base their observations on their experience of the child in many familiar and unfamiliar contexts, this assumption is, to say the least, shaky. I would not wish to set up a competition for validity between parents and professionals: either can be, and often are, mistaken in their interpretation of information. However, they are much less likely to be mistaken if they pool their knowledge, each with respect for what the others can give, and try to come to a conclusion which is congruent with the child as seen by both of them.

Along with the assumption that parents' observations have poor validity goes the professional belief that to parents 'all their geese are swans'. Parents are very aware of this belief. A recurrent anecdote, told ruefully or bitterly by the many parents we have talked to in the course of doing research on handicapped children's upbringing, concerns telling the professional of some ability that the child shows at home, though not in the clinic, only to be met with an amused 'Oh yes . . .?', in which it is clear that the parent is disbelieved. Parents find this both humiliating and frustrating: it is hurtful to find both their child's capability and their own powers of observation discounted. Yet, beyond this, they feel that there is something significant in the child's 'best' performance which the specialist ought to know about. In this, of course, parents are absolutely right: if we are to remediate effectively, it is vital that we should have some idea of the child's top performance, in order to design our goals realistically. It does not matter that the child's 'best' is produced only under the optimal conditions of relaxed, familiar environment in the bosom of his own family and perhaps only when Granny is there; if we know what his best is, and what those optimal conditions are, we can begin to set up or simulate the optimal conditions more often, produce his best more frequently, and eventually shape the situation in such a way that he will tolerate the less-than-optimal. It has in fact been our experience that parents who are taken seriously do not make exaggerated claims for their children's abilities: indeed, when as part of a research project we gave a group of parents video facilities so that they could film their children at leisure in their own homes, we too began to see on the screen a level of behaviour in some handicapped children which had never been seen in the clinic.[5]

Creating a Facilitating Environment

Once we appreciate the necessity of not wasting the resource we are offered in parents, it becomes the clinician's responsibility to consider how an environment may be provided in which parents can fully assume their expert role – which essentially means that it must be made possible for them to structure and define the information they have. We can do this in a number of ways.

Learning to Ask the Right Questions

[. . .] The proper understanding of a child's condition, particularly a child whose cognitive and social development is anomalous and complicated, depends upon being able to draw out from the parents a richly detailed description of the child's progression so far and his behaviour pattern at the present time, and upon being sensitized to pick up from the narrative those tiny indicative fragments which might be significant, and follow them as far as they lead. Interviewing parents for information thus becomes a creative and intensely intellectually demanding business (not least because it must feel relaxed, though never casual), which also needs to be backed up outside the interview by more leisured but deliberate consideration of how questions can best be framed in order to be fruitful. [. . .]

Because so much research time has been spent in our Unit in devising interview schedules which can be used repeatedly, and therefore comparatively, with large samples of children with particular handicaps, we have been forced to think hard about how to frame questions effectively: it has been an excellent discipline, with enormous clinical benefits. It compels us to listen to our own questions from the parents' point of view, and to evaluate them in terms of how rich a response they elicit. [. . .] [One mother said at the end of the session 'I've told you things I didn't know I knew'; and this indeed is what we must try to facilitate.]*

The parents may also not know the *significance* of what they know, which is why it is the clinician's responsibility to draw it out; for one child, with severe attentional and behavioural problems, the *best* indication of his good intellectual status when we first saw him at $3\frac{1}{2}$ was the systematic and abstract nature of his obsessional and compulsive acts in his home setting, and these proved highly prognostic of his ability to profit exceptionally well from the specialist school for which, on this apparently shaky basis, we recommended him. In the case of an 8-year-old developmentally dysphasic child, unrecognized as such, a feature of special significance was the sign system which she had evolved for communicating effectively with her father; since both of them were shy of doing this in public, there was no way of learning about it except by asking him directly and at length.

Teaching Parents to be Good Witnesses

By asking parents the right questions and in sufficient detail to be useful to us, we very quickly also begin to make them aware of the nature of evidence. We can do this quite deliberately by starting off with a general question about some topic, and gradually making the questions more and more specific. For example, we may ask 'Does he understand any gesture?' 'Oh yes, he understands when I point.' Now we take this further: 'All right; if he is beside me, and I point ahead of us, he can follow along my arm and finger with his eyes and see what I'm pointing at?' 'Yes, he would.' 'Right. Now suppose I point behind him and say "Look, it's over there", will he turn round and have a look?' Obviously, it is useful to us to know whether the child can understand this much more abstract concept of gesture; and it is even more useful that the parent should understand that there are different degrees of complexity in gesture, because through this kind of insight we teach parents to become good sources of information now, good analysts of information in the future, and therefore good remediators.

Another very common example concerns the context-dependence of the child's understanding. In a discussion of verbal instructions to which the child responds, the mother may say 'Well, he understands when I say "Go and get your coat, we're going out", because he does it.' 'Yes. Now what's usually going on when you say that? Can he see that you've got your coat on, and the baby ready in the pram?' Often this is enough to make the mother think very carefully, but we can help her if necessary: 'Suppose you were sitting by the fire at seven in the evening, and suddenly said to him "Get your coat, we're going out" – would he do it then?' And again the mother begins to become more aware of what evidence is: what we are trying to get at, and how we are trying to 'home in' closer and closer to what the child actually does and what it implies. [Professionals often complain of parents saying 'he understands everything I say to him'; they seldom use the parents' knowledge by answering 'Fine, but *what* are you saying, and in what context?']* As the mother settles into membership of the team, and feels herself to be a part of the investigation, she does in fact become increasingly professional in her ability to answer questions more and more precisely and to give us real evidence concerning her child: and therefore she becomes more and more useful, both to us and to him.

Giving Parents a Job to Do

[. . .] Some features in the child are especially difficult to map adequately during the observation session; in particular, it is often impossible to obtain a full range of the child's speech. Where the child is producing rather limited speech, parents can be asked to make detailed notes of a sample, or even a complete record, over a week or so. Here again, because the parent is respected as a member of the team, in our experience a very competent job will be done. Sometimes, although the child does not talk much during the session, it will be clear from the interview that there are times when he is considerably more vocal. In such a case, parents can be asked to use a tape recorder to tape the child at his most productive. From a tape cassette recorded by his parents, we were able to obtain and analyse four pages of transcript of the quite sophisticated, if obsessional, speech patterns of one young autistic boy; since this child's talkative period occurred when lying relaxed in bed at night, we could hardly have learned this valuable information without his parents' help. [. . .]

Giving Parents Tools

If we ourselves find certain tools useful in coming to understandings about children, why should we not share such tools with parents? Some of these tools are of course in terms of skills and techniques, which help us to work out balance sheets of positive and negative in the child's behaviour, to structure and make sense of information. But there are also tools in the sense of 'hardware' which help in arriving at insights and which we can make available to parents. Two examples will be enough.

The first is the one-way screen, which I have already mentioned. We use the screen because by doing so we can observe the child without distracting him. (This is the *only* function of the screen, so far as my Unit is concerned, in the sense that the screen is never used in order to observe children's secret behaviour which they might want to hide from us. In fact the child knows very well what kind of screen it is – or at least, he has been given the opportunity to see both sides of it; whether he makes anything of that experience is another matter.) But using the screen has spin-off benefits which I am still becoming aware of. One is that observers are sitting in twilight, and this in itself has a very relaxing effect upon parents, while also by contrast focusing attention on the child. Another benefit of which I was only half aware was put into words by a child's mother. We had been sitting for about an hour watching her child and talking about him, when she suddenly said 'You know what, this is the first time I've brought my child to an expert and not had to protect the expert from my child.' [. . .]

This small degree of distance not only allows parents to give their whole attention to the job in hand – getting as much information worked out between us as we possibly can – but it also allows a sense of perspective on the child. Parents frequently seem to come to a new and more realistic appraisal of the child's condition as a result of *standing back and looking at him* in a way they do not normally have a chance to do.

A second kind of hardware is video. I have already mentioned that video allows us to see on the screen behaviour filmed at home which, with the best will in the world, we cannot expect to see in the clinic, however hard we try to make the clinic homely and attractive: behaviour which depends on optimal familiar conditions. Equally important, video also allows us to see some extremely disruptive behaviour occurring at home which also may not occur in the clinic; and this too is necessary for us to see. Yet again, video can sometimes tell us when, with the best of intentions, management has gone seriously wrong. When blind 3-year-old Janie's mother told her paediatrician 'Mealtimes are a battle, Doctor' and he answered reassuringly (as he thought) 'Ah well, you'll just have to get it down her as best you can', he would never have known that this was interpreted as 'Get it down her or she'll die' if he had not seen videotape of the thrice-daily feeding scene: Janie bound in a sheet, arms against her sides, preventing both struggles and balance; tipped backwards, force-fed one spoonful on top of another, throat firmly stroked to push the food down – and a mother with tears in her eyes.

Video also has the effect of 'distancing' which I have referred to in talking about the one-way screen: it allows parents to look at their child with more objectivity and insight. Professionals have a very similar experience: that the screen somehow allows us to 'focus in' on the child[6]. This seems to be partly because the screen frames the child and cuts out distractions, so that we begin to be aware of the *patterns* in the child's behaviour which might not be so clear-cut when we look at the child himself in the midst of his immediate environment. Parents themselves can recognize on the screen patterns (for instance, the 'curling inward' of the young blind child) which they may not have been conscious of previously because they are normally distracted by their own attempts to relate to the child; and this may help them to direct their efforts better. Or they may suddenly see on the screen some error in their handling which they had not noticed: for instance, one mother, who had wondered why her spastic baby rejected spoon-feeding so violently, realized immediately when she filmed herself feeding that the little girl could not see the spoon on its way to her mouth, so that every mouthful was a shock; correction of the angle of approach solved the problem.

In addition, video allows us to retain a 'living' record of a child's progress; for children whose gains are small and slow, this is important for parental morale, and it also forms a useful basis for progressive assessment and rethinking of remediative strategies.

Giving Back Information

The final part of the clinician's responsibility in making it possible for parents to assume their expert role is to make information available to them in a clear and structured form. Let me say what this means in my own clinic.

First, it means that at the end of the session the other observers will withdraw to make tea for everyone, which gives the parents a private opportunity to say anything else they wish to. Often what they want at that moment is a brief summing-up discussion about what we have seen and what possibilities might be before them. At this point there is an enormous obligation on the clinician to answer questions honestly; at the same time, it is understood between us that the discussion can only be tentative in some ways, as the team have not yet compared notes. Whatever is said now will be spelled out more thoroughly once that has happened.

Secondly, reports are written by both observers, and by the person working with the child, and these reports are dovetailed together and combined with the information which has been gained from parents, the whole being summed up and commented upon in a final section. This completed report, usually about six pages long, is then sent to the parents, who are invited to comment if they wish, and particularly asked to say if they disagree with anything that has been said, or feel that anything else should be added. They are also told that, whether or not the Unit continues to be in contact with their child, they are welcome to discuss any further problems or implications either now or later.

The parents are the first people to receive the report, because they are regarded as the most essential recipients of the information it contains. Obviously there are likely to be professionals involved or about to be involved with the child, including the referral agent; any of these may receive copies with parental permission. The reports sent to other people are precisely the same ones as the parents receive.

It is interesting that sending reports to parents, particularly unabridged reports, is regarded by many clinicians as extraordinary and dangerous. I would personally take the opposite view: that to spend a lot of time assessing a child with great care, and then to send out reports to all sorts of people *with the exception of those who are most closely and permanently concerned with the child*, is bizarre in the extreme, and is only considered reasonable because of the way clinical work has developed historically: if we were inventing it from scratch, would we now, I wonder, include this almost paranoid secretiveness?

In fact, to refuse a report to parents at once suggests two implications: it endows the report with *spurious* significance, as a document which is so explosive that it must not be seen by those to whom it might matter; and it also devalues it, as something which is of no use to them. But as I said at the beginning of this paper, there is no point in an assessment unless it offers some guidelines for the future. To whom should such guidelines be of use, if not above all to the child's parents?

If parents are seriously to be considered as a resource for the clinician, then they clearly have a right to receive the report which they have helped to produce. What is more, parents who are brought into the team in the ways I have described will be capable of understanding not only what the report means but *by what processes it was arrived at*. All too often, the reports from which parents are excluded are based upon observational procedures from which they were also excluded; and occasionally, let us admit, neither will stand up to a critical appraisal.

A child comes for assessment because there are uncertainties and confusions in people's minds as to what are his capabilities and how his needs can best be met. Parents do not necessarily expect all to be clear by the end of the assessment; but they do hope for some move towards clarification. What often happens, however, is that they are given other kinds of ambiguities in exchange: uncertainty as to what has been written down in their child's casenotes, uncertainty as to what was done with the child by the various people who have seen him, how the child reacted and how his behaviour was interpreted. They also wonder how far their own behaviour has been interpreted and included in the notes. Is it not possible that we might all do a better job if we know that parents will see both what we do and what we say about what we have done? Why are we so defensive?

Obviously reports are not all cut-and-dried; we all suffer uncertainties as to prognosis, and our suggestions as to guidelines must often be couched in tentative terms. Sometimes it is asserted that parents will find it difficult to accept reports which are tentative. My own experience is that they will find it easier to accept tentativeness when they have been allowed to share in the reasoning process that lies behind it than to accept vagueness which has no explicit basis. It must be remembered that parents suffer an additional and rational anxiety: that professionals may be hiding something from them in order to shield them. [. . .]

Postscript

Because my own situation as a clinician is an unusual one, perhaps it should be said finally that I cannot see why the principles which I have discussed should not be met in any clinic that attempts assessment of handicapped or delayed children. Occasionally I am told that this kind of assessment could not be carried out elsewhere because it is labour-intensive, the implication being that we have a cheap source of labour in our trainees. The question must be asked, however, how much labour to derive how much information? If this is the ratio that we are considering, then I do not think the input is uneconomical. By exploiting to the full our most valuable resource, the parents, four professionals in one admittedly long afternoon derive a body of useful information which appears rarely to be significantly improved upon by multidisciplinary teams working many more man-hours in a more fragmented way. The joint session, I should add, is always followed by an hour's discussion of what we have seen: originally organized in this way because of the needs of training, in that it seemed important that what was observed should be immediately discussed in terms of its implications, this collaborative discussion is of such immense value in focusing our conclusions that I would retain it if serving the needs of the child were our *sole* function. Four professionals and two parents working as a united team are a more powerful investigative force than a much larger 'team' working separately behind closed doors. As I conclude this paper, I hear in my mind the words of the mother whose child we worked with 2 days ago: 'It's been a fantastic afternoon. I'm absolutely worn out, and I should think you are too.' Yes, we were all exhilarated and exhausted; our labour had been thoroughly intensive, and this is as it should be if what we are doing is for real.

Note

[* Indicates author's additions to compensate for editorial deletions made for reasons of space.]

References

1 NEWSON, J., and NEWSON, E. (1963) *Infant Care in an Urban Community*. London: Allen and Unwin; (1968) *Four Years Old in an Urban Community*. London: Allen and Unwin; (1976) *Seven Years Old in the Home Environment*. London: Allen and Unwin; *Perspectives on School at Seven Years Old*. London: Allen and Unwin.
2 HEWETT, S. (1970) *The Family and the Handicapped Child*; London: Allen and Unwin; WOOD, H. (1970) Problems in the development and home care of pre-school blind children. Ph.D. thesis, University of Nottingham; GREGORY, S. (1976) *The Deaf Child and his Family*. London: Allen and Unwin.
3 A full discussion of interviewing method in general will be found in NEWSON, J., and NEWSON, E. (1976) 'Parental Roles and Social Contexts'. In M. Shipman (ed.) *The Organisation and Impact of Social Research*. London: Routledge and Kegan Paul.
4 NEWSON, J., and NEWSON, E. (1979) 'Play-Based Observation for Assessment of the Whole Child.' *In Toys and Playthings in Development and Remediation*. London: Allen and Unwin; Harmondsworth: Penguin Books.

5 PRYOR, C. (1973) Working with parents: a behavioural approach. Ph.D. thesis, University of Nottingham.

6 EVANS, R., and CLIFFORD, A. (1976) 'Captured for considerations: using video-tape as an aid to the treatment of a disturbed child.' *Child: Care Health and Development*, 2, 129–37.

23 Peter

M. Ainscow

D. A. Tweddle

This is the story of Peter Blakey's first year in the junior department of a primary school. Most teachers who have taught in a primary school will probably know a child like Peter – some may know many.

Peter moved into Mrs Jones's class in September. Fairly quickly she realized that Peter was some way behind the others and raised the subject in conversation with Miss Nolan, Peter's previous class teacher. Miss Nolan confirmed that this had always been the case, but said that Peter seemed happy enough and had made some progress during his year with her, albeit rather slow. Mrs Jones decided to keep a careful eye on the situation. [. . .]

Mrs Jones decided to ask the headteacher's advice. She described the problems she was having with Peter to Mr Walker, the headteacher, who decided first to talk to Miss Nolan and then later asked Mrs Jones to prepare a full written report over the Christmas holidays so that consideration could be given to Peter's needs. Mrs Jones presented the following report to the headteacher on the first day of the new term:

Report on Peter Blakey

Peter is a pleasant and likeable little lad, despite the fact that it is almost impossible to keep him working for more than a few minutes at a time. He needs constant one-to-one supervision. Otherwise his mind seems to wander and eventually he begins interrupting the other children. I feel as though I have tried absolutely everything. I have shouted at him and tried kindness, but it doesn't seem to make much difference to his attitude.

As far as work is concerned Peter can only read six or seven words on the Burt Word Recognition Test. He can recognize his own name and is currently reading Ladybird 2A, although he doesn't always seem to understand what the book is about. In arithmetic it is much the same story! He is a long way behind the rest of the class, he can count reasonably well and do simple sums (on a good day and provided he can use counters), but again he doesn't seem to really understand the processes involved. In group and class language lessons Peter rarely contributes.

I have thought a lot about Peter in an attempt to get to the bottom of his problem by finding what is really the matter with him. I have wondered whether he has difficulty hearing because his speech is still very immature

Source: M. AINSCOW and D. A. TWEDDLE (1979) *Preventing Classroom Failure*. Bristol: John Wiley (extracts from chapters 1 and 2).

and he invariably fails to carry out any instructions that I give him. I just cannot decide whether he has difficulty hearing properly, doesn't understand what is said to him, or is simply lazy.

I have not met Peter's mother as she did not turn up to the parents' meeting last term. Miss Nolan told me that Peter has no father – apparently he died before Peter was three. I have wondered whether this may have affected his work in some way.

Peter's favourite activities in school are painting and PE, and he says that he likes watching TV at home. He loves to paint or crayon and he will sit doing this all day if I let him.

I hope that some special help can be provided for Peter as soon as possible. I feel very sorry for him, but I am afraid I just don't understand his difficulties and don't know how best to help him. I think that it is an urgent problem because his behaviour in class is getting steadily worse.

Mrs P. Jones, Classteacher

[. . .] Eventually, a meeting was arranged between Mr Walker, Mrs Jones, and Mrs Blakey. Apparently, Mr Blakey had died in a road accident just before Peter's third birthday and whilst Mrs Blakey was pregnant. Susan, Peter's sister, was now nearly five and attended a local nursery school full-time. It appeared that Mrs Blakey had not attended parents' evening because she had been let down by the baby-sitter at the last minute. Both Mr Walker and Mrs Jones were impressed by Mrs Blakey's genuine concern for Peter and her eagerness to help as much as possible at home. Mrs Blakey was not surprised to learn that Peter was some way behind the other children in his class because, in her words, he had 'always been slow to catch on' [. . .] Mr Walker was particularly interested to hear that Peter's birth had been a difficult one. Mrs Blakey said that forceps had been used and 'his head was a funny shape'. He wondered if mild brain damage had been sustained, or if Peter was suffering from dyslexia. He said nothing about this to Mrs Blakey, however, but decided to mention these details to whoever subsequently came to see Peter. Mrs Blakey agreed to Mr Walker's suggestions that advice should be sought from the Remedial Service. She was less happy about referring him to the school medical officer, since she was sure that Peter's hearing was normal and felt that the exercise was rather pointless. Nevertheless, consent for the referral was given.

Afterwards, Mrs Jones and Mr Walker discussed the interview, which they both felt had been helpful. A number of points had been raised which might at least partly explain Peter's problems. It was possible that Mr Blakey's death had had some kind of long-lasting effect upon Peter, and Mrs Blakey had said that 'Peter often asks about him'. Mr Walker felt sure that the difficult birth was an important factor and thought that mild brain damage had probably been sustained. And finally, while Mrs Blakey seemed a caring and well-intentioned mother, she clearly was not very bright herself, and maybe this was a factor. Whatever the cause of the problem, Mr Walker agreed with Mrs Jones that expert help should be sought immediately, and so he wrote to the Remedial Service and asked the school medical officer to check Peter's hearing. [. . .] Eventually, Mrs Blakey was asked to take Peter to the school clinic for a hearing test. This she did, and the results of a thorough audiometric investigation indicated, as Mrs Blakey had anticipated, that Peter's hearing was normal. [. . .]

In the meantime a speech therapist had visited the school to see another child and Mr Walker took the opportunity of mentioning Peter. The speech therapist kindly agreed to see him that morning and, after talking to him for some time, reported back to the headteacher that, although Peter's speech was rather immature for an eight-year-old, there was certainly no sign of any abnormal articulation. The problem would solve itself with time, she said, and she could not justify giving him regular, individual, speech therapy.

Just before the Easter holidays, Mr Thompson, a teacher from the Remedial Service, visited the school to see Peter. [. . .]

Before leaving, Mr Thompson discussed his findings with Mr Walker and Mrs Jones, and later submitted a detailed written report. A number of interesting points came out of the discussion. First of all, test results indicated that Peter might be in need of special education. [. . .] He therefore suggested that a referral for a full psychological assessment should be made immediately, but pointed out that this could only be done with parental consent. [. . .]

It was late June before the psychologist arrived at the school. [. . . She] saw Peter in the medical room and the interview lasted most of the morning. A meeting was held that afternoon after school between Mrs Armitage, Mr Walker and Mrs Jones to discuss the results of the assessment. The first important point to come out of the discussion was that Peter apparently did not need special education. He was not educationally subnormal. [. . .] Mrs Armitage felt that segregating Peter would not be in his best interests. She pointed out that 'sending Peter to a special school would deprive him of the opportunity to interact with normal children'. Peter was apparently a good deal brighter than the children at the local ESN school and anyway, 'his reading age is now over six, and so he is obviously making some progress'. [. . .]

Mrs Armitage asked about Peter's home circumstances, and Mr Walker provide the background information he had collected during his interview with Mrs Blakey six months earlier. The psychologist then explained that it was difficult to determine exactly *why* a child was having learning difficulties in the same way as a doctor, for example, might diagnose a physical ailment. The truth was, she explained, that all of these factors were probably involved in some way.

Mrs Jones then raised the question of dyslexia. Was Peter dyslexic? Mrs Armitage explained that she had reservations about the use of this term, again because it was difficult to know exactly what people meant by it, and in any event, she said, 'there are no special teaching methods which are particularly suitable for the treatment of dyslexia'.

Three practical suggestions were made by Mrs Armitage before she left. First, she said that she could probably arrange for a peripatetic remedial teacher to visit the school once a week from September to take Peter out of his class for individual reading lessons. Secondly, she suggested that language work for Peter was as important as reading, and in a subsequent written report to Mr Walker she listed three books containing useful suggestions and a language development programme which she felt would be appropriate. And, finally, regarding Peter's deteriorating classroom behaviour, Mrs Armitage emphasized that the classteacher should praise Peter's efforts generously, no matter how modest his achievements were, compared to his peers. [. . .]

Despite the conscientious attention of the classteacher, the prompt and proper attention of the headteacher, and the helpful suggestions from all those who eventually become involved, our system for dealing with slow learners seems somehow to fail Peter Blakey [. . .]

The purpose [here] is to look closely at some of the important features of the approach adopted in the case study, with a view to identifying those aspects that might be improved. [. . .] There are clearly certain factors which influence a child's educational progress over which the teacher can have little or no influence. Since nothing can be done about these, there seems to be little point in focusing too much attention in their direction. It is factors which are within teacher-control that must be our primary concern. This is a practical classification with which to structure the development of the argument, and one which leads to interesting conclusions.

Factors Outside the Teacher's Control

There is a natural desire among those who teach slow learners to know *why* a particular child is having learning problems. The discussion between Mrs Jones and Mr Walker was probably fairly typical in that they were speculating about the reasons for Peter's difficulties. The death of Mr Blakey, Mrs Blakey's subsequent struggle to raise two children, her own limited ability, the difficult birth and the possibility of mild brain damage were all mentioned as possible contributory factors. It will also be recalled that the issue was never clearly resolved, the psychologist suggesting that probably *all* these factors in some way influenced Peter's development.

What if Mrs Armitage had been able to solve the riddle and specify which of the suggested possible causes was largely responsible for Peter's difficulties? How useful would this information have been? Certainly the staff of the school could do little to improve Mrs Blakey's domestic situation, and significantly influencing Mrs Blakey's intellectual competence was also outside their control. Although parent–teacher cooperation can, to some extent, influence a domestic situation or parental attitudes towards schools, it is unrealistic to have expected Mr Walker to do much more than he had already done in that direction. There already existed good parent–teacher liaison and special efforts had been made to have Mrs Blakey continue at home the work which Mrs Jones was doing in her classroom. It seems that in Peter's case at least, if family history or domestic circumstances were a significant causal factor, there was little more that Mr Walker or his colleagues could do about it.

What about the question of mild brain damage, or 'minimal cerebral dysfunction' as it is sometimes called, possibly caused in Peter's case by the forceps delivery? If Mrs Armitage could have confirmed that this was at the root of his difficulties, would any particular action or treatment necessarily follow from the diagnosis? The condition is a difficult one to diagnose reliably, it is not something which can be rectified surgically, and there is no evidence to suggest that children with minimal cerebral dysfunction should be taught differently from those without it. (Bateman, 1974). Even if we were able to confirm that this was the root cause of Peter's problem, therefore, we would still be no further forward in knowing how best to help him. In other words, brain damage might or might not be a significant causal factor, but in any event it is beyond the control of the class teacher.

It would appear that the causes, or aetiology, of Peter's problems in particular, and of mild to moderate learning difficulties generally, are elusive. Furthermore, in the search for a cause, there seems to be a tendency to speculate about factors which are largely beyond teacher control and consequently have minimal prescriptive value. If this is true, why do teachers persist in seeking the cause? It is as if there is an implicit assumption that a knowledge of the cause will lead directly to an understanding of what to do about it. This kind of approach resembles the medical model of diagnosis and prescription, and in fact may have derived from that source. Whilst it may suit medicine admirably, it seems to lead teachers up a series of blind alleys, and succeeds only in setting questions to which invariably there are no definitive answers and in inadvertently focusing attention on factors which are outside teacher influence.

A medical-style approach is apparent too in other ways. Mrs Jones thought that Peter might be dyslexic, and Mrs Armitage addressed herself to the question of whether or not he was educationally subnormal. Classifying children's difficulties by the use of descriptive labels, such as 'dyslexia', 'ESN', 'maladjusted' or whatever, is not unlike the medical labelling of physical ailments. But again there are problems, since what seems to work in medicine is not automatically useful in the field of education. First of all, there are enormous problems of definition. [. . .] Consequently, a child classified as ESN by one psychologist may not be so deemed by another. And the same is true of dyslexia. Secondly, and perhaps more important, there are no specific prescriptive implications associated with either diagnosis. That is to say, there is no evidence that ESN children learn, or should be taught, in a fundamentally different way from children who are not ESN. And the same with dyslexia. In fact Keogh (1975) wrote ' . . . with the possible exception of children with sensory deficits or severe physical conditions, where modification of curricular materials is required to enhance availability of information, there is little evidence that exceptional children learn differently from normal children, or that they require dramatically modified instructional techniques.'

[. . .] There is another important repercussion of the labelling process. The work of Rosenthal and Jacobsen (1968), Pidgeon (1970), and Nash (1973) seems to indicate that providing teachers with information about a child's *predicted* progress may influence the progress that is *actually* made. It has been demonstrated that children described to their prospective teacher as 'bright' seem to make more progress than those described as 'rather dull' – even when no such differences exist. If this is so, describing a child as ESN, dyslexic or brain-damaged not only has the disadvantage of telling us little or nothing about what or how he should be taught, but may also establish expectations of slow progress and limited achievement.

[. . .] Mrs Armitage used an intelligence test with Peter, and, as a result, stated that he was not educationally subnormal. It is important, therefore, to spend some time examining this aspect of the psychologist's contribution.

[. . .] An intelligence test usually consists of a wide range of tasks that have been standardized on a large number of randomly selected children of various ages. The purpose of doing an intelligence test with a child is to see how he or she performs on those tasks compared to all the other children of a similar age who were tested during the standardization. [. . .] It is important to realize, however, that this is all an IQ can do. It does not purport to indicate what, or how, a child should be taught, and again there is no evidence to suggest that a child with an IQ of 69 learns, or should be taught, differently from a child with an IQ of 91.

It seems, therefore, that IQ is another factor beyond the teacher's control. [. . .]

So far a number of important aspects of the approach used with Peter have been examined. They have been found to have one important feature in common in that none of them seem to provide any detailed indication of what, or how, Peter Blakey should be taught, and it has been suggested that the reason for this is that they involve focusing on factors which are outside the teacher's control. [. . .]

Factors Within the Teacher's Control

The analogy between medicine and the traditional remedial style of intervention can be extended a little further. Both approaches are curative. When a child is seen to be having difficulties the remedial expert or psychologist is called in to diagnose the problem and prescribe appropriate remedial treatment, rather like the GP who is called in to the sick patient to diagnose the complaint and prescribe a treatment. [. . .]

Keogh (1975) quotes research indicating that ' . . . children with long histories of school failure . . . bring a generalized expectation of failure to new problem-solving tasks. Self-perceived inadequacy and a "set" for failure may explain at least part of their school problems'.

If a complaint can be made against Peter's school it would be that it was two years before help was called, and almost a further year before any practical change occurred in Peter's circumstances. For almost three years he made 'painfully slow' progress, and was exposed to the failures and frustrations which that involved. This is a factor over which it is possible to have complete control. The headteacher could have referred the problem at least a year earlier, and it is even possible that the reception classteacher may have been able to predict that these difficulties were likely to occur. [. . .]

This then represents the first fundamental difference between the approach used with Peter and the approach described in later chapters of this book. Instead of waiting for failure to occur and using external support services to formulate curative strategies, the intervention should be geared toward preventing failure by taking immediate action as soon as it is seen that a child is having difficulty.

It must be mentioned that the notion of early identification has been criticized because this too can influence teacher expectation, the prediction of failure becoming a self-fulfilling prophecy and actually limiting the child's prospect of success. This is a real danger, but one which can be overcome. It is being suggested that children with learning difficulties should be spotted as early as possible in order that subsequent classroom failure can be averted. It is certainly *not* suggested that we predict educational failure and then wait to assess the accuracy of our predictions. [. . .]

An influence on the thinking of many teachers is the notion of the natural distribution of ability which assumes that, given children of a full range of ability for whom a standard lesson is prepared, some will succeed with ease, some will steadily plod through, and others will be largely incapable of success. This kind of thinking is detrimental to the child with learning difficulties in many schools, where subjects are taught for a set amount of time, at a predetermined point in the child's primary school career. [. . .]

Bloom (1975), at the University of Chicago, has developed the idea of 'mastery learning'. [. . .] Bloom suggests that we should *not* teach a topic for a predetermined time, assuming that all the children in the class will learn it to a varying degree of competence. Instead, in mastery learning, the amount of material to be learnt thoroughly is held *constant* and teaching time becomes the *variable* which is manipulated. [. . .]

This is the second factor over which teachers have a direct control and which might be manipulated to benefit the child with learning difficulties. He can be given enough time to master essential areas of learning. [. . .]

What about the way in which Mrs Jones introduced the work and presented the tasks to Peter? Very often children who have difficulty with learning do so because, for whatever reason, they fail to understand the instructions that are given. It will be recalled that Mrs Jones was worried about Peter's hearing because of his apparent lack of understanding of oral instructions. Understanding of language is an area of crucial difference from pupil to pupil. Therefore, it is vital that teachers pay careful attention to the way that tasks are explained, ensuring that each pupil understands the vocabulary used.

What records were being kept in the classroom about Peter's progress? Again there was no mention of this in the case study. If there existed an accurate record of the work set, the teaching methods used, the skills already acquired, the areas of particular difficulty to Peter, it could provide invaluable data for the formulation of an appropriate programme of intervention. What about Mrs Jones's management of Peter on those occasions when he was being rude, interrupting other children or avoiding settling down to do his work? Could praise be used more effectively to maintain Peter's interest for longer periods and encourage his efforts?

This brief discussion of aspects of Mrs Jones's classroom is not intended to imply that she was necessarily doing anything wrong. It is merely suggested that her planning, teaching methods, and classroom organization are within her control but were not considered in any detail when Peter was being investigated. Instead there was a preoccupation with Peter himself, the state of his brain, his family background, test results, diagnosis, and classification – none of which provided Mrs Jones with any specific and detailed practical advice. [. . .]

Further Reading

BATEMAN, B. (1974). 'Educational implications of minimal brain dysfunction,' *Reading Teacher*, 27, 662–8.
  Argues that there are *no* educational implications in a diagnosis of minimal brain dysfunction.
BLOOM, B. S. (1975). 'Mastery Learning and its Implication for Curriculum Development'. In M. Bolby, J. Greenwald and R. West (eds) *Curriculum Development*. London: Croom Helm.
  Outlines the fundamental issues involved in mastery learning.
BROPHY, J. E., and GOOD, T. L. (1974). *Teacher-Student Relationships*. New York: Holt, Rinehart & Winston.
  Reviews recent research that has demonstrated the effects of teacher expectation.
CLEUGH, M. F.(1968). *The Slow Learner, Some Educational Principles and Policies*. London: Methuen.
  An introduction to the policies and principles underlying the accepted approach to the education of slow learners.
DELAMONT, S. (1976). *Interaction in the Classroom*. London: Methuen.
  Includes an introduction to teacher and pupil expectations and the notion of the self-fulfilling prophecy.
FURNEAUX, B. (1969). *The Special Child*. Harmondsworth: Penguin Books.
  A useful and readable survey of work with exceptional children in special schools and ordinary schools.
GULLIFORD, R. (1969). *Backwardness and Educational Failure*. Slough: National Foundation for Educational Research.
  An introductory text dealing with the nature and sources of educational failure.

HOLT, J. (1964). *How Children Fail*. Harmondsworth: Penguin Books.
Uses classroom observation to argue that 'school is a place where children learn to be stupid'.

KEOGH, B. K. (1975). 'Social and Ethical Assumptions about Special Education.' In Wedell, K. (ed) *Orientations in Special Education*. Chichester: Wiley.

NASH, R. (1973). *Classrooms Observed*, London: Routledge and Kegan Paul.
The behaviour of teachers and pupils observed in an attempt to demonstrate and explain how teacher expectations can act as self-fulfilling prophecies.

PRESLAND, J. (1970). 'Who should go to ESN schools?', *Special Education, 59*, 1, 11–16.
A psychologist examines the issues involved in deciding which children should be placed in ESN schools.

24 Behaviourism and the Environment

Ann Brechin

Behaviourism and the Individual

Behaviourism has arisen from attempts to understand the relationship between observable behaviour in man and animals and observable features or events in their environments. It thus concerns itself with noting how behaviour changes in relation to external changes, and forbears to attempt explanations for such changes which call on hidden thought processes or the assumption of conscious choice. In much the same way as people reacted against the introduction of the Freudian ideas which implied that human behaviour was often somewhat less than rationally based, and indeed was determined considerably by quite unconscious motivations, so many have reacted against the growth of behaviourism which once more detracts from the image of rational man, and suggests this time that behaviour is considerably under the control of environmental events, indeed that it is conditioned by our experiences. An alternative view such as Kelly (1955) has proposed counters such apparent denigration of humanity, by focusing on the very mental processes of deduction and construction which the others have appeared to discount.*

It is important to recognise, however, that, contrary to the impression one gets from the kind of 'debates' that take place between individuals espousing different schools of thought, such interpretations of human development are not mutually exclusive. In this paper, the focus is on behaviourism not as an attempt to portray it as of greater or lesser significance than other models, but as an attempt to examine its particular contribution. As a theory with direct practical applications, the potential of behaviourism was quickly realised. It can be said to have revolutionised much psychological practice, and is being increasingly taken up by other professions. Inevitably, perhaps, it is brought to bear particularly on those individuals whose behaviour is seen to deviate in some way from normality, in an attempt to return them to the fold, or resolve their difficulties, depending on which way you look at it. Handicapped people particularly have been seen in this light, and it is in this area that this paper will be considering the contribution of behaviourism.

Essentially the application of behavioural techniques is founded on the following tenets:

1 That individuals learn to behave, or change their pattern of behaviour as a result of environmental consequences. For example, if an action is followed by a pleasant consequence, the action is more likely to be

* [See also Bannister's article in this Reader (p. 230)]

Source: Previously unpublished Paper written for this Reader.

repeated. A child who makes a joke resulting in adult laughter, goes on repeating the joke *ad nauseam* having *learned* that it can produce a pleasant result. Conversely an action which does not result in any particular consequence is less likely to be repeated. Of course, the details are more complex and cannot be pursued here.**

2 This being the case, it can be supposed that individuals who behave in 'unacceptable' or 'inappropriate' ways have learned to do so as a result of faulty conditioning of some kind; i.e. their exposure to inappropriate learning experiences has caused the problem.

3 If it is possible to modify behaviour by environmental consequences, then 'faulty' learning can be put right by exposure to more appropriate and carefully controlled consequences, to teach the individual new behaviours.

Such an approach has had outstanding successes. Perhaps the greatest impact has been in the field of mental handicap. See, for example, Kiernan (1978). Previous assumptions that levels of development, or disturbed or disruptive behaviour were direct and unalterable results of a physiological impairment, did not accord with behavioural assumptions about the modifiability of behaviour. In line with behaviourists' expectations it proved possible both to improve levels of functioning (e.g. by teaching new skills such as self care, cooking, literacy) with enormous implications for educational practice and to reduce 'behaviour problems' (e.g. aggressive or non-compliant behaviour and self destructive behaviour, such as hair pulling or eye poking). Such 'behaviour problems' have for a long time been one of the biggest difficulties for families and care staff trying to cope. They also have serious implications for the individual's development. A blind and retarded child who becomes obsessed with eye poking, is limiting the opportunities available for taking part in other learning experiences. In more complex ways, an aggressive and disruptive individual is likely to become unpopular, and be involved in fewer positive learning experiences with others as a result. The availability of techniques which can frequently and demonstrably improve things, often quite dramatically, has had enormous impact on ideas and practice. The nature of this impact will be raised again later.

Identifying Goals

First it is worth thinking more carefully about the implications of using such techniques. The use of inverted commas in the previous section anticipates one of the key issues which can be raised, namely how are the targets of behavioural techniques to be identified. Who will decide whether behaviour is appropriate or problematical, and, if it is to be changed, what it should be

** For an outline of a behavioural approach see, for example, Blunden and Revill (1980), Morris (1974) Carpenter (1974).

replaced by. Behaviourism carries with it no built in guidelines for identifying its aims but rather provides techniques grounded in learning theory for changing behaviour. Theoretically it would be quite possible to develop psychopathic behaviour in everyone if that were deemed appropriate.

Very often, of course, there are consensus views within a society as to what is acceptable behaviour and what is not. Few, for example, would suggest that a mentally handicapped adolescent girl who keeps undressing in public should not be stopped. All societies have developed overt sanctions of some kind to deal with transgressors of social rules. What is more, everyone is subject from birth onwards to a process of behavioural conditioning which includes sanctions and is in effect a way of socialising each individual to 'fit into' the given society. Is the use of behavioural techniques any different?

One clear difference lies in the fact that these are consciously determined processes, controlled and administered by any of the professionals, parents, volunteers or individuals who have been taught to use the techniques, and yet there are none of the safeguards which exist in other legally determined sanctions. No agreed code of conduct exists as to how problems should be identified and goals set. The difficulty this causes is basically an ethical one, which only becomes fully apparent when disagreements are noted between the goals of the two individuals involved. Brechin and Liddiard (1981) have illustrated how seriously the view points of professional and individual *may* diverge in identifying desirable goals.

Some professionals are very conscious of this problem, and will make efforts to establish the individual's wishes. It is naïve to assume that this solves the problem, however, as we know too much about the ease with which people are overawed and influenced by a wish to comply with the 'expert'. He or she does, after all, have specialist knowledge to draw on to provide advice. Mentally handicapped people may find it particularly difficult to give voice to their wishes or goals. It is not difficult to conceive of an adult, who has developed a special relationship with the nurse who feeds her, being quite distressed by the introduction of a self feeding programme, known by the experts to be for her own good. Her view of what is good may differ from theirs. The existence of such serious ethical problems should not be forgotten, however much one may justify such interventions in terms of an ultimate vision of greater independence and happiness. Their expert status and skills to implement changes, does not confer on those professionals using behavioural techniques the right to determine what changes should be made.

While it is impossible to generalise about the problems and consequent goals as perceived by handicapped people, we can get an impression from publications such as the statements of the Union for the Physically Impaired, (1980), or the compilation of interviews with young spastic people (Davidson 1977), or again papers such as Williams (1978) in which he gives voice to feelings he has heard mentally handicapped people express. The clearest difference which stands out between the behavioural view and the individual view is the direction of focus. A behavioural approach tends to concentrate on the individuals' problems and develop goals which involve changing the individuals' behaviour. Individuals tend to think mostly in terms of the problems caused to them by other people, circumstances and environments.

Identifying Changes

We can return at this point to a consideration of the impact of behaviourism. The current impression of behaviourism is that it focuses attention on the individual. Terminology varies, but the common usage of 'behaviour therapy' as applied generally in a psychiatric setting to the treatment of disturbed behaviour, or 'behaviour modification' as applied more often to the application of the same range of techniques to handicapped people, both reflect a pre-occupation with the behaviour of the individual. As such it comes frequently under fire from other professionals for purportedly ignoring the significance of other factors affecting the individual's present state whether historical, emotional or social/environmental.

The behaviourist responds typically with a defence which draws attention to the interactional nature of behaviourism. Behaviour is not seen in isolation, but is analysed as part of a functioning system (i.e. functional analysis) in which the aim is to identify those features of the environment which maintain the undesirable behaviour. Only then should appropriate changes be suggested which may bring about an improvement. Furthermore, it is argued, particular attention must be paid to perpetuating such changes once they have been achieved. Implicit in that is the need to pay attention to those long term environmental factors in the individual's situation. Reading through theoretical accounts of behaviourism these arguments are reinforced. One is impressed again and again by the importance attached to examining the environment in relation to behaviour.

Yet when it comes to accounts of specific behavioural interventions, one looks in vain for a reflection of this orientation. It is as if one of the great values of behaviourism, namely its capacity to be applied usefully in the most extreme of circumstances (e. g. toilet training mentally handicapped inmates in a long stay hospital), also becomes a pitfall, in that it makes it possible to lose sight of the wider contexts of behaviour. A pre-occupation, for example, with 'poor motivation' in a remedial context, may lead to the instigation of a behavioural programme of built-in rewards to increase a patient's level of activity, with no account taken of what he may expect his home circumstances or employment future to be, i.e. what his future environment is offering, or failing to offer in the way of naturally occurring rewards. Without such a maintaining environment, the skills will simply be lost again.

And yet experience tells us that quite often programmes may be set up with groups or individuals where perhaps little can be done to alter the environment, but which lead, nevertheless, to successful outcomes. What exactly happens when a behaviour programme is set up? Observations are limited by what we select to look at, and behaviourists are typically focusing their observations in very specific ways. They may often, therefore, be failing to draw enough attention to other important effects of their interventions, seeing them as side-effects rather than critical factors.

Consider one example. A mentally handicapped nine year old girl with autistic behaviour is living in a large subnormality hospital. The child, Jane, has become increasingly withdrawn and involved in self stimulatory activities: initially rocking and chewing, but eventually hair pulling to the point of baldness and a constant packing of her mouth full of anything she can find, mainly torn bedclothes. A psychologist decides to intervene using behavioural techniques. Having observed Jane's behaviour in the context of her environment, he evolves a programme which he feels will alter the consequences of her behaviour sufficiently to reduce such self destructive behaviour. But in order to implement it, certain changes are necessary. Firstly, it is essential that one or two members of staff should accept responsibility for carrying it out. The details are complex and they must be able to get to know Jane and she them. Within the normal nursing rotas of hospital wards that is impossible. Secondly she must have activities available which can gradually replace the present ones. She needs people who can respond to her, altering the consequences of her behaviour, and she needs circumstances within which she can learn to be active. These are the minimal essentials to allow the programme to be put into practice, but in trying to achieve them the obstacles of hospital ward life prove insurmountable, and eventually a small unit is set up in the hospital grounds to cater for a group of severely disturbed children including Jane. Here with regular staff and normal daily activities available, the programme can be operated effectively. Jane improves – not surprisingly. The programme continues to evolve and increase her capacities, and is clearly working, but everyone knows too that something about the change of environment has been critical.

Essentially what seems to have happened is that the behavioural analysis has pinpointed the necessary contingencies to change Jane's behaviour. In attempting to make such contingencies available according to a prescribed programme, a far wider range of contingencies has also incidentally been made available. Reinforcement in the form of adult approval is now available, not just contingent upon specified behaviours, but also generally where before it was not. In the same way, not only specified activities are built in as a part of her programme: a range of activities have become available as a part of the life she is now involved in.

Even without such dramatic changes as the setting up of a separate unit, important effects can occur. Any individuals called upon to observe carefully and respond contingently to specified behaviours are being, in their turn, taught new ways of interacting. Reinforcement for *them* may come in the form of approval from the initiator of the plan; from pleasure at the success they have; or from the approval of others around them. They are likely, as a result, to learn to be more alert, sensitised and reinforcing to behaviour in general. Not only the specified contingencies will occur, therefore, but also a general increase in the responsiveness of the environment they provide. In Jane's case, for example, the simple fact that adults were now responding more to her actions generally, led to the beginning of verbal communication, although no specific language programme had been set up at that point.

Behaviourism and the Environment

Changing the behaviour of individuals by altering the contingency behaviour of those around them, tends, as we have seen, to draw attention to the context of *that* behaviour in turn. One may thus come to ask why the behavioural environment of the individual was maladaptive for him/her in the first place. Tharp and Wetzel (1969) present a useful interpretation in these terms of a chain of factors, culminating in community traditions, which may serve to maintain behaviour nevertheless defined as undesirable.

This focus can be seen as particularly relevant in disability. Cultural definitions of disability provide a behavioural context in which access to routine sources of reinforcement is disrupted: access to educational or job opportunities is curtailed; mobility may be restricted by inaccessible buildings and transport; choice of housing or living conditions is reduced, and personal relationships are distorted. The reinforcements available for a growing child in the form of parental approval, acceptance by peer groups, and the rewards of a growing mastery of the environment, may all be reduced for the child with a mental or physical disability. Such a view of the failure of the environment to provide an appropriate context for learning to live in a social world coincide with the tendency of disabled people also to define problems in this way.

Studies in which such a perspective is specifically adopted are growing in number, and have so far emerged largely in the field of residential care and mental handicap. As patients are increasingly moved out of subnormality hospitals to live as people in a more 'normalised' environment, attention is drawn to the nature of that environment. Wolfensberger and Glenn (1975) have evolved an evaluation battery, Program Analysis of Service Systems (PASS), as a tool for assessing the nature of the new environments provided for mentally retarded people, much as King, Raynes and Tizard in 1971 developed a scale of child centredness for residential homes. Kushlick (1975) has set up community residential provision for children to evaluate their success in meeting children's developmental needs in comparison with hospital settings.

Recently Demaine *et al.* (1980) and Crawford *et al.* (1980), for example, have stressed the importance of examining the environmental characteristics of such substitute homes in direct relation to their degree of success in maintaining mentally handicapped people in the community. This notion again reflects the move away from more conventional, but largely unsuccessful attempts which focus on individuals and try to determine which personal characteristics will make them most likely to succeed in the community.

Such moves suggest that the potential does indeed exist for behavioural analysis to contribute, in a much wider way than it does at present, to our understanding of the nature of the social and physical environment of handicapped people. A shift in focus from the individual to the environment will allow new possibilities to emerge, more in line with the perspective of disabled people, for the identification and modification of processes which at present produce for them such a disabling learning environment.

References

BLUNDEN, R., and REVILL, S. (1980) *A Behavioural Approach*. Unit 5 of P251 – 'The Handicapped Person in the Community'. Milton Keynes: Open University Press.

CARPENTER, F. (1974) *The Skinner Primer*. New York: The Free Press.

CRAWFORD, J. L., AIELLO, J. R., and THOMPSON, D. E. (1979) 'Deinstitutionalisation and community placement: clinical and environmental factors.' *Mental Retardation*, *17*(2), 59–63.

DAVIDSON, M. B., (ed) (1977) *You Tell Me*. Edinburgh: Scottish Council for Spastics.

DEMAINE, G. C., SILVERSTEIN, A. B. and MAYEDA, T. (1980) 'Validation of PASS 3: a first step in service evaluation through environmental assessment.' *Mental Retardation*, *18*(3), 131–4.

KIERNAN, C. C. (1978) 'Behaviour Modification' In A. M. Clarke, and A. D. B. Clarke *Reading from Mental Deficiency – The Changing Outlook*. London: Methuen. (University Paperback edition.)

KELLY, G. A. (1955) *The Psychology of Personal Constructs*. Vols 1 and 2. London: Norton Bailey.

KUSHLICK, A. (1975) 'Improving the Services for the Mentally Handicapped.' In Kiernan, C. C. and Woodford, F. P. (eds) *Behaviour Modifications with the Severely Retarded*. Amsterdam: Associated Scientific Publications.

MORRIS, P. (1974) *Behaviourism*. Block 3 of DS261, 'An Introduction to Psychology'. Milton Keynes: Open University Press.

THARP, R. G. and WETZEL, R. J. (1969) *Behaviour Modification in the Natural Environment* New York and London: Academic Press.

'The Union for the Physically Impaired against Segregation' (1980) *Community Action*, January/February.

WILLIAMS, P. (1978) *Our Mutual Handicap: Attitudes and Perceptions of Others by Mentally Handicapped People*, Campaign for the Mentally Handicapped.

WOLFENSBERGER, W. and GLENN, L. (1975) *A Method for the Quantitative Evaluation of Human Services*. Toronto, Canada: National Institute on Mental Retardation, York University.

25 Resettlement Services of the Employment Services, Manpower Services Commission: Some Observations

Joseph Stubbins

California State University, Los Angeles

Introduction

I have long suspected that individualized approaches in vocational rehabilitation had been over-emphasized in the United States while social and programmatic methods that facilitated and created job placements for disabled citizens were meagrely provided for. More specifically, I wanted to assess the relative values of the clinical attitude as practiced through various diagnostic and remedial procedures which professionally trained counsellors usually employ in working with handicapped clients, as against such statutory approaches as the quota scheme and similar ones aimed at favorably influencing the client's employment prospects. With that in mind, I spent a sabbatical year in England at the Employment Rehabilitation Research Centre in Birmingham beginning with July, 1979. My project could not have been carried out without the generous co-operation of the Centre's Head of Research, Paul F. Cornes, the Centre's staff and numerous personnel in the Employment Service Division both at Headquarters and the West Midlands Area.

The complete report is titled *The Clinical Attitude in Rehabilitation: A Cross-Cultural View*. Three of the ten chapters deal with the British scene. [. . .] I made this abstract with the hope that it may stimulate discussion of the issues implicit in this brief presentation.

The Disablement Resettlement Officer as a Vocational Rehabilitation Clinician

A major focus of the study was the Disablement Resettlement Officer (DRO). [Here I] considered the question of the clinical skills of the DRO. A clinical attitude toward a client requires that the practitioner be objective, regard the client's problematic behavior as naturally occurring events, that he arrive at a diagnosis and employ remedial procedures in a discriminating way. Integral to the clinical attitude are also certain value attitudes of positive regard for the client, suspension of moral judgments, and a belief in the reconstruction potential of people under appropriate conditions.

Source: Abstracted from Part II: 'The Clinical Attitude in Britain.' In J. STUBBINS *The Clinical Attitude in Rehabilitation: A Cross-Cultural View* (in preparation).

The DRO was assessed with respect to six components of the clinical attitude. It was concluded that the DRO could not be considered a clinician. However, within the limits of their designated functions DROs are considered to be doing their work satisfactorily – a consideration underlined by the fact that reviews of the resettlement service in the past thirty years resulted in only minor modifications of their training and job descriptions.

Through their employment at Job Centres and Employment Offices, DROs are strategically located to identify, analyze, sort out and refer clients to needed services and to develop hypotheses about facilitating their employment. Naturally, to carry out these functions they must have the co-operation of other professional functionaries and agencies. Primarily because they lack clinical training, they tend to have a limited status with doctors, social workers and others with whom they work closely. Further, the majority of DROs and managerial personnel have a limited appreciation of the potential impact that psycho-social clinical skills could have in advancing the employment interests of disabled citizens. Perhaps this is most evident in the reluctance with which DROs face clients with a history of mental illness, a group which constitutes about 50 % of all handicapped job seekers.

Other consequences of DROs lack of clinical training are the following: their value attitudes tend to resemble those of employers and leaders in the busy community rather than scientists and practitioners in the biological and social sciences; nationally, DROs have no voice in and make no contribution to social policies concerning the disabled; most of them do not maintain contact with those constituencies concerned with improving the lot of disabled citizens.

Practically, DROs spent most of their time attempting to match their clients with available job openings. They have an excellent knowledge of jobs in the local labor market and surpass American rehabilitation counsellors in this regard. As a group, they are conscientious civil servants trying to perform gigantic tasks with meagre training and under inappropriate organizational auspices. They treat their clients with dignity, seem free of racial prejudice and appear to maximize what is possible through common sense approaches to job placement. Within the constraints of their official job description, it would be unfair to criticize them.

For the most part, DROs operate outside the mainstream of the techniques of vocational rehabilitation e.g. job analysis and job redesign, taxonomies of occupations, behavioral techniques of modifying client behavior, group counselling and self-help modalities, and other ways of raising the morale of severely disabled persons.

Use of Community Resources for Vocational Rehabilitation

Because of the limited geographic mobility of most British workers, DROs tend to have meagre occupational information outside the local labor market. This could be a handicap in their working with middle-class, educated clients. They appear to under-utilize resources for training and re-training; perhaps because British workers are not motivated to undertake such training or perhaps because DROs lack techniques of triggering their motivation.

DROs regard doctors with great deference though sometimes their own assessments of clients' physical and psychological limitations are more realistic because they are based on first-hand information of industrial conditions. Physicians (except those in occupational medicine) should only be expected to state restrictions in functionally generic terms rather than job terms. This would enable the client to take advantage of job openings on the least restrictive basis. There was considerable stereotyping of disability categories which violated that principle. For example, clients with a prior psychiatric label were invariably assigned to work which was routine and not stressful. It was remarkable that this stereotyping even occurred in the presence of medical consultation.

The most frequently used rehabilitation resource was the Employment Rehabilitation Centre [ERC]. I thought referrals were made on a non-discriminating basis and I was forced to change an initial impression that the ERCs were reserved for clients with complex or very difficult problems arising from their disabilities. Some DROs felt under pressure actively to recruit clients. My limited observations tended to confirm that the majority of ERC clients could not be classed as seriously disabled though they all had difficulties in finding or holding jobs.

The range of rehabilitation techniques employed within the ERCs was limited to positive encouragement, work hardening, work discipline and vocational training in basic engineering and clerical work. Considerable information was collected on clients. But it was not exploited for the purposes of career guidance, selection of training objectives and job placement in the client's home community. I found the environment low key but strongly supportive to clients. Clients are made to feel comfortable. However the division of labor within the ERC subjected the client to a succession of interviews and handling which surely diluted the potential of the ERC experience. The status hierarchy within the ERC with the client at the bottom also limits the rehabilitation impact.

My overall impression of the ERC was that its strong commitment to its present structure of an eight week course and existing procedures not only shut out other rehabilitation modalities but also the kinds of personnel who delight in experimenting and require a minimum of autonomy with which to do so.

The Quota System

Probably, the quota system has been more discussed than any other feature of the resettlement service of the Employment Service Division [ESD].

Because of this, I shall not review the literature which I covered in Chapter 4 of the full report, and go directly to my personal observations.

The majority of personnel in the resettlement service favored repeal of its mandatory features. With even greater unanimity, the disabled and their organizations favored retention. This difference in viewpoint might suggest the great divide between career civil servants concerned with employment rehabilitation and those who experience disability directly. Personally, I thought it remarkable that ESD persisted in fomenting another review of the quota scheme in 1979–80 despite the fact that there was plenty of evidence that the rehabilitation community itself believed its continuation was essential. There was a suggestion that officials consistently attributed more importance to the views of employers and the trades unions than to the broad constituency of the disabled. This is undoubtedly proper when considering matters relating to the provision of general employment and training services. However, it was surprising to find that, where specialist services were concerned, more weight was not given to the representatives of potential clients, the disabled themselves.

The cost of inducing seriously disabled workers is greater than that for the non-disabled and there must be some way of distributing these additional costs equitably. Presumably, the Job Introduction Scheme and similar devices by themselves are adequate. Also, the British need not ignore the American experience with the voluntary approach to the employment of the disabled. Despite a vast network of Employ-the-Handicapped Committees reaching down to the local level and a small army of professional trained rehabilitation counsellors, the level of unemployment among the disabled runs at about four or five times that of the general population. Perhaps, that is why practically every West European country has some kind of system that mandates the employment of qualified but disabled job applicants. Many of the seriously disabled were injured in the course of employment; they represent part of the social costs of a complex industrial system. From this viewpoint, there is no more reason to make their re-employment 'voluntary' than there would be to place the continued employment of older workers on a purely voluntary basis.

In the course of my painstaking review of reports on the quota system, I was struck by the academic impartiality with which the employment problems of handicapped persons were discussed. It would be difficult to sustain such Olympian objectivity except in the absence of any existential encounter with live disabled persons. But even such objectivity may be tempered under certain circumstances. A physician who was routinely reviewing the vocational objectives of clients in rapid succession noted that a previous physician had restricted a particular client from driving on account of diabetes. 'Oh', he said, 'Remove that restriction. I've had diabetes all my life. I couldn't carry on without driving my car.'

The quota scheme continues to contribute to the employment of disabled citizens despite its half-hearted enforcement in recent years.

The Disablement Resettlement Officer and his Organizational Setting.

This chapter delineated the DRO's job satisfaction, professional status, career ladder, administrative relations, community relations and civil service status as functions of the organization of which he is a part. I considered it necessary to do this as a response to the marked tendency of government bureaucracies everywhere to respond to suggestions for improved services through changes in the lowest echelons.

Resettlement work is not highly esteemed in the Employment Service Division. Most of it is considered well within the competence of almost anyone at the clerical officer level. In fact, it is sometimes considered a mark of disfavor to be assigned the work of DRO, though it is not uncommon for upwardly mobile young persons to volunteer as a means of attaining breadth of experience. Typically, the post is considered a transitional phase in a career within the Employment Service Division and those who remain for more than three or four years either develop status anxiety or become reconciled to their modest civil service position. The reader can draw his own conclusion from the fact that Senior DROs and Area Supervisors need not have had line experience though they serve as consultants, and in some sense professionally supervise DROs. The DRO is essentially a job adviser, and differs little from those who work with the non-disabled clientele.

The DRO's service functions were analyzed with respect to several basic criteria of professionalism. The DRO does not meet any of these because he is not credentialed for having mastered certain knowledge and skills relevant to career advisement, he lacks an exposure to the more or less systematic body of knowledge known as vocational rehabilitation, has a minimum of formal education, enjoys little autonomy, and therefore has little scope for the exercise of critical judgment. Finally, even if DROs were to share a common code of ethics, it is far from clear what it might be and how they could assert it in the face of the tight guide lines under which they operate. Indeed, the position of the ESD is that the DRO's work is not and need not be professional in nature.

The civil service has no system of rewards for DROs or for anyone else to develop a high level of expertise concerning the employment implications of physical and mental disabilities. Considering the high level of development of British social science and social welfare programs the level of psycho-social expertise in vocational rehabilitation within the resettlement service is low. This is partly due to a philosophy of management that places much more importance on the selection and development of generic leadership as compared to specialized technical expertise. This subject has been widely discussed. I would like to add, however, that psychological studies in the US which attempted to identify generic dimensions of leadership have not been successful. There is more warrant for postulating a range of leadership types. Thus, a very successful sales executive or a leader of a research organization is not necessarily equally successful in other spheres. In the light of the relatively low esteem in which technical expertise is held within the civil service, changes in the training and status level of DROs might make only a modest improvement in the quality of services.

Ultimately the services available to disabled workers can be most fruitfully understood as an organization product. By taking this view, we are less likely to beguile ourselves into thinking that programs of in-service training or updating the titles of DROs would improve employment rehabilitation significantly. Vocational rehabilitation is a complex of social service functions that is difficult to carry on in an organization committed to filling job orders, many of which go unfilled even in periods of high unemployment. The vast majority of disabled who present themselves to DROs do not only lack a job; they suffered a series of developmental mishaps. Unemployment is simply the most visible of such mishaps of which government policy takes note.

British resettlement services operate in relative isolation from several constituencies with which they might be in closer communication. ERCs, for example, might offer training and research opportunities for university programs in psychology, social work, medicine and para-medical occupations. I found little evidence that the work of private rehabilitation agencies had influenced the work of the resettlement service. One of the structural features of the ESD which militates against close informal relations with outside non-governmental personnel is its status hierarchy. If a line functionary such as the DRO or Senior DRO wishes to set up some mutually satisfactory procedure, he must either do it on his own and run the risk of censure or go through the long and tedious process of convincing his superior officers for whom rehabilitation is a minor responsibility. It is no wonder that almost everyone in the resettlement service minds his own business![. . .]

26 Designing for the Disabled

R. J. Feeney

M. D. Galer

The Market Place for Consumer Goods

Any analysis of problems concerning the design of consumer goods is confused by the different views of the market that are held by those on the one hand who make and sell the goods, and those on the other hand, who buy and use them. The confusion is multiplied by the lack of agreed meanings of different key words. An immediate example springs to mind in the use of the word 'need'. To the consumer or purchaser, this means that which is needed in order to fulfil activities in daily life which are considered necessary, e.g. eating and drinking, personal hygiene, entertainment, transportation. To the businessman making and selling the goods, any attribute or appeal strong enough to affect purchasing is considered to reflect a legitimate need.

Other words for which there are widely differing meanings are: 'information' – is it advertising or consumer advice? 'Competition' – is it price difference or product difference? And even the word 'product' itself: is it a functional device or a means of expressing an individual's personality or status?

The reason for such different perceptions stems from the different goals and expectations of people in the market place. If the goal of manufacturer and marketing is the financial return on money invested, such a goal may not be consistent with the goal of consumers who want to satisfy their demands with the smallest financial outlay possible.

Certain assumptions which are commonly made in relation to the economics of society tend to ignore the existence of these differing views of the market-place. For example, it is commonly assumed that the consumer guides production; that competition is a safeguard of the consumer; that consumers are rational and alive to their own interests, and that there are market-place mechanisms to ensure that the consumer's interests are heard and acted upon.

However, in the interests of manufacturing and selling products which can be produced as cheaply as possible and sold in sufficient number to ensure return on investment, the demands of peripheral groups whose needs may be significantly different from the marketing target, may well be ignored. There are several examples to illustrate how the requirements of these groups in the population are ignored in the interests of a major section of society. People who are left-handed have great difficulty in using ordinary

Source: Previously unpublished Paper written for this Reader.

scissors which are designed for use with the right hand. Only a small number of manufacturers make left handed scissors and usually these are at the higher end of the price range. In the interests of providing for a mass market, cars are designed for 'average' people who often also have to be fairly agile and fit. Anyone who is over 6′4″ or less than 5′0″ will find difficulty in operating the foot pedals comfortably and conveniently in most cars on the market.

Designing for the 'Standard' Man

One would imagine that the aim of product design is to design goods and services which are suited to the users i.e. the range of people who are going to use these products in their everyday lives. This is not always possible and the reasons are that a balance must be struck between the knowledge available about the product and its likely use, the complexity and constraints of the manufacturing process and the market forces which apply. This means that very often products are designed for a particular section of society whose interests are served when this market balance is struck.

Unfortunately such a section of society very often comprises the 'average' or 'normal' members of the population. The implication of this is that, in a mass market, design has to be aimed at 'standard' men and women who are not 'different', who are not fat, tall, short, weak, or disabled. Those people who do not conform to the designers' concept of 'standard' men and women are disadvantaged in that they are restricted in the extent of the world with which they may interact and may have to make special arrangements.

Ergonomists* tend to talk of designing for a pre-determined percentage of the population which can be described statistically. For example, in determining the optimum height of kitchen work surfaces elbow height is the prime consideration, and the variation in elbow height of say 90% of the population would be taken into account. This would include people with elbow heights between certain limits selected from a statistical distribution. It would exclude all people whose elbow heights were outside the heights determined by these limits. The same approach can be used in relation to other human factors in the design of products involving characteristics such as strength, energy consumption, reach etc. If such an approach were adopted by all designers this would go some way towards ensuring that consumer goods and equipment are more suited to the characteristics of people that use them.

Most ergonomics data on body dimensions and strengths of human beings tend to describe the fit, unimpaired and generally more able members of the population, sometimes based on data that has been gathered from

* Ergonomics is concerned with the matching of machine and equipment and environment characteristics to the characteristic and requirement of the user. Its application involves analysis, evaluation and design aimed at ensuring an optimum match.

measurements of military personnel. Another more serious shortcoming is that the data tend to describe single body dimensions only rather than combinations of dimensions. To return to our earlier example, it may be easy to design kitchen work surface heights according to the distribution of elbow heights within the population; but surfaces are worked on, reached over, and so on, so girth and arm length are also important dimensions to be considered. The implication of this line of thought is that even where a more magnaminous view of variation in body characteristics within the population is taken in the design process, certain 'non-standard' people whose combination of body dimensions, or other characteristics are untypical, are left out because they do not fit. It is not difficult to see that the disabled, because of factors like body deformity, differential growth patterns, muscular weakness, amputation etc. possess a combination of body characteristics which do not 'match' the design of products and environmental fittings for the standard man and therefore appear to require special design.

One of the most common producers of 'handicapping' design is 'styling' particularly where style takes precedence over function. In such situations the adaptability and flexibility of the human form is taken advantage of, and in the interests of novel looks and styling the consumer may have to accept some inconvenience and discomfort in order to use the product.

The 'standard' man can often cope with these vagaries of styling because he can adapt his behaviour, he is not using all his capacity. Unfortunately difficulties for our 'standard' consumer are considerably magnified for 'non-standard' groups within the population such as the elderly, the disabled and even those who are just 'different' in that they are too tall, too short or not strong.

Designing for the 'Non-standard' Man

It can be seen from the foregoing discussion that a principle problem for any designer of consumer goods is the lack of usable data on people who do not conform to the ergonomists' '5th to 95th' percentile concept. Some attempts have been made to rectify this situation. The dimension and reach capacities of wheelchair users has been studied[1], the grip strength of people with different disabling conditions has been measured[2]. It must be recognised however that measurements of single variables may not be appropriate and measurement is needed of total function in relation to the basic component activities associated with more general activities. A study of the optimum height for wall switches and power points illustrates this point[3]. By studying large numbers of disabled people, including those in wheelchairs, to determine the maximum and minimum comfortable height at which power plugs could be inserted and switches operated, it was demonstrated that one single height (1000 mm) could accommodate the needs of the majority of the disabled and incidentally, the non-disabled.

The approach to designing for the disabled should not be any different from that of designing for any other section of society. The design process involves,

the analysis of the requirements and capabilities of the potential user population,

the design and development of goods to meet those requirements,

the testing and evaluation of the goods to assess how well the requirements have been met,

the carrying out of any necessary modifications to the goods prior to production to ensure that the users' needs are being met in a satisfactory fashion.

This is second nature to any good designer. But the question is how many manufacturers follow this process and employ good designers. The back-of-the-envelope process is still commonplace and as was suggested above, an 'average' or standard person only is considered in formulating the design of the product.

What are the Consequences for the Disabled?

It has been argued earlier that consumer goods for standard people do not take into consideration the requirements of non-standard people and what may produce difficulties for many people who are not disabled often creates impossibilities for many who are disabled. For people with poor strength and poor agility, who are different, everyday goods such as household machines, cars, kitchen utensils and bathroom fittings are often unsuitable, and gadgets and aids have to be resorted to, to make standard equipment usable.

An overall consequence of all this is that opportunities to participate in ordinary everyday pursuits are often denied to disabled people. Their chances of engaging in education and work are hindered particularly where the design problems involve the buildings. Access to public buildings is often hindered by the inevitable steps leading to the main entrances. These cause severe difficulty to the semi-ambulant and are impossible for wheelchair users to negotiate alone. Also these same people are often restricted to the use of one floor only in many buildings, because they cannot negotiate internal stairs and no lifts are provided.

The production of special aids, by definition, caters for a relatively small market. The consequence of this is that often there is a cost penalty compared with mass produced goods. The unit cost of special aids is higher. Good design skills are even less likely to be used in this area in order to keep costs down, and there is often a lack of variety and choice when purchasing aids to suit specific requirements. In other cases the purchaser is confronted with an overwhelming array of almost identical products the qualities of which are totally unknown.

The gadgets and aids themselves are often of poor design, are also of poor quality and do not have the durability of many ordinary consumer goods. In a study by the Institute for Consumer Ergonomics carried out for the Department of Health and Social Security 1974–1979[4] a large number of aids to assist with personal hygiene activities such as using the toilet and bathing were evaluated. In technical and user tests it was shown that many of the aids lacked sufficient technical and design quality to render them suitable and safe for use by disabled people.

An important side-effect of designing specially for the disabled is that the difference between non-disabled and the disabled is emphasised. Disabled people cluttered with gadgets and aids around their house are singled out as different.

How Can Non-standard People Be Catered for?

The Short Term Approach

The short term approach is to improve design for non-standard people to ensure they have the advantage of as many facilities as other people expect. This can be helped by the provision of information about the suitability of standard consumer products and by the provision of aids and adaptations.

Indeed, an important ingredient to market change is that the consumer should be informed in order that he may differentiate between design features and qualities which suit his requirements. This is the essential purpose of the testing programmes developed by consumer organisations. Unfortunately, testing goods with the handicapped in mind has not, up till now, been a feature of most testing programmes. One exception to this is the testing arrangements carried out by the Institute for the Handicapped in Sweden. Standard goods such as vacuum cleaners, washing machines, typewriters and so on are provided free for those who are unable to function in certain essential daily activities without technical aids. Panels consisting of persons with different impairments who are themselves actual or potential users of the equipment under test are observed carrying out the complete range of tasks associated with normal use of the equipment. From the results of these observations and from the subjective responses of the panel, judgements are made on the ease of operation comfort and convenience of the various user features of the equipment. The results of the testing provide the basis for a list of specific products which are eligible for subsidy and are prescribable by rehabilitation doctors. As this presents a potential increase in the market for manufacturers' equipment, considerable interest has been shown by manufacturers in the possibilities of incorporating features which are both acceptable to handicapped and non-handicapped sections of the population.

The process of testing products with panels consisting of handicapped persons is identical to that used by consumer organisations, such as the Consumers Association in the UK in their testing with non-handicapped persons. It is conceivable therefore that as a logical extension to present programmes of testing, panels in future could comprise representatives of both the handicapped and the non-handicapped population.

In the short term such evaluation studies will only demonstrate the unsuitability of many standard consumer products, and so the provision of special aids and adaptations will be paramount. There is, therefore, a need to provide consumers with information on the qualities of these products. An example of such an evaluation was the study quoted earlier in which aids for personal hygiene activities were tested. Testing of special aids and adaptations for impaired people follows a similar pattern to that already described for standard consumer products. The main problem, however, involves the provision of resources to carry out such testing regularly. Whilst charitable funds are sometimes available in the long term governmental responsibility cannot be avoided.

The outcome of such evaluations, whether for consumer products or special equipment, is two-fold. First, information is available for the purchaser on the qualities of the products, both technical and user related. In addition, information is made available for use by designers and manufacturers, about the requirements and characteristics of the user population and also the deficiencies of the products currently on the market. This information is an excellent starting point for the design and development of more satisfactory products. Certainly there is no room for complacency in these exercises. Evaluation is not enough, very often better products have to be developed to meet the needs of the users. An example of this is a study carried out by the Institute for Consumer Ergonomics for the National Corporation for the Care of Old People.[5] Twenty-five alarm systems 'designed' to assist elderly people to call for help in an emergency were tested from technical and user points of view. All of the twenty-five products on the market in 1974 had major shortcomings which rendered them unsafe, unreliable or unsuitable for use as alarm systems. It was essential that products were developed which would fulfil their design purpose. The report on the evaluation has been the basis of a specification from which manufacturers and designers have worked for several years now.

The Long Term Approach

In the long term approach the emphasis should be on designing standard goods and services which consider the requirements of all the potential users at an early stage. The consequence of this would be that fewer people would be 'handicapped' in their use of these goods and services. The process would be the same as that described earlier for designing and evaluating consumer products and special equipment.

Design starts with a systematic assessment of the task to be achieved, the potential user's needs and requirements, his capacities, capabilities and limitations, the conditions under which the product will be used, the constraints of the environment, the technology available and the cost. The design process should pay particular attention to the interface between the user, the product and the environment. Very often if a novel product is envisaged much of this vital information is not available, or only available in a restricted form.

Prototype products should be developed to the best possible specifications based on existing information. These prototypes should then be tested with users representative of the total potential user population. No longer is it acceptable to design for small groups of potential users. All groups should be included. This is the ultimate goal of designing for low handicap. If products are initially designed for use by a larger proportion of the population: the elderly, the fat, the tall, those temporarily disabled and the permanently disabled, then the number of people handicapped by their environment will be reduced, the need for special aids and adaptations will be reduced and dependence on the rest of the community will be reduced.

References

1 FLOYD, W. F. *et al.* (1966) 'A study of the space requirements of wheelchair users.' *Paraplegia 4*, 24–6.
2 MCCLELLAND, I. (1972) *Bath Aids for the Disabled – An Ergonomics Evaluation.* Loughborough University of Technology: Institute for Consumer Ergonomics.
3 CUNNIFF, P. (1972) 'The optimum height of domestic electric sockets.' Report to the Consumers Association. *Which*, November 1972.
4 PAGE, M. E., GALER, M. D., BHANDARI, V. K., and FEENEY, R. J. 'Evaluation of Home Aids.' Reports 1–30 to the DHSS, 1974–1979 Loughborough University of Technology: Institute of Consumer Ergonomics.
5 FEENEY, R. J., GALER, M. D. and GALLAGHER, M. '*An Evaluation of Alarm Systems for Elderly and Disabled People.*' Loughborough University of Technology: Institute of Consumer Ergonomics.

Further Reading

FEENEY, R. J., GALER, M. D. (1978) *Selecting Aids for Disabled People*, National Corporation for Care of Old People.
GALER, M. D., (1977) 'The need to consider psychological and social factors in the conception of new devices.' *Responaut.*

27 Honeylands – A Family Help Unit in Exeter

M. J. Rubissow

Honeylands is an institution which has evolved within a district general hospital paediatric service to meet the needs for family support, residential relief and medical care of the young child with chronic illness, mental or physical handicap, and social deprivation. Families whose children's longterm problem is not appropriately cared for within the acute hospital system are referred to Honeylands for extended care by consultant paediatricians (Brimblecombe 1974).

The population served is that of East Devon, roughly 350,000, including the city of Exeter. The age limits which have evolved are birth to puberty. There are at present about 150 families on the active list. Surveys done in the paediatrics department show an incidence in this population of one in every hundred births resulting in a child with a major handicap, so that we expect about twenty new children each year. This is a practical number for our small team of therapeutic staff to handle in a thirty-bed unit.

In addition to support for families with major problems, Honeylands also provides a therapeutic environment in which to solve some of the minor problems of child-rearing, in a short-term period. It is particularly helpful when there are feeding or sleeping difficulties in the first year, maternal depression, and convalescence after serious acute illness.

The provision of services has developed as the needs of the families using Honeylands have been expressed; there has been no particular *imposed* design or plan. The location is advantageous – in spacious grounds close to the centre of Exeter, on main bus routes.

Honeylands is nominally a children's hospital, and staffed as such, with a basic staff of six trained nurses, three State Enrolled Nurses, six nursery nurses and six auxiliaries. Also on the staff are a play therapist–psychologist, physiotherapist, occupational and speech therapists and other specialized staff, who share their Honeylands work with other community obligations. The matron and the medical social worker are the core organizing force, and together work out each child's attendance, while the therapists, nursery nurses and voluntary helpers are responsible for their activities.

Activities

Parent relief is a major goal, and thus babysitting, overnight stays, weekend and holiday stays are provided for all the children enrolled, their use

Source: T. E. OPPÉ and F. P. WOODFORD (eds) (1977) *Early Management of Handicapping Disorders*. Amsterdam: Associated Scientific Publishers.

depending on the needs of the family. When plans can be made ahead, the matron books beds in advance, rather like making hotel reservations. Much of the demand occurs suddenly, however, and the doors are open at all times as a refuge. The sleeping arrangements are by age groups: the older children sleep in a large room of ten to fifteen beds, the younger ones and those requiring special care in smaller rooms closer to the night sister. Two rooms are occasionally used for parents to stay overnight with their child.

Meals are arranged in a family atmosphere, with tables of several children together with one parent figure. Babies are fed by volunteers or by other children's mothers as well as by staff. The general atmosphere is one of a large extended family.

Daytime activities are co-ordinated by a play therapist, and include nursery groups morning and afternoon, individual or group therapy sessions, outdoor romps and swimming. Groups of mothers meet regularly with the medical social worker – sometimes the group will be one of children who all have similar handicap, such as Down's syndrome; at other times the mothers will have children with various problems. A new venture is to bring together two groups of mothers and their infant twins to share the management problems.

For several years a classroom of the Exeter school district has been at Honeylands. To this class come children with asthma, diabetes, heart disease, cystic fibrosis, malignancies – i.e., potentially serious or lethal illnesses, who need a period of fairly intense medical supervision but whose ultimate educational prospect is to join a regular school in the community. These older children usually come by day; a few board weekly. They will attend from one to several terms.

For most of the children – younger ones in playgroups and babies – an individual programme of developmental goals is suggested by the staff, shared with the parents, and implemented as far as possible by everyone concerned. Any specific therapy is given individually, with schedule and frequency determined by the therapist involved, and often with the mother or nursery staff in attendance. These younger children generally come in by the day, but if they live a long distance away may stay overnight regularly once a week and thus spend two days at Honeylands.

On any one day an average of thirty-five children attend. The use to which the 150 families currently enrolled put Honeylands is distributed roughly in thirds – one third use just the residential relief help, one third use day care only, and the last third use both day care and relief. The particular disabilities in the children also fall roughly into thirds – one third are socially disadvantaged without major physical or mental handicap, one third are physically handicapped or chronically ill, with normal or near-normal intelligence, and one third are mentally handicapped. Many children, of course, have a combination of all three.

Every attempt is made to return a child to community services whenever possible, so as not to duplicate or confuse efforts. Thus many children are referred into community play groups after a period of group work at

Honeylands. The peripatetic teachers' work with deaf and mentally handicapped infants is vigorous in Exeter and their work in the homes might be supplemented by residential relief or socialization in groups, at Honeylands, if necessary. Informal 'case conferences' take place frequently, either by telephone or visit. Formal conferences are rare. Medical clinics are held at Honeylands and the progress or lack of it is reviewed by the paediatrician (ophthalmologist, community specialist in hearing and speech, etc.) and parents at intervals of a few months. At these visits, Honeylands staff are often present to share with the parents the interpretation of advice given.

Family Involvement

Children are usually referred to Honeylands at a time of stress for the child and family. They are visited immediately at home by the social worker, who begins to introduce the types of services offered. Often, with a parent reluctant to accept help, there may be quite a long time between referral and arrival on the doorstep. This is kept under review by the social worker and referring paediatrician.

When she does agree, the mother visits Honeylands with the referred child and often her other pre-school siblings, sometimes with the father. She is encouraged to continue short visits with them until she feels content to leave her child. Some mothers take months or years to feel enough confidence. Once the initial familiarization phase is completed, the amount of relief, support or practical help the family needs tends to be worked out between themselves and the staff. The doctor is rarely involved at this stage.

Mothers have various ways of using Honeylands. Some stay away completely, some stay at Honeylands most of the time and help with the work of the day. Chat with other mothers, often for hours and hours, performs a vital function of 'densensitizing' the new mother and making her feel comfortable. We have found that the initial contacts for the mother within Honeylands are easiest when they are made by other mothers, and some of the more frequent and steady attenders have taken it upon themselves to help regularly in this way. Strong friendships develop between mothers and between mothers and others' children, as well as between staff and mothers. Once a month there is a coffee morning to which all mothers are invited. This is attended by newly referred mothers, those whose children have 'graduated', and sometimes by mothers whose children have died, as well as many of the mothers whose children are in regular attendance. It is a very popular function with mothers from the middle social classes. The higher- and lower-class mothers often do not attend, and may respond better to staff members than to the other mothers.

A father's involvement is less evident at Honeylands, but opportunity is always sought for a chat or a cup of tea when he picks up the family or the child. Fathers are often called on for practical support by the staff – for repairs, toy-making, alteration of equipment, etc., which they seem pleased to do. Regular evening functions are attended by an encouraging number of the fathers.

A League of Friends gathers volunteers and funds and has recently raised enough for a splendid covered, heated swimming pool. Members volunteer regularly in the work of the day, and some concern themselves with particular families and problems. They are active in running the summer holiday play schemes for handicapped children which occur in outlying communities.

The most recent addition to the help available to the parents has been the provision of weekly home visits by 'developmental therapists', to babies under eighteen months referred with a major developmental problem such as cerebral palsy, Down's syndrome, mental retardation, blindness, etc. The paediatricians are encouraged to refer babies early, prior to definitive diagnosis – indeed as soon as a serious problem has been suspected or described to the parents. The goal is to bring a positive approach into the home soon after bad news has been given. The 'developmental therapists', who are traditional therapists or nurses experienced with families of the young handicapped child, are then supported by a multidisciplinary team in designing their programme for the mother and child at home. Each developmental therapist acts in her usual capacity (speech, physio, occupational therapist or nurse) as a member of the multi-disciplinary team. The therapist visits Honeylands with her mother and child four to six weeks after referral, and thereafter at intervals of six months. At these morning-long visits, the team sees the family, makes written suggestions in each of their areas of expertise (movement, communication, cognition, etc.) to the therapist, who then shares them with the mother at her discretion. A record of progress is kept at home.

This has become a training programme in problems of infant development for all those participating, and the professional interchange is lively. No one therapist in this project works with more than one new family per three months, and these home visits are a part of her regular working week. This distributes the responsibility for new patients among several experienced therapists, and in particular brings the impact on the family in their home into a different focus for the therapist, accustomed to working in a clinic or hospital.

Work with the Community

Study days are held at Honeylands for playgroup leaders and health visitors, and individual lectures are given to nurses, family practitioners and educational psychologists at various Exeter courses. Schoolchildren doing community service and Exeter University students (from the Departments of Education, Psychology, Educational Psychology and Drama) often work individually with children. A combined physiotherapy and swimming 'clinic' is held weekly in a health centre in the other major town in the area, Exmouth.

Discussion

There are several convictions behind the evolution of the services at Honeylands:

1. that practical help, emotional support and occasional residential relief lessen the burden imposed on the family by a handicapped child;

2. that the type and amount of such help required is apt to be different for each family, and that the service team must be sensitive and flexible;

3. that the specific handicap or functional disability in each child requires an individual approach to his development which is best started in the home, where parents can retain their natural confidence as the true experts for their own child, and then continued with information and teaching from specialists as necessary;

4. that a single kindly skilled therapist representing an extended family in society, with primarily an educational role but prepared to answer calls for help, is a good form of aid to the family of a handicapped infant;

5. that by distributing severely handicapped infants for home visiting among the available therapists, so that a new family is encountered every three months or more, we more fairly distribute the necessary emotional investment which these situations command, and which parents often complain in retrospect was lacking in their early medical care;

6. that it is the responsibility of society in general, and of paediatric services in particular, to nurture and protect a family's emotional health, to facilitate the natural bonding of mother and baby by not interfering with their relationship more than is absolutely necessary. This bond, so often tenuous after adverse birth events, can break down with the separation of frequent hospitalization, with the management problems of an irritable or uncommunicating baby, with the uncertain pessimism of doctors trying to make an accurate assessment and with the variable advice of relatives and friends. To strengthen this bond is our obligation to the handicapped child and his family;

7. that most families will maintain their concern and support for their own child throughout his lifetime better than any statutory service, and that it is in the community's best interest to facilitate this whenever possible, rather than to provide substitutes; and

8. that perhaps the most important quality needed for this type of work is respect – respect for the ability within each family to find their own best way of living with their handicapped child, and respect for the capacity within each child for growth and development, given love and a responsive environment.

In this way the normal life style for the sibs and parents can be largely maintained without the withdrawal from normal society so often observed in families with a handicapped child in other circumstances (Mac Keith 1976).

Outlook

Honeylands provides one type of system within which a community can support and educate a family with a handicapped infant or young child. It is surprising that its facilities are not overused, but this may be an indication of its effectiveness.

Over the next two years an evaluation, both economic and sociological, will be undertaken, supported jointly by the National Fund for Research into Crippling Diseases and the Department of Health and Social Security.

The home visiting programme is a separate three-year project supported by the Mental Health Foundation and the NFRCD, and is being studied for effectiveness in achieving parental information and satisfaction plus developmental progress in the child commensurate with his abilities. These are broad goals not easily assessed, but an attempt will be made. A control group of handicapped infants and their parents in North Devon has been identified and is being compared with the home therapy group at Honeylands.

Examples

A girl born with tracheo-oesophageal fistula was unwanted by her single mother. Major surgical procedures and illnesses at the acute hospital alternated with months at Honeylands in the first years. The mother has gradually assumed care, married when the child was five, and the child, now eight, attends normal school and lives comfortably at home with her mother, stepfather and stepbrother, with no obvious handicap. Honeylands' role with the mother was encouraging and friendly at all times.

A full-term infant seen for routine check-up failed to gain weight in the first three months. The excellent health visitor was visiting daily, helping the mother with feeding. Acute hospitalization revealed no metabolic or nutritional reason for failure to thrive. The mother was young, inexperienced and anxious, with a supportive older husband. After three months of attendance at Honeylands all day for mother and baby, both are thriving. Mother did all the caring and feeding. Feeds were not altered. Mother visibly appeared to relax and enjoy herself and the baby, and now visits once a week or less (the baby is now seven months old).

A girl of two years was referred by Social Services for not walking; there was some suspicion of neglect. She was silent and depressed, and would move only with apparent pain. She attended Honeylands three days a week and then as a weekly boarder for a year. Walking and talking were both achieved in that time; no organic problem was ever detected. Her family disintegrated further and she was fostered at age three. She is now four and, apart from shyness and slight emotional instability, appears quite normal. The foster family felt no need for further support and only attend for check-ups.

An extremely retarded boy was referred at one year. His mother had rejected him on hearing the bad news, and later experienced deep depression for which hospitalization was necessary. He stayed at Honeylands full-time for several months. Mother began visiting, and gradually began to take him home on weekends. He is now six and has one normal younger sibling. He has just learned to walk, but has no effective speech. He sleeps at home two or three nights a week, is at Honeylands the other nights, and attends the ESN(S) school (school for the severely educationally subnormal) by day. Parents have come to terms with his condition and are planning for residential placement when he reaches adolescence.

A boy with Down's syndrome and cyanotic congenital heart disease was abandoned at birth by his young teenage mother. He spent his first year at Honeylands or in the acute hospital because of the severity of the heart disease. A volunteer mother with a husband and older son met him there and now fosters him. She began taking him home at about eighteen months, and he now at age three lives at her home, with one weekly visit to Honeylands for speech therapy. She uses regular holiday relief for him: 1–2 weeks every few months.

A bright little 2½-year-old girl with quadriplegia who lives on an isolated farm attends two days a week and stays overnight. Physiotherapy and speech therapy, as well as socialization in peer groups, seem to have facilitated her development. At eighteen months, when she was referred, she had no head control, speech or independent movement. She has now mastered all three, and her speech is normal for her age. Her mother visits rarely and regular home visits by the social worker have been necessary to keep her in touch. The child accepts her schedule completely. She will attend the nursery class of the physically handicapped school when she is three and live at Honeylands during the week, returning home at weekends.

References

BRIMBLECOMBE, F. S. W. (1974) 'Exeter project for handicapped children.' *Br. Med J. 4*, 706–9
MAC KEITH, R. (1976) 'Advantages and disadvantages.' *Dev. Med. Child Neurol. 18*, 143–4

28 Personal Social Work

Peter Durrant

It is regularly argued that social work is in a state of crisis. In these first years especially of the nineteen-eighties its critics, internally[1] and externally,[2] are in full cry. Social workers themselves may well have contributed to this state of affairs; the wish and the need to reform the world might be said to amount to a somewhat dubious motivation. Nonetheless there also seems a fair case to be made for arguing, significantly perhaps at a time when the economy is in difficulties, that those who opt to put into practice social welfare legislation encounter too much public scapegoating.[3] Be that as it may, the face of social work is clearly undergoing enormous change. Whether or not it survives what Adrian Webb has called 'the disengagement of the state' remains to be seen and much, if not all, will depend upon how social workers re-adapt their contribution to a fast-changing society.

Social work, leaving aside for the moment the vexed question of defining what it actually *is*, takes place in a number of arenas. These include the voluntary sector with its wide diversity of field, day and residential provision, and the major possessor of social work resources, the much-maligned social services departments. Over the years they have become known more specifically as the personal social services in an attempt to identify and clarify their individual style of operation. To what extent they have succeeded in this aim remains contentious. Some, particularly members of the medical profession, remain convinced that 'Social Services is a Department and a doctor is a person.'[4] Yet the reality is different. Bureaucratic constructs do not negotiate referrals, enter peoples lives and encounter pain. Personal social services departments are only sums of their parts and it is people who face other people at the grass-roots:

At the age of three, Hamid, for whatever reason, fell from a high chair and sustained hemiplegia of the right side. Many accusations and case conferences later he spent three years in a long-stay childrens home before being shipped back to a relative in Calcutta. Four years on, a period of his life about which we know little, he was abruptly returned to a family that had learned to live without him.

It is a curious business to be in when a father can offer *you* his child. In so doing he and his family allow a glimpse into their culture, and nothing more than a glance at their reasoning. In spite of attempts to confront, counsel and refer their minds are made up. Overtly the child no longer fits. Covertly the events of the early years, culled from the dusty earlier file, stubbornly intrude.

Overlaps in time between the private decision to accept, and the public

Source: Previously unpublished Paper written for this Reader.

decision to take, need to be spent in marshalling resources. It is at this stage that colleagues who have been quietly and creatively working at alternative ways of caring show their mettle. It is at this stage too that we need to admit our absolute dependence on the new caretakers. It is they, the foster-parents, who must make the major contribution now. Yet this implies no devaluation of role for the social worker since by now she or he will have become an integral part of a widening circle of help and the skill is in preparing for, and working on, the child's future. Physical separation may have taken place but it is the social worker who must work hard at the interface of the boundaries as they lengthen and take form.

Hamid, we all agreed as our partnership took shape, was a survivor. He had to be after all he had been through. Reassuringly, as though to vindicate our judgement, he seemed to grow in trust and slowly began to blossom. His thin frame filled out and our hopes began to rise that his academic slowness was due to cultural differences rather than some degree of mental handicap; the undersized arm and leg eased back into his functioning and the loving foster-parents ingeniously built on the physiotherapist's advice.

The middle time is about contract-making. With parents it is about legality and loss. With foster-parents, superbly professional in their own right, it is about sharing the decision-making without confidentiality becoming too impaired. With the professionals, who needed no persuasion to give of their time and knowledge, it is about making sure that their contributions fit. The middle time is also the phase when objectives need to be clarified and adhered to; when values need to be made more explicit and shaped around our priorities for, and as much as possible with, the child.

Social work today has matured more than we sometimes give ourselves credit for. Not so long ago a series of childrens' homes might have awaited Hamid, dedicated residential workers notwithstanding, but now it is adoption first with everything else rightly seen as second best. The reason that we can afford to be more confident about outcome for this handicapped child is because successive generations of child care and other workers have painstakingly mapped out new territories. The current inheritors of this knowledge are the Barnardo's New Families Project and it is their expertise that we now need to commission.

In *his* middle phase Hamid rose magnificently to us, and our first prospective adoptors, examining his teeth and inspecting his fetlocks. He *must* have known, as he surpassed all our expectations, that this was his bid for happiness. But for the best of reasons the attempt, five months in the making by a dozen people, failed to take. Our disappointment must have been projected on to Hamid as his behaviour became less mature and the bed-wetting re-emerged.

Barnardo's, however, had just completed their early discussions with a couple who had selected Hamid from their 'brochure'. First indications looked good and the helping machinery moved cautiously forward a second time. Almost a year on success came upon us with startling suddenness. The carefully designed Barnardo's/local authority operation, scrapbook[5] and all, eased smoothly into place with the new family proving everything that we could have wished for him. He too began to sense and accept the unconditional love which was directed towards him and it was as much as the social workers could do to continue to stress the possible problems and the probable obstacles. The only real snag came when the closure of yet another manufacturing company left the new father on a reduced working week. But fostering may prove advantageous for us all in the short-term. The long-term will depend upon a government of whatever hue getting the economy right and the hastening of assisted adoption.[6] But following visits which naturally expanded themselves it was obvious that this resilient and courageous little eleven-year-old had found himself, with a little help from his friends, a new home.

Personal social services departments *are* capable of personal work. The helping of Hamid is what social workers, amongst other things, *do* in spite of their bureaucracies. They are not 'the welfare' nor should we allow them to become so. Instead we should be directing them towards more creative activities as a means of releasing their vast potential. The discussion that follows will examine the changing face of social work from a personal social services base, seek to provide evidence that progressive change can, and is, taking place and finally will attempt to identify the ingredients necessary for local authority social work to alter radically its perspective. This will include, as an integral part of its philosophy, the involvement of people on the receiving end.

A whirlwind tour around the history of social work would find its antecedents in the Elizabethan Poor Law, its birth in the nineteenth century Charity Organisation Society and its infancy spent struggling out of the mass of social legislation of the post-war years. With such a long period of gestation it was not surprising that its collective values became saturated with large amounts of paternalism which have only recently been diluted by more radical prescriptions. Effectively the personal social services are the children of the Seebohm Committee's deliberations of 1968 which led to the three major social work agencies in local government amalgamating, unwillingly, in 1971.[7] The predominant method of intervention was social casework, an approach very much influenced by American experience; but as the seventies wore on it became apparent that a style of work based largely on psycho-analysis was inadequate. At the same time the build-up of welfare law meant that personal social services resources although starting off from a low base-line, expanded rapidly. This pressed into being an urgent need for a new management infra-structure and drained, almost overnight, the field of its experienced practioners. In turn their clientele, especially the visually handicapped and the mentally ill, experienced a sudden jolt.[8] Familiar services often geared to local needs no longer existed and a brave new generic animal had taken their place.

No sooner had the first organisational dust settled than the fledgling departments were off again, this time ripped apart by local government reorganisation.[9] In its wake came the scandals of old people dying alone, the side-effects of homelessness and the tragedies of children being abused by their parents. Not surprisingly the onslaught of media criticism contributed to a defensive withdrawal accompanied by a rigidity of thinking which now seems so characteristic of much of their public image. At their worst local authority services for people with varying degrees of handicap are simply that: *services* which warehouse clients rather than sympathetically using their power to redefine need in a contemporary fashion. The large gymnasia-like buildings masquerading as day centres, and the purpose-built hostels which advertise their differentness daily from the rest of the street, typify this approach.[10] At their best they are capable of a sensitive appraisal of need which uses as its beginning value the expressed views of its customers:

Wandsworth social services *Project 74* set out 'to enable the mentally handicapped using their training centres and hostels to speak for themselves about their experience there and at home.' The whole enterprise soon became a cooperative experience involving trainees and their parents, staff at the training centres and hostels, and volunteer interviewers from both within and without the social services department. Three-quarters of Wandsworth's 155 trainees and hostel residents were successfully interviewed and provided ample evidence that the views of people with varying degrees of mental handicap can play an important part in contributing to better services.

The results were enlightening with 76 per cent of trainees expressing a desire to get a job outside the centre whilst six out of ten men of a sample of trainees said they would like to do activities at the centre generally associated with the opposite sex. Hostel residents appeared to be dissatisfied with the amount of freedom and individual choice they had and many trainees expressed the need for more autonomy at home.

Another outstanding example of how consumerism can, and should, be put into operation comes from further north:

The sad death of Stephen Menheniott at the hands of his father was one of the reasons why Durham social services have published and sent a Guide to every child in their care. The attractively produced booklet carefully explains why children come into care and contains a stamped, addressed postcard to the Director. This is for use if 'you feel that you are being ill-treated by anyone, either inside or outside the place where you are living.' The Guide was written with the help of children in care 'to try and help you know what being in care is about'. It explains how the department is organised and the names of the people immediately involved with their lives; what the purpose of the six monthly reviews are and provides realistic advice on what to expect if the child wants to be present. Throughout it attempts to help young people play their part in choosing their own clothes and involves them in their health affairs. Finally it helps prepare for the important time when care comes to an end and the outside world, often a difficult and lonely place, looms large.

The last five years have seen the casework ethic increasingly under attack with social workers seeing themselves less as therapists and more as enablers and facilitators. This momentum, given a hearty shove by critical sociologists, the rise and fall of the Case-Con movement, and the influence of community work have led to a less precious view of the world and its excluded citizens.[11] Social work's inbuilt critical faculty, often painfully injected during training, could be its salvation yet, through providing the impetus to pose basic questions about its sense of direction. Should the route be fully professional, aim high at its own esoteric body of knowledge, and control and limit entry to those who would enter? Or should it take an occupational path which accepts its responsibilities whilst attempting to share and redefine the nature of the task?[12]

At the same time the bulk of social work seems firmly attached to its local authority home with some arguing that, as an activity, it cannot exist out of context.[13] Nor are the personal social services made up of social workers alone although they may retain a dominant position.[14] Increasingly they are composed of a number of professional and occupational groups each jockeying for space in a diminishing territory. Legislative shifts of emphasis, particularly the Chronically Sick and Disabled Persons Act of 1970, have meant that occupational therapists are now often key workers for people with varying degrees of physical handicap. Hard on their heels are specialists in visual handicap and, initiating some of the most imaginative help for people with severe handicaps and chronic sickness, the home help service. Whilst at the centre they are ultimately governed by elected committees sometimes capable of making their own marks on services.[15]

Meanwhile back at the grass-roots, the need has been to put into practice ways of working which avoid the one-sidedness of the past. Task-centred work built around the notion of a reciprocal contract is such an approach.[16]

Carmel, who continually has to evolve ways of coping with a crippling heart disease, approached the department for advice on how to negotiate her way through the maze of welfare benefits. Ian, who continually has to evolve ways of coping with a department that overloads its workers, accepted the commission. The negotiations and interactions which followed had implications for them both:

Carmel writes: 'It was suggested to me that Ian would work on my behalf on a 'contract' basis with set aims and ambitions. This seemed an excellent idea as I needed practical help; not a father figure or a shoulder to cry on. . . . I only had the "use" of Ian for a short time but the encouragement, ideas and hope he gave me will definitely have a long-term effect. I am now better equipped to put plans into operation myself. . . . After my initial suspicion I came to accept Ian as an ally whom I could trust not to fob me off with platitudes. If I hadn't trusted and respected him as well as liking him I'd probably have had him "running around in circles" just to amuse myself. As far as I was concerned we had an agreement and specific goals were identified and set.'

Ian writes: 'The details of the contract are not relevant here but I came away feeling very threatened. I was unsure of Carmel's commitment to the project and even felt she was playing games with me. Other colleagues put it down to "manipulation" but looking back I realised this was a somewhat trite explanation. What had happened was that in offering to negotiate with the client I had altered the power balance in our relationship in favour of her. No longer could there be any one-sided definition of goals. I had to accept that perhaps she did not want to go where I wanted her to. At first this is very threatening as you are giving people permission to say "I do not want what you have to offer but I want x and y instead." However the benefit is that once you have agreed on where you are going, and who is responsible for what, then the chances of achieving the goals are considerably increased. . .

'Since my initial attempt at contract making I have tried to adopt this style of working for all my cases. Not everyone is happy to actually write down a formal contract but by negotiating goals and means of achieving them, I am finding that relationships with clients are greatly improved, there is more trust, on both sides, and we certainly seem to be making considerably more progress.'

The time has come for local authorities to take some risks. And some are. Others are beginning to develop the debate and hopefully innovation may be emerging as a force to be reckoned with sometimes in partnership with the voluntary sector.[17] But the encouraging thing is that we now know enough about social work to make a clear choice of route and the main directions should be well sign-posted.

a There needs to be a rationalist starting point from which to plan. The personal social services have been bedevilled by incrementalist reactions which see a gap and in-fill it; rarely stopping to think about an overview, or the relationship of one part to another. In order to achieve this the individualist nature of social work needs to be confronted and replaced by a broader style of operation. 'Case-loads' label and compartmentalise need; 'workloads' enable action research, monitoring and discussion to take root.
b Rationalist thinking needs to be complemented with competent social auditing; what resources there are and what function they serve. The starting point is to identify, and become familiar with, what already exists; buildings, equipment, finance and labour. Only then is it possible to scan and analyse the usefulness, or not, of what there is. But except for a few examples[18] the skill of creatively assessing, why, what and where organisations are at is still remarkably under-developed.
c One of the reasons for this is because personal social services, poised uneasily on local and national political tightropes, are hesitant to clarify the values which underpin their work. Yet no public or private provision can deny its historical evolution and its current assumptions about how it operates. Values are *always* present and the art may lie in making ideologies

sufficiently explicit in order that they may stimulate debate about principle and function. The focus might then alight on concepts such as fairness, natural justice, relative poverty and normalisation in opposition to clumsy attempts at political points scoring.

d What agency objectives do survive have too often been used as professional camouflage to avoid conflict and fuller discussion of issues. Terms such as 'community care,' and 'participation' have become so global as to mean everything or nothing. One side effect has been that the people actually putting policies into action become uncertain about their role. Another is that consumers begin to distrust the agency's commitment to follow through legislative promises.[19] Just as social work practice is hopefully moving towards greater explicitness so should organisational aims begin to state precisely what they hope to achieve, over what period, and what the consequences might be if objectives fail to be realised.

e One conceptual framework which might further this process is the integrated approach. Currently a controversial development in social work, it aims to clarify problem-solving machinery through identifying client, target, action and change-agent systems. This systems theory approach which helps broaden the areas of choice seems well-suited to the needs of the personal social service. Used with verve it may even represent 'a shift from a predominantly individualistic conceptual model of practice to an inter-actionist one'.[20] The model is still regarded with some suspicion in the field, yet at the very least, it can provide the means whereby badly needed information is fed back to the centre. If holistic work is to take off not only descriptions of emotional distress need to be taken into account. Monetary, housing and environmental poverty too, the main ingredients of societal exclusion which then attract and justify professional intervention, must also be included.

f It follows that the actual siting of helping networks can only be within communities which are easily accessible to consumers. Their philosophy should embody the principle of normalisation and they should be continually striving towards preventative approaches.[21] Whatever 'face-to-face' work was still required should be subject to strict contractual agreement between those concerned so that offers of help might be clearly understood. It would then be possible for community, group, *or* case-workers to make their contribution *provided* the method and probability of outcome are on open display. Equally, those occupying inferior power positions need to be able to scrutinise the small print, assess the worker's claim to credibility and have a full stake in the proceedings. None of this is achievable unless systems are 'open' and the provision of information seen as integral to the whole.[22]

Contemporary needs *are* slowly producing more ideas based on 'mutuality' and conviviality. Co-counselling, disclosure and eclectic case-work are examples.[23] In social work education too a lively debate is taking place about the merits of 'de-schooling' and learning on the job.[24] But there are perhaps two main indicators that would really demonstrate that reform *is* actually taking place.

The first might be when we find more appropriate ways of referring to each other. As Louis Battyre has bitingly remarked of such terms as 'wardens' and 'superintendents,' 'the nomenclature is disturbing'.[25] He was right! The truth is that titles *are* ways of ascribing authority and local government 'officers' and their 'clients' are no exception to this rule. In essence it is *people* with varying degrees of handicap who need to negotiate, as of right, what is available. Deliberately blurring the boundaries between helpers and helped has immense benefits for us all, if only the former can screw up their professional courage and let go. The last word really belongs to Diana Paulopolis, a MIND volunteer: 'It's nice to get it across to someone who is mentally ill that we are all screwed up mentally, but that some are better at hiding it than others.'[26]

The second might be when consumer groups begin to emerge in their own right confident of their ability to direct and manage their own affairs. The evidence is that this is happening:

In America 'one of the most exciting and politically powerful developments in recent years has been the establishment of 'self-advocacy' groups. These are groups of mentally handicapped people (sometimes including people with other handicaps) who have been taught to organise their own affairs, run meetings, take decisions and carry them through, with minimal help from non-handicapped people.'[27] A major advance has been the second *People First of Nebraska* Convention in 1979 where workshop topics included 'Rights and Responsibilities,' 'How to Stick Up for Yourself,' and 'How to Start Your Own Group'.

In England the Union for the Physically Impaired Against Segregation argues that both 'inside and outside institutions, the traditional way of dealing with disabled people has been for doctors and other professionals to decide what is best for us. Sometimes, of course, we need medical help or therapists. But we are *people* first, not "patients," "cases," "spastics," "the deaf". We reject the idea of medical or other experts telling us how we should live or withholding information from us.' Wary of outsiders taking over, and history provides plenty of precedents, membership is only open to physically impaired people who support its aims. The help and support of sympathetic and able-bodied people is needed and welcome but 'because it is society which disables physically impaired people . . . it follows that exclusion can only be put right by disabled people themselves taking a more active part in society.'[28]

Social workers, or anyone else employed in the 'helping professions,' need not be alarmed at these developments. Society itself is built on an interlocking and interdependent model. Commerce cannot survive without customers and neither can people in service industries. The existence of the helped justifies the income of the helper. Social workers and others need to accept this and use their abilities to complement, not undermine, the right of the disadvantaged to rid themselves of disadvantage.

The activity of social work needs to take place at two levels. The first OU course on the handicapped person in the community put it nicely. 'Any worker with handicapped people has a double duty: to provide the best possible service for his client within the options his community currently offers; and to question continually the adequacy of those options and to work for extension of them.' In the past social work has found itself ladling out a weak version of the former and almost totally denying the latter. If we really want to stay in the helping industry, and time is short since the golden years for professionals of all sorts are fading fast, we need to learn from our mistakes. We must remember also the things we do *well*, for we should not write ourselves off too quickly. Occupying a conscientious and accountable centre role is of prime importance and we should have no cause to apologise for being there. And we might at times even remind our critics that preparing for, staying with and carrying through difficult work well is an eminently worthwhile contribution to make to society's present state of play.

Notes and References

1 Recent years have seen a number of social workers, and social work educators, becoming increasingly critical of existing practice. See, for example, *Justice for Children*: Morris, Giller, Szwed and Geach (Macmillan Press, 1980). Also *Radical Social Work*: Roy Bailey and Mike Brake (Edward Arnold, 1980).

2 See *Can Social Work Survive?*: by Colin Brewer, who is a psychiatrist and June Lait, who is a university lecturer (M.T. Smith, 1980).

3 Press criticism, particularly from the *Daily Mail* which misses few opportunities to crudely lambast social workers, is sometimes justified but occasionally blatantly unfair. See, for example, the *Daily Mail* 4 November 1980 which not only had a banner headline 'I blame the welfare workers' but also contained a front-page photograph of the startled social worker concerned who had clearly just opened the front door of her own home.

4 'Prescribing more than medicine.' *Community Care*, 9 November, 1980.

5 It is now commonplace for progressive adoption agencies to circularise carefully selected mailing lists with written details, including a photograph, of 'hard-to-place' children. Once children are placed with prospective adopters, 'life-stories' or 'scrapbooks' are compiled as a means both of helping the child adapt to a new environment and of providing a record of the past. See *Working with Children who are Joining New Families* (ABAFA).

6 At the time of writing the government seems at last on the brink of implementing measures on adoption that have lain dormant on the statute book since the passing of the *Children Act 1975*; including an allowance for couples who adopt children they are already fostering. The *Guardian*, 5 November, 1980.

7 'Seebohm' the *Report of the Committee on Local Authority and Allied Personal Social Services* was mandated to 'secure an effective family service.' The legislative result was the *Local Authority Social Services Act 1970* which was generally implemented in 1971. This brought together Children's, Health and Welfare depts into one allegedly generic body.

8 According to a letter in *Social Services* 13 April 1974 John Wilder, Director of the Psychiatric Rehabilitation Society, 'the generic doctrine' meant that 'the mentally ill are receiving less attention since Seebohm.' In the early seventies

parents of mentally handicapped children and people with visual handicap, who even organised a protest march, were also dismayed at the loss of specialised services.

9 Following the reorganisation of local government in 1974, departments are now situated in 39 non-metropolitan county councils, 34 metropolitan districts and 6 metropolitan counties and 33 boroughs in London. See *The Personal Social Services:* Eric Sainsbury. (Pitman, 1977.)

10 E. J. Miller and G. V. Gwynne in *A Life Apart* (Tavistock, 1974) posit that the warehouse model, the attempt to translate the model of the hospital into the setting of the residential institution, requires residents to remain dependent and depersonalised. 'Any attempts by the inmate to assert himself, or display individual need other than those arising from his specific disability, are . . . constraints on task performance. They are therefore to be discouraged.' See also *No Place Like Home:* Ann Shearer (Campaign for the Mentally Handicapped).

11 (a) For a comprehensive analysis of the relationship between sociology and social work see 'Uneasy bedfellows' *Social Work Today.* Vol 5, No. 1. by David Wilson. (b) *Case-Con:* 'a revolutionary magazine for social workers' prospered both in terms of sales and local networks in the first half of the seventies. Its Manifesto is reprinted in Bailey and Brake, *op cit.* (c) An evergeen debate is whether or not social work is community work. See *'Community work and social work as separate disciplines':* Joan Matthews and Dave Ward. *Social Work Today.* Vol 10. No. 15.

12 From a small number of professional organisations in the 1930s grew the *British Association of Social Workers:* (BASW) which initially restricted but, following internal pressure, eventually widened its membership. It publishes its own weekly magazine, *Social Work Today* and a quarterley journal, *The British Journal of Social Work.* Amongst its policies it is committed to the establishment of a General Council to regulate and accredit social workers. The seventies have also seen, not least as a result of the impact of *Case-Con.* a counter-move towards unionisation as a conscious rejection of what is seen as BASW's elitism. Membership of NALGO or NUPE would be seen then as a means of identifying, and working with, the massive trade unions which represent the bulk of local authority workers.

13 With much of social work closely allied to legislation it appears to David Howe: 'Agency function and social work principles': *Brit. Jnl. Soc Wk.* that 'there is no social work task as such. It is just that some tasks derived from carrying out agency functions, and conducted with more or less skill, are pursued with certain principles in mind. It is this which causes people to feel that social work is going on.' Pruscilla Young, too, argues in the foreword to *Towards Practice Theory:* Kathleen Curnock and Pauline Hardiker, that she finds 'it difficult to identify social work as a professional activity separate from the functions of the agency.'

14 In a fascinating, and for social workers reassuring, essay in the *British Medical Journal.* 12 January 1980 Rudolf Klein: 'Doctors and social workers' maintains that the 'social work profession has the dominant role in the personal social services, just as the medical profession has the dominant role in the NHS'.

15 (a) At least eight groups, in addition to field social workers, can be identified in personal social service departments. They include residential social workers of all sorts; social work assistants; day care personnel; home helps and their organisers; occupational therapists now sometimes known as advisers to the disabled; playgroup organisers; family aides and administrators. (b) Of these E. Matilda Goldberg *et al., Ends and Means In Social Work (Allen and Unwin, 1979)* found that

the occupational therapist was involved in over half of the allocated client group which comprised 'the physically disabled under 65'. (c) The home help services are increasingly developing schemes such as Hammersmith's '*Home Carers*' which provide 'a caring service for the severely handicapped, chronically sick, or frail elderly people to enable them to stay at home and at the same time give relatives a much needed break.' (d) In Strathclyde working groups with equal numbers of councillors and officers have produced a number of reports including one on mental handicap and another on addiction. See *Social Work Today*. Vol 10. No. 26. 'Officer-member groups in Strathclyde.'

16 The first major piece of research which indicated that clients of social workers sometimes failed to share the worker's view about the nature and the resolution of the problem was *The Client Speaks:* John Meyer and Noel Timms (Routledge, 1970). The book has been immensely influential in persuading social workers that tasks need to be clearly identified and explicit agreements made about who will, and in what way, carry through the work. See also 'Exploring the task-centred casework method:' Matilda Goldberg, *et al*. *Social Work Today*. Vol. 9 No. 2 and *The Use of Contracts in Social Work*. BASW Practice Notes No. 1.

17 (a) Sheffield, in a job description for a social policy strategist (November 1980) committed themselves to stating that 'Much of the Strategies will be highly "political" in that the council is strongly committed to policies which will discriminate in favour of the most needy.' (b) Kent's *Community Care Project*, by paying carefully selected helpers from the community, is attempting to make possible the more effective care in their own homes of frail, elderly people requiring residential care or even more intensive provision. The analysis of data showed that the experimental group fared better in a number of important ways; and that the gains appear to have been made at no extra cost to the social services department. See *A new approach to community care:* David Challis and Bleddyn Davies. *Brit. Jnl Soc Wk*. Vol. 10, No. 1. (c) After reviewing specialist child care facilities in the north-west in the early seventies, Barnardo's in cooperation with the local authorities concerned built new residential units in Liverpool and Salford. This was followed up, with the support and encouragement of Lancashire social services dept., by the *Chorley Project* which now has four full-time social workers and provides a comprehensive service for families with children who have varying degrees of mental handicap. See *Support Service for Families:* Alan Kendall, and *Barnardo's Chorley Project:* Ann Shearer.

18 See 'Enabling practitioners to contribute to practice:' David Anderson. *Social Work Today*. Vol 10. No. 39.

19 One of the first charities to take a local authority to court was the *Fellowship of Workers for the Handicapped*. They took proceedings against the London Borough of Hillingdon under common law in conjunction with section two of the CSDP Act 1970 on behalf of a disabled couple. Since then there have been a steady stream of legal actions by voluntary societies.

20 'Some implications of an integrated model of social work for theory and practice:' Roger Evans. *Brit. Jnl Soc Wk*. Vol 6. No. 2. The major American theorists of unitary, or integrated, theory are Howard Goldstein: *Social Work Practice: a Unitary Approach* and Allen Pincus and Anne Minahan: *Social work practice: model and method*. The first British text is *Integrating Social Work Methods:* Harry Specht and Anne Vickery. For a critique of unitary theory see Bill Jordan. *New Society*. 2 June 1977: 'Against the unitary approach to social work'.

21 For a discussion of (a) how social workers are increasingly working in

communities see 'The patch system:' *Social Work Today*. Vol 15. No. 16. (b) The principle of normalisation in action in Nebraska where 'the goal is to serve mentally handicapped people of all ages and degrees of disability in their home community' see *ENCOR – A Way Ahead* (Campaign for the Mentally Handicapped). (c) Of primary and secondary prevention see the chapter on the theme by John Barter in *Seebohm Across Three Decades* (BASW publications).

22 Some personal social service departments are extremely competent at providing information. *Camden*, in particular, in 1974 commissioned two journalists Judith Stone and Felicity Taylor to write the *Camden Handbook for Parents with a Handicapped Child*. Distributed free, and beautifully printed with the now famous pink mouse by a child from a special school on the cover, the handbook has been widely imitated. But rarely surpassed. Camden also provide a comprehensive folder *Camden Can Help You Help Yourself* which won a silver jubilee access award in 1978.

23 (a) The basic principle in *co-counselling* is that both participants give and receive help by one talking and the other listening attentively followed by the roles being reversed. (b) *Disclosure* is concerned with the sharing of personal experiences, see *Self-disclosure*: Gordon J. Chalune and Associates. (c) Joel Fischer, a long-standing critic of what he regards as the ineffectiveness of social casework, has produced an account *Effective Casework Practice: an Eclectic Approach* (McGraw, 1978) which sets out to include the four components which seem to be best proven and efficacious. They are (a) the use of structure in intervention (2) behaviour modification (c) cognitive procedures and (4) the core thera-peutic conditions of empathy, warmth and genuineness.

24 See 'De-schooling social work': Martin Richardson and Peter Beresford. *Community Care*; May 1978. The continued growth of the Certificate in Social Service (CSS) has also attracted comment through combining its teaching between college and the agency. See 'Qualifying for social work: the unresolved dilemma of the CSS.' *Social Work Today*. Vol 12. No. 7.

25 Louis Battye, author and playwright, lived in a Cheshire Home for much of his life. On the twenty-fifth anniversary of the homes he took a critical look at their organisation and methods. See the *Guardian*. 28 September, 1973.

26 MIND pamphlet: *Where Do You Draw the Line?*

27 *Make us Citizens and See Us Grow:* Paul Williams and Alan Salomon (Campaign for the Mentally Handicapped.)

28 *Community Action:* January/February, 1980.

29 Construing a Disability

D. Bannister

George Kelly's personal construct theory (Kelly 1955 and 1978, Bannister and Fransella 1980) has only a limited popularity with psychologists, perhaps because it demotes them to the level of people, or, put the other way round, it promotes people to the level of psychologists. Kelly started from the notion that all men and women are scientists. Clearly he did not mean that all men and women have PhDs or wear white coats or are interminably dull in their discourse. He meant that all of us have theories about the nature of humankind. If we are official psychologists we refer to them as our theories. If we are only people, then our view of the world may be referred to as our central nervous system or our prejudices or our unconscious complexes. From theories scientists derive 'hypotheses' while mere mortals have 'expectations'. Members of the Science Club acting in terms of their theories are said to be 'experimenting' while men and women are said to be 'behaving'. On the basis of the outcome of their experiments, psychologists 'reformulate their theories' while the humble citizen is 'subject to change'. Kelly argued that we are all active and purposeful even though conventional language dignifies only the official scientist.

Given this view, psychology becomes a way of making sense out of the way people make sense. It becomes a way of exploring people's theories about their own nature and the nature of others. The name Kelly gave to your personal philosophy, stance towards the world, picture of yourself, values, feelings and motives was 'a personal construct system'. Perhaps we can get at the nub of his argument by examining just those words – a personal construct system.

Personal

Personal, because although there is a real world out there we can only contact it by individually interpreting it. The instant that you say that what you are now holding in your hand is 'paper' or 'an interesting argument' or 'rubbish' or 'an example of modern typesetting' or 'something that might come in handy for lighting the fire' you have construed a part of your universe. That such interpretations are personal and individually different becomes evident if we consider a daily occurrence, namely that two people can respond quite differently to the same situation. Peter and Paul, in the same job, contrastingly refer to it as 'boring' or 'exciting'. Jane and Joan, meeting the same person, respectively refer to him as 'a creep' or as 'charming'. Kelly's

Source: Previously unpublished Paper written for this Reader.

argument is that the two people are not in the 'same' situation. The situation is only the same looked at through the goggles of yet a third person outside it. From within the situation, seen through the eyes of the two different people, there are two different situations, to which they respond differently.

This is not to deny that we share, communicate and dispute our personal construct systems through the way in which they have been embodied in our community – as language, as art, as scientific theory, as folklore, as custom, as religion, as history and so forth.

Construct

A *construct* is our way of distinguishing same from different. It is a bipolar discrimination. It is our interpretative tool. Some of our constructs have verbal labels, north-south, nice-nasty, coming-going, hard-soft, expensive-cheap, man-woman and a few million others. Many of our constructs have no verbal labels. We construe music busily for hours on end without necessarily involving ourselves in the business of words. Kelly chose to see constructs as bipolar to highlight the fact that we never affirm something without negating something at the same time. If we say that Albert is an honest man we are not (as the conventional logic of concepts would have us believe) saying that Albert is an honest man as distinct from being a dahlia, a contour map, a dwarf, a prime number, or any other of the millions of things that he could be. We are saying Albert is an honest man, he is *not* a crook. Often the import of what we say is mainly carried by what we simultaneously deny, as in the case of the ship's officer who entered in the log the statement that 'the captain was sober tonight'.

System

System, because our constructs are linked and related into a complex, hierarchical structure. Language is simply an attempt to chart a kind of average relationship of constructs. We denote our hierarchy of constructs every time we produce an ascending chain of reasoning. You must wash your face little Jimmy because people do not like to see dirty faces so you won't grow up to be admired and important and then you won't go to heaven. Our personal construct systems are not just stories we tell to each other late at night by the fire. They are us. They are our guidelines for living. They can be smashed. A man or woman who construes a razor blade thin layer of ice as 'thick enough to skate on' comes to grief when they put their construing to the test and if they survive will have to reconstrue.

Psychology Through the Looking Glass

Unlike many psychological theories personal construct theory is reflexive. That is to say it accounts for its own construction, it acknowledges that it is simply an act of construing; an interpretation placed on nature; one more guess. Psychological systems are rarely reflexive. The Freudian who explains *your* behaviour in psychoanalytic terms rarely suggests that his explanation is merely his own attempt to sublimate his sex drive. The behaviourist who argues for learning theory is not presenting his belief in it as simply the haphazard result of his personal reinforcement history. Most psychologists argue that human behaviour is *caused* while claiming that their behaviour in so arguing is the outcome of *reasoning*. The quality of reflexivity in personal construct theory makes it a system of self examination, not simply a system for evaluating others.

'The Disabled' or 'a Disability'

Some of the ideas which we can derive from construct theory about disability are not unique to the theory: they could be derived from other points of view. The advantage of trying to examine the problem from Kellyan perspective is that it might eventually yield a consistent and integrated way of viewing disability.

Let us examine the construct of 'disablement'. From a Kellyan point of view we need to know three things about any construct: firstly, what its contrast pole is (since all constructs are argued to be bipolar); secondly, how superordinate the construct is, how widespread its implications are; thirdly, what kind of construct it is: pre-emptive, constellatory or propositional.

Clearly, the construct of 'the disabled' can be used in a way which imprisons those who are construed as such. To begin with it has an odd contrast, 'the able', which rather conceals the fact that none of us is, in any sweeping sense, 'able'. For all of us there are many things we cannot do, dare not do, have never thought of doing. Perhaps we are tempted to refer to 'the disabled' because it makes us feel, by contrast, relatively able. Again the construct may be used too superordinately, so that we are letting disablement carry far too many implications. Thus some seem to see any severe disability as implying very wide ranging limitations for the person with the disability, e.g. limitations on sexuality, on travel, on work capacity, on independence, on toughness, or responsibility and so forth. Thirdly the construct may be used pre-emptively. A pre-emptive construct is a 'nothing but' construct, i.e. if this person is disabled then he is *nothing but* disabled. Clearly, if we start to use the construct in this pre-emptive way we are in danger of seeing the disabled person as somehow less than a person. There are many ways of using a construct pre-emptively without explicitly saying 'nothing but'. Perhaps the reverence with which we often speak of disabled people, our inability to be humourous or argumentative with them may be a sign that we are identifying them totally with their disability.

Perhaps we can limit the power of the construction (the nature of its contrast, its superordinacy and its pre-emptive quality) by thinking of 'a disability' rather than a disabled person. No person is, in any fundamental

Even identifying something as 'a disability' should leave open the question of how far it may *ultimately* prove to be a disability: the extent of a disability is constantly being put to the test. Kelly once referred to that most dread disease, 'hardening of the categories' and maybe in thinking of 'the disabled' we have contracted the disease.

Self Image and Disability

Talking about how people view someone with a disability raises the contrasting question of how the person with the disability views himself or herself. This in turn must involve the question of what their total picture of themselves is, what they value about themselves, what they think life is about for them. A person who sees life as about *nothing but* achievement, success in competitive, practical spheres, may find that their disability has, in a major sense, invalidated their life and significantly reduced their value as persons. A person with the *same* disability, who sees life as also and importantly about personal relationships, about reflective experience, about what you are rather than what you do, might find the same disability truly less disabling.

The notion that each of us has a personal construct system suggests that we can only understand the nature of a disability (our own or someone else's) in terms of our total outlook on life, our whole image of ourselves, our feelings about what is important and what is unimportant.

Dependency

Much is made of the issue of dependency in relation to disabilities but, again, from construct theory point of view, the problem of dependency is essentially the same whether we suffer from a labelled disability or not, if we use the word dependency in a truly psychological sense. Kelly designed a particular technique (grid technique, see Fransella and Bannister 1977) to examine the ways in which a person's constructs are linked together. As part of this work he designed a 'dependency' grid.

Take a piece of squared paper and list down the left hand side a number of situations in which you might need help. These could range across situations involving financial difficulty, feelings of personal rejection, periods of depression, serious problems at work and so forth. List along the top the names of people within your circle, family members, friends, other significant figures. Each square now represents the intersection of problem situation and a person and you can ask the question 'would I turn to that person for help in that situation?' You can signify if the answer is 'yes' by putting a tick in that square, or if the answer is 'no' by leaving it blank. You can go on to fill the whole of the matrix of squares in this way. Even if we analyse this matrix in only the very simplest way, by looking directly at the of our dependencies. In psychotherapy, it is often noted that such grids show one of two kinds of *undistributed* dependency. Sometimes virtually all the squares are ticked, which suggests that the person would turn to everyone for help in every kind of difficult situation – a kind of *undiscriminating* dependency, which is likely to meet with a fair amount of hurtful rejection. Another kind of undistributed dependency is manifest when virtually all the squares are blank except for one column of ticks. This suggests that the person would turn to just the one particular person for help in all situations. Clearly the person thus chosen might become heavily overburdened.

All of us are dependent in a variety of senses and our problem is to *distribute* our dependencies so that we call appropriately on different people for different kinds of help. It is in this sense that the problem of dependency is the same for the person with a disability as it is for the allegedly 'non-disabled'.

Psychological Movement

Having asserted earlier that the way in which a person handles or fails to handle their disability is necessarily related to what they think their life is about, it follows that the way *we* look at people with disabilities will be an integral part of what we think life is about. From a construct theory point of view life is about development, exploration, movement. Kelly defined (re-defined) aggression as 'the active elaboration of one's construing' and by active elaboration he meant *experiment* in the living sense of that word. This suggests that we should not be too ready to urge people to *adapt* to their disabilities. Adaptation may be construed as meaning that the person should regard the style of their life as fixed by their disability or that those who are trying to help should regard the person with a disability as someone who needs their life fixing into a comfortable frame.

This can more easily be seen when choices are being made directly in terms of a disability. I recall a young woman suffering from spina bifida who at one point had a choice between proceeding swiftly and easily in a wheelchair or slowly and clumsily with calipers and sticks. In terms of point to point progress the choice was simple. But if we widen our construing of the situation (as she did) then we have to take into account questions like her height relative to other people in a wheelchair or on sticks; questions like the fairly fixed boundaries of movement possible in a wheelchair as compared with the possibly extendable boundaries of movement with calipers and sticks; questions like the differences in the response of other people to a person in a wheelchair or a person on sticks and so forth. Construed in another way the issue has to do with the temptation to live with the devil we know rather than the devil we do not.

Again, it should be noted that personal construct theory does not make a special case out of disabilities. The issue of whether we want life to be comfortable and fixed or challenging and changing is an issue for everyone.

Construing Constructions

For those who are directly involved in working with people with disabilities the most significant of the eleven corollaries of personal construct theory is perhaps the sociality corollary. This reads: 'to the extent that one person construes the construction processes of another he may play a role in a social process involving the other person'. Helping is surely playing a role in a social process involving the other person. Thus, the helper needs not simply to know *about* the disability or to sympathise. The helper is faced with the much larger task of trying for some understanding of the personal viewpoint of the man or woman with the disability and to be understood in turn. The help that we can give is necessarily circumscribed by what the person with the disability considers is appropriate as help, what they accept does not infringe their rights as a person, what they see as a fair relationship between themselves and others.

Equally it means that we cannot regard a disability, pre-emptively, as *nothing but* a disability. We sometimes acknowledge the extending power of the *experience* of a disability. We acknowledge that the blind have a more subtle perception of sound than the sighted. But we may fail to realise that any disability opens up some aspects of the world just as it closes down others.

Research

A primary method of exploring the way in which a person construes his or her world and situation, derived from personal construct theory, is repertory grid technique and it may offer us a way of investigating the meaning of a disability both for a person with it and for those trying to relate to him or her. The assumption underlying grid method is essentially a simple one: the way in which a person relates their constructs can be roughly estimated from the way particular judgments they make are statistically related. Thus, if you divide up twenty people known to you into those you consider selfish and those you consider unselfish and then re-divide them into those you consider honest and those you consider dishonest, then we may find there is a clear statistical trend in your judgments. Perhaps those you judged selfish are much more likely to be classified as dishonest. We can argue from this that there is a conceptual link, in your implicit psychological theory, between honesty and unselfishness.

It would clearly be possible for a given individual or for a group, to examine the way they see disability by having them make judgments on elements such as kinds of disability, or activities restrained by disability or experiences related to disability, in terms of the constructs they habitually use to comment on disability. There is a field of formal research and individual exploration which can be carried out using techniques of this kind. Such research could be extended by bringing into relationship the construing of the person with the disability and the construing of stranger, friend, relative, helper or whoever.

However varied and wide-ranging such modes of research might be the central aim would be to examine the *meaning* of the disability both for the person who has it and for the people who relate to him or her.

Conclusion

Even from such a sketchy outline as this it should be seen that the broad implication of personal construct theory for viewing disabilities is that always what is being talked of is *a person* with *a disability*.

The construct of 'the disabled' is menacingly superordinate and pre-emptive (to say nothing of its curious contrast pole) and thereby an oppressive categorisation. This is manifest even when intentions are good, as in the provision of special features in architecture, transport, entertainment and so forth 'for the disabled'. It would be better if such features were not special case additions but standard and customary aspects of public design. Such reconstruing might mean forsaking the construction of a few wide doors and ramps for wheelchairs and accepting that all our doors are socially too narrow and that our addiction to steps is arbitary.

Neither publicly nor privately is a disability an identity. We are identified by our presence as persons.

References

BANNISTER, D., and FRANSELLA, F. (1980) *Inquiring Man*, 2nd edition. Harmondsworth: Penguin Books.

FRANSELLA, F., and BANNISTER, D. (1977) *A Manual for Repertory Grid Technique*. London: Academic Press.

KELLY, G. A. (1955) *The Psychology of Personal Constructs*, Vols. 1 and 2. New York: Norton.

KELLY, G. A. (1978) In B. A. Maher (ed.) *Clinical Psychology and Personality: Selected Essays of George Kelly*. New York: Krieger.

SECTION FOUR
Integrated Living

This final section focuses on the politics and economics behind the thrust for change in the 'quality of life' for disabled people. It looks both at the official channels in legislation and the provision of services, and at participation by disabled people in the processes and decision-making which shape their lives.

DeJong, in the first paper (30), outlines and analyses the background to the exciting and challenging developments in the USA under the 'Movement for Independent Living'. This movement, we are told, has sprung from two main sources (both of which are apparent in this country): the efforts of disabled people to seek a more fulfilling life in an able-bodied world, and the efforts of professionals to reach severely disabled people. This paper is not included to suggest that the 'Movement for Independent Living' could or should take place in this country, but rather as an analysis with which developments and approaches in this country can be compared.

This is followed by extracts from two of the recent Government Reports (other examples being the Warnock Report, the Court Report and the Black Report) which have direct implications for disabled people. The main focus in the extract from the report by the Social Services Committee (31) is on the allocation of resources. The Committee put forward their economic arguments for improvements in perinatal 'preventive' measures. The extracts from the Jay Report (32), on the other hand, set out the basic stipulations the Committee had in mind as fundamental to an adequate provision of care and life-style for mentally handicapped people. In this report priorities, in terms of allocation of financial and manpower resources, were seen to lie in 'prevention': a non-medical form of prevention conceived as an improvement in the social circumstances of disabled people.

One approach to change is through legislation. The next two readings each illustrates a major concern. The extract from the DES White Paper (33) is an example of a Government response to a major report (in this case, the Warnock Report). Accompanying this are the ACE comments on the White Paper. A major question here is the effectiveness of a series of reports as a basis for legislation, with each considering a particular aspect of health, education or the life-style of disabled people, and each arguing for priorities in resources. Even if legislation is passed, it may not be enforced (or even enforceable) as illustrated by Topliss and Gould (34) in relation to the Chronically Sick and Disabled Persons Act.

The papers by Bayley (35) and Simkins (36) focus on the provision of services to support disabled people, and their families, living in the community. A crucial issue, raised by Bayley, stems from the problems of cooperation between the helping professionals and those *already* providing care in the community, i.e. family and friends. Simkins examines economic questions. She shows how an inadequate system for financing 'disabled families' is itself disabling and argues for a complete renewal of the system.

The unifying theme of the remaining readings is the direct involvement of disabled people in decision-making and processes which shape their life-style. They cannot be said to represent a consistent view of disability, but they each challenge common assumptions and definitions. De Jong (30) sees the thrust behind self-help as the opportunity for disabled people to exercise control over their own lives and the services they use. Loney (37) while recognising the challenge to professional assumptions within the self-help approach, analyses self-help and community care from a political viewpoint and argues that these are not cheap alternatives. The paper by Jones (38) outlines a programme developed by a self-help group of parents of handicapped children, 'Kith and Kids', concentrating particularly on the group's use of voluntary help. The papers by Finlay (39), Davis (40) and Davis and Woodward (41) describe three interesting projects in this country, each initiated by disabled people. In these projects, covering research, a housing scheme and an information service, the problems faced by disabled people are defined by disabled people themselves. Full integration, that is the overcoming of those features in the nature and organisation of our society which segregate disabled people from the mainstream of social life, involves a social world geared *for* and through participation *by* the whole population.

30 The Movement for Independent Living: Origins, Ideology, and Implications for Disability Research

Gerben DeJong

Medical Rehabilitation Institute, Tufts-New England Medical Center, Boston, Massachussets

Origins and Legislative Background

It is difficult to point to an exact time when, or a place where, the movement for independent living began. The movement has sprung from two main sources. The first source is the efforts of disabled persons to seek a more fulfilling life in an able-bodied world. The second source is the efforts of rehabilitation professionals to reach disabled persons for whom a vocational goal was, until recently, unthinkable. While the efforts of both groups often converge on specific legislation, their interests and origins are sufficiently different to warrant separate consideration.

Indigenous Origins

The disabled students program at the University of Illinois at Champaign-Urbana was among the first to facilitate community living for persons with severe physical disabilities. In 1962, four severely disabled students were transferred from a nursing home isolated from campus to a modified home closer to campus. The disabled students program has emerged as a significant self-help effort and has helped to make the University of Illinois one of the most architecturally accessible institutions of its kind.

It was not until the early 1970's that the movement gained greater visibility and momentum with the creation of the Center for Independent Living (CIL) in Berkeley, California. The Berkeley CIL incorporated itself in 1972 as a self-help group to be managed primarily by persons who were themselves disabled. The center provides a wide range of related services such as peer counseling, advocacy services, van transportation, training in independent living skills, attendant care referral, health maintenance, housing referral, wheelchair repair, and others (Brown, 1978, p. 24; Stoddard, 1978, pp. 2–3). Unlike other centers that have since emerged, the Berkeley CIL has no residential program. The Berkeley CIL serves persons with a greater variety of disabling conditions than do many other existing centers.[1]

Source: Occasional Paper No. 2. Michegan: University Centers for International Rehabilitation.

On the East Coast, the Boston Center for Independent Living (BCIL) began its activities in 1974. BCIL emphasizes transitional housing and attendant care services (Corcoran, *et al.*, 1977). Similar centers and organizations have sprung up in Houston, Columbus, Ann Arbor, and in other locations. New centers seem to emerge almost weekly. Each center offers its own unique blend of advocacy and consumer services. The various centers have given the movement for independent living both an organizational focus and a vehicle for realizing some of the movement's more important goals.

The movement's organizational efforts have not been limited to centers for independent living. Allied organizations such as the American Coalition of Citizens with Disabilities (ACCD), mentioned earlier, have been instrumental in monitoring federal legislation affecting disabled persons. The ACCD also helped to organize the coast-to-coast demonstrations that goaded the US Department of Health, Education and Welfare (HEW) to promulgate regulations implementing Section 504 of the 1973 Rehabilitation Act.

Professional Origins

Developing concurrently with the organizational initiatives of disabled persons were the efforts of rehabilitation professionals in the formulation of national legislation. [. . .]

In 1972, Congress passed H.R. 8395 amending the Vocational Rehabilitation Act to provide independent living services to those individuals 'for whom a vocational goal is not possible or feasible.' [. . .][2]

The 1973 Rehabilitation Act did contain other breakthroughs important to those in the movement for independent living. First, it mandated that those who were most severely handicapped were to receive first priority for services under the Act. Second, Title V extended new statutory rights to handicapped persons. Sections 501 and 503 mandated affirmative action programs for the employment of disabled persons within the federal government and by organizations contracting with the federal government. Section 502 created the Architectural and Transportation Compliance Board. And Section 504 banned discrimination on the basis of handicap in any program or activity receiving or benefiting from federal financial assistance. Together, these four sections comprising Title V have sometimes been referred to as the civil rights title of the Act.

Differing Views of Independent Living

The concept of independent living services raises two important issues. First, the concept of independent living rehabilitation has changed since it was originally introduced to Congress almost two decades ago. Since then, medical and rehabilitation technology has advanced significantly. Those who would have been targeted for independent living rehabilitation services 15 years ago are now routinely prepared for gainful employment by state vocational rehabilitation agencies.

Second, vocational rehabilitation professionals, as reflected in the legislation reviewed here, have a different conception of independent living than do their consumer counterparts in the movement for independent living. For many vocational rehabilitation professionals, independent living services are for those for whom a vocational goal is thought to be impossible. Independent living is seen as an alternative to the vocational goal – thus, the term 'independent living rehabilitation' as distinct from 'vocational rehabilitation.' Independent living rehabilitation refers to those medical and social services that enable a disabled person to live in the community short of being gainfully employed. From this perspective, independent living and rehabilitation are seen as competing policy goals. Throughout the history of the legislative debate on independent living, there has been the fear that independent living would dilute the specificity of the vocational outcome. Some professionals feared that independent living services would result in the same charges of nonaccountability often levied against more ill-defined social services such as those administered under Title XX of the Social Security Act.

Others in the movement for independent living, whose involvement does not originate in the vocational rehabilitation tradition, reject the conception of independent living and employment as competing policy goals. To them, such a conception is potentially sinister: it implicitly places an arbitrary upper limit to the goals a disabled person might set for him or herself. No upper limit should be set. Limits tend to be self-fulfilling. Instead, the vocational objectives should be seen as an integral part of the independent living goal, not as a competing goal.

Other Legislation

The movement for independent living has also been shaped by (or has shaped) legislation outside the vocational rehabilitation tradition. [. . .][3] [Legislation has] opened up educational opportunities for disabled children and helped to make housing, public buildings, highway facilities, and public transportation more barrier free (Parsons and Counts, 1978, p. 8).

Future Legislation

The legislative goals of the movement for independent living have centered on issues such as discrimination, architectural barriers, and specialized services. Much of the enabling legislation is in place. The legislative agenda of the movement is by no means complete. One priority for the movement is the careful monitoring of governmental agencies to assure full compliance with the legislation's stated purposes. A second priority is the advocacy and development of new legislation, particularly in the funding of independent living support services and the removal of employment disincentives within various health and welfare benefit programs.[4]

Relation to Other Social Movements

The movement for independent living has flourished at a time when several other complementary social movements have also developed. [. . .] Each has influenced the movement for independent living to one degree or another. [. . .]

Civil Rights

The movement for independent living has been similarly concerned with both civil and benefit rights. The movement's interest in civil rights is reflected in Title V of the 1973 Rehabilitation Act prohibiting various forms of discrimination, particularly in the area of employment. However, the concern for civil rights has not stopped there. Persons with severe mobility impairments are insisting that architectural and other environmental barriers in effect deprive them of their civil rights when these barriers prevent them from participating in the political life of the community. In like fashion, disabled persons have become aware that their benefit rights are prerequisites for living in a community setting. Without income assistance benefits or attendant care benefits, many disabled persons would be involuntarily confined to a long-term care facility.

The civil rights movement has not only had an effect on the securing of certain rights but also on the *manner* in which those rights have been secured. When traditional legal channels have been exhausted, disabled persons have learned to employ other techniques of social protest such as demonstrations and sit-ins.

The black movement that eventually grew out of the civil rights movement has had its own effect on the movement for independent living. According to the critique offered by the civil rights movement, racial discrimination was an American anomaly that could largely be removed through the enactment of new legal protections. The black movement saw the issue as one of racism that was central to the definition of white America and beyond the scope of simple legal remedies. The movement for independent living has come to recognize that prejudice against disability is rooted in our culture's attitudes about youth and beauty, and in the able-bodied person's fear of vulnerability to physical disability. The black movement has inspired the movement for independent living to search more deeply for the sources of attitudes and behaviors toward persons with disabilities.

Consumerism

[. . .] Basic to consumerism is a distrust of seller or service provider. It is up to the consumer to become informed about product reliability or service adequacy. Consumer sovereignty has always been the hallmark of free market economic theory. In practice, however, it is often the professional who has been sovereign.

With the rise of consumer sovereignty, professional dominance in disability policy and rehabilitation is being challenged. In vocational rehabilitation, for example, the professional counselor does not necessarily have the final word in case planning as he/she once did. Instead, the Rehabilitation Act of 1973 provides for an 'individualized written rehabilitation plan' (IWRP)[5] to be drawn up jointly by client and counselor. Outside vocational rehabilitation, the movement for independent living has spawned new advocacy centers to advise disabled persons of their legal rights and benefits. With the awareness generated by the movement for independent living, the disabled person with several years of disability experience is often better informed about governmental benefits and regulations than his/her professional counterpart in the human services system.

Self-Help

[. . .] Among disabled persons, centers for independent living have become the primary self-help unit. The various centers seek to serve both as an adjunct to the present human service system and as an alternative service provider. As an adjunct to the system, the centers at times serve as conduits for funding human services such as attendant care. As an alternative to the system, the centers may provide peer counseling and advocacy services not provided by mainline human service organizations.

The self-help movement is fueled by the same distrust of professionally dominated services mentioned in our discussion on consumerism. Self-help organizations are intended to give people the opportunity to exercise control over their own lives and the services they use. They are the knowledge-giving, awareness-providing organizations that help to confer sovereignty on the consumer.

Demedicalization/Self-Care

'Demedicalization' is a trend that is challenging the dominance of medical professionals in selected spheres of human life. The trend is supported by well-known critics such as Ivan Illich (1976) who have expressed the concern that too many social problems and life conditions are being unnecessarily 'medicalized'. [. . .]

The movement for independent living is very much a partisan in the medicalization/self-care debate. At issue for the movement for independent living is the extent to which the management of disablity should remain under the aegis of the medical care system once medical stability has been substantially obtained. Today, most public policy with respect to disability requires some type of professional medical presence, whether that be in the acute stages of disability, in the determination of eligibility for income maintenance benefits, or in long-term institutional care. The movement for independent living asserts that much of this medical presence is both unnecessary and counterproductive.

Central to the goals of the movement for independent living is the belief that the management of medically stabilized disabilities should be demedicalized. Disabled persons are insisting that the management of their disabilities is primarily a personal matter and only secondarily a medical matter. A constant medical presence in the lives of disabled persons is said to entail behaviors on the part of both medical practitioners and disabled 'patients' that induce dependency and thus are in conflict with rehabilitation and independent living goals.

The Medical Model

To understand how these behaviors arise, it is helpful to turn to the concept of the 'medical model,' a loosely used concept that often varies with the context in which it is discussed.[6] As used here, the medical model consists of the following assumptions and role expectations in the provision of medical care:

The physician is the technically competent expert.

Medical care should be administered through a chain of authority wherein the physician is the principal decision maker, i.e., accountability for the care of the patient is centered on the attending physician.

The 'patient' is expected to assume the 'sick role' that requires him/her to cooperate with the medical practitioners caring for him/her.

The main purpose of medicine is the provision of acute/restorative care.

Illness is muted primarily through the use of clinical procedures such as surgery, drug therapy, and the 'laying on of hands.'

Illness can only be diagnosed, certified, and treated by trained practitioners.

Like most models, this version of the medical model is a rather rigid construction of what is supposed to exist and happen in the provision of medical care. The model does not attempt to be exhaustive; it focuses primarily on those elements that can also help us understand what the demedicalization of disability is all about.

Before evaluating the role expectations of the medical model, it is worth noting some of the model's other features that have been unpalatable to the movement for independent living. One important reason for demedicalizing disability, the movement implicitly argues, is that many of the assumptions of the medical model do not fit or apply to the needs of disabled persons. For example, the model's emphasis on acute/restorative care is not in keeping with the needs of long-term disabled persons well beyond the acute phase.[7] Likewise, once beyond the acute phase and living independently, disabled persons are not in need of surgery, drugs, or the laying on of hands that characterizes clinical medicine. Disabled persons often develop sufficient familiarity with their disability in order to adequately monitor their medical treatment. Hence, experienced disabled persons are often not in need of the diagnostic, certification, or treatment services of medical professionals.

The Sick Role

The movement for independent living has been particularly critical of the behavioral expectations of the medical model as defined in the sick role. [. . .]

The sick role consists of two interrelated sets of exemptions and obligations:

A sick person is exempted from 'normal' social activities and responsibilities depending on the nature and severity of the illness.

A sick person is exempted from any responsibility for his/her illness. He/she is not morally accountable for his/her condition and is not expected to become better by sheer will.

These exemptions are granted conditionally. In exchange:

A sick person is obligated to define the state of being sick as aberrant and undesirable, and to do everything possible to facilitate his/her recovery.

A sick person is obligated to seek technically competent help and to cooperate with the physician in getting well.

The sick role is intended to be a temporary one. But for the long-term or permanently disabled person there is no immediate recovery in the sense of being restored to one's original physical condition. Because the disability is often an irrevocable part of his/her existence, the disabled person, as a result of the sick role, begins to accept not only his/her condition but also his/her own very personhood as 'aberrant' and 'undesirable'. Moreover, he/she begins to accept the dependency prescribed under the sick role as normative for the duration of his/her disability. Thus, the sick role removes from the disabled person the obligation to take charge of his/her own affairs.

The Impaired Role

This critique of the sick role is affirmed in the concept of the 'impaired role' articulated by Gordon (1966) and by Siegler and Osmond (1973). The impaired role is ascribed to an individual whose condition is not likely to improve and who is unable to meet the first requirement of the sick role, the duty to try to get well as soon as possible.[8] Occupants of the impaired role have abandoned the idea of recovery altogether and have come to accept their condition and dependency as permanent. In the words of Siegler and Osmond (1973, p. 56), the impaired role 'carries with it a loss of full human status:'

> . . . the impaired role does not require the exertions of cooperating with the medical treatment and trying to regain one's health, but the price of this idleness is a kind of second class citizenship.

The impaired role is not a normative one or one prescribed by the medical model, but is a role a disabled person is allowed to slip into as the passage of time weakens the assumptions of the sick role. [. . .]

The movement for independent living rejects the behavioral expectations created by both the sick role and its derivative, the impaired role, by saying that the disabled do not want to be relieved of their familial, occupational, and civic responsibilities in exchange for a child-like dependency. In fact, this 'relief' is considered tantamount to denying the disabled their right to participate in the life of the community and their right to full personhood.[9]

Deinstitutionalization/Mainstreaming/Normalization

The dependency creating features of the medical model and the impaired role are most pronounced in institutional settings. Institutions are self-contained social systems that allow house staff and various practitioners to exercise a substantial measure of social control with little outside interference. [. . .]

Severely physically disabled persons and their advocates are latecomers to the deinstitutionalization thrust. This is understandable. Unlike mentally impaired persons or ex-offenders, their disability is more difficult to conceal. Moreover, the deinstitutionalization of the severely physically impaired requires substantial environmental or architectural modifications not required by others.

The movement for independent living has adopted many of the same money-saving arguments for deinstitutionalization used by other groups. The only problem is that many of these arguments are beginning to wear thin with representatives of the taxpaying public who have not witnessed any significant decrease in human service expenditures. As latecomers to the deinstitutionalization thrust, severely physically disabled persons are less likely to benefit from the money-saving argument. Public cynicism about deinstitutionalization may prove to be yet another barrier to independent living.

Closely related to the deinstitutionalization movement are the concepts of normalization and mainstreaming. These two concepts have been discussed mainly in connection with developmentally disabled children and young adults. At one time it was thought that the interests of disabled children were best served by confining them to institutions or segregating them into special education classes. Now, the thinking is that a disabled child or young adult becomes more 'normal' when 'mainstreamed' with his/her able-bodied counterpart. However, normalization goes beyond mere deinstitution-alization. According to Dybwad (1973, p. 57), it assumes that:

normal on our earth is trouble and strife, trial and tribulation and the handicapped person has the right to be exposed to it. Normalization . . . includes the dignity of risk. . . .

Hence normalization takes deinstitutionalization one step further to include the possibility of failure – a fact which the deinstitutionalization movement has not always been prepared to accept.

The dignity of risk is what the movement for independent living is all about. Without the possibility of failure, the disabled person is said to lack true independence and the mark of one's humanity – the right to choose for good and evil. [. . .]

Notes

1 Since 1974, nineteen independent living programs have surfaced in California alone.
2 [Details about earlier legislation in America have been omitted.] (Eds)
3 [As 2 above.] (Eds)
4 It is this author's contention that the work disincentives, caused by the sudden loss of needed health and welfare benefits when a disabled person becomes gainfully employed, are among the most important determinants of independent outcomes.
5 See Sections 101(a)(9) and 102 of the Rehabilitation Act of 1973 (P.L. 93–112).
6 The term, 'medical model,' is used in at least two ways: (1) as a set of criteria to determine whether a particular form of social deviance should be defined as a 'medical problem' (Veatch, 1973), and (2) as a set of assumptions and behavioral expectations considered typical or normative in the provision of medical care. The second use of the term is the one employed here.
   The concept of the medical model is strangely absent from much of the medical sociology literature. The concept is more often discussed in the psychiatry literature (e.g., Siegler and Osmond, 1974), in part because psychiatry operates at the boundaries of medicine where it is not always clear whether a form of social deviance or mental aberration should be labeled a medical problem.
7 Working with chronically disabled patients who have little or no hope for full recovery (in the conventional sense) is considered by most medical practitioners to be less glamorous and less rewarding than the heroic life-saving and health-restoration activities involved in acute care.

8 Others (Kassebaum and Baumann, 1965; Safilios-Rothschild, 1970; Segall, 1976; Twaddle, 1969) have also acknowledged the limitations of the sick role as a theoretical construct and have suggested the need to develop alternatives to the sick role concept for the patient/person with a chronic illness or disability.

9 Safilios-Rothschild (1970: 73–81) has proposed the concept of a 'disabled role' or a 'rehabilitant role.' This role requires the individual to resume 'normal' social roles within the limits of his/her physical impairment. As Safilios-Rothschild (1970: 80–81) suggests, the rehabilitant role is an ideal social role often undermined by the rules and regulations present in the institutional environment in which rehabilitation is supposed to take place.

References

BROWN, B. M. (1978) 'Second generation: West Coast.' *American Rehabilitation*, *3*, July–August, 23–30.

CORCORAN, P. *et al.* (1977) In P. Reich, (ed.) *The BCIL Report*. Boston:Tufts-New England Medical Center, Rehabilitation Institute, July.

DYBWAD, G. (1973) 'Is Normalization a Feasible Principle of Rehabilitation?' In *Models of Service for the Multihandicapped Adult*. New York: United Cerebral Palsy of New York City, Inc.

GORDON, G. (1966) *Role Theory and Illness: A Sociological Perspective*. New Haven, Connecticut: College and University Press.

ILLICH, I. (1976) *Medical Nemesis: The Expropriation of Health*. New York: Random House.

KASSEBAUM, G. and BAUMANN, B. (1965) 'Dimensions of the sick role in chronic illness.' *Journal of Health and Social Behaviour*, *6* (Spring), 16–17.

PARSONS, M. C., and COUNTS, R. (1978) 'Historical Development of the Independent Living Movement.' Omaha, Nebraska: mimeo (May).

SAFILIOS-ROTHSCHILD, C. (1970) *The Sociology and Social Psychology of Disability and Rehabilitation*. New York: Random House.

SEGALL, A. (1976) 'The sick role concept: understanding illness behavior.' *Journal of Health and Social Behavior*, *17*, June, 162–9.

SIEGLER, M. and OSMOND, H. (1973) 'The sick role revisited.' *Hastings Center Studies* *1*(3), 41–58.

SIEGLER, M. and OSMOND, H. (1974) *Models of Madness, Models of Medicine*. New York: Collier Macmillan.

STODDARD, S. (1978) 'Independent Living: concepts and programs.' *American Rehabilitation*, *3*, July–August, 2–5.

TWADDLE, A. C. (1969) 'Health decisions and sick role variations: an exploration.' *Journal of Health and Social Behavior*, *10*, 105–15.

VEATCH, R. M. (1973) 'The medical model: its nature and problems.' *The Hastings Center Studies*, *1*(3), 59–76.

31 Screening and the Prevention of Congenital Disease

Perinatal and Neonatal Mortality. Extracts from the Second Report from the Social Services Committee

We have above average neural tube defects in the West Midlands. I would like tests to be brought in to prevent such terrible suffering to these women (A Midwife).

343. The evidence we received on screening related both to screening for fetal and maternal problems, and it became clear that the term was used to refer to two different types of antenatal screening. On the one hand, the term as used by Dr Dunn and many others, covered the whole of antenatal examinations, including such tests as blood pressure readings and urine testing for the early detection of toxaemia. On the other hand there was a tendency to reserve the term largely for screening for evidence of immunity from rhesus haemolytic disease, from rubella (German measles), and more importantly for evidence of certain congenital defects of the fetus, particularly neural tube defect and Down's syndrome and of poor fetal growth. It was explained to us that screening of this kind involved special investigations, be they specific laboratory tests, or the use of ultrasound examinations which make possible visualisation of the fetus at quite early stages of development. Two features that are common to the situations in which screening is introduced are that some preventive action can be taken and, in each case, that the tests need to be carried out at specific stages before or during pregnancy. These developments are now dictating much of the pattern that antenatal care and care before pregnancy needs to take, and this needs to be made explicit during the course of the health education of adolescents and young adults.

Before Pregnancy

344. From the evidence provided by the DHSS it would appear that the problem of congenital rubella could be abolished by providing all girls and young women with full protection. This can be done both by increasing the uptake of rubella immunisation in schoolgirls and by screening for susceptibles and immunisation before pregnancy. The latter could be carried out in family planning clinics or at parenthood classes given by GPs. Although the evidence showed that congenital rubella was numerically a small cause of perinatal and fetal death, these deaths, and the more tragic

Source: SOCIAL SERVICES COMMITTEE (Session 1979/80) *Perinatal and Neonatal Mortality, 1*. London: HMSO (extracts from chapters 18 and 19).

survivors of the disease, are potentially preventable. The Report from the Expenditure Committee on Preventive Medicine had already recommended the full implementation of this programme.

345. Prospective parents should also be fully aware of the steeply increasing risk of Down's syndrome (mongolism) with advanced maternal age, particularly after the age of forty. Apart from these risks which are common to all, the presence of a congenital or genetic defect in a close relative may indicate an increased risk, and prospective parents in this situation should seek advice about the size of this risk and the possibilities of prenatal diagnosis before undertaking a pregnancy.

346. In certain ethnic groups, such as those of Mediterranean origin, there are particular hazards of specific blood disorders, for example, thalassaemia and sickle cell disease. We understand there have recently been important developments in detecting individuals at high risk of carrying these defects and affected fetuses. Leaders of such communities should be kept abreast of modern developments, and should keep their members fully informed.

In Pregnancy

347. In pregnancy there are various tests for detecting mothers at high risk of carrying fetuses with congenital defects, and no doubt new tests for other defects will be developed in the future. These tests differ considerably from each other, as does the action which follows from them, and it will become increasingly important and difficult, to keep prospective parents fully informed. The most important of these were explained to us and are outlined below.

348. Where susceptibility to rubella before pregnancy has not been assessed it can be tested for in pregnancy, even though immunisation cannot be carried out until after delivery. Those shown to be immune can be assured that their fetus is in no danger if they are exposed to rubella. Mothers unfortunate enough to have developed the disease can be offered termination of the pregnancy.

349. Prevention of rhesus haemolytic disease has become possible since the discovery by a British team of prophylactic treatment of susceptible mothers after delivery. This disease may result where rhesus negative mothers and rhesus positive fathers conceive rhesus positive babies. In such cases the mother may, unless treated immediately after delivery become sensitised to the fetal cells, and such sensitivity will lead to a destruction of rhesus positive fetal blood cells in a future pregnancy. This disease is now preventable, but we understand that there are still gaps in the organisation which can allow susceptible mothers to slip through the system without this protection being given after delivery.

350. We recommend that health authorities make every effort to ensure that no case of fetal rubella infection, or of newly established rhesus sensitisation occurs, and that regular checks are made to ensure that preventive action is universally carried out.

351. We were informed that there are many congenital defects of which the cause is still quite unknown, and which we are therefore unable to prevent. However we were told that the diagnosis of fetal defect in pregnancy is now possible in an increasing number of conditions, most leading to very high rates of perinatal and neonatal mortality and often causing serious handicap in survivors.

Neural Tube Defects

352. The most important of such conditions in this country are those following the failure of the normal development of brain and spinal cord, leading to a spectrum of malformations with the lethal form, anencephaly, at one end and minor degrees of spina bifida at the other. A simple test on the maternal blood, if carried out between 16 and 20 weeks of pregnancy, can now select out those women at substantial risk of neural tube defects, even if they have not already been identified as being at high risk because of having had a previous affected baby. The presence of an affected fetus can then be determined with a high degree of accuracy with a combination of a biochemical test on a small quantity of fluid withdrawn from around the fetus (amniocentesis), and examination using ultrasound.

353. It was explained to us that there was considerable geographical variation in the incidence of neural tube defects in the British Isles, it being most common in Scotland, Ireland and South Wales, so that the incentive for mounting a screening programme will vary from place to place.

354. The DHSS gave evidence on the cost-benefit of these tests, and selective termination, done on a population basis. This showed that as far as tests for neural tube defects are concerned, in a high risk area such as South Wales the annual savings from avoiding the care of severely handicapped survivors exceed the annual cost in the second year and every year thereafter, and the accumulated savings exceed the accumulated costs by the end of the third year.

355. A recent report by a DHSS committee headed by Sir Douglas Black summarised the evidence and concluded that such screening programmes could be justified in many regions, but did not recommend that any extra resources be made available for this. **We recommend that these programmes for screening for neural tube defect be considered by each Regional Health Authority which must decide where in their own priorities this would come. A decision would depend**

on the level of risk, which will vary with geographic and demographic features, and their risk of perinatal death and handicap in the Region from other preventable causes which might take priority for resource allocation.

356. Prenatal diagnosis for Down's syndrome is carried out by examining fetal cells obtained by amniocentesis, but is only warranted in mothers at high risk by reason of their age, or a history of a previous affected infant, since the procedure itself carries a risk to the fetus. **We do however recommend as did the Expenditure Committee in the report already referred to that all mothers whose babies are at high risk of Down's syndrome be offered prenatal diagnosis and termination of affected pregnancies.** The level of risk (or age cut-off point) at which screening can be offered will be determined largely by the available resources locally, of which the most critical are cytogeneticists to analyse the fetal tissue. However, it is generally agreed that a maternal age of 40 or more is an indication for amniocentesis. [. . .]

359. **We recommend that each Region should, as a matter of urgency, establish whether their staffing levels and organisation of genetic services are appropriate to our current state of knowledge. They and the DHSS should also ensure the continuing education of the medical and nursing professions as well as that of the public in the problem of hereditary diseases.**

Cost-effectiveness of the Prevention of Handicap

The question of whether more money for perinatal care could result in early and measurable savings is something which you have received a lot of evidence about and it will be very important for us to study the outcome of your report (Secretary of State for Social Services).

360. Mr Nodder told us '. . . the measures being taken to reduce perinatal mortality are expected to have an effect on reducing the incidence of handicap. This seems to be generally accepted by the professional people, probably in the order of every death saved meaning one or two handicapped babies being saved [from handicap] . . . perhaps three. There is no specific statistic available . . .' This is only one example of the many statements we received regarding the relationship of perinatal death to chronic handicap, but we found it surprisingly difficult to obtain a clear picture of the number and type of handicaps one might expect to avoid with improvements in care. Nevertheless, and in spite of Dr Chalmers' trenchant criticism of the use of crude perinatal mortality statistics as a ' . . . surrogate measure of the incidence of handicap', we have been convinced that certain perinatal hazards contribute both to the risk of perinatal death and of handicapping disorders. If a specific risk could be removed altogether, both perinatal death and handicap from this cause would disappear.

361. The only detailed 'cost-benefit' data we were given relating to the prevention of handicap were exercises into the financial cost and benefit of avoiding the serious congenital defects of anencephaly and spina bifida (neural tube defect) and Down's syndrome (mongolism). These estimates were for mounting screening programmes to make possible prenatal diagnosis and the offer of selective termination of affected pregnancies. A by-product of such programmes, though not the primary aim, would certainly be the reduction of perinatal mortality due to the lethal forms of these disorders, and they are examples of measures in which mortality and long-term handicap are reduced simultaneously. The savings to be made from such prevention of long-term handicap from these causes can be shown to outweigh the costs of specific avoidance programmes. [. . .]

364. The immediate hazards that cause perinatal and neonatal death in normally formed newborn infants are usually (as in the case of infants with congenital malformations) the same as those that cause long-term handicap in survivors. Hazards in potentially normal babies are however transient and if they can be surmounted, the baby will survive to become a normal healthy child, unlike the situation with a baby born severely congenitally malformed. Prominent among transient hazards are birth-asphyxia, and problems associated with preterm birth. Witnesses agreed that the provision of proper facilities for the avoidance of intrapartum asphyxia, for swift resuscitation at birth, and for the special and intensive care of newborn infants should lead both to an increase in the number of normal children surviving and to a reduction in the proportion of survivors who are handicapped.

365. Professor Papiernik told us 'The cost of intensive perinatal care is very small if you compare that to the cost of a handicapped child which could live for 80 years now'. As we have already stated Professor Hagberg in reviewing the fall in the incidence of cerebral palsy in Sweden that paralleled the decreasing perinatal mortality rate over the past 20 years concluded 'The significant gains in surviving and non-damaged infants during the last 25 years in Sweden mainly refer (sic) to decreasing damaging factors in the perinatal period, defined as the day of delivery and the first neonatal week. Advances in obstetrics and particularly in neonatology may be credited for this'. [. . .]

367. It was clear to us, though, that if a baby was born who was at high risk for developing a derangement that could lead either to death or handicap – as in the case of a small preterm baby – innovations in care could reduce the risk of perinatal death, whilst at the same time the risk of handicap in survivors might fall, remain high, or even, on occasion, be increased. Dr Wigglesworth went on to describe this situation very clearly when he put it to us that the skills which might be keeping tiny babies alive but sometimes damaged, are also keeping bigger babies alive and intact whereas previously they too might have been damaged. ' . . . One really

wants to get the balance such that one is doing obviously more good than harm. This is why one has constantly to examine the quality control of what goes on, in both the special care baby units and the neonatal regional intensive care units.'

368. We received no evidence to suggest that at the present time more handicapped babies survived than babies in whom handicap had been prevented and a good deal to suggest the balance was favourable, but we agree about the importance of constant 'quality control'. This is the reasoning behind our recommendations in Chapter 20 [of Report] that infants at high risk of handicap be followed up and the ascertainment and registration of those with chronic handicapping disorders be improved. Only in this way will it be possible to obtain hard evidence about the quality of babies who survive perinatal hazards. [. . .]

370. One area of perinatal medicine that seemed to us likely to be very expensive was neonatal intensive care. Since no information was available from Departmental witnesses about the cost of intensive care, Mr Winterton asked, in a parliamentary question ' . . . what is the cost per week of treating a baby in the neonatal department of University College Hospital, London; and how [does] this compare with the average adult patient cost per week in the same hospital and in hospitals in the United Kingdom as a whole?' Mr Moyle, in a written answer replied 'Current approximate costs per neonatal and in-patient care are £340 and £342 respectively. The in-patient cost per week in England for 1976–77 (the latest period for which figures are available) for acute hospitals with over 100 beds was £250'. The neonatal unit at University College Hospital is a combined special and intensive care unit and is a regionally designated NICU. Similar estimates of the cost of looking after babies in two other major combined special and intensive care units are known to us. We realise that these figures are approximations, but it nevertheless appears – surprisingly – that the average cost of caring for an infant in a combined special and intensive care unit (or NICU) is no greater than the cost of caring for adult patients in the hospital service as a whole. We accept that the cost of providing prolonged intensive care will be several times greater than the average figures quoted.

371. Costs of caring for handicapped individuals are hard to estimate. The Spastics Society stated ' . . . A place in a Spastics Society home now costs £4,329 a year – 40 years at current prices will cost £173,000. Add to this 40 years of lost earnings at £5,000 a year (the actual value of lost production will be much higher), and the minimum cost of a full adult life destroyed at birth is £373,000. The cost of providing proper maternity services is infinitesimal by comparison'. Professor Butler said that the French had estimated the social security cost of a handicapped individual throughout life as ' . . . one hundred and twenty-five thousand dollars, and the United States Government figure is more like half a million'. [. . .]

378. We became convinced that there are very substantial savings to be made as a result of improved prenatal and perinatal care, even though only

a fraction can be realistically estimated. And this estimate is not straightforward, for it is likely that as a consequence of improved perinatal care the incidence of handicap will gradually fall over time – parallel with improvements in care. We could postulate that if perinatal mortality fell at a rate of one death per thousand births per year for the next 10 years, the rate of severe handicap would be likely to fall at a similar rate at 0.1 per thousand per year. Table 1 shows that if this were so the number of individuals spared severe handicap would be 69 in the first year, in the second year 145, and by the tenth year there would have been 3,529 less such handicapped individuals than if no reduction in perinatal mortality and morbidity had occurred. In reality it is probable that the rate of fall would decrease, but new advances in prevention of handicap might well be introduced during this period, so that this estimate is reasonable. For this calculation we have used the number of annual births projected over the next ten years. Table 6 shows how with an increasing number of births but no change in handicap rate the number of handicapped individuals would increase.

379. The Spastics Society's estimate of the minimum cost of a life destroyed at birth – £373,000 is without discount, and makes no allowance for the cost of medical and nursing care which is bound to be great in the case of severely handicapped individuals. If we multiplied just the current cost of a year in a Spastic Society home for ten years by the number of individuals in whom handicap had been prevented, as calculated in Table 6 the saving would be £4,329 × 3,529 × 10 = £152,770,800. This is without taking into account lost earnings or tax. If however, the handicap rate stayed unchanged, a rise in birth rate would result in a large additional financial burden for the country to bear. Plainly, at a time when the birth rate is on the increase, it becomes increasingly important to ensure that the incidence of handicap falls as fast as possible.

Table 1   The prevention of handicaps with a falling rate of 0.1 per year per 1,000 births.

Year	Projected births/year (thousands)	'Preventable' severe handicaps				
		Constant rate/1,000	Nos handicapped	Falling rate/1,000	Nos handicapped	Nos Prevented
1980	648	1.5	972	1.5	972	0
81	685	1.5	1,028	1.4	959	69
82	721	1.5	1,082	1.3	937	145
83	750	1.5	1,125	1.2	900	225
84	769	1.5	1,154	1.1	846	308
85	780	1.5	1,170	1.0	780	390
86	788	1.5	1,182	0.9	709	473
87	795	1.5	1,193	0.8	636	557
88	800	1.5	1,200	0.7	560	650
89	802	1.5	1,203	0.6	481	722
Total			11,309		7,780	3,529

380. We have thought it necessary to go into the complex question of cost-effectiveness in some detail, because of the paucity of information available. We also needed to establish in our own minds that improvements in antenatal, perinatal and neonatal care are not likely to result in a net increase in the number of severely handicapped individuals, who would become a burden on their families, on society, and on the finances of the nation. Having attempted this exercise we are firmly persuaded that improved services will bring about an overall reduction in the incidence of mental and physical handicap in the community. We think – but have no proof – that money spent improving the maternity services is likely to be quickly repaid as a result of the consequent reduction in handicap rate. We remain very concerned about the lack of information upon which firm conclusions can be based. **We recommend that the DHSS initiates further cost-benefit studies of the effect of interventions designed to reduce death and handicap of prenatal or perinatal origin. We recommend that priority for resources be given to those interventions which are most likely rapidly to lead to a reduction in the incidence of both perinatal death and handicap, rather than just death alone. [. . .]**

32 Philosophy and Model of Care

Extract from the Jay Report.

Principles

[. . .]

89. As a Committee we have identified three broad sets of principles which in combination underpin our thinking:

    (a) *Mentally handicapped people have a right to enjoy normal patterns of life within the community.*

    (b) *Mentally handicapped people have a right to be treated as individuals.*

    (c) *Mentally handicapped people will require additional help from the communities in which they live and from professional services if they are to develop to their maximum potential as individuals.*

90. These principles can in turn be interpreted more specifically to give guidance concerning key questions such as: where should mentally handicapped people live, what kind of living environment is required, and how should services be organised?

Living Like Others Within the Community

    91. (a) *Mentally handicapped children should be able to live with a family.* The first question to be asked must always be 'How can we provide support which will allow the child to continue to live with his own parents and his own brothers and sisters, in his own home, in his own community?' If this proves impossible, we must look first to a long term placement with a substitute family.

    (b) *Any mentally handicapped adult who wishes to leave his or her parental home should have the opportunity to do so.*

    (c) *Any accommodation provided for adults or children should allow the individual to live as a member of a small group.*

    (d) *If they so wish, mentally handicapped people should be able to live with their peers who are not mentally handicapped.* The corollary is that non-handicapped members of the community have a right to grow up and learn to live with their less able fellow citizens.

    (e) *Staffed accommodation should wherever possible be provided in suitably adapted houses which are physically integrated with the community.*

    (f) *These homes should be as local as possible to help the handicapped person to retain contact with his own family and community.* This means that we

Source: *Mental Handicap Nursing and Care, 1*, (The Jay Report) (1979) London: HMSO, Cmnd 7468–1. (Extracts from Chapter 30.)

need a highly dispersed system of homes. Clustering a number of
living units together, whilst it might still allow small group living,
would inevitably infringe this principle of *locality* (or localness).

(g) *Mentally handicapped people should be able to live in a mixed sex
environment.* For adults this would include the right and opportunity to get married.

(h) *Mentally handicapped people should be able to develop a daily routine like
other people.*

(i) *There should be a proper separation of home, work and recreation.*

Individuality

92. What about specific extensions of *the right to be treated as an individual?*
Here we would list again, as with our explanation of 'as normal a life style as
possible', but without intending to be exhaustive:

(a) *The right of an individual to live, learn and work in the least restrictive
environment appropriate to that particular person.*

(b) *The right to make or be involved in decisions that affect oneself.*

(c) *Acceptance that individual needs differ not only between different
handicapped individuals, but within the same individual over time.* [. . .]

(d) *The right of parents to be involved in decisions about their children.*

Service Principles

93. The two groups of principles (on a normal lifestyle and on
individuality) outlined above involve value judgements about the human
rights of handicapped people in society. If they are to make full use of these
rights and to contribute as members of society the majority of handicapped
people will need considerable help – sometimes throughout their lives. It is
important that the service system we develop should not be based on
historical accident, that it should facilitate rather than hamper the
integration of handicapped people into society, and should help the
community to accept differences in their peers rather than reinforce
prejudices. For these reasons we believe that:

(a) *Mentally handicapped people should use normal services wherever possible.*
Special provisions tend to set apart those who receive them and
may therefore increase the distance between mentally handicapped people and the rest of society.

(b) *Existing networks of community support should be strengthened by
professional services rather than supplanted by them.*

(c) *'Specialised' services or organisations for mentally handicapped people
should be provided only to the extent that they demonstrably meet or are
likely to meet additional needs that cannot be met by the general services.*

Often these specialised services will be required only intermittently or as one component in a more general service. Often the aim will be to provide 'back-up' to a more general service. Wherever possible the special services should be delivered in integrated settings. In the past such services have often been specialised only in name, they have not met defined special needs.

(d) *If we are to meet the many and diverse needs of mentally handicapped people we need maximum co-ordination of services both within and between agencies and at all levels. The concept of life plan* seems essential if co-ordination and continuity of care is to be achieved.*

(e) *Finally, if we are to establish and maintain high quality services for a group of people who cannot easily articulate and press their just claims, we need someone to intercede on behalf of mentally handicapped people in obtaining services.* [. . .]

The Components of the Model [of Care]

[. . .]
Support to Families

103. When a child is assessed as mentally handicapped it is imperative that parents get the best possible information and counselling at this sad and fearful time in their lives. Sometimes, the child's handicap will be obvious from birth, but in many children it will be possible to make such an assessment only as the child grows older and it is established that his development is slower than that of his peers. There is evidence that, as professionals, we have mishandled the 'telling' (what, when and to whom); that we have been slow to enlist the help of other parents; and that we have often communicated our own prejudice and ill-founded predictions about eventual development rather than offering skilled practical advice on how to meet the child's current developmental needs. In the early years those in the closest contact with parents will be 'generalists', such as GPs, health visitors and midwives who have been involved in the ante-natal period, and sometimes also paediatricians and others including nurses and midwives in the maternity and child health services. Attitudes in the professions and among the general public are changing; the general community services are demonstrating their ability and willingness to help mentally handicapped people. This development should be encouraged and the community staff should be offered training to prepare them to work with their new clients.

---

* A 'life plan' means that for every mentally handicapped individual the delivery of services should be mapped out in advance. At any one time the aims of the present care regime and the options which will be open in the future should be well known to all those involved.

104. It would be fruitless to list all the general services from which mentally handicapped people could benefit but the Primary Health Care Team (PHCT) of GP, Health Visitor, District Nursing Sister and Midwife will be an important resource for families. The Health Visitor should provide continual support but the services of other members of the PHCT will be needed at intervals throughout the mentally handicapped person's life. The team has close links with families and is traditionally the first source of help; families with a mentally handicapped member should find in the PHCT a quick and informed response in times of difficulty. We would like to see all members of the PHCT being given additional training in mental handicap.

105. Our model envisages that parents who decide to care for their child at home will quickly find themselves supported by a range of appropriate help, with competent helpers drawn from the whole range of services we have already remarked upon. The important issue is that the support is available, effective and consistent and that it provides a sense of hope. The elements and staff which go to make up this support will depend on what is needed and what is available. The most urgent requirement is for answers to the parents' questions, skilled and compassionate interviewers, health care help and a sense that now and in the years ahead parents will not be alone in facing the care of a handicapped child. Parents themselves speak movingly of their need for practical and emotional support in caring for their children and of their past difficulties in obtaining such help. These problems might be alleviated by the appointment of a specifically named worker. This person, who would be a member of one of the agencies already involved with the family, would be both acceptable to the family and clearly identified by all the other professionals involved. He would be responsible for helping the family to articulate their needs, personally representing them where necessary, and, in co-operation with other professionals, for marshalling the required service.

106. The existing system has often forced parents into making desperate choices: many have cared for their children at home almost entirely unsupported, others have found the burden too great and have seen no alternative but to make a complete separation from their child and request for him to be placed in an institution. But already there are encouraging signs that major changes have occurred in the pattern of admission of children to hospitals and other forms of residential care. Those children who do come into long-stay care now do so at a much later stage in life. We think that, in part, this reflects changing professional and public attitudes and beliefs about the best place of care for mentally handicapped children. More important the provision of education as a right to all children has, in our view, made a significant impact on the lives of families with a severely handicapped child, as have some of the new financial allowances.

107. Domiciliary care of the most wide ranging kind may substantially change even further the number of parents who choose or are able to keep

their child at home. The active care which we envisage will consist of the most imaginative range of service which can be devised. From the general services will come the best of child care and understanding of the issues facing the parent and child. From the specialist services, the advice and help which gives the parents a chance to take an active part in furthering their child's development. From the local community networks, the understanding and support which the professionals cannot always provide. Money advice and skilled family counselling may also be needed and there will be occasions when help will be required urgently. The services will include short-term relief of various kinds, providing the parents with a chance to go shopping or to the hairdresser and longer-term relief to allow the family to have a holiday. [. . .]

Alternative Care for Children

111. Even with support of the kind described there will be some children for whom alternative homes will have to be sought. On the whole, as we have indicated, these will be older children. At the moment, the main alternative is a mental handicap hospital. We find this quite unacceptable. Our first choice would be long-term care in a substitute home. The substitute parents or professional residential care staff will need much the same order of service as the real parents; it would be sad if substitute care or care in a children's home broke down because it was seen as some final solution which could then be left unattended.

112. The conditions for the success of such care seem to be:

(a) the availability of a good support system;
(b) opportunity for the training of substitute parents;
(c) a reasonably high financial allowance which takes into account the responsibility and work involved in caring for a severely handicaped child; and
(d) a positive commitment and enthusiasm on the part of the social services, local education authority and NHS support staff operating the programme.

113. Another alternative would be to offer children places in homes where children without handicap live. We realise that if this form of care is to be successful it will require careful attention to the behaviour and needs of the group which the child will join, and to the skills and interest of residential care staff. As with substitute family care it will require good support both from colleagues within the same discipline and from members of an interdisciplinary team. We believe that increasingly children of all degrees of handicap could be accommodated in the normal provision of residential care for children provided by voluntary and statutory agencies.

114. The needs of a small number of mentally handicapped children will, however, best be met by small, special homes which are locally based. Our

preference is for such homes to be in specially adapted private houses. We are beginning to realise the influence of architecture on the nature of the social environment and we need to investigate whether the style of the new purpose-built homes for mentally handicapped people is in fact perpetuating the old 'institutional' approach to care. The problems of size and economy of scale will have to be solved. Views on the optimum size of living accommodation for mentally handicapped people have followed a consistent trend in favour of 'smallness' in recent years. But whereas a 40 bed ward was regarded as small by comparison with a 70 bed ward 15 years ago, many people now think of 'small' as meaning a maximum of 6 children in a house. There is little or no experience of highly staffed homes for 4 to 6 residents and the nearest equivalent, the family group home for disturbed children which was popular a decade ago, is a completely different concept. Our model envisages a home with a small number of residents and an appropriate staffing ratio plus the availability of support from interdisciplinary teams.

115. The clustering of a number of units may allow small group living but the very small numbers of children whom we see as needing residential accommodation will inevitably mean that the units could not be truly local. This would make contact with families of children in long stay care more difficult, would hamper the use of the home for short-term care for children in the locality and would restrict some of the outreach work from the home.

116. The small unit which we envisage is a place where residents and staff live together as a unit, a place where meals are cooked, washing-up is done and tradesmen are seen. In such small homes, whether general or special, the child will experience as normal a life as possible and he will be cared for by staff, both men and women, trained in the care of children living separately from their parents. The home will not be seen as a substitute family, since a key feature will be that the environment is planned to nurture the child while providing him with a group of adults to whom he becomes accustomed and with whom he has consistent (but not constant) close contact and shares a warm life.

117. In this home the small group of familiar people who care for him will provide opportunities for the child to develop emotionally, by recognising what particularly pleases the child and responding to his personality; physically (by physical contact, cuddling, helping the child to play with special aids, teaching him special exercises); socially (by building up a relationship with the child, helping him to relate to other children and adults, singing to him and giving the child personal attention at mealtimes and bedtimes); and intellectually (by providing general stimulation, creating a stimulating environment and implementing well-designed learning programmes to teach colour, shape, texture and language). The

picture we have drawn is one which is needed by all children whether they are cared for in their own homes or elsewhere, but our model requires staff to change their attitudes so as to admit that severely handicapped children can be stimulated and can learn and develop, and it relies on the methods which are now available and are being used to make the special effort necessary to help the mentally and often physically handicapped child to set out on his developmental path. [. . .]

Adults

127. Our pattern of care leads at different speeds and in different ways forward into adult life. We believe that with the increasing effectiveness of foundation work in the early childhood years, as the mentally handicapped individual moves forward into young adult life the choices open to him or her can be greatly widened. Much of what happens at present is rescue work for those who have not been offered appropriate experiences much earlier in life.

128. Adult life will present a new set of challenges for the handicapped person, for his family and for society as a whole. Our model requires that the family should not continue to be regarded as the central agent in care and support until parents are old and infirm. We think that the community and the professional services must assume a far greater responsibility than at present. In particular we think that accommodation ranging from highly staffed homes to unstaffed houses and flats should be provided. This would allow the handicapped person to make a choice, jointly with his family, to move on and to establish a life independent of the parental home. This is the normal pattern within our society. [. . .]

130. We as a Committee propose that adults – no matter how handicapped – should be treated as adults, and whenever possible provided with the kinds of experiences which their non-handicapped peers enjoy. We realise that this is quite a difficult idea for many people to accept, especially when the handicapped person's developmental level is that of a child. We accept that in some cases it is highly unlikely that a handicapped individual will appreciate the social significance of the actions of those who are interacting with him. We consider it even more important however that the person should, for instance, have clothing appropriate to his age, and to be addressed in a manner appropriate to his age and the social circumstances – in other words that he should be interpreted to others as an adult. We must start to listen to those who are less handicapped talking about themselves. A report of a survey in which mentally handicapped adults living in Wandsworth[1] were encouraged to talk about their experiences, relationships and aspirations provides clear evidence that they are more like us than they are different.

Families

131. Some mentally handicapped people will choose to remain with their families or foster families even when alternative accommodation is offered; we do not envisage that support will be withdrawn from these families. On the contrary they will continue to need help to construct what Michael Bayley[2] in his study of families in Sheffield, has called 'Structures for Coping' and 'Structures for Living'. To these we would add our own 'Structure for Development'. Families and handicapped people will need the services of counsellors, advocates in obtaining welfare benefits, medical help of general or specialised kinds, advice or help with work, opportunities to be away from home during the day through day centre or other provisions, and encouragement in finding leisure activities. According to the nature of their disability mentally handicapped adults may need encouragement or support to extend their lives outside the home, but profoundly handicapped adults too need to be given the stimulus of active programmes when they are at home. Parents will also need skilled advice concerning teaching goals and methods appropriate to adults. We totally reject the pessimistic view that if handicapped people have not learned important personal and social skills as children they are unlikely to show progress as adults. This belief has no empirical foundation whatsoever. Short-term care will be of vital importance for those families who decide to continue to care for an adult relative. [. . .]

Day Care Options

132. There will also need to be a wide range of work and further education opportunities ranging from sheltered employment within open industry to special centres with carefully developed objectives and programmes of the kind described in the National Development Group pamphlet 5[3]. We are particularly anxious that those who are most severely handicapped should all be offered places and we find it totally unacceptable that someone who has been in full time education should not be offered a place in a community-based programme of this kind. We hope, however, that many more adults will be able to choose where they live and where they spend their day. For those who have grown up in some form of residential care the issues are the same, they will share with their peers who have been living at home decisions about where their adult place of residence should be and how they should live their lives.

Residential Accommodation for Adults

133. The principles stated at the beginning of this Chapter [of Report] require that mentally handicapped adults should have the opportunity to

leave their parental home. They also suggest that the accommodation we provide should be, in terms of size, design and location, as much like the accommodation we ourselves would wish to live in, but at the same time should meet a continuum of individual need ranging from maximum support and protection to minimal professional involvement in the life of an essentially independent person. In short, handicapped adults must have the opportunity to live in the least restrictive home environment which they as individuals can manage at a particular point in time. [. . .]

Independent Living

137. What kind of options do we visualise? First we expect that in the future many more people who are mentally handicapped will live in flats and houses which they themselves have rented from local councils, housing associations or private landlords, or in houses which they or their families have purchased. This they may do as single people, as married couples, or in small groups. We know from our own experience how successful this kind of truly independent living can be. In many parts of the country the opportunity to move into an unstaffed group home has allowed the handicapped person to develop the confidence and the ability to initiate a move beyond supported accommodation into truly independent living.

Group Homes

138. For others, placement in an unstaffed but supported group home will represent the maximum kind of independence that they will be able to manage. Here we want to emphasise that we have no set ideas about what constitutes a group home – it may involve two people or it may involve five. Similarly we would wish to emphasise that this is not an option which we see as appropriate only for the most able. We have been very impressed by the imagination of those staff who have been willing to give handicapped people, some of whom may have been in hospital for very many years, a chance to move into this kind of home. Often in a mixed ability group one member is able to complement another in terms of household management or personality. For a person who has lived in staffed accommodation for many years, where he or she has had to make few decisions, and interpersonal difficulties with friends have often been 'solved' by staff members, living in a group home can initially be a source of great anxiety. At the same time it can provide an opportunity for the development of skills that have remained latent for decades. Some homes may involve a lot of visiting from highly skilled staff whilst others will require infrequent visiting. The amount of support that a particular group needs may vary over time and flexibility must be built into our programme. The first solution to the problem of an individual who is not doing too well should not be to look for

an alternative placement in a staffed home. That should be the last. Making homes of this kind work will demand a lot from support staff. Institutional approaches of the kind described by King, Raynes and Tizard[4] are not confined to institutions. They can emerge in professional practice in the community. Even though an agency may hold the rent book or own the home, we see the residents having the major say in who comes in and leaves their *home*. Where there is incompatibility amongst members of the group, the provision of a number of such homes may allow groups to split up and reform spontaneously. [. . .]

Accommodation Shared with Non-Handicapped People

140. We also see the sharing of accommodation with non-handicapped people as an important element in our continuum of residential care. This could take a number of forms. We are, for instance, aware of programmes in this country and abroad where non-handicapped people contract to share a house or flat with one or two mentally handicapped people. As with the substitute family schemes we have advocated for children, it seems entirely acceptable that a financial allowance should be made available in return for friendly supervision and support. [. . .]

Staffed Accommodation

141. It is clear that many mentally handicapped adults will need considerably more help than could sensibly be offered by the kinds of accommodation we have described above. But are the choices currently available to these people acceptable? We have already indicated that they are not. In particular, we cannot support policies on the provision of residential care which attempt to distinguish, on the basis of degree of handicap and/or degree of personal and social adjustment, those mentally handicapped people who need care in community based homes, and those who need hospital care. Our OPCS survey indicates that local authority homes tend to accommodate only the more able adults. We do not wish to deny that many mentally handicapped people will need very intensive and highly skilled staff support, nor that some mentally handicapped adults will be unresponsive or difficult and that interactions with them may often be unpleasant and may bring little direct reward to the staff caring for them, but our model requires that the residential accommodation which we offer to the more severely and indeed profoundly handicapped people should conform just as closely to the principles we have described as would the accommodation for those who are less severely handicapped. In other words the accommodation should be small, should serve a local community and, wherever possible, should use suitably adapted ordinary houses. The homes we envisage should also be capable of acting as a resource to the families in the locality.

142. These staffed homes would allow for people with varying degrees of intellectual handicap. Each home would be for men and women and would be staffed by men and women. We cannot hope to help mentally handicapped people to acquire normal behaviour patterns unless we can provide examples of normal behaviour and relationships. Too often in the past we have compounded the problems of handicapped people and of those caring for them by grouping together those with similar handicaps and denying mentally handicapped people the possibility of learning from each other *and* helping each other.

143. As with the children's homes we would envisage meals being cooked in the house and residents having personal space, with individual bedrooms (except in the case of those who expressly wanted to share their sleeping accommodation with someone else). The climate of experience for adults, depending on their personal, social and physical development, would be one in which personal competence and personal identity were continually strengthened; in particular, in making decisions, as much freedom as possible would be normal. The practicalities or difficulties involved in making it possible for mentally handicapped adults to decide when to go out and when to return, who they should be friends with, how they should spend their money and what they should eat would be seen by residential care staff as exciting problems to be solved, rather than barriers to progress.

Specialised Staffed Homes

144. We found no valid reason for a distinction between 'treatment' and 'residential care' since in our thinking an active developmental programming is required by mentally handicapped people with all degrees of handicap and all kinds of problems. Nor, in practice, did we find persuasive evidence that the accommodation currently provided, which is separate from the community, is in most cases meeting the identifiable and justifiable needs of handicapped people or of the community. There were, however, members of the Committee who argued that even the well staffed local homes described in our model would not be able to meet the needs of a small minority of mentally handicapped adults and children, those who we have described elsewhere as 'the most severely handicapped'. This might include a small minority of those who are profoundly handicapped and who also have associated physical and/or sensory handicaps and those with very severe behaviour disorders whether mildly or severely intellectually handicapped.

145. The arguments, as we have already indicated earlier in this Chapter, are complex ones. The rights and needs of individual profoundly handicapped people to live in the most normal environment possible have to be finely balanced with the needs and rights of their handicapped peers to

enjoy a life that is not continually disrupted. Similar considerations also apply to the community and to residential care staff. [. . .]

147. In the end we agreed that our model would encompass the possibility of some small specialised residential accommodation. This would have to be provided on a regional or sub-regional basis – for instance a home for profoundly handicapped blind-deaf people or a home for seriously anti-social mentally handicapped people. Wherever possible these homes should share as many of the characteristics of normal living which we envisage in our staffed local homes as possible. Again we saw little merit and many disadvantages in clustering a number of specialised homes on a single site. Where separation from the community and a degree of security are needed these should, if possible, be provided through staff; the siting and design of accommodation should augment this rather than compensate for lack of staff or lack of skills.

148. We believe that those planning services at a local level should be required to justify any request for specialised accommodation and the nature of the care programmes to be offered should be clearly defined. When an individual was considered for placement in such a home the expected benefits should be clearly stated, the programme to be provided clearly described, and the progress of the individual regularly reviewed. In all cases where an individual was identified as having a special problem the first response should be to attempt to deal with that problem *in situ*. Those people transferred into specialised homes should be taken back into their own 'home' as soon as possible. Since there is so little documented empirical evidence on the need for and effectiveness of such specialised homes we urge that appropriate research programmes be undertaken. We believe as a matter of principle that the onus is on those who believe in such specialised programmes to demonstrate their value.

Elderly Mentally Handicapped People

149. In the later years of life the problem of age will be added to the problems of mental handicap. In the future, more people with a mental handicap are likely to survive to a greater age. It is hard to tell how many severely mentally handicapped people will live on to old age, but some caring Units will be required for these people. Questions of retirement, admission to suitable accommodation and the right to live at home are problems which society must face for all elderly people and the solutions should benefit mentally handicapped old people too. We hope that more and more elderly people who are mentally handicapped will have recourse to normal provisions and services and that many of these people will be so well established in their way of life that they can move smoothly into their old age.

The Residential Care Staff

150. The model presents issues which must be further developed and poses questions to which answers must be found. The first among these is this: What sort of worker in residential care could help to make the model a reality and what will be expected of such a worker? Those who gave evidence to us found it hard to express what the tasks of the residential care worker consisted of, except in very broad terms. The analysis of professional work to be done, undertaken by the Health Care Evaluation Research Team in Wessex[5] was, however, very useful to us in our deliberations. Our model envisages a growing number of mentally handicapped adults and children resident in accommodation not especially designed for them. There must clearly, therefore, be some attitudes, behaviours and skills common to all residential care staff working with all possible groups of clients. For both specialised and general skills we will be describing a cluster of attributes which should be available among staff rather than trying to designate levels of accomplishment or responsibility. There is no doubt among us that residential care staff should receive training which helps them to feel confident in their professional world and provides them with the sense of belonging to a respected group in society.

151. The first general attribute required is one which is hard to define because it has so often been hidden by professional roles, large organisational systems, inadequate expectations of individual staff or rigid specifications of the role to be filled. It is the quality of naturalness or individuality and freedom from restricted ideas of one's self in a post, role, hierarchy or profession. (The study by King, Raynes and Tizard[4] develops this idea.) Its absence has led to criticisms of training and of professionalism and the demand for what could (impertinently) be called a 'back to nature' approach. We understand some of the despair which has given rise to these criticisms but think this despair is unfortunate. We believe that the naturalness and spontaneity of the residential care worker can be left intact by training and that the additional knowledge, skills, sensibilities and intelligent thought which good training brings can help to create a caring person who would himself be nurtured by the model of residential care which we postulate. [. . .]

152. The staff will also need a belief in the capacity of all handicapped people to move forward, and a sense of their own contribution to this process. We recognise that at our present state of knowledge a few mentally handicapped individuals are unable to make significant or perceptible developments. Although their numbers are small such people still need respect from those who care for them. The residential care staff will need help from others to sustain them in their continued attempts to reach these profoundly handicapped individuals; the ability to keep trying will be the important thing. [. . .]

154. Among the other attributes of residential care staff should be the capacity to make the environment agreeable and relaxed and yet at the same time appropriate to the age of the residents. This is really not a difficult goal to aspire to; sadly we often fail to reach it in our present institutions. [. . .]

155. Engagement is a word which is often used to describe a concept of care which goes beyond merely keeping the residents warm, safe, clean and well fed. We are not merely in favour of engagement, we regard it as an essential component of our model, but we feel that there is a danger that the word is becoming a hollow term. Our model does not envisage engagement at all costs. Part of the skill of the residential care staff will be in recognising peaceful and contented inactivity and in discovering from the residents (if necessary by asking them) what activity they would prefer to be engaged in. The imposition of knitting or other well meant devices on a group of otherwise idle residents may be done with good intentions but it is no substitute for a good knowledge of the resident's likes and dislikes.

156. Above all each residential care worker must be able to learn to plan and take part in whatever developmental programmes are designed for individual residents. This will be the medium through which the resident's maximum potential is developed. [. . .]

157. To complete our model we need to focus on three important concepts. The first concerns an individual life plan for each handicapped person; the second, the need for a specialist inter-disciplinary team which can provide a back-up service to the residential care staff; the third concerns parental involvement.

An Individual Plan

158. We have stated as a basic principle that mentally handicapped people have a right to be treated as individuals. We have also recognised that meeting individual needs is not to do with finding a category or label for the individuals and linking it with a matching facility within existing services. Rather we believe that it is to do with clear identification of needs within each individual and the careful development of a programme in which general and special services are appropriately balanced and co-ordinated. Each mentally handicapped person's life should be assessed at regular intervals and key questions should be asked:

What needs to be done in this situation, at this time?

Where, how and by whom should it be done?

How is the work of several people to be co-ordinated?

How is progress to be evaluated?

Inter-Disciplinary Teams

159. It follows from our beliefs about the needs of mentally handicapped people, the way in which they vary from one person to another, and the way in which the needs of an individual will change over time, that no single profession could possibly begin to provide a total service. Instead, our model envisages a network of services within which certain professionals may, through close personal contact, come together, sometimes as a generic team, for instance as outlined in the Court Report[6], or at other times in a more highly specialised form of team, for instance a Community Mental Handicap Team.

160. If professional staff, parents and substitute parents are to live and work with mentally handicapped adults and children they need the support of inter-disciplinary professional teams. The members of these teams would come from many fields and would probably include experienced residential care staff, nurses, occupational, speech and physio-therapists, social workers, psychologists and psychiatrists, but should not be limited to these people and should be constituted according to local needs. The team members would work across administrative boundaries without status-seeking or tension. They would bring their advice, knowledge and skills to the assistance of residential and day care staff. They might be called in to observe a particular behaviour problem which the residential care staff could not cope with or to advise on a suitable programme. The aim of the teams' interventions would be to ensure that residential care staff were not left with problems which they did not understand. Members of the team might also take an active part in therapeutic endeavours. We envisage a two-way traffic whereby the residential care staff themselves would be called on as experts in certain circumstances. [. . .]

A Partnership with Parents

162. When decisions are being made about the future of a mentally handicapped person it is important that, wherever possible, both he and his family should be fully involved and in agreement with the final decision. It is not sufficient to assume that professional staff, however well trained, automatically know what is best. Mentally handicapped people should be offered expert advice on future care and treatment by professionals with specialist knowledge of the facts and the prognosis of the case; they would then be able to accept or reject this advice in the normal way. Staff will need to accept that they are advisers as much as residential care staff and that parents have a right to be involved in decision making. In the past it has often been difficult for families and staff to make contact; families have felt (with or without justification) that they were outsiders. Some have lost contact with their children, not for selfish reasons but because they could

find no place for themselves within the scheme of care. It has been suggested that families who have seemed to drop away have re-established their links when their mentally handicapped relative has been placed in a smaller, more informal setting, nearer to home. Two moving comments, made by mothers at the recent opening of a local home in which parental involvement is actively encouraged, illustrate this point: 'No one will ever take away the gift of kissing my daughter, Victoria, goodnight again' and 'It is almost like having my daughter back home again. I feel as though I nearly lost her'. [. . .]

Conclusion

164. It is from the principles and the model of care described in this Chapter that our recommendations about training, manpower and organisation have been developed. Taken together, as they must be, we believe they form the basis of a new deal for all mentally handicapped people and their families and for those who provide the care. *But to achieve our vision will require major new initiatives and commitment at both local and national level over and above that already shown over the last few years.* [. . .]

References

1 LONDON BOROUGH OF WANDSWORTH (1976) *Project 74: A Research Study in which Mentally Handicapped People Speak for Themselves.* Social Services Department Research and Planning Section.

2 BAYLEY, M. (1973) *Mental Handicap and Community Care*, London: Routledge and Kegan Paul. (Paragraph 131.)

3 NATIONAL DEVELOPMENT GROUP FOR THE MENTALLY HANDICAPPED. (1977) *Day Services for Mentally Handicapped Adults*, Pamphlet No. 5. London: HMSO. (Paragraph 132.)

4 KING, R. D., RAYNES, N. V., and TIZARD, J. (1971) *Patterns of Residential Care.* London: Routledge and Kegan Paul. (Paragraphs 138, 151.)

5 KUSHLIK, A., FELCE, D., PALMER, J., and SMITH, J. (1976) *Evidence to the Committee of Inquiry into Mental Handicap Nursing and Care from the Health Care Evaluation Research Team, Winchester.* Winchester: HCERT. (Paragraph 150.)

6 DEPARTMENT OF HEALTH AND SOCIAL SECURITY. (1976) *Fit for the Future: The Report of the Committee on Child Health Services.* Cmnd. 6684. London: HMSO. (Paragraphs 159, 311.)

33 Special Needs in Education

Extracts from a White Paper presented by the Department of Education and Science with comments on the Paper by ACE.

Integration

35. There are legitimate differences of view over where and how a child with special educational needs is best educated. The Government takes as its starting point the principle that children and young people who have such needs should be educated in association with those who do not. But this principle must always be applied so as not to frustrate the aim of giving the child or student, within the limits of what is practicable, the greatest possible opportunity to benefit from the education process. The right placement for a child with a serious disability can only be properly determined after careful assessment of his needs by competent professionals and in close consultation with his parents. For some children with special needs association, or full association, with other children is the wrong solution and to impose it would be unfair to the child, his parents, other children and the taxpayer. In such a case the arguments for full association must give way to other arguments which are more valid in that case. [. . .]

37. The Government intends that the process of planned and sensible integration of handicapped children into ordinary schools should continue. However, children with serious difficulties must not be obliged to attend ordinary schools if these cannot fully provide for their needs. In the Government's view, it will continue to be necessary to provide places in special schools and classes, and to make other special arrangements, e.g. through education at home or in hospital, for some of the most seriously handicapped children.

38. The development of the education service will need to take place within the finanical limits set by the public expenditure plans which the Government has announced. Present arrangements for handicapped persons make relatively modest calls on local authority budgets. In the Government's view, authorities will be able to give progressively fuller expression to the new approach outlined in this White Paper by the gradual redeployment of resources. The good practice already achieved by some authorities provides a substantial base on which to build. The Secretaries of State will also be ready to advise authorities about meeting proposed new responsibilities.

Source: *Special Needs in Education* (August, 1980) London: HMSO.

The Government's Proposals

39. In accordance with the approach outlined [in Section II], the Government proposes legislation which will do away with the present system of special educational treatment for children ascertained as belonging to a category of handicap. Instead it proposes in this area to base the duties and powers of LEAs and schools, and the rights and duties of parents, on the concept that certain children have special educational needs. A minority of such children will, as the Warnock Committee recommended, be the subject of a formal record, on the basis of which the LEA, in the interest of the child, will take special steps in regard to his education and keep his progress under regular formal review. But most such children will be educated without the formality of a record. It is likely that, at least initially, 'recorded' children will roughly correspond to those who at present have been ascertained as requiring special educational treatment. It will be for the LEA to decide whether a child's needs are such that he ought to be 'recorded'; and it will not be able to decide that he should, except on the basis of a multi-professional assessment carried out in accordance with rules prescribed by the Secretary of State.

Definition of Special Educational Needs

40. The Government envisages a broad definition of special educational needs, to include those needs which are attributable to a physical, sensory, or mental disability or an emotional or behavioural disorder and which call for special provision in respect of such matters as the location, content, timing, or method of education, and any other needs which are similar in their effect. Within its general duty to secure a sufficiency of schools for its area the LEA will have a duty to have regard to the need to secure adequate provision for pupils with special educational needs, instead of, as at present, for pupils who require special educational treatment because they fall into a defined category of handicap.

Integration: Statement of Principle

41. The Government proposes that a child with special educational needs who is not a 'recorded' child should normally be educated in an ordinary school; and that a 'recorded' child shall also, wherever this is reasonable and practicable, be so educated. Accordingly the proposed legislation will provide that a child with special educational needs shall be educated with children without such needs, provided that the arrangements are capable of meeting his needs, are compatible with the efficient education of the children with whom he is to be educated, and with the efficient use of public resources, and take proper account of the wishes of his parents. This provision will replace section 10 of the 1976 Education Act.

Special and Independent Schools

42. The adoption, on this basis, of the principle of integration makes it necessary to ensure that where a 'recorded' child cannot be educated at an ordinary school, alternative arrangements can be made available. The Government therefore proposes to retain the present system of maintained and non-maintained special schools whose arrangements are subject to the approval of the Secretary of State; and to augment it by a new category of independent schools which will be approved by the Secretary of State as suitable for the admission of 'recorded' children. As in the case of the special schools, approval will be conditional on the school's compliance with regulations governing its general conduct, staffing, premises and educational standards. The Secretary of State will maintain a list of all independent schools suitable for the admission of 'recorded' children. A LEA will not normally be allowed to place a 'recorded' child in an independent school which is not on this list.

43. The Government is consulting non-maintained special schools about alterations to the composition of their governing bodies to bring them into line with the requirements for the governing bodies of maintained special schools under the Education Act 1980. The Government has also considered whether independent schools approved for the education of 'recorded' children should, as the Warnock Committee recommended, be required to have governing bodies. The Government has decided that such a requirement would be neither fair nor practicable. Many independent schools are commercial enterprises and their proprietors could not reasonably be expected to surrender control to persons whom they did not themselves appoint. The Government considers that the power to approve an independent school for the admission of 'recorded' children adequately protects the public interest. But it will encourage such schools to appoint advisory committees to help them discharge their highly specialised task. [. . .]

Identification of Children with Special Educational Needs

45. The present duty of LEAs to discover children requiring special educational treatment can in practice be fully discharged only in respect of children registered at a school maintained by the LEA. The LEA is in no position to inform itself of the potential educational problems of every child in its area who is under compulsory school age or attends an independent school. Under the proposed new legislation a LEA will only be required, in relation to children between the ages of two and five who are not receiving education in a school maintained by the LEA and children attending independent schools, to follow up cases which come to its notice (e.g. through the parents or a health visitor) of any child whose special educational needs might justify his being 'recorded'; in relation to pupils of any age in a school maintained by the LEA there will be a duty either on the

school or on the LEA to identify all children with special educational needs, and not only those who should be 'recorded'. Once a child with special needs has been identified, there will be a duty on the LEA or school to meet his needs in accordance with the arrangements set out in paragraph 47 below.

46. Since it is sometimes desirable to tackle special educational needs when children are under two years of age, it is proposed to empower LEAs to 'record' such children and to arrange for their education. But this power will be exercised only with the consent of the parents.

Meeting Special Educational Needs

47. In the case of the ordinary schools which it maintains, the LEA will be required, in consultation with school governors and head teachers in the case of county and voluntary schools, to keep under review the arrangements made in these schools for meeting the special educational needs of the pupils. Each county and voluntary school, in accordance with the respective responsibilities of the governors, the head teacher and the LEA, will be under a duty to meet the special needs of its pupils having regard to the resources available to the school, including the advisory and support services provided by the LEA and by the health and personal social services. Where a school considers that it cannot meet the special needs of a pupil, it will be required to inform the LEA, who must then consider, in consultation with the school and, as appropriate, the parents, whether the child's needs are best met by arrangements under which he remains at the school or by other arrangements. In the case of nursery schools it will be for the LEA to ensure that special educational needs are met. [. . .]

Recording

54. For children whose special educational needs call for formal recording by the LEA, the Government proposes the following arrangements. As was explained in paragraph 39 above, the decision to 'record' a child will lie with the LEA. It is the Government's intention that a LEA should not 'record' a child if his special educational needs can be met by attendance at the ordinary schools maintained by the LEA without the need of systematic annual review by the LEA. The LEA will first have to decide whether there is a prima facie case for recording which is sufficiently strong to justify the multi-professional assessment which will be a prerequisite of recording. It will take this preliminary decision in the light of information which it receives about the child, e.g. from his parents or school. The parents of a child aged two or over will have the right to request a multi-professional assessment, and the LEA will have to meet that request unless it is unreasonable.

55. The exact nature of the multi-professional assessment will depend on the circumstances of each case. But the Secretary of State will prescribe broad rules which will govern the assessment. These will include the requirement that the medical, psychological and pedagogic aspects must each be covered by a qualified professional person. If the child is two or over, the parents will be required to submit him for the examinations involved in the assessment and will have the right to attend them.

56. The LEA will have to consider the assessment and also take into account any relevant reports or other information about the child. In particular it will have to consider any views expressed by the parents. If it decides that the child should be 'recorded', the record will be in a form prescribed by the Secretary of State and will have two parts. The first will be a description of the child's special educational needs stemming from the multi-professional assessment and other information received by the LEA; the second part will set out the educational arrangements which the LEA proposes to make to meet these needs; in making the proposal in the second part the LEA will have to have regard to the description of special needs in the first.

57. The Government agrees with the widely-held view that it would be wrong to require full disclosure to parents of the professional reports lying behind the record. Professional reports must remain confidential if they are to give the LEA fully and frankly the information it needs in assesing and meeting special educational needs. Parents have an absolute right to know how the LEA judges their child's educational needs in the light of the multi-professional assessment and the Government acknowledges this. It proposes that the LEA will have to give the parents an opportunity to see the record which it proposes to make in respect of their child, and will have to consider any comments they make on the record. If the parents argue that their child should not be 'recorded' and the LEA does not accept this, the parents will have the right to refer to an appeals committee, in accordance with the provisions set out below, the question of which school should provide for the child. Parents will similarly have the right to take their case to an appeals committee if the LEA decides that their child should not be 'recorded', but they wish him to be. In such cases the parents will have a right to be informed of the LEA's reasons for its decision not to 'record' the child.

Appeals

58. Once the LEA has made a record, it will have a duty to act in accordance with the second part of the record, unless it is satisfied that the parents are making adequate arrangements. The LEA will normally carry out this duty by arranging to place the child in a particular school. This may be an ordinary school, possibly in a special class or unit of the school; a special school; or an independent school approved for the admission of

'recorded' children. The placement will require the consent of the parents if the child is below compulsory school age. If the child is of compulsory school age and the parents dispute the placement, they will have the right to bring the matter before a LEA appeals committee established by the Education Act 1980. But in this class of case, since the circumstances may be very special and the decision may have substantial resource implications, the committee's findings will not be binding on the LEA but will be in the nature of a recommendation to it. This difference in the committee's function will affect its operation. For example it will have to be able to consider the child's record and to comment on its contents. But subject to this, the Government intends the provisions governing this part of the committee's work to be as close as possible to those which govern its other work. [. . .]

Review of the Record

60. In the Government's view, it is essential to keep the progress of 'recorded' children under regular and systematic review. The child's teachers should be continuously aware of how he responds to the education he receives, and this should be the foundation of a periodic formal reappraisal. The Government therefore proposes that LEAs should review each child's record annually and inform the parents if as a result it proposes a change of arrangements. [. . .]

Access to Information and Advice for Parents

61. Parents often encounter very real difficulties in gaining and under-standing information about their children's special needs and the nature of possible solutions. The Warnock Committee suggested that for 'recorded' children there should be a 'named person' at each stage of the child's life to whom the parents could look for information and advice. The Government does not consider it appropriate to prescribe such an arrangement by law but looks to local authorities to consider ways in which parents can gain access to information and advice in the most effective way possible. [. . .]

Comments on the Preceding Report by Advisory Centre for Education (ACE) 'An Insult to the Handicapped'

The Government White Paper, *Special Needs in Education*, is an insult to handicapped students and their parents, and to those who produced the detailed recommendations for a better deal for handicapped young people in the Warnock Report.

Britain already lags behind the United States and Scandinavian countries by perpetuating and tacitly encouraging segregated education for students with handicaps, and by denying parents access to all the records and reports on which decisions about handicapped students' schooling are based. (In the US, the Education of All Handicapped Children Act, 1975, states that handicapped and non-handicapped will be educated together to the maximum extent possible, and the handicapped only placed in special or separate classes 'where the nature or severity of the handicap is such that education in regular classes, even if they are provided with supplementary aids and services, cannot be achieved satisfactorily'. The Act also gives American parents the right to examine all relevant records and reports).

It is hard to see how the changes in the law which the White Paper proposes would have any beneficial effect on the educational opportunities offered to handicapped children. In certain ways the proposals, heralded as a 'parents' charter', reduce parents' rights. Local authorities and professionals are to be given further powers to decide what should happen to children with special needs, and the proposed appeals procedure is inadequate. The White Paper says that the Government's plans to reduce total public expenditure on education assume that spending on special education will not be reduced in real terms up to 1983–4, despite falling rolls. But this statement conceals the fact that many LEAs have been forced by central government cuts to reduce their spending on children with special needs.

Integration

While the White Paper recognises that more and more people believe that young people with handicaps should receive an integrated education with those who are not handicapped, it fails to make any clear statement on the need for LEAs to move away from segregated education. The lukewarm references to handicapped children being educated in ordinary schools, the emphasis on the very special provisions that must be made for 'recorded' children to be allowed into ordinary schools, and, over-riding all, the repeated and – in this context – offensive references to the lack of resources lead ACE to conclude that the White Paper does nothing to advance the cause of non-segregated education, and may even set it back.

The White Paper is an open invitation to recalcitrant LEAs which have done nothing to end unnecessary segregation, to continue to do nothing.

Recording

The proposed system of 'recording' some children with special needs, and placing them in schools selected by the LEA pays insufficient regard to the rights of handicapped students and their parents: while parents are to be given the right to appeal against an LEA's decision to 'record' a child, this will happen after the event, and they are to be compelled to submit the child for any examinations which the LEA regards as necessary.

If parents disagree with an LEA's decision to 'record' a child, or disagree with the suggested placement, they may appeal to the LEA Appeals Committee set up under the 1980 Act, but unlike appeals against ordinary school placements, the decision of the Committee will be merely a recommendation, and not binding on the LEA: this could hardly be described as a charter for parents of handicapped students.

Access to records

While the Government has agreed that parents of 'recorded' children should be given access to the two-part record, setting out the child's needs and how the LEA intends to meet them, parents and students are to be denied access to the multi-professional reports on which assessment will be based. The White Paper refers to the 'widely held view' that such reports should be confidential: it may be widely held in government and some professional circles, but it is certainly not widely held by parents. The White Paper recognises that LEAs must have access to all these reports in order to fulfil their duty to meet special educational needs. Parents have the primary legal duty to see that their children receive suitable education, and the Government must recognise parents' right to be given access to all the information on which school placement decisions are made.

The White Paper implies that parents should become more fully involved in their children's education: the Government cannot pretend to be encouraging cooperation while it allows professionals to write and circulate secret reports on the basis of which vital and often irreversible decisions about children's futures are made.

Independent schools

By allowing LEAs to use a new category of 'approved' independent schools for placement of 'recorded' children, the Government is by implication discouraging LEAs from providing adequately for children with special needs. And by rejecting the Warnock Report's recommendation that such independent schools should have to have properly constituted governing bodies, it is putting some handicapped children at risk in commercially-run institutions with little or no accountability and with inadequate inspection.

Further Reading

Special Educational Needs (Report of the Warnock Committee) (1978). London: HMSO.
ACE Summary of the Warnock Report, (ACE). Available direct from ACE.
Parents' Rights in the Education of Handicapped Children (ACE Information Sheet).

34 Improving Welfare Services for Disabled People

Eda Topliss

Bryan Gould

[. . .]

The emphasis of the *Chronically Sick and Disabled Persons Act 1970* was on the disabled person who was living in a private household. This is understandable, because the vast majority of disabled people does live in ordinary households. It also reflected the view, which was being increasingly, and somewhat uncritically, accepted in the nineteen-sixties, that institutional care was always and intrinsically less satisfactory than living at home, almost regardless of the home conditions, for every individual who did not need elaborate hospital therapy.

The Act therefore concerned itself very little with residential facilities, and concentrated instead on the provision of welfare services to disabled individuals living in their own homes. Section 1 of the Act imposed a duty on each local authority to discover how many such persons there were in the authority's area, and to inform them of the services available to them. Section 2 specified the services which local authorities were required to provide to those of their disabled and chronically ill citizens who needed them.

Local authorities were making some welfare provisions for disabled people even before the Act, but the coverage was very uneven and inequitable from one part of the country to another. The assumption of many who supported Alf Morris's Act was that some local authorities were evading their moral duty to their disabled population by refraining from exercising the powers to provide welfare services to handicapped individuals which had been conferred on them under Section 29 of the National Assistance Act 1948.

Consequently Section 2 of the Chronically Sick and Disabled Persons Act imposed a duty on all local authorities to provide a specified range of supporting services to any of their disabled citizens in need of them. The survey of impaired people in Great Britain being conducted by the Office of Population Censuses and Surveys at the time when Alf Morris was preparing his Bill, collected information on such matters as whether the impaired person had a television, a radio, a telephone, opportunities for leisure activities and holidays, and help in the house. These are the facilities which Alf Morris sought to ensure for all handicapped people who could benefit from them, and the services which Section 2 made mandatory are as follows:

Source: TOPLISS, E, and GOULD, B. (1979) *Charter for the Disabled*. Oxford: Basil Blackwell.

(1) Practical assistance for disabled people in their own homes.
(2) Assisting those who could not otherwise afford them to obtain radio and television facilities, and help to obtain library or similar recreational facilities in the disabled person's own home.
(3) Provision of similar recreational facilities outside their homes and assistance with use of educational facilities.
(4) Provision of travel facilities to facilitate participation in such recreational, educational, or other similar facilities.
(5) Assistance with home adaptations and the provision of additional facilities to secure the greater comfort, safety or convenience of the disabled person at home.
(6) Assistance in taking holidays.
(7) Provision of meals, either in the individual's home, or elsewhere.
(8) Assistance in obtaining a telephone and any necessary special equipment for its use by the disabled person.

Continuing Variability of Provision

The Act therefore introduced considerable specificity as to the type and range of services to assist disabled people which local authorities had a duty to provide. Whatever hopes there may have been in 1970 that this would eliminate the unacceptably wide differences in provision between one authority and another, must be badly shaken by the evidence of continuing inequities.

Table 1   Variations between authorities in provision of specified services (Numbers helped expressed as a rate per 1,000 of the population in the relevant area).

Service	Average all England	Highest Provider	Lowest Provider
Practical assistance *Home Help service	90.8 clients per 1,000 pop.	193.6 clients per 1,000 pop.	37.8 clients per 1,000 pop.
Private property adaptations	0.7 per 1,000 pop.	8.3 per 1,000 pop.	0.0 per 1,000 pop.
local authority	0.7	3.8	0.0
Personal Aids	4.7	17.9	1.0
Radio and TV	0.9	63.0	0.0
Telephone and attachments	2.1	18.3	0.3

* In the case of the Home Help service the figures indicate the number of clients over 65 (among whom will be many handicapped persons) as a rate per 1,000 of the population over 65 in the relevant area.

The [preceding] table, based on the Department of Health and Social Security statistics of local authority personal social services for the twelve months from April 1st 1977 to 31st March 1978, shows how great a gap still existed between the most helpful and the most niggardly local authorities in respect of each of a number of services for disabled people. Cuts in social services budgets since 1978 have ensured that the low spending authorities could not begin to close the gap, even if they had wished to do so.

Some local authorities were at the top end of provision across a whole range of services, while other local authorities were as consistently near the bottom end of provision for most services to disabled people. Unfortunately it is not possible to be sure that these differences in the general level of performance in respect of help to disabled people have persisted over time, because local authority statistics have not been kept in such a way as to permit comparison across the range of services over the years. It is only possible to look at earlier performances in respect of the Home Help service and residential care provision for elderly people, among whom are found many of the chronically sick and disabled population. As far as these two areas of provision are concerned, it appears from Table 2 below that the low

Table 2   Consistency of high or low performance by local authorities across a range of services for Disabled people

Authority	Service (expressed as a rate per 1,000 of the population in the relevant area)				
	Telephone	Aids	Adaptations L.A. Private	*Home Help	*Res. care
Low Performers:					
Buckinghamshire	1.7	2.0	0.0 0.0	68.9(61.7)	14.2(15.3)
Cambridgeshire	0.1	2.9	0.1 0.2	74.3(60.6)	13.9(16.3)
Lincolnshire	0.4	4.5	0.1 0.1	78.3(73.6)	17.2(**)
High Performers:					
Oldham	3.2	10.5	1.1 0.9	161.5(149.5)	20.8(21.9)
Camden	9.8	8.1	1.6 0.8	124.9(131.8)	32.8(24.9)
Hammersmith	4.2	6.7	1.4 1.0	92.2(92.9)	24.6(22.6)
Islington	18.3	9.8	2.4 0.7	127.4(116.0)	30.0(25.1)
Lambeth	5.6	5.7	2.2 1.5	124.5(120.3)	24.0(29.4)
Lewisham	10.9	6.9	2.7 1.7	149.2(137.9)	20.2(24.7)
Tower Hamlets	3.8	7.1	2.9 0.2	135.7(146.5)	27.2(28.1)
Wandsworth	14.5	17.9	3.4 2.0	127.4(114.4)	21.8(30.7
All England	2.1	4.7	0.7 0.7	90.8(82.5)	17.5(17.3)

* In the case of the Home Help service and residential care, the figures indicate the number of recipients over 65 (among whom will be many chronically sick and handicapped persons) as a rate per 1,000 of the population over 65 in the relevant area.
** There were no figures for residential care for the county of Lincolnshire as a whole for 1974–75.

performers among local authorities in 1977–78 were low performers in 1974–75, and had not brought the level of their services nearer to that of the better authorities in the intervening years. The rates for 1974–75 are given in brackets.

The inescapable conclusion is that, notwithstanding the obligatory and specific duties imposed on local authorities by Section 2 of the *Chronically Sick and Disabled Persons Act 1970*, great differences in provision by local authorities continued. Furthermore, it is apparent from Table 2 that even some of the high performers among local authorities were, in 1977–78, providing a Home Help service, or residential care facilities, or both, at a lower rate per 1,000 of the relevant population than was the case in 1974–75. Any increases in provision which they may have made must have been more than swallowed up by the increase in numbers of their elderly populations.

Increased Provision and Increased Need

There is a general problem of relating the increased expenditure, in real terms, made by local authorities as a whole on services for disabled people, to the increase in need which took place over the same period. Some of the increase in need was due to the growth in the numbers of elderly people, among whom many disabling conditions are to be found. In addition, however, the emphasis placed by Section 1 of the *Chronically Sick and Disabled Persons Act* on identifying the numbers of disabled people in the population meant that the total of handicapped people who were identified as potentially likely to require supporting services increased as fast as, or faster than, the provision of services. Consequently the proportion of people known to be disabled who received assistance from local authority services probably did not increase much, if at all. Neither, it seems likely, has the level of help given to each disabled recipient increased significantly since the passing of the Act.

Nonetheless, there is no doubt at all that there has been an increase in the numbers of people receiving some assistance from local authorities in respect of needs created by disability. The numbers of households with a disabled member receiving some assistance under Section 2 increased by almost 60 % between 1972 and 1978. It is true that the initial base from which the development of services has been measured was extremely small at the beginning of the nineteen-seventies, so that even quite minor increases in provision showed as large percentage improvements. [. . .]

It is also pertinent to note that during the period in which the numbers of people receiving local authority services under Section 2 had increased 60 %, the numbers of handicapped persons entered on local authority registers increased by 100 %, so that the expansion of services did not permit the maintenance of the same level of help to all people discovered to be disabled as had been available to the smaller number previously identified.

It is possible, of course, that the more heavily disabled people would have come to the notice of the local authority soonest and therefore would be among those earliest registered. Later additions to the register would then include a higher proportion of lesser disabled people who might not require services. There is some evidence that the majority of disabled individuals who receive no welfare services, do not want to make use of any of the local authority services currently available.[1] If this is the case, the 60 % increase in provision of services should mean that there has been a real reduction in unsatisfied demand among disabled people, despite the increased number of handicapped individuals now known to be living in the community. This was indeed the picture revealed in a study carried out in one local authority area, which showed that between 1971, when the Act first began to be implemented, and 1974, there had been a marked reduction in unsatisfied demand for services among both those known to be disabled in 1971, and those who became classified as handicapped at a later date.[2]

One could therefore be cautiously optimistic about the extent to which the increased provision of local authority services since 1970 represented a real increase in the welfare of a greater percentage of handicapped people. At the same time, there seemed to be no grounds for complacency, since the evidence suggested that even before the economic cuts of 1979–80, unsatisfied demand persisted for such basic assistance as the provision of rails round the WC or bath, for telephones, holidays and library facilities. Above all, there remained considerable inequity of provision according to the local authority area in which a disabled person happened to live.

Problems of Enforcing the Provisions of the Act

Quite soon after the *Chronically Sick and Disabled Persons Act* reached the Statute Book, a degree of unease began to be expressed about the way in which local authorities were implementing, or failing to implement, Section 2. Hansard records a number of questions asked on this topic in the House of Commons during the Session 1971–2. The replies to these questions by spokesmen for the Conservative government which was returned in the election held immediately after the Act was passed, were bland and evasive. Some early questioners were told that it was too soon to be able to assess the response of local authorities to the Act.[3] [. . .]

In fact statistics have been collected by the Department of Health and Social Services on local authority personal social services, and those relating to the provision of the *Chronically Sick and Disabled Persons Act* appeared for the first time for the twelve month period from April 1st 1972 until March 31st 1973. The form in which information has been collected and presented has varied from year to year, making comparisons and the detection of trends difficult, if not impossible. Some areas of provision, such as leisure opportunities and transport facilities for disabled people, are not documented at all in the statistics available, and the figures given of numbers of people assisted with holidays do not permit the identification of handicapped beneficiaries. [. . .]

Unfortunately, the Act carried no provisions for enforcement, so that even if the central government had the will to secure the full implementation of the Act, it was not clear what, if anything, could be done about recalcitrant authorities. In any case, the largely uninformative and unhelpful replies which Conservative government spokesmen gave to questions about implementation during their period of office from 1970 until 1974, throws considerable doubt on their enthusiasm for coercing niggardly authorities into greater expenditure on services for disabled people.

In 1974, however, a Labour government was returned, and Alf Morris was appointed the country's first Minister of State with special responsibility for the welfare of disabled people. [. . .]

There was a mood of renewed optimism among organisations of and for disabled people about governmental intention to ensure the full implementation of the *Chronically Sick and Disabled Persons Act*.

Quite early in the new parliamentary session, the Minister for Disabled said, in answer to a question about how policies for community care were reflecting the large increases in numbers of disabled people on local authority registers:

'It is my policy systematically to build up services . . .' but he added . . . . 'as resources permit'.[4] [. . .]

No such caveat about the availability of resources was made by the Parliamentary Commissioner for Health and Social Services, Sir Idwal Pugh, when later in the same year he investigated a complaint by the father of a disabled girl whose local authority was not providing her with services under Section 2 of the Act and of which she was in need. The Ombudsman declared that a local authority could not plead lack of money as a reason for not meeting need.

Once again, there was a small upsurge of confidence among disabled people that at last niggardly local authorities would be compelled to discharge their duties under Section 2. The later years of the decade 1970–1980 showed this confidence to be unfounded. Despite the Ombudsman's unequivocal statement, local authorities continued to fail to meet a number of requests for services under Section 2 expressed by disabled people, and there appears to be no legal remedy open to a handicapped individual thus denied, so long as the local authority concerned avoids acknowledging that he has a need for the service in question.

The Chronically Sick and Disabled Persons Act 1970 is ambiguously worded in a number of places. The haste with which the measure was drafted and the lack of expertise in such matters available to private members in framing their Bills, may account for some of the ambiguities. On the other hand, it is also clear from the records of meetings of the ad hoc group formed to assist Alf Morris in the development of the Bill that some wording was deliberately imprecise in order to avoid disputes and delays which might prove fatal to the passage of the Bill through both Houses of Parliament in the limited time available for private members' measures.

This was certainly the case in respect of the terms 'chronically sick' and 'disabled' and 'chronic sickness' and 'disability', where some members of the ad hoc group who favoured giving a precise definition to the term were persuaded that to attempt to do so would almost certainly delay the Bill and cause it to be lost. The concept of need was likewise recognised to be susceptible of differing interpretations, but no definition was attempted and the determination of need was left to local authorities. Doubtless a degree of ambiguity was necessary in order to facilitate the Bill's passage into law, but it has meant that the Statute thus established has been largely unenforceable.

In respect of Section 2, not only is there no precise definition of who is to be regarded as chronically sick or disabled, but neither is there any definition of what constitutes a need for a service. Consequently the Ombudsman's ruling that a local authority could not plead lack of resources as a reason for not meeting need, only warned local authorities to be extremely careful not to admit need on the part of any disabled person unless the authority was in a position readily to provide the necessary specified service or facility. Refusal on the part of a local authority to recognise a need expressed by a handicapped person had not, up to the end of the first decade of operation of the *Chronically Sick and Disabled Act*, been challenged in any way; nor is it easy to see the constitutional channels for making such a challenge.

It may be argued that even the eminently worthy aim of improving services to disabled people must be tempered by an understanding of practicalities, and that lack of resources simply must be a factor in any discussions as to whether or not to make a service available at all, or available to a particular individual in particular circumstances at a particular time. Two points must be made in this connection. One is that the avoidable social disadvantages suffered by disabled people as a result of social neglect of their needs over past years, has meant that they often lack the opportunity to make their views clearly heard in discussion about priorities in the allocation of resources. The second is that the evidence of considerable disparities between local authorities in the matter of help provided for disabled people, shows that the constraints on resources which affect all of them alike, have been dealt with very differently by the different authorities. This is because moral choices, attitudes, and values are involved in deciding priorities, as well as, perhaps as much as, practical exigencies.

Notes

1 See EDA TOPLISS, (1979) *Provision for the Disabled*, 2nd edition. Blackwells & Martin Robertson, for a report of a survey of disabled individuals, indicating that

while only a third received any local authority services, three quarters of those who did not receive services, did not want any.

2 WARREN, M. D., KNIGHT, ROSE, and WARREN, J. L., (1979) *Changing Capabilities and Needs of People with Handicaps*, Health Service Research Unit Report No. 39, University of Kent, Canterbury, pp. 47–50.

3 H. C. Deb. Vol. 805 Col. *282* and H. C. Deb Vol. 811 Col. *250*.

4 H. C. Deb. Vol. 882, Col. *682*.

35   The Community Can Care

Michael Bayley

Lecturer in Social Administration, University of Sheffield

A staggering amount of self-help is achieved by the families of the handicapped. The job of official services should be to fit in with that.

'I have to wash and dress her. I like a good hour. If I have my own time I am not breathless. I am getting a bit short of breath now you see.' This is not surprising because this mother was aged 91.

What is community care?

It is often considered in terms of services *in* the community rather than the care and support already given *by* the community. In fact, the community itself tends to be disregarded. A view of community care which includes human organisation and the realities of our political and administrative system, means considering society at four levels: the client and his family; the social network of the family's kin, friends and neighbours; the social worker and other local authority workers and services; and some form of residential care – which may, of course, be provided by the Area Health Authority.

A study I completed in 1973,[1] explored the first two levels: the client, his family and the social network they lived in. I considered the official services in relation to how they can help and strengthen the care by family and friends.

I first analysed the files of all the mentally handicapped people known to the Sheffield Mental Health Service. These showed that difficulties with behaviour, some major physical handicaps, gross social incompetence and the need of a lot of supervision, were strongly associated with hospital admission. I then selected a deviant group which, according to the data on file, *should* be in hospital. I visited this group to see what compensating factors had helped the families to keep the handicapped person at home. My visits were limited to families where the handicapped member was over the age of 15. In all, I made 53 successful visits. The average age was 29, though the oldest handicapped person was 71.

The disabilities of the people I visited ranged from the two most severely disabled, who could do virtually nothing at all themselves, not even hold their head up, to one of the least disabled – a woman in her middle forties, who needed some help with dressing and washing. These were her only handicaps apart from her mental retardation and her rather limited speech.

Source: *New Society*, 25 October, 1973.

Her handicaps were mild compared with the more severely disabled. But one effect that all the mentally handicapped had on their families was the way they restricted the family's freedom of action, especially the mother's. Most of the families were subject to the sort of restrictions associated with a pre-school child. However, this was not just a stage through which the family passed, but had persisted for the mentally handicapped person's lifetime.

The impact of this constant restriction on freedom of choice and movement cropped up in many interviews. One widow I saw had a daughter who was quite unable to dress or wash herself, suffered from epileptic fits, could only walk when supported and, most distressing of all, could not really speak ('I would give anything if she could speak'). The mother admitted that 'sometimes I feel these four walls are just like a prison.' In all, 24 out of the 53 mentally handicapped were not left in the house on their own for more than five minutes, 19 were not left for more than an hour and only ten were left for over an hour. Nine were not even left in a room on their own for more than five minutes.

The families, however, had to deal with a great deal more than just restrictions on their freedom of movement. Ten had their sleep disturbed severely. 'She can sit up all night and all day and all night and all day again; it's unbelievable the sleep she can do without.' Another 17 found this a lesser problem. Slightly under half the families found it a struggle getting their handicapped member up in the morning. Bathing was especially difficult with the severely disabled (29 were unable to wash themselves at all) and half had some problems with washing clothes. Incontinence, naturally, made the problem worse and 30 of 53 were at least partially incontinent. For eleven families, keeping the handicapped person occupied was difficult and in eight cases it appeared to be a severe problem – for instance the mother who said, 'He can't do anything. He looks at my clubbook. Apart from that, there's nothing he can do really. He can't use his hands enough.'

The interviews showed how the mundane business of living, the daily grind, dominated the lives of the families. A friend of the mother of a very severely disabled young man came in near the end of one interview. (The young man in question could walk, but do almost nothing else for himself and was often, and thoroughly, incontinent.) The friend summed up the position pretty accurately. 'The main problem is boredom for Richard [the mentally handicapped son] and monotony for her [his widowed mother]. You know it's never going to alter.'

It was equally evident that the families coped with the sometimes very heavy burden of caring for their mentally handicapped member by working to a routine. As one mother said, 'We have a system, and everybody falls into that system . . . We've just organised things, we've lived together until we just blend.'

Sometimes this routine was rigid and sometimes it was flexible. But all the families had created a structure within which the family could cope with the handicapped person. His care was only possible within that structure –

which was generally based on continuing care by one person. This was normally the mother though sometimes both the parents.

Two major elements made up the structure. First, there were routines which involved the help of another person or persons. I saw many examples of such routines. There was the father who took a job where he was permanently on the night shift, so that he was at home when his totally disabled son needed lifting out of bed in the morning and into bed in the evening. There were husbands and friends who carried the handicapped person upstairs; sisters who helped with bathing; and husbands, relations and friends who helped with shopping. One widow, whose daughter could do nothing whatsoever for herself, and who received highly efficient help from various members of her family and friends regularly every week, summed up her situation by saying, 'We all sort of live in a circle.'

Second, there was official help. This included incontinence pads being provided: help with bathing; day care or twice a week; and attendance at training centres.

Structural help must fit in with the daily or weekly routine. That means that it must be regular, reliable and punctual. It was in this respect that the official services often failed – for instance, in irregularity in the time at which a home nurse called to help with bathing. Much of the informal help, however, had been given absolutely regularly over a number of years – usually by people who lived close at hand.

Structural help with the daily grind of caring for the mentally handicapped person is not the only type of help that is needed. But if adequate help is not given at this level, the family is unlikely to be able to cope. The handicapped person will then be admitted to hospital or, if no bed is available, the family's standard of living and quality of life can suffer seriously and irreparably.

This same 'idea of structure' can be used in regard to wider aspects of living. The social life of most of the families I saw was severely restricted. As one father said, 'The thing is we just don't get any life, it's the same thing over and over again, year in, year out.' The restrictions that the care of a mentally handicapped person imposed on the life of the family meant that friends who did keep up relationships with the parents needed determination to do so. One mother who had had the distressing experience of her apparently normal daughter progressively losing her faculties until she could not even speak, felt they had become rather isolated. 'I think you do get a bit that way, you see we've got that we don't make the effort to go to a film. We used to visit different friends. We've dropped them all. In time I suppose people get tired of asking. No, it's difficult. But socially you do get outcast. I don't mean people get nasty or cut you off. It's yourself. You build up a kind of barrier. I think we all do it with any handicap.'

Because of this difficulty, those parents who had worked out some form of routine, or were members of some club, were more able to retain social contacts. Although this 'structure of living' overlaps with the structure for coping, it can be considered by itself. But the emphasis again is on structure.

If the family has to make gigantic efforts in order to remain in touch, the effort required will probably lead to a gradual loss of contact. It is a question of what is taken for granted and what happens as a matter of routine. It was interesting that part-time work, a matter of regular routine, gave a few mothers a great boost. Seven mothers worked part-time (in three cases as barmaids) and two full-time.

Where there was no one readily available to look after the handicapped person, the parents usually had to do a great deal of organising to go out together by themselves. Only nine did so at least once a fortnight; nine occasionally (at least once in six months); and 16 did not at all. In 19 cases there was no husband or wife with whom to go out. Two of the 19 were widowers, both of whom went out regularly by themselves. But out of the 17 widowed or single women, only four went out regularly, three occasionally and ten never. The sheer effort involved, on top of an already demanding daily routine, was often a crucial factor in limiting the parents' social activities. The parents who managed to go out usually did so as a matter of regular *routine* – that is, as part of the structure of living.

The ways in which friends and relations fitted into this structure varied a great deal. There was the old woman, whom one mother used to visit every week. 'We don't gossip or anything like that,' said the mother, 'we discuss astrology and things like that which we both enjoy.' There was the niece who came on Thursdays ('And then me and her mother have an hour at tombola'). And there was the sister of severely disabled Tom (who was prone to biting the flex of the hoover). She looked after him every Saturday, while his parents met other members of the family at a pub. There was the son and daughter-in-law who looked after the very severely disabled Judith overnight once every fortnight while her parents went out. (Judith was subject to frequent epileptic fits: 'It sounds as if you have put a red-hot poker on her.') And there was the aunt who looked after the severely disabled Jennifer for a whole fortnight, while her sister went on holiday.

This doesn't mean that the help that these families received was necessarily adequate. If one just considers the informal support from family, friends and neighbours, it seemed that out of the 53 families, 13 received poor support, eleven shaky support and 29 good support. Even if support from family and neighbours was good, this does not necessarily mean that it was enough.

There is one other important point about the informal help and support given to these handicapped people and their families. It is important that, whenever possible, help should be reciprocal. One mother gave her granddaughter dinner every day when she came home from school; another had a telephone which neighbours used; several, perhaps through what they had experienced themselves, were sympathetic listeners. Whatever it was, the fact that the families were not always on the receiving end, but had something to give, made a big difference to the family's morale. There were three important aspects of this reciprocal help. First, it let some mothers accept the help they needed. Second, it made the mothers (and fathers) feel they were needed, and that they were valued as people, apart from just looking after the mentally handicapped person. Third, it helped them to feel they were part of life, not just people condemned to social euthanasia.

I have emphasised in this article the structure within which these mentally handicapped people and their families live for 24 hours a day, seven days a week, for anything up to half a century or more. When one considers the care that they need, it is obvious that any serious planning about community care must be based on the vast amount of care that is already given. This is not to argue that statutory help is not needed. It is needed desperately. Many of these families were paying dearly, both financially and in terms of their own health, for the care they were giving. But I think it is quite wrong to consider voluntary, informal help as 'supplementing official services' (to use the words of the 1971 white paper, *Better Services for the Mentally Handicapped*). This phrase shows inadequate appreciation of the fact that the basic caring is the care and help *already* being given by countless relations and friends. It is on this that all other help should be seen to be based. This needs a different approach by the helping professions and services on the lines suggested by the Seebohm report. This saw that the caring already done, and the caring of the official services, need to be 'complementary and inextricably interwoven.'

But how could caring become 'complementary and inextricably interwoven'? This means not thinking of just multiplying services, but of supporting and strengthening the structure for coping, and the structure for living, that the families had worked out. In many cases, much could be done simply by providing more physical aids. For instance, incontinence pads were mentioned by several mothers as a great help, but it seemed unreasonable to ration them, and not all those who could have used them had heard about them. There was a whole range of physical aids such as cot beds, ramps, rails, gates, telephones, special clothing, the right type of wheelchair, which could have lightened the burden.

More personal help was given in the case of the mother who was helped with bathing her severely disabled daughter by a bathing aide. But the aide only came once a fortnight and this was the only family to receive the service. Short-term care for the handicapped person, while his parents had a break or went on holiday, was a great help – but only a third of the families had used it at least once in the previous five years. Attendance at a training centre was also much appreciated. This fitted in with the structure worked out by the families, but only 17 out of the 53 attended. It was also not available for the very severely disabled, of whom only four received day care in hospital once or twice a week.

It will be better when these services are more generally available but this will still leave the bleakness of the lives of some of the families largely unrelieved. In the homes I visited, this was not just a question of whether the parents ever went out by themselves but the extent to which variation, interest, support, friends and social meetings, were part of their daily routine. I therefore cannot finish by just listing certain specific steps which are needed. What is needed is a different approach to the details of the daily care of handicapped people. For instance, would it be possible to establish a link between a young overactive handicapped man and a group of young people in his neighbourhood, who would be prepared to kick a football around with him every day? Would it be possible to arrange for a neighbour to come in to carry a heavy handicapped man upstairs on the evening that his father went out? Would it be possible to arrange for the ambulance to arrive punctually to take a handicapped woman to day care in hospital? Would it be possible to arrange regular and reliable relief for the families?

Would it be possible to deliver all the various services so that there was the maximum possible contact with local people – for instance, having a local person as a home help? And possibly most critical of all, would it be possible to provide residential services so that existing contacts with family and friends were maintained?

Community care for the chronically handicapped has got by largely by exploiting the families of handicapped people. But for the care given by families and friends, many of these people would be in hospital. If they were, care would be provided for 24 hours a day. The care of those at home needs to be considered in the same terms.

However, there is no possibility of the statutory agencies being able to provide the supportive services needed to cover 24 hours a day for half a century. It can only be done in close cooperation with the caring that is *already* being done, plus patient, systematic and sensitive encouragement and support. In some cases, what is needed is the payment, and some training, of people who live nearby.

In administrative terms this means a closer coordination between residential and domiciliary services. But, more fundamentally, the helping professionals need to see their task as being to support the informal and generally local help already being given, rather than the other way round. The community can care. It is up to the professional helpers and helping services to help it to do so.

Postscript to the preceding article written for the Reader by Michael Bayley, January 1981

Eight Years On

The article above first appeared in 1973. (The visits were carried out in 1970.)[1] Unfortunately it requires very little alteration. As far as the mentally handicapped and their families are concerned there have been no radical changes. Of course there have been some changes, for example, adult training centre places and local authority hostels have increased in number and there are even a few group homes, but the date when the goals set down in *Better Services for the Mentally Handicapped*[2] are going to be achieved recedes ever further into the future[3]. Two changes which made a real difference to quite a number of families were the Attendance Allowance and the money which became available through the Family Fund. The latter showed an especially imaginative approach to providing help on the scale that was needed in ways that improved the 'structure of care'. The past tense is not to suggest that the Family Fund is short of imagination now but it does not have funds on the same scale.

At a broader policy level, however, there has been a major development. In 1973 informal care was hardly mentioned. It now figures large in official thinking. The Wolfenden Report (1978)[4] with its distinction between the informal, the commercial, the voluntary and the statutory systems of care played an important part in this. Shortage of money has probably played an equally important part. Mr Patrick Jenkin, the Secretary of State for the Social Services, said on 15th September 1980, 'My colleagues and I . . . have stressed the key role of the family, of friends and of neighbours. We have sought to persuade social service departments to try to build partnerships with voluntary agencies, and with informal caring networks'.[5] Official encouragement of the development of support for voluntary and informal care at a time of high and growing unemployment linked with fierce cut backs in public expenditure makes the development of community care a highly sensitive political area. Is it to be a sensitive development of carefully considered ways in which the statutory sector can give informal carers the support they need (for example the Kent Community Care Project)[6], or is it going to be a crude exploitation of the goodwill of those who care? 'Cutting home helps or meals-on-wheels may bring the desired result – people's caring instincts aroused and the vulnerable maintained in the community. But at what cost to sons, daughters, parents? How much physical strain, emotional stress and disruption of normal life?'[7]. But however difficult it may be and however politically sensitive the issue may have become, informal care remains the true primary care and professional workers have to work out how they are going to relate to it.

References

1 BAYLEY, M. J. (1973), *Mental Handicap and Community Care*, London: Routledge and Kegan Paul.

2 DEPARTMENT OF HEALTH AND SOCIAL SECURITY (1971), *Better Services for the Mentally Handicapped*. Cmnd. 4683. London: HMSO.

3 TYNE, A., and WERTHEIMER, A. (1980) *Even Better Services? A critical review of mental handicap policies in the 1970s*, Campaign for Mentally Handicapped People.

4 WOLFENDEN, SIR J. (1978), *The Future of Voluntary Organisations* (Report of the Wolfenden Committee). London: Croom Helm.

5 JENKIN, P. (1980) Press Release by Department of Health and Social Security, 15 September.

6 CHALLIS, D. and DAVIES, B. (1980) 'A new approach to community care for the elderly.' *British Journal of Social Work*, *10*(1).

7 *Involve* (1980) (Journal of the Volunteer Centre). Editorial, Summer 1980.

36 Financial Provisions for Disabled Families

Jean Simkins

Senior Research Consultant, The Economist Intelligence Unit

[. . .]
'A family that includes a disabled person becomes a disabled household'. Those are the words of Alf Morris, [then] Minister for the Disabled [*No Feet to Drag*. 1972, p. 29] – and one critical factor in such disabling is very often finance.

I was fortunate enough to take part in a United Nations expert group meeting on economic aspects of rehabilitation. I heard there a story I want to pass on to you now. (To my infinite regret, I cannot really do justice to it – you must imagine it told by an elderly gentleman of generous proportions and enormous humanity, who has a large family of his own and an immense wisdom and kindliness, and who has spent many years bringing into being a rehabilitation service in a country which is both tropical and poor.)

He was once faced with the problem of how to rehabilitate a man, paralysed from the waist down and dependent on a wheelchair, whose family lived in a remote village where the only means of livelihood for those without special skills were growing crops on the small plots of cleared land, or taking produce to the nearest market. The terrain was a mixture of jungle and rocks and both occupations were clearly inappropriate for a man in a wheelchair. After talking to the man, and the village elders, it emerged that virtually every household grew maize and every household pounded its own coarse flour to make the tortillas which are a standard part of the diet. So a small hand-mill was bought, and the man taught how to use it, and it was agreed that villagers would bring him their maize for grinding, and pay him for the service, in cash or in kind.

Later, going back to see how he was getting on, they were astonished at the success of the venture. Not only was he supporting his family – and to a better standard of living than they could ever have hoped for when he was fit – but the man had become the hub of the community: everyone came to him bringing their grain . . . and their gossip. He knew all that went on, and was respected, and his advice sought, as a man of experience. He was a happy and a busy man.

Sadly, he was so happy, and so busy, that he forgot the warnings he had been given: a neglected infection got out of control, and he died.

Now, it was never the practice of the authorities to *give* equipment to people they rehabilitated (they had found from experience that relatives

---

Source: Paper presented at the Second European Conference of Rehabilitation International, September 18–21, 1978. Sevenoaks; Naidex Conventions.

were apt to sell it in emergencies!). It remained officially 'on loan'. So, when they heard of his death they sent a man to the village to bring back the hand-mill. Chaos! The villagers were horrified. They said 'you can't take away the mill – it has changed the whole pattern of our community. Not only here, but in other villages nearby, nobody pounds their own maize any more. And now you want to take it away?'

Puzzled, the official said 'surely, now the man is dead, it is not being used?' There was great dignity and a certain scorn in the reply: 'He had a ten-year-old daughter. We gave it to her and she is now supporting the family'.

The mill was allowed to remain – a form of 'death benefit' rare in its genuine usefulness.

That story may seem to belong to a different world, but many things about it would strike a chord of recognition among disabled families in our own community: the impact on the whole family's way of life of the disablement, and then the rehabilitation, of the breadwinner; the passionate desire to be self-supporting, independent, and have a place in the community; the fact that the *right* help can achieve this at relatively little cost. It would have been very easy to spend much more in an inappropriate way and waste it all if the approach to the problem had been less sensitive.

Handicapped families would also appreciate – perhaps somewhat wistfully – the sensitivity of that official help, first, in understanding the background; in consulting with those involved and having the imagination to devise the scheme.

Notice they are quite realistic about human nature, with their insistence on loaning equipment. But notice also the flexibility of the official response to the villagers' action in giving the mill to the daughter – it is not hard to envisage a system which would have said 'you can't do *that* – it's not in the rules!'

I would like you to keep that story in mind in considering the good and the bad about cash benefits for handicapped families in the UK today. [. . .]

Let us look first at the good news. The UK system of cash benefits is intended, especially since the Chronically Sick and Disabled Persons Act, the appointment of a Minister for the Disabled, and the efforts in recent years to improve the Supplementary Benefits scheme, to assist all such families. Its provisions should theoretically, in one way or another, reach handicapped wage earners (or male heads of households who would otherwise be the breadwinners) and their dependants. Single parent householders, themselves handicapped (or their children), should also be covered, and most benefits, be they age-related or arising from industrial or services injury or sickness, carry additional allowances for dependants. Finally, Supplementary Benefit was intended to provide a safety net for any who fall through the rest of the system.

So why is it that when locating the homes of disabled families the unpainted house, the overgrown garden, are so often the first of many signs of financial struggles more difficult than those of their neighbours, even in a generally low-income area?

To begin to understand the present situation it is essential to remember that the 'system' we have is not something that was designed and constructed for the job it is doing. A patchwork of provisions has grown up, based on a mixture of principles. Central to the present system is the *insurance principle*, under which what you get is affected by what you have been able to contribute in the past. This, however, was grafted on to provision for the (often patronising) *'relief of destitution'* – which was much older. The extension of the idea of *compensation*, first introduced by War Pensions, into civilian industrial injury benefits brought yet another principle into the mix.

And the bad news? The resulting structure does not deal with disablement or handicap *as such* – only as an incidental aspect of poverty, or interruption of earnings, or of having reached the particular point on the calendar designated as 'retirement age'.

Another of the basic problems is that there is no adequate or coherent financial recognition of the unavoidable extra expenses of disablement. I am not, now, speaking of those costs which are recognised by Supplementary Benefit regulations, such as extra bed linen for incontinence, extra heating bills (though even for these the 'recognition' may be woefully inadequate for the extra cost). Extra costs for the disabled person include getting someone else to do all the things he or she can't do: the cost of paid help to do every little do-it-yourself job in the house and garden (this is 'saved' when the jobs are not done – hence the visible signs I spoke of earlier); the cost of paying others to collect, escort, or care for children; the extra expense of not being able to 'shop around' but having to pay the higher prices of the nearest shop and the specified item, in order to save the Home Help's precious time (rather than the cheapest shop and the change of intended menu open to householders shopping for themselves); and the item-by-item cost of mobility, never remotely guessed at by those who can use their own feet and public transport or who have transport of their own.

In 1976, commissioned by the Disablement Income Group, the Economist Intelligence Unit carried out a study, published earlier this year under the title *'Whose Benefit?'* We used the files of DIG as our starting point, but also drew on the experience of welfare rights workers, social services staff and researchers – any who were in touch with handicapped people – up and down the country. Our report includes many examples given to us by them. There were families whose financial problems had mushroomed over three or four years on an income never designed for long-term support, because the law says that if eligible for more than one benefit, they must be paid the higher, and a few pence difference had prevented them ever getting started on the two-year qualifying period at low-rate Supplementary Benefit and thereby reaching the substantially higher long-term rate. The only 'solution' offered had been to dub them 'problem families' and send in a battery of social workers, when the most basic need was for an adequate income.

Many people felt that, although staff on the ground may work together quite well, there is a need for a system which really dovetails the *services* of local authorities with the *cash* benefits available from central government. At present they sometimes overlap, sometimes conflict, and occasionally leave gaps across which the disabled family is helplessly passed back and forth.

Sometimes the result is top-heavy administration. One man, who only wanted four door-handles of a particular type, wrote wistfully that if he had had the money he would have bought them, but that required resources either to get to shops or to telephone suppliers, as well as to pay for the handles themselves. They were 'available' through the local authority, but at a cost in delay and administration which is out of all proportion to the items needed.

There is a whole category of people who struggle to carry on working, but unlike the man with the hand-mill, they find themselves hindered by the system . . . like the mentally handicapped 36-year-old who had lived on Supplementary Benefit (or its equivalent) since he was 16. His day centre instructor found him a job, in the belief it would help him. For fifteen weeks he managed to cope, but then he became ill. When he gave in and re-applied for his Supplementary Benefit he was given the significantly lower short term rate – as though this were some new illness – because the period of employment had exceeded thirteen weeks. True, when his case was taken up, the Supplementary Benefits Commissioner said such cases would now be 'looked at more sympathetically' but that is waiving the rules, not making them more appropriate.

The recent news that a comprehensive disability benefit is being actively considered makes it imperative to draw attention to the need to incorporate into any new scheme more realism regarding handicapped people. The present system does not acknowledge in those of working age anything between 'sickness' (which qualifies for the appropriate benefits) and 'fitness' (when benefits depend upon 'availability for work'). A person quite significantly handicapped, e.g. by cerebral palsy or the after-effects of childhood polio, may be advised to go on to sickness benefit even if seeking work, because this relieves him of the often expensive obligation to visit the employment offices regularly. But if he does this, he is technically no longer 'available for work' and experience suggests he will tend to be overlooked for job opportunities. Perhaps more serious, he is creating a false impression of his own health record for possible future employers, and the doctor's written declaration that he is sick is an expedient nonsense which some doctors may, with every justification, object to signing. Officials, doctors and the handicapped person are all obliged to put themselves in the wrong because the system does not recognise that one may be *fit* and yet still handicapped.

The same shortcoming in the system causes some people who have made great efforts to re-train as their disabilities have increased, to find they cannot take work they could manage (for example, on a part-time basis), because of the economic effect upon their families. By so doing they would not earn enough to support the family, but they would earn enough to cut off their entitlement to benefit.

Since we finished our study, attention has been focussed on the housewife's Non-contributory Invalidity Pension. Leaving aside the actual demands on the family budget for special needs derived directly from her disability, the costs to a family of a disabled mother and marriage-partner arise in the most practical ways – the fetching and carrying, cooking and cleaning, washing and mending and 'making do', escorting and chauffeuring, gardening and secretarial functions, among others, not performed. Who pays bills at offices that are never open when a worker is at home if his wife can't go out alone? Or takes things to the cleaners or repairers (other than on a Saturday, the busiest day, implying in itself an uneconomic use of the fit partner's already over-committed time)? Or makes arrangements with gas, electricity or other services if there is no telephone and the housewife cannot go? Yet the decision whether to pay this benefit depends on proof of inability to carry out 'household duties' narrowly defined and recently argued in a court of law in terms of how much sugar a woman can lift. Not, you will notice, whether she can safely walk about while carrying it, or cook with it – other than in a step-at-a-time fashion. That takes far longer than for someone who can pour things into a bowl with one hand while stirring with the other – *and* turn quickly if something boils over while she is so doing. The concept is both impractical and humiliating, but the real shock was for those who succeeded in qualifying, despite this rigmarole, and then found they were no better off, or a few pence only, precisely because they were worse off to start with. Those whose husbands are earning, whatever the salary, receive the full allowance. For those whose husbands are on state benefits – such as the many who are at present suffering unemployment – only the difference between the appropriate dependant's allowance and the new housewife's benefit is payable. Yet the act of qualifying for HNCIP proves that they have expenses not incurred by the ordinary 'dependant' who, under the rules for unemployment benefit, could actually be earning and contributing to the family's resources.

Moreover, because it is so contentious, the HNCIP has again highlighted the cost to the client involved in repeated applications, medical examinations and appeals. The complexity of the system and the futility people see in having to battle for their theoretical entitlement only to find that it is of little real benefit, lead to millions of pounds remaining unclaimed. Do not be misled, however: apart from the question whether we really want to economise by making the benefits so troublesome and so trifling, or the procedures so humiliating, that people do not take them up, as a community we do not in this way escape the cost. It may frequently be *more* in the long run, when the result is the break-up of families or greater dependence on expensive professional care services, themselves already overstretched.

Our conclusion was that the addition of more minor changes only adds to anomalies, administrative problems and the confusion of the people intended to benefit. A complete renewal is required. The only time the

British benefits system has come near to this was in 1942, with the Beveridge report. We need a new Beveridge, to produce a system of support that is purpose built to meet the real needs of handicapped people and their families with something of the sensitivity and flexibility reflected in our original story.

We also believe that the early stages of such a new scheme must include (a) a change in the rules concerning fitness and work; (b) must provide for the unavoidable extra costs of disabled living; and (c) must adapt to the changing role of women in our society.

Until we achieve this, families will continue to carry the double burden of economic disablement and the disabilities of individual members.

Further Reading

Social Insurance and Allied Services (The Beveridge Report) (1942). Cmnd 6404. London: HMSO

MORRIS, A. (1972) *No Feet to Drag – Report on the Disabled*. London: Sidgwick and Jackson.

SIMKINS, J., and TURNER, V. (1978) *Whose Benefit – the Legislative Background*. London: Economist Intelligence Unit.

37 The Politics of Self-Help and Community Care

Martin Loney

Self-help might, at first glance, appear to be one of those rare issues which attracts universal support. It accords well with Conservative philosophical principles, representing those admirable characteristics of initiative, self-reliance, and economy. Libertarians might find in self-help a welcome resistance to the steady encroachment of the state and bureaucracy into ever larger areas of social life. Socialists might turn to the cooperative tradition to vindicate a claim for the authentic radical roots of self-help movements. Professionals, constantly under pressure to meet increasing demands with steady or diminishing resources, might be expected to welcome any assistance. Critics of professional dominance, like Ivan Illich (Illich, 1977), can be expected to support the reassertion of people's ability to tackle their own problems.

An issue which attracts such wide support, from groups which do not usually find themselves in agreement, clearly invites closer examination. Self-help contains all the elements I have mentioned but their combination, and the dynamics of self-help groups create an extremely diverse spectrum of activity.

Some groups may see themselves as attempting to stand on their own two feet, whilst the nation undergoes a bit of painful, but necessary, belt-tightening. Others may combine precisely to more effectively pursue their demands for significant increases in spending on social service facilities.

Some groups unite, like Alcoholics Anonymous, to tackle what members experience as a common failing or difficulty. Others, like the Campaign for Homosexual Equality, see the problem as lying, not in the characteristics of group members but in ignorance and social prejudice in society as a whole.

Individuals who experience a common social, physical or mental disability join self-help groups for a wide-range of reasons. Contact a Family, which, for the last five years, has been setting up neighbourhood self-help groups across London for families with a handicapped child, provides a clear illustration of the diverse objectives sought by self-help groups. Contact a Family summarises its aims thus:

To give families with a handicapped child living at home contact with other families who are in the same situation and area as themselves.

To bring together these families so that they can exchange information and share experiences; give each other mutual support, understanding and practical help.

Source: Previously unpublished Paper, written for this Reader.

To enable these families to meet as near as possible to their home; to have frequent contact and somewhere central to meet and share activities.

To give parents, through being part of a local group, the opportunity to press for better services and say collectively what their group needs are.

To encourage families to organise services that they need locally, e.g. holiday play-schemes, babysitting and transport schemes etc.

To enable families with handicapped children to benefit as a whole, not just the handicapped child but also the parents and brothers and sisters.

To give these handicapped children and their families the opportunity to take more active part in their local community.

Self-help is as old as humanity but its formalised expression in group activity, directed to health and welfare objectives, is a more contemporary phenomenon. Robinson and Henry (1977, p. 11) summarise some of the reasons:

Disillusionment with the established helping services, anti-professionalism, changing ideas about what medicine is or can do, a decline in the traditional systems of social support and rejection of an over-individualistic and pragmatic world are some of the reasons given for the emergence of self-help.

The last decade has seen a major increase in the number of self-help groups and also in the attention devoted to self-help by politicians and researchers.

Stewart and Stewart (1979) trace the development of the popularity of self-help, in the UK, to the American influence. They argue that it is a relatively recent phenomenon but one which has grown rapidly, with the formation in Britain of three national co-ordinating bodies for self-help groups in 1977 – the Mutual Aid Centre, the Self-Help Clearing House, and the Association for Self-Help Community Groups. The authors argue that in the context of scarce resources there are considerable dangers in the self-help phenomenon.

The political implications of the 'self-help phenomenon' arise from the way in which it is open to interpretation as a policy development which could threaten those elements of universalism which currently exist, however inadequately, in the statutory personal social services. The reality of this threat is brought home by the ease with which the concept of self-help fits into party political debate, and the unusual and growing interest in the subject which is to be seen throughout the political spectrum.

They draw attention to the Central Policy Review Staff's *A Joint Framework for Social Policies* which called for the exploration of:

The possibly declining capacity and willingness of the family and local community to care for their own social casualties, the implications of this for institutional care, and the scope for *reversing the trend*.

Hadley and Hatch (1977), in contrast, see self-help as a positive antidote to the bureaucratisation and insensitivity of state welfare provision which, they argue, frequently denies the consumer any real choice:

The current system stresses the dependence and passivity of the user or client. It obstructs the development of alternative forms of social service in the voluntary sector by allocating relatively tiny resources to it. And it reduces the opportunity of the citizen both to give service, and to exercise choice when he is seeking service.

Hadley and Hatch see a particular role for self help:

Perhaps the major growth point is in organized mutual aid: witness, for instance, the spread during the past decade of organizations for handicapped people like stroke victims and the hard of hearing, whose members consist predominantly of the handicapped themselves and their relatives. As well as representing the consumer in pursuit of better statutory provision, such organisations provide, in the face of deprivation and often of stigma, support of a special quality obtainable from no other source . . . One of the more valuable functions of mutual aid groups is to reinforce the caring capacity of these informal networks, spreading the load and giving psychological support.

Self-help groups may provide tangible services to members, which supplement wider welfare services or which fill gaps in existing service provision. They may provide members with information about available provision and entitlement and offer support to members who experience difficulty in obtaining various welfare benefits. Perhaps the most important characteristic of self-help groups is the assurance of a sympathetic reception for members difficulties. Group members understand the experience of a particular social, physical or mental handicap as only those who share it can. This provides important self-affirmation for members and combats the stigma attached to many handicaps. Social attitudes play a crucial role in the experience of handicapped people and may in fact constitute the major difficulty. An article in 'Honey' magazine, *Big Problems for Little People* drew attention to the importance of social prejudice for those of restricted growth.

The physical limitations of restricted growth are relatively easy to overcome – or at least learn to live with. Clothes can be made to measure and household appliances and even cars, can be specially adapted to suit the little person's need. Telephone kiosks, door handles and shaver points can, of course, present problems, but Mr. Pocock carries a neat briefcase which opens into two steps for just such eventualities.

Robinson, who quotes the article, argues: 'Clearly what turns technical abnormalities into major problems is the way they are interpreted by the people themselves or by others'. (Robinson, 1978). The problems of living with a handicap are not restricted to the handicapped themselves but also affect their friends and relatives. Self-help can again play an important role in enabling group members to respond to the problems they encounter with more confidence and understanding. Wordsworth (1979, p. 23) describes the work of the Honeylands Family Support Unit, which worked with a group of mothers of children suffering from Downs Syndrome:

The group not only devised practical schemes of mutual support but played an important part in reassuring group members about the progress of their children and in undermining irrational feelings of guilt. It was reassuring for the mothers in the group to find that the experiences of their child were not unique and that the difficulties experienced in early development were shared by the children of other group members.

Wordsworth stresses the supportive role the group was able to play in helping the mothers come to terms with some of the insensitive social reactions to their situation:

> In our groups one afternoon we were able to live through the experience of one of the mothers who took her child to a doctor's clinic, where she sat in a room full of bright chubby babies each with their proud mother comparing notes. What do you say when they come to yours and there is a silence followed by 'never mind dear, better luck next time' or 'well, she's quite sweet really!' What do you do, run out in tears, shout and scream at them? No, you sit politely with a smile on your face though your insides are falling apart and wait for the time when you can share this experience with people who know what it feels like and can offer the comfort and support to enable you to recharge the emotional battery.

The role which self-help groups play in improving the self-confidence and self-esteem of their members is generally uncontentious but the ostensible purpose of many groups is concerned with service provision. This may be directed towards the running of services by the group itself, towards securing improved provision by the statutory sectors, or both. The objective is frequently to provide compensatory support to enable the handicapped individual to function more autonomously in the community. Groups of relatives of the handicapped may be concerned both with the quality of existing services and with the burden which is placed on those providing care in the family. Wheatley, for example, has drawn attention to the stress experienced by the relatives of those who care for mentally infirm old people at home. Some 75 % of the mentally infirm elderly are cared for by their own families generally with inadequate outside support. (Wheatley, 1980).

In principle the goal of enabling the handicapped individual to function more autonomously enjoys virtually universal public support. Institutional care is expensive and, over time, may decrease the ability of those in care to function independently. It invites attack from progressives who support the 'normalisation' of conditions for those who experience a handicap and from politicians concerned at spiralling costs. Residential care is labour intensive. Labour intensive activities experience relative increases in costs compared to other sectors of the economy, which may gain greater output per employee through investment in new technology. Demographic changes, notably a significant rise in the proportion of the frail elderly, caused by a general increase in longevity, create greater demand for residential care. The response of politicians has been to seek less expensive remedies and to advocate a return to community care. Since there is no suggestion that we return to the 'idyllic' villages of feudal society, which this imagery frequently seems to conjure up we must assume that what is being proposed are policy measures which relate to more modern communities.

David Ennals, Labour Secretary of State for Social Services said in 1976:

The thought that the responsibility for an elderly person is not their's – that 'mum' is not their's but is the Social Service Department's – that's not right . . . People must themselves as individuals and members of the community try to play a bigger part in it themselves. We need more self-help.

(Stewart, 1978)

His Conservative successor told that Age Concern Conference 'Ageing in the '80s':

We must put the responsibility for day-to-day help back where it firmly belongs, into the communities in which elderly people live.

(*Community Care*, 1980, p. 6)

Community care strategies are not however free of financial implications and it is arguable that it has been the unwillingness of government to accept these that has limited the effectiveness of community based approaches. Finch and Groves (1980, p. 491) have argued that there is little evidence that the viable neighbourly communities which would be required to provide an effective informal welfare service, exist. In practice a policy of community care may simply mean that women, in the family, are required to provide the care:

An examination of the reality of community care, in a situation where there is minimal input of statutory resources, reveals that the provision of primary caring falls not upon 'the community' but upon identifiable groups and individuals, in a way which is not necessarily equitable. Indeed, this can be best expressed in terms of a double equation – that in practice community care equals care by the family, and in practice care by the family equals care by women.

Finch and Groves (*ibid*) note that the provision of domiciliary services, which would make the home-based care of various groups of the frail and handicapped more realistic, remains low:

In 1976, the current provision of domiciliary services was commonly at about half the level recommended by the guidelines of the Department of Health and Social Security (DHSS) itself.

There is ample evidence that governments, at both local and national level have failed to put adequate resources into community care, in spite of the proclamation of policies to extend this area of provision. For the last twenty years successive governments have been committed to a policy of community treatment, wherever possible, for the mentally ill or handicapped, yet many thousands are still confined to institutions, not because they need to be there but because local authorities have not provided sufficient services outside the hospitals. Handicapped children are still being admitted to hospital because of the absence of suitable community facilities (White, 1980). A 1980 survey by the Association of Directors of Social Services showed a further restriction on community resources in this area.

The 1970 Chronically Sick and Disabled Persons Act placed a responsibility on local authorities to provide specific assistance to the disabled living in the community, to enable them to live fuller lives. Ten years after the passage of the Act many councils still make little provision and the Association of County Councils was, in 1980, pressing to make the obligation to provide help permissive, rather than mandatory. Given the Government's failure to enforce the provisions of this Act, and the reluctance of many local authorities to implement the Act there is ample reason to express considerable scepticism about future community care policies. Community care slogans may well serve to legitimise an effective reduction in public support for the handicapped.

One of the objectives of self-help groups is to increase the autonomy of the handicapped and mobility may be a key factor in this. Successive governments have fought to limit the amount of, and entitlement to, mobility allowances. For many years attempts to phase out invalidity tricycles and replace them with safer, four wheeled vehicles were resisted. Simultaneously the government attempted to restrict entitlement to a mobility allowance to a narrow group of the disabled. Mobility needs are clearly not affected by ability to drive but this was retained as a crucial criterion until 1976. Before that date those who could have used the allowance to improve mobility, perhaps by having a relative or a friend drive, were denied assistance. Susy Large has documented the complex interests involved in the mobility issue and the miserly attitude of the governments and civil servants involved. (Large, 1977).

A more recent study has shown that the DHSS has attempted to restrict pension rights to disabled married women by applying a household duties test in addition to the simple test of incapacity to work. Again both Labour and Conservative Governments have been complicit. (See Disability Alliance, 1980.)

These examples of austere and inflexible national policies can be duplicated at a local level. In Cardiff a group of undergraduates took five severely mentally disabled teenagers from Ely Hospital to share a large house with them and to live in the community. The intention was to provide a relatively normal environment and to increase the capacity of the handicapped patients to live on their own. Instead of the dependency which is fostered by institutional care the students intended to steadily increase the competence of the patients, whether in learning to run a house or in improving verbal and social skills. The project was a dramatic success but in late 1980, six years after it opened, it faced imminent closure because of a shortage of funds. (Drinkwater, 1980) The cost of a place on the scheme was less than half the cost of a place in hospital but, whereas money was committed to the latter, the demands of the Cardiff project required, at least in the short term, additional expenditure.

What these examples suggest is that self-help groups, who demand the resources necessary to enable members to live fuller and more independent lives, may not necessarily receive the warm embrace from politicians that their statements on public platforms would lead us to expect. Adrian Webb (1980) has argued that we face a growing problem:

from the tendency of an inadequately financed policy of community care to transfer the burden of care to the families, neighbours and friends of the people in need of care – or to volunteers.

An American study concluded:

> The alternative to the institution has been to be herded into newly emerging 'deviant ghettos' sewers of human misery and what is conventionally defined as social pathology, within which (largely hidden from outside inspection or even notice) society's refuse may be repressively tolerated. Many become lost in the interstices of social life, and turn into drifting inhabitants of those traditional resorts of the down and out, salvation army hostels, settlement houses and so on. Others are grist for new, privately-run profit-oriented mills for the disposal of the unwanted – old age homes, half-way houses and the like.
>
> (Scull, 1977, p. 153)

From the vantage point of a local group the link between self help and community care policies is immediately apparent. The withdrawal of residential or other state welfare services has immediate implications for the scale of provision that the group may be expected to make and it may increasingly involve groups in direct conflict with the public sector over declining resources.

Many self-help groups would welcome a move to shift resources into the voluntary sector and particularly to place greater control in the hands of service users. Provision made by large bureaucracies tends to be slow, impersonal and insensitive to the idiosyncracies of individual service users. It also increases the degree of professional control in determining and labelling client group behaviour. Those who experience the disability may have a unique perspective. Robinson and Henry (1977, pp. 13 and 14) cite the views of the founder of SHARE:

> Well (I'd) been drawing a war pension since 1940 and I'd experienced all the business of being in hospital for 2½ years rehabilitation, going from social workers, departments of employment, assessment and all that business and also the attitudes of people, public, doctors and others. Quite frankly, for me, there was something lacking. I felt that the thing lacking was that the whole problem of the difficulties of disabled people was looked at from, what I might say, the medical-technical point of view as to how the services were to be applied to the people or the person. Few people had a look at the person and said; 'What potential might this person have?' 'How can we assist it to develop?' 'To what extent can they be self-dependent?'

Self-dependence, self-help and, where possible community based approaches are worth while goals but it is important that the intentions of their advocates are made clear. There is a fundamental difference between humanistic concerns to enable the handicapped to live full and relatively autonomous lives and economistic concerns which are primarily focussed on cost-cutting. Policy measures which seek to meet the real needs of the handicapped and their families, in the community, would not be cheaper. They would permit resources to be used more efficiently and in a way which maximised the opportunities open to the handicapped.

Policies which actively seek the social integration of the handicapped must necessarily recognise the vast amount of unmet need which currently exists. This is reflected in the low take-up of benefits, the continued failure of local authorities to identify the disabled and to provide services, and the inadequacy of services offered. Westland (1980, p. 86), a former Director of Social Services has noted that, against an estimated 3 million handicapped people:

We know only one million of these in our local authority records; and we know that they are often not receiving all the services they require. So even if the services continue at their present level, they are in many ways inadequate and are not yet reaching the majority of those who would be eligible to receive them.

Marion Johnson, whose son had muscular dystrophy, offers a consumer perspective on what this means, and attacks the failure of the medical and social work professions to provide adequate help (Johnson, 1980):

Having handicapped children turned me from a timid shy person into an aggressive tiger. All my life I seem to be fighting. Other handicapped parents tell me the same story. Do we have to fight for everything?

When I started the Hugh Johnson Club the parents were adamant that no social workers should be asked to help.

Not all self-help groups take a militant approach to campaigning for improved services or a highly critical stance towards conventional service providers. Nonetheless the tensions in self-help are real. The attractiveness of groups of handicapped people meeting together, across the country, to provide their own services are obvious. No doubt the poor could be asked to do the same. The concern for economy would be met but let us not pretend that this is synonymous with social justice.

In the context of a maldistribution of national resources and a continual attempt to restrict assistance to the handicapped – whether by inadequate services, limited entitlement, deterrents to take up or refusal to recognise need – self help strategies must attempt to meet the immediate needs of group members and to tackle the long-term tasks of changing social and professional attitudes and increasing welfare provision.

References

DISABILITY ALLIANCE (1980) *After Working All These Years*, London.

DRINKWATER, C. (1980) 'Life on the outside with mental handicap.' *New Society*, 23 October.

FINCH, J., and GROVES, G. (1980) 'Community care and the family: a case for equal opportunities?' *Journal of Social Policy*, October, 9 (4), 494.

HADLEY, R., and HATCH, S. (1977) 'Why our social service volunteers deserve more official backing.' *The Times*, 23 November.

ILLICH, I., *et al.* (1977) *Disabling Professions*, London: Marion Boyars.

JENKIN, P. (1980) Reported in *Community Care*, 14 February.

JOHNSON, M. (1980) 'Personally speaking.' *Community Care*, 20 November, p. 12.

LARGE, S. (1977) 'Mobility for the Physically Disabled.' In Jones, K. (ed.) *The Yearbook of Social Policy in Britain, 1976*. London: Routledge and Kegan Paul.

ROBINSON, D., and HENRY, S. (1977) *Self-Help and Health, Mutual Aid for Modern Problems*, p. 11. London; Martin Robertson.

ROBINSON, D. (1978) 'Self-help groups.' *British Journal of Hospital Medicine*, September.

SCULL, A. (1977) *Decarceration, Community Treatment and the Deviant: A Radical View*, p. 153. New Jersey: Prentice-Hall.

STEWART, G. (1978) 'The politics of community care.' *Community Care*, 23 August.

STEWART, G., and STEWART, J. (1979) 'The self-help phenomenon.' *Social Work Today, 10* (47).

WEBB, A. (1980) 'The Personal Social Services.' In N. Bosanquest and P. Townsend, (eds) *Labour and Equality*. London: Heinemann.

WESTLAND, P. (1980) 'Protecting the disabled.' *Municipal Review*, July.

WHEATLEY, V. (1980) 'Relative stress.' *Community Care*, 28 August.

WHITE, T. (1980) 'Matters beyond our control.' *Community Care*, 18 September.

WORDSWORTH, E. (1979)'Helping parents help each other.' *Community Care*, 5 April.

Further Reading

CHISHOLM, J., and GILLIE, O. (eds) (1975) *The Sunday Times Self-Help Directory* London: Times Newspapers.

'Grapevine', The BBC TV series, provide a number of relevant, free information sheets. For details send a large SAE to: 'Grapevine,' BBC TV, London, W12 8QT.

THE PATIENTS ASSOCIATION. (1978) *Self-Help and the Patient: A Directory of Organisations Concerned with Particular Diseases and Handicaps*, London.

ROBINSON, D., and ROBINSON, Y. (1980) *From Self Help to Health*. London: Concord.

38   Volunteer Teaching: Kith and Kids

*Ann Jones**

The needs of handicapped children cannot be fully met under the present educational system. But 'Kith and Kids', a revolutionary group of London parents, has shown just what can be achieved through imaginative two to one teaching with volunteers. Ann Jones, child psychologist, describes the programme.

If there is resistance in the field of normal education to the idea of unqualified helpers being used in the teaching situation, there is a great deal more of it in the field of subnormal education.

Teachers feel that because of their qualifications they alone can teach the child efficiently, and efficient teaching should be the child's entitlement. How can an unqualified volunteer be efficient?

Teachers of handicapped children believe even more strongly that their specialist skills and qualifications are absolutely necessary for handling the particular and often very severe difficulties of their pupils. Volunteers do not have specialist skills. How can they be given a teaching role?

An understandable reaction, but given a recognition of the need of most handicapped children for individual tuition, and given that no authority could reasonably consider the expense of providing such tuition on the basis of one professional to each child, how can a satisfactory teacher/child ratio be achieved?

Parents of handicapped children face the dismal fact that as things stand their children's educational needs can never fully be met, and that their children cannot be helped to reach their full potential.

Most parents accept this position, albeit unwillingly. But three years ago one group of parents decided to do something positive to help their handicapped children. The group, calling themselves Kith and Kids, were already meeting once a fortnight for Sunday lunch. This gave them supportive help for themselves through discussion with other parents in a similar position; and at the same time a social environment for the handicapped children with normal brothers and sisters and friendly adults. The handicaps of their children vary widely, but nearly all have severe disabilities. They include ESN and SSN children, autistic children, cerebral palsied children, mongols, brain damaged children and even two partially sighted and one deaf child of normal intelligence. Out of their discussions grew a shared conviction that their children could all benefit from consistent

* [Ann Jones is now Ann Brechin.]

Source: *New Psychiatry*, 14 November, 1974, vol. 1, No. 5.

one-to-one attention over a period of time aimed at helping each child to progress in whatever area seemed most crucial for that child. No modest ambition, but an awareness shared by most parents of handicapped children. Kith and Kids have a way of turning their ambitions into reality and, faced with the impossibility of providing qualified help on a one-to-one ratio for their children, they had the courage and determination to try out their own revolutionary ideas. With the support of two professionals they rounded up a group of volunteers prepared to work for a period of a week on a one-to-one basis with a handicapped child. That was in 1972 and the experiment was a success. In 1973 it was repeated, and this summer 46 volunteers worked on a two-to-one basis with 23 handicapped children for a fortnight. The projects have been organised with increasing confidence, increasing efficiency and increasingly encouraging results.

The volunteers are unqualified, inexperienced and mostly young, usually senior schoolchildren or students but all are expected to fulfil a much more ambitious role than the usual unqualified helper of handicapped children who is restricted to a role of supervision and entertainment. The two-to-one ratio that has been achieved for the last two years may sound overwhelming for the child, but in fact it makes for an ideal situation. Working together, two volunteers give each other mutual support which is very necessary coming as they are to a new and challenging situation. It also enables each to observe the other working with the child, to make written observations, and to have time to plan what he might do with the child next.

Under the guidance of two professionals the volunteers aim to teach the child new skills. With the intention of making the child's adjustment to society easier, the emphasis is on social skills, an area often neglected in busy schools.

Achievements like tying one's own shoe laces, going on a bus journey, buying a packet of crisps, using a public toilet, knowing which clothes to wear on a hot day, or how to pour a drink of orange, how to cross a road or use a telephone are all skills which add one small measure of independence to the life of a child who is going to be basically dependent on others for the rest of his or her life. Skills normally acquired automatically with no conscious effort on the part of the adult who teaches or the child who is taught, pass by these handicapped children unless they are consciously and carefully taught.

The development of social skills was thus the main aim of the fortnight, but given such a wide range of disabilities, no blanket formula could be produced for the volunteers to apply to every child. Each child needed an individual written work-programme. These were drawn up by the two professionals, Mary Arkwright, an educational therapist, and myself, a child psychologist, and were based on Gunzberg charts completed by the parents, and in most cases on a personal knowledge of the child.

The volunteers therefore found themselves with widely varying tasks. Those assigned to Ian (an ESN 9 year old) worked generally on trying to slow down his impulsive behaviour and bring it under his control;

specifically on shoe lace tying and the handling of small amounts of money. By the end of the fortnight Ian was going to the toilet only three or four times a day instead of literally every ten minutes; he had also learnt to tie his own shoelaces and could add $\frac{1}{2}$p's, 1p's and 2p's. The helpers working with Gary (SSN, aged 8) tried among other things to teach him to ride his two-wheeler bike – an important matter of pride for a boy that age. They did not quite succeed, but he did learn how to start and stop without falling off, and how to use the brakes and the bell.

With Daniella, a talkative 14-year-old mongol, time was spent trying to direct her chatter on to comprehensive, communicative lines. Progress on teaching her how to use the telephone was aided by the discovery of her total confusion over the fact that the numbers on a telephone dial go the opposite way from numbers on a clock. With a much younger child, Vicky, aged 4, the helpers' task was to increase her attention span, her interest in voices and in making noises, and her manipulation of objects. They also tried to improve her ability to feed herself.

The essential thing was that the volunteers, who came to the project inexperienced but with boundless enthusiasm, were helped to channel that energy into systematic and structured activities geared to the individual needs of each child.

The support they had was two-fold. On the one hand there were the professionals. We held training sessions at which we explained the ideas and methods that would be used, and discussed the individual children and their work programmes with the volunteers. We were also present throughout the fortnight, watching, commenting, suggesting and answering any problems that arose, and holding an hour-long group discussion at the end of each day.

Richard Landis, a trainee teacher, was another source of supportive help and advice, operating from a resource room which contained everything from paint, paste and sticky paper, to boxes and newspapers. On the other hand there were the parents. The contact maintained between volunteers and parents was an essential part of the project. Only by constantly passing information to parents about problems or progress could the helpers have the feedback to know how realistically they were seeing the child. Vicky's helpers thought they were getting nowhere with language stimulation until they heard that she had started saying 'Da da' at home. Sometimes apparent progress was just a settling down to behaviour that was normal at home, or apparent difficulties were due to the child playing up a bit to a new adult. Often it was helpful to know how parents handled a tantrum, or introduced a new activity, and equally reassuring for volunteers to know that sometimes parents had found no way of coping with some behaviour problems.

One of the most valuable results of this constant two-way flow of information between volunteers and parents was that the volunteers ended up full of admiration for the way parents coped with having a handicapped child in their family. The intensive 'one-to-one' handling of children in this situation led to a real awareness of what it means to have a handicapped child – a sympathetic awareness too often lacking in teachers of the handicapped, who have a tendency to dismiss parents as either over-possessive or rejecting, without considering the problem from their point of view.

If the volunteers became more aware, they also became more skilled in handling their child: in understanding what they were trying to achieve and how to go about it. The nervousness of the first day was, without exception, replaced by enthusiasm and often great excitement as they shared the satisfaction of a new achievement, however small, with their child. It meant just as much that Simon moved over to help himself to a packet of biscuits, or that Victoria followed a dropped toy with her eyes, as it did that Ian and Kim both learned to tie their shoe laces, or that Mark remembered a three-item shopping list, helped to find the items in the confusion of a supermarket, and learned the fundamentals of telling the time. In the daily discussions it was clear that the volunteers were becoming adept at identifying their child's difficulties and were engrossed in finding realistic methods of dealing with them.

It all sounds like hard work for the children, but it had to be fun for it to work. And it was fun! Just how much is shown by Kim, up and dressed with shoes all laced by 6 a.m., pestering her parents to take her to the Two-to-One. The sheer enjoyment the children got from the fortnight was apparent above all else. Specific achievements apart, all the parents found their children becoming more alert, more responsive and more interested in what went on around them.

So within the fortnight the inexperienced volunteers became demonstrably useful in an educational role. Of course, given 46 qualified teachers to 23 handicapped children, the results might have been even more startling, though I doubt if professionals could have matched the volunteers for verve and enthusiasm, or created the same atmosphere of give-and-take with the parents.

If the experiment succeeded on one level – in stimulating individual development – it also succeeded on another level – in stimulating group development. Many handicapped children are unable to relate to others in a group, and a group game every afternoon was remarkably successful in many cases in producing an awareness of other children that did not exist before. It worked for the individual, it worked for the group, and, as an unforeseen bonus, it worked for the community. This approach has enormous implications for the possibility of a community approach to the problem of handicapped. As a result of this one fortnight alone 46 young people will never again shy away from a handicapped child. More specifically many of them are actually keeping in touch with their child and family, a fact of enormous importance to such socially isolated children. If holiday schemes like these spread, they could make all the difference to the success or failure of the current Government trend towards community care. Parents will go to great lengths to cope with their handicapped children, but they need help. Above all they need society to recognise their children's existence and to make a place for them, however minimal the child's contribution to society might be. Schemes like these would go a long way towards increasing public awareness of the needs of handicapped children.

As Kith and Kids see it, they started out with an idea so simple that it had to work – and it did. All it took was a group of determined parents asking around to find volunteers who were interested in spending a week or two in the summer with handicapped children; a kindly disposed school (in this case the Sainte Union de Sacre Coeur) to make premises available; a bit of fund-raising and some grant-seeking (Camden Council gave £500 and the Inner London Education Authority Youth Services £100) to cover professional fees, expenses for volunteers, and the cost of toys and equipment; and professionals prepared to work closely with parents and lay helpers, passing on their knowledge, in an attempt to find practical solutions to everyday problems.

So, this simple but revolutionary idea worked – and not only were all those involved in the project amazed by how well it worked, but the many visitors from various professions could not fail to be impressed by what they saw. The problem now is how to spread the idea. Already one meeting has been held for interested professionals. Parents can achieve a lot, as Kith and Kids have shown, but they also feel it is time more professionals (psychologists, educationalists, or any who see themselves as concerned with the development of handicapped children) stopped hiding behind the protective veil of their professional role and faced the much more exacting challenge of finding realistic solutions for the problems of handicapped children.

39 Housing and Disability

Bill Finlay

[Due to restrictions in space, we have been unable to include the results or conclusions of this survey in the extracts below. The findings represent a detailed and comprehensive account of 'housing disabilities' and interested parties are strongly advised to consult the original report.]

Introduction

This Report on the Housing Needs of Physically Handicapped People is based on the findings of a research project conducted in the Rochdale Metropolitan Borough between November 1977 and September 1978.

The investigation was restricted to this particular local authority's area because of the 'historical accident' which led to the formation in Rochdale of a group of physically impaired people, their relatives and friends, who were concerned at the existence of housing disabilities, rather than because the Sub-Committee believed that the experiences of physically handicapped people living there were significantly different from those experienced by similar people living in other local authorities' areas.

This group, which became the Housing and Disability Sub-Committee of Rochdale Voluntary Action in May 1977, successfully applied to the Manpower Services Commission, under its Job Creation Programme, for a grant to finance the research which they felt was needed. [. . .]

Naturally, the Sub-Committee's role as a locally-based pressure group also affected their decision to restrict their first venture into the world of research to an investigation within an area with which they had strong links. Despite the fairly small-scale at which the research was attempted, the Housing and Disability Sub-Committee believe and hope that the findings presented in their Report will prove to be of interest to bodies and individuals who will understandably be more concerned with the subject area of Housing and Disability as a whole, or as it manifests itself in their own areas or organisations, than they are with the particular experiences of physically handicapped people living in the Rochdale Metropolitan Borough. [. . .]

The Report is concerned with the interaction between physical handicap and that aspect of the physical environment which we call 'housing'. This interaction is referred to as 'housing disability' in those cases where innappropriate housing adds to the disabilities experienced by physically handicapped people. In the context of the Report, disability is defined as a

Source: *Housing and Disability* (1978) A report on the housing needs of physcially handicapped people in Rochdale, Rochdale Voluntary Action.

social rather than physical or medical phenomenon which takes insufficient account of the needs and potential abilities of people who are physically handicapped. Taken outside of the Report's context, 'disability' as a generic term could be used to describe any situation in which society takes insufficient account of the needs and potential abilities of any of its component minority groups. The housing disabilities identified by the research team were therefore only one facet of the disabilities experienced by that minority group within society who are identifiable by their physical handicaps. Moreover, these housing disabilities can be distinguished in that they are generated at two distinct but complexly inter-related levels of social interaction.

The more easily identifiable and demonstrable 'first level' is that at which there is an interaction between the physical needs and capabilities of individual physically handicapped people and their housing environments, which as a physical entity (in terms of such things as its range of sizes, layouts, fittings, component parts, and locations of houses, and markets provided for), represents the physical expression given to the aspirations and demands of the majority of the population for adequate shelter. At this level, the research objectives would be best met by emphasising the physical nature of housing, and measuring in some way or other the disabilities experienced by physically handicapped people in managing their own housing environments. The less easily identifiable and demonstrable disabling social interaction occurs at the 'second level' where the housing environments, occupied by physically handicapped people are combined into a distinguishable housing market composed of households with one or more physically handicapped members, which are initially disabled by their inability to manage their own housing environments but which are also and further disabled by both their own individual and collective inabilities to manage their housing 'sub-market', and also by the unresponsiveness of the managers of the various markets involved in providing accomodation more suitable to their needs and capabilities. At this level, the research objectives would be best met by emphasising the social role of housing, and assessing in some way or other the attitudes held by, and resources available to, the individuals and organisations responsible for providing and managing accommodation for physically handicapped people.

In practical terms, these two levels of disabling social interactions operate jointly. Thus research of one level of social interaction in isolation from the other cannot be expected to identify all of the factors at work which combined lead to that phenonemon defined as 'housing disability'. Unfortunately, it has not been possible to research both these levels of social interaction at the same time. This is because the grant, which was made available by the Manpower Services Commission, was not large enough to finance a research project which could investigate the total phenomenon of 'housing disability'. With the resources available, the Housing and Disability Sub-Committee was therefore obliged to establish and manage a research project into the more identifiable level of 'housing disability', that is the interaction between the capabilities of individual physically handicapped people and their own housing environments.

The Housing and Disability Sub-Committee do not believe that the findings presented in this Report are the only kind of contribution needed for physically handicapped people in order to promote and ensure an improvement to their housing conditions, although a sympathetic reading of these findings, and perhaps even more importantly a sympathetic understanding and appreciation of the concepts of handicap and disability employed in preparing this Report, might do much to reduce the 'political' need for an investigation into the 'second level' – i.e. the management of the housing needs of physically handicapped people – while at the same time not reducing the 'academic' value of such a complementary research project. But who are the 'managers' to whom this Report is therefore in part addressed?

Because of the limited resources available, the Housing and Disability Sub-Committee decided at an early stage in the research process that it would not be feasible to provide a framework for collecting data that would be equally applicable to both the housing needs of physically handicapped people living in a normal domestic situation (albeit in a house purpose-built or adapted to their particular needs), and those of similar people who for a variety of reasons might find themselves in a non-domestic situation, such as special residential or hospital-based accommodation.

It was therefore decided to restrict the research to an investigation of the needs of physically handicapped people living in the community rather than in partial or total physical isolation from it. Hence while technical and administrative details of housing disability were collected, that most fundamental housing need – the need for a suitable house and domicilary support services that would allow an institutionalised physically handicapped person to embark on a process of re-integration into the community – was not dealt with. Such people nonetheless can be seen to have a pressing housing need, which in fact is tantamount to homelessness, and for that reason the Housing and Disability Sub-Committee strongly believes that the Report is of as much relevance to the work of managers of accommodation provided for physically handicapped people in situations such as special hospital-based units, as it is to those involved in the management of the more typical housing markets relied upon by the majority of handicapped people.

The Report to some extent deals with the actual and potential overlap of support provided by the housing environment itself and the domiciliary services required to satisfy any needs left unmet by that housing environment. Many of the findings presented would seem to suggest that the present policy as to where the 'break' between the support roles of the physical housing environment and complementary domiciliary care should lie is not in a position best suited to the needs and capabilities of physically handicapped people themselves. But as argued above, there is also by implication an overlap at the 'second level' of social interaction which spans the interface between the provision of suitable accommodation for physically handicapped people in normal domestic and residential institutional-ised units of 'shelter'. Hence the reduction of housing disabilities achievable at the 'first level' of social interaction, via the provision of more thoughtfully designed units of housing that would reduce the disabilities experienced by both physically handicapped people and their helpers (whether the latter group contains paid domiciliary carers or not) would also necessarily create the potential for a complementary reduction in housing disabilities at the 'second level' of social interaction as it becomes increasingly more practical to re-integrate into the community physically handicapped people who previously had been obliged to rely upon the providers of special residential accommodation in their capacity as 'landlords of last resort'. The ways in which these reductions in housing disabilities might come about is outlined below.

At the 'first level' of interaction (i.e. that between the physical housing environment and the needs and capacities of individual physically handicapped people), housing disabilities would tend to be reduced with a switch in priority away from housing physically handicapped people in unsuitable accommodation and helping to compensate for the disabilities created by this action through the provision of domiciliary care support, towards providing the most suitable possible built environment and thereby reducing both their physical disabilities, as well as their social disabilities, i.e. their dependence upon someone else to perform tasks on their behalf.

By reducing these physical and social disabilities, stresses felt by the handicapped person, other members of his or her household, and helpers, would also probably be reduced. In those cases where stress might be a contributory factor to the disabilities experienced, such a policy if implemented might prove to be positively therapeutic. The reduction of physical disabilities through the provision of suitable accommodation might also lead to a situation in which the increasing sophistication of technical and domiciliary care support facilities, developed through the experience of implementation, makes it possible for the various authorities concerned to be able to provide for the housing needs of even the most severely handicapped and disabled people in their own domestic environments. Recent events such as those of the Younger Disabled Unit at Withington Hospital, Manchester, point to the possibility that this decision might already be capable of being realistically made.

At the 'second level' of interaction (i.e. that between the housing needs of all disabled people and the managers and providers of their accommodation and domiciliary support), housing disabilities would tend to be reduced with a change in emphasis from spending on current account; e.g. wages, salaries, administration, and so on, to spending on capital account; e.g. adaptations, fixtures, fittings, and purpose-built accommodation. While the latter course of action might involve considerable additional outlays in the short-term, the spending would be increasingly beneficial through the medium to long-terms as the overall stock of suitable accommodation increases and the demands for further capital expenditures decrease accordingly. The former course of action offers no prospect of increasing returns and benefits on expenditure, however, since by its very nature it relies upon the provision of services funded recurrently. Furthermore and with specific reference to the role of special residential institutions as 'accommodation of last resort', social disabilities will tend to reduce as physically handicapped people achieve the freedom to realistically choose between a continuing stay in such institutions and re-integrating into the community. It must be borne in mind that such institutions in general, and Younger Disabled Units in particular, do not exist in order to reduce the physical and social disabilities of handicapped people, but rather serve to increase them, for while certain aspects of their physical environments may be technologically suited to the needs of handicapped people, for example the provision of ramps for wheelchairs, extra-wide doorways, and lifts, their organisational regimes tend to socially and physically disable through the assumed dependence of the handicapped residents on the professional staff, and the expected submissiveness of the former to the latter. Thus any physically suitable attributes in their environments tend to be provided as aids to the staff rather than as opportunities for independence to the residents. Such regimes can therefore be seen to be disabling in themselves, in that they deliberately provide personal support to physically handicapped people even when it may be unnecessary in those cases where personal independence is a practical alternative. The social facet of this form of disability is commonly referred to as 'institutionalisation'. It cannot be compensated for by any amount of personal support, and in fact will tend to increase as the level of care support provided increases.

One final point concerning the role of the 'landlords of last resort' is that in attempting to compensate for housing disabilities, they are not so much providing for the most severely handicapped people, but rather for people, regardless of the nature of their handicaps, who are most disabled by the physical unsuitability of their present homes.[. . .]

Research Objectives and Concepts

The Housing and Disability Sub-Committee of Rochdale Voluntary Action was established in May 1977. Among the reasons which led to its formation was the opposition of its members to the proposal to build a Younger Disabled Unit in Rochdale. This opposition was prompted by their belief that the needs of disabled people, as they themselves perceived them, had not been solicited before the scheme had been adopted. At the same time, the Sub-Committee was becoming increasingly aware that the housing needs of all disabled people, and not just those who were severely disabled, had not been investigated properly. It believed that this lack of information had led to a situation in which the Local Authority and the Area Health Authority were obliged to base their policies on little more than rough estimates of the housing needs of disabled people, and that these estimates were themselves based upon records of expressed demands rather than actual needs for assistance. Unfortunately, the Sub-Committee was unable to attempt to satisfy all of its research objectives within a single project. It therefore decided to concentrate on those objectives that could be researched with a consumer survey of disabled people living in the Rochdale Metropolitan Borough. By way of a 'bonus', the survey method adopted also provided the potential to produce estimates on the total number of disabled people experiencing housing disabilities throughout the metropolitan district.

The Sub-Committee believed that an important contributory factor leading to the lack of information on housing needs was that the statutory bodies most directly involved were using concepts of handicap and disability that were both inadequate and misleading. In order to produce more useful estimates, its members believed that terms such as 'physical impairment', 'physical handicap' and 'physical disability', would have to be strictly defined so that any information obtained would be capable of analysis within a rational theoretical framework. It also believed that the attempt already made by the Office of Population Censuses and Surveys to define these terms was not very useful given their own research objectives, since these difinitions tended to suggest that the physical attributes of the housing environment (which the Sub-Committee believed to play a major part in the creation of housing disabilities) should be taken as given, and that the physical capabilities of disabled people should be measured against these constants. Taken to their logical conclusions, such definitions, when applied to policy formulation, would accommodate only those recommendations which could in some way improve the performance capacity of people, rather than that of their environments. The Sub-Committee, however, believed that a more useful approach would be to accept the physical capabilities of disabled people as given, and to measure against these the capacity of their housing environments to both accommodate these capabilities, and to compensate for any remaining incapacities. It therefore decided to accept and promote a re-definition of the terms that would incorporate these important concepts.

A number of possible approaches to conducting a survey of the housing needs of disabled people were considered. For a variety of reasons, the Sub-Committee finally decided to adopt an alternative which was based upon a house-by-house survey in certain parts of the Borough. These areas would be chosen so that, when combined, they would be fairly representative of the social, economic and housing characteristics to be found throughout the metropolitan district. This type of survey would both identify disabled people who might be prepared to respond to a second detailed questionnaire consumer survey into their housing needs, and would also provide information from which the incidence of housing disabilities, experienced throughout the Borough, might be estimated.

40 28–38 Grove Road: Accommodation and Care in a Community Setting

Ken Davis

Founder Member of the Disablement Information and Advice Line

Introduction

In Great Britain we have a habit of providing for 'difficult' minority groups in segregated institutions and those suffering traumatic tetraplegia are no exception. It is a tradition which has roots in the Poor Law and which comes down to us today virtually unchanged. Only rarely can someone who depends heavily on others for personal help, and who for some reason does not have the support of – or wishes to live independently of – his or her family, find an alternative system of accommodation and care: 28–38 Grove Road is a fresh approach and this paper attempts to convey a little about the tenants' view of the scheme; the objectives it set out to achieve; and how the scheme works in practice.

Physical Features

On the surface, 28–38 Grove Road appears merely to be a group of six fairly ordinary two storey flats. They occupy a corner-plot at the junction of Grove Road with another undistinguished street in a typical Midlands industrial town. Underneath however, things are not quite as ordinary as they at first appear.

The three ground floor flats are specially designed for occupation by physically handicapped tenants. They are linked to the three first floor flats by a speech intercom system which is sufficiently flexible to allow any given tenant to communicate with any other tenant in the building. The upper flats are designed to be let to the ablebodied 'supporting families' who are willing to co-operate with all the other tenents in providing a background of personal help to those tenants who happen to be physically handicapped.

The interior design of the ground floor flats contains features nowadays becoming more common in 'wheelchair housing.' For instance, the corner worktop in the kitchen allows access to sink and hob unit without the need to move position. But the generally unobtrusive nature of the design features and items of equipment tends to conceal the careful thought underlying them. The level top of the hob allows hot pans to be slid across to the sink –

Source: Paper presented at the Second European Conference of Rehabilitation International, September 18–21, 1978. Sevenoaks: Naidex Conventions.

an important point for people with paralysed hands and fingers. And details such as the shape and siting of knobs, switches and handles were all important for the same reason. The electric hoist, in combination with the integral WC/douche, exerted a considerable influence on the design of the units. It was necessary to provide a method of transfer from bedroom straight to bathroom and thus the track hoist dictated the relationship between these two rooms.

There are too many design details to enumerate here, but it can be judged from this very brief description that a good deal of effort was made to create an environment which would enable the fulfilment of a specific goal. That goal was to provide a living situation for people hitherto considered too physically handicapped to live in their own homes in the community. It hinged on the simple idea that there should exist ordinary families willing to co-operate with disabled people in providing support not otherwise available.

Objectives

The immediate reason for the development of this idea stems from an attempt by a tetraplegic couple, and others, to find a practical solution to their accommodation and care problems which could enable them to get married. Marriage, in itself, is still a fairly familiar story – but dependent, handicapped couples approaching such a point in their relationship, rarely carry it through. Without going into personalities, that was not the chosen approach. As a consequence, there began a long and sometimes very difficult search for the solution which is the subject of this paper.

The character of this solution came about for a number of definite reasons. I have already noted the propensity in our society to provide the socially neat and tidy institutional means of solving the accommodation and care needs of dependent handicapped people who may be without family support. It is probably not surprising to find that some of the disabled people initially involved in the concept of this scheme were already in institutional care, and that the concept was a reaction to that situation.

With this in mind, it is interesting to refer to the objectives formulated by the disabled (then prospective) tenants of the scheme. They attempted to analyse the situation they were in, drawing out what they saw to be desirable objectives, as follows:

1 Institutions disable physically impaired people by taking them out of the community and aim to cater for their physical needs in batches, under the same roof and under the same regime.

   Thus the design of the scheme should not make the building stand out as 'special' for the disabled and should blend into the local community. It should cater for handicapped tenants' physical needs in the privacy of their own homes, in a way which encouraged and supported their independence and individuality.

2 Institutions are provided ostensibly because, in the absence of family support, statutory domiciliary services are insufficiently comprehensive and flexible to meet the physical needs of severely handicapped people in their own homes in the community.

Thus the community based alternative had to embody a system of help sufficient to make up for the deficiencies in locally available services in meeting tenants' physical needs.

3 Institutions have a hierarchy of paid staff who organise and provide help which is theoretically available to inmates all the time – whether or not it is wanted by them, or appropriate to their real needs.

Thus the help provided in the scheme should correspond to the help needed. The handicapped tenants should best know their own physical needs but, since any dependency situation involves a relationship between helper and helped, the organisation of – and payment for – help should be decided co-operatively between the people concerned.

4 Institutions are dependency oriented. Staff see themselves primarily in a helping role and inmates as the dependent recipients of care. Comprehensive aids to independence are rarely provided or, if provided, used, by either residents or staff.

Thus the scheme should be oriented towards independence through inter-tenant co-operation. Helpers should see themselves primarily in a supporting role, and aids and equipment appropriate to the individual needs of handicapped tenants should be provided.

5 Institutions occasionally allow inmates the opportunity to present limited views on aspects of organisation. But fully democratic participation in areas where inmates can usefully contribute is often actively discouraged.

Thus there should be maximum opportunity for all tenants to bring their personal resources into the scheme and exercise effective democratic control in clearly defined areas over their living situation.

The initiators drew on their wider experience of disability in formulating guiding principles to help them gain these objectives. Aware that disabled people and their families frequently have to put up with what other people thought best for them, they decided to rely heavily on their own experience in formulating an answer to their problem – and seek to create the conditions for consultation and participation with any party who could help them produce a solution.

Aspects of Participation

Four years elapsed from inception to completion, an eventful period which holds a story of its own. There were key events along the way: gaining the interest and co-operation of the (then) Inskip St Giles Housing Association; obtaining the agreement of the local church to the sale of the site of the derelict St Bartholomew's Mission; gaining loan sanction from Ashfield

District Council; receiving the support of the Social Services Department; and participating with the architects of the Wyvern Partnership on aspects of the design.

The Architect's view on the value of participation is very clear. He notes that contact with the real client (the user) as well as the actual client (the Housing Association) is of the greatest assistance in solving problems which otherwise would be left to the architect to work out in unsure isolation. He observes that, in the Grove Road project, having contact with the spokesman and co-ordinator for individual requirements (one of the tetraplegic tenants) was particularly helpful in providing detailed solutions for those tenants who were known in advance.

But problems can follow from this point about known potential tenants for schemes in process of development. For tenants there is the real problem of holding a number of people together over a long period, where the hope of a tenancy lies at some unspecified future date. The Architect, aware of this problem, notes how important it is to adopt plan arrangements and fitment details which are sufficiently flexible to allow for changes of prospective tenants. For the Housing Association, there is the possibility that a given participant could develop views different from those of the other prospective tenants on how the scheme could operate and, notwithstanding, attempt to lay legal claim to the implicit promise of a tenancy. All of these problems had to be faced during the development of the Grove Road Scheme. With the benefit of hindsight, it is important that everyone connected with innovatory schemes should be agreed on and subscribe to the concept and objectives as early as possible in the development.

The Scheme in Operation

The scheme has now been operating successfully for two years. During this time the tenants have dealt with matters of common interest through the medium of their association, the St Bartholomew's Tenants Group. The main business handled by the Group concerns the management of services to the common parts of the building, various functions which serve to foster good neighbourly relations in the local community, the organisation of, and payment for the 'supporting family' element of the support system, and initial tenant selection. Concerning the latter, advertising for, and initial screening of potential incoming tenants is conducted by the Group, who then make recommendations to the Housing Association for follow-up in accordance with their own tenancy selection procedures. Meetings of the Tenants Group are also a general forum: a medium for mutual education of individual and group needs.

Clearly it is necessary to have the right tenants, who understand the concept and objectives of the scheme, if it is to function properly. Because of the importance of this, special conditions of tenancy were drawn up which make it clear that occupancy of all flats in the scheme is dependent on all tenants accepting a co-operative basis of giving and receiving assistance.

The support system gives an indication of the extent of fall-back in the event of care failure at any point:

1 Locally available statutory services, eg, District Nurses and Home Helps.
2 Three supporting families co-operating with the handicapped tenants to give help not covered by statutory services.
3 Local voluntary support, eg, WRVS, the Community Service Scheme and local schools community projects.
4 Neighbours, relatives and friends living locally.
5 Selective hire of agency nurses.

However, the handicapped tenants regard their own self-sufficiency as the first line of support. But overall, the intention is to 'spread the load' and avoid the typical situation which arises where there is disability in the family, where breakdown occurs because of the unremitting strain borne principally by one or two people.

It has never been necessary to resort to the fifth tier, and it is interesting to note that the disabled tenants greatly over-estimated the amount of help they would need. The case of the tetraplegic couple is typical: prior to moving in, and based on their experience of institutional care, they anticipated a combined weekly need of 2 hours from the District Nurse, 4 hours from the Home Help, and almost 20 hours personal help from supporting families. From their first day in residence, they were able to manage without help from the District Nurse. Whilst their assessed need for the services of the Home Help was realistic, their call on supporting families in the first week totalled only 8 hours – a figure which gradually reduced to an average of $1\frac{1}{2}$ hours a week by the end of the first year.

Nevertheless, the de-institutionalisation process is difficult and exhausting: breaking conditioned dependency patterns does not happen without effort. Many factors help the process along however, including a degree of individual motivation. But plain, practical considerations lie at the heart of the matter. Good basic design coupled with aids and equipment appropriate to individual needs, reduce the need to call for personal help and maximise potential for independence. This in turn maintains harmony within the scheme: calls for assistance are seen to be necessary and supporting families know they are not simply being 'used'.

Examples of new-found independence are many: typical is the example of two female tetraplegic tenants. Over a combined institutional experience of 23 years, neither had ever dressed or undressed or been able to transfer to or from wheelchair to bed or WC. Now, using the track hoist in conjunction with ingeniously designed clothes and fastenings, both perform these functions completely independently. Or again, people previously considered too disabled to look after themselves, now prepare and cook meals as a matter of course.

The 'supporting family' element of the support system is readily adaptable to meet changing needs. These needs now consist mainly of help with shopping, small emergencies, minor help with dressing, and other personal needs. Still important for handicapped tenants is the security of knowing that there is always someone available to help, if necessary. A payment system has evolved to compensate the first floor tenants for help given and inconvenience caused.

As the tenants have remarked: a touch of flair and a lot of know-how on the part of the Housing Association, combined with patient, empathetic co-operation on the part of the architect, has gradually turned a simple idea into a reality. That reality is a home of their own, on the same terms as other people – and the benefits are almost beyond calculation.

Bibliography

CENTRE ON ENVIRONMENT FOR THE HANDICAPPED (1978) *Design for Special Needs*, May–August, No. 16.
ST BARTHOLOMEW'S TENANTS GROUP (1977) '28–38 Grove Road, Sutton in Ashfield.' Paper to accompany ATV 'Link' programme, 1977.

41 DIAL UK: Development of the National Association of Disablement Information and Advice Services

Ken Davis, Co-ordinator

James I. Woodward, Development Officer

Open information is the raw material of knowledge. Knowledge is the basic tool needed to participate effectively in any activity or social organisation. The movement in the United Kingdom to provide a network of local information and advice services promotes the provision of free access to open information.

In the absence of open information disabled people cannot effectively participate in their society. Few people would deny the need for such active participation and therefore the need to supply open information. We contend that the most effective way to disseminate such information is to provide it at the local level. Here, at the local level, free and impartial information can be given direct to anyone concerned with disability. This basic commodity is what the National Association of Disablement Information and Advice Services offers, inter alia, through its associated local groups.

A lack of information is a situation generally shared by most citizens in the UK. We have no legislation which provides for free access to information, such as in the USA, or elsewhere. In Sweden, for example, hospital patients have the right of access to their case notes, as well as ward meetings to discuss their case. Such restrictive practices in the UK exacerbate the situation of physically impaired people who have specific information needs. The National Association has come to recognise that the way such information is collated, presented and disseminated – or sometimes deliberately suppressed – actually disables physically impaired people.

We have, therefore, developed a concept of 'information disability' which breaks with the traditional medico-sociological models exemplified by Jefferys[1] or Agerholm[2]. This tradition is illustrated by its attention to the individual and his or her functional impairment. The effects on the individual of the social organisation within which he participates are largely ignored. To focus on the nature of our social organisation produces a fresh perspective on our circumstances. The physically impaired person who vitally needs open access to specialist information frequently finds mystification instead of matter-of-factness; complexity instead of clarity; secrecy instead of salience or ignorance where there should be knowledge.

Source: Paper presented at the Fourteenth World Congress of Rehabilitation International, Winnipeg, Canada, 1980.

These facts are deeply embedded in our social relations.

As I have implied, to the extent that most people in the UK are denied access to open information, most people are disabled by it accordingly. But for those such as people who are physically impaired, where access to specialist information is crucial to meaningful participation, there is a significant distinction. Information disability is a specific form of social oppression. In practice, it results in the disadvantage or restriction of activity caused – not by the impairment of the individual – but by the way in our society we present, or withhold, information and prevent opportunity for full participation in the mainstream of social life. Within the field of rehabilitation moves towards social definitions have not been so generally aired. Within the U.K. the social definition of disability has been expounded mainly by the Union of the Physically Impaired against Segregation.[3] In their booklet '*Fundamental Principles of Disability*' they state:

In our view it is society which disables physically impaired people. Disability is something imposed on top of our impairments by the way we are unnecessarily isolated and excluded from full participation in society. Disabled people are therefore an oppressed group in society. To understand this it is necessary to grasp the distinction between the physical impairment and the social situation, called disability, of people with such impairments. Thus we define impairment as lacking part of or all of a limb, or having a defective limb, organ or mechanism of the body; and disability as the disadvantage or restriction of activities caused by a contemporary social organisation which takes no or little account of people with physical impairment and thus excludes them from participating in the mainstream of social activities. Physical disability is therefore a particular form of social oppression (these definitions are based on those of Harris but differ from them significantly).

Three points arise from these definitions, one, that disability is extraneous from physical impairment, two, that disability is imposed upon the individual by the society which does not accommodate his situation. [. . .] The third point arising from the social definition of disability, is that it is a phenomenon which can be *overcome*. Therefore the situation facing DIAL UK is the challenge of struggling to overcome 'information disability'. The organisation of specialised information which is its concern, has to be made thoroughly intelligible and accessible to all with an interest in this field. [. . .]

It is worth noting that in the case of the Union of the Physically Impaired, [. . .] and in the case of the growth of DIAL UK, we have instances of disabled people participating in matters affecting their lives and, through such participation, they themselves are defining their own problems and discovering solutions to them. Therefore, this Paper is describing a developing scenario of which DIAL UK is an integral part. Disability is now defined in terms of specific spheres of life and is seen as an imposition by society upon the individual whose circumstances society does not accommodate. Finally we find the scene describing a state in which the physically impaired person may be equated to other disabled people in society who find themselves in the same situation, although for different reasons.

Within the United Kingdom there has been an organisation for several years which tries to provide information and advice to a multitude of people with different problems. This organisation is called The Citizens Advice Bureau. However, as society becomes more and more complicated information resources become more and more numerous and knowledge becomes more and more technical and specific, there is a need, to-day, for this general information service to have as a back-up several information services of a more specific nature.

Within the field of rehabilitation the historical development from the policy of institutionalisation of the physically impaired, to that of an integrated care system within the community, has, as its wake, a growth of services and provisions which are extremely complicated for the individually impaired person to comprehend. Warren[4], for example, has stated the necessity for an educational imput within rehabilitation to aid such comprehension. He states:

the one thing which is certain about any person who suddenly becomes disabled is that after the accident they are going to rely more on their brains than they did previously. In spite of this almost all active time in hospital is devoted to physical training and in between physical sessions most patients sit about bored. As part of the programme on increasing reliance on the mind there should be more information and communication outlining the confusing array of welfare services for the disabled

In this article he describes the intricate network of health and welfare organisations, passage through which is full of danger. One can so easily get lost or left up a blind alley or completely fall through the net.

This was the situation in 1976 which Ken Davis discovered for himself when he was living in an institution. He became aware of the additional problems caused by lack of information among his fellow inmates and users of the Centre. He realised that, in the community, it was even more likely that information disability would be more prevalent among those isolated from contact with the Centre or other services. He, therefore, set about with others, in establishing a telephone information service specialising in matters related to physical impairment. Over a six months period the idea developed more comprehensively to embrace the notion of a free, impartial and confidential service of information, advice, practical help and counselling to anyone–lay or professional, able or disabled in the local community. DIAL Derbyshire was born, the letters standing for Disablement Information and Advice Line.

The service caught the imagination of others. It was by no means the first specialist information service for the physically impaired, but it came at a time in the UK of a general growth of interest in the subject. In October, 1977, a seminar was held to explore and exploit this interest. The result was the beginning of a national network of DIAL-type services. By June, 1978, a Steering Committee was elected from representatives of local DIAL groups to form a National Association of Disablement Information and Advice Services – now known colloquially as DIAL UK. Its aim is to facilitate the spread of a network of local services so that physically impaired people are not disabled due to lack of intelligible information and informed advice anywhere in the UK.

At the same time a further committee known as DIAL Information was set up to co-ordinate up-to-date and accurate information necessary to local services to operate efficiently.

These developments culminated in the appointment of a Development Officer and the opening of a National Office in Derbyshire, England, to cover the whole of the United Kingdom.

The future of DIAL UK lies in the growth of the network of local groups. It is essential that disabled people actively participate in these groups and that the groups are independent and autonomous. The development of a democratic regionalised structure ensures a service of high calibre by the constant appraisal of minimum standards through the regional study days and conferences. Cross-fertilisation of ideas is not only maintained through such meetings but by means of a house journal which channels the multiplicity of information sources into the DIAL network.

In the close future there are plans to link every DIAL office to a central computer which can be regularly updated *pari passu* with information changes. Ready access will be by a simple telephone call to the computer and the required information will be received on a TV terminal situated in each office. The advantage of this system is that the enquirer has an interface with the computer and can therefore request interpretation of the information on the spot.

By using this system, called 'Prestel', DIAL UK will be able to integrate its service with other information-providing services using the same system.

In this manner a general information service can accommodate the specific requirements of any individual, disabled in any form in any sphere of life.

References

1 JEFFERYS, M. *et al.* (1969) 'A set of tests for measuring motor impairment in prevalence studies.' *The Journal of Chronic Diseases, 22.*
2 AGERHOLM, M. (1975) 'The identification and evaluation of long-term handicap.' Paper delivered to the Medico-Legal Society, London, 10 April.
3 *Fundamental Principle of Disability.* Union of the Physically Impaired Against Segregation and Disability Alliance, London.
4 WARREN, J. R. 'The Incurable Optimist.' (1972) Disablement Income Group Occasional Paper No. 14.

INDEX

Subject

Author

Copyright Acknowledgements

The editors and publisher wish to thank the following for permission to reprint copyright material in this book:

University of Pittsburgh Press for extracts reprinted from Constantina Safilios-Rothschild, 'Disabled Persons' Self-Definitions and Their Implications for Rehabilitation,' in *The Sociology of Physical Disability and Rehabilitation*, Gary L. Albrecht, Editor. Published in 1976 by University of Pittsburgh Press; Lexington Books for extracts from *Social Aspects of Mental Retardation* (1977) by Richard Kurtz; Marion Boyars Publishers Ltd for extracts from 'Professionalized Service and Disabling Help' by John McKnight from I. Illich *et al* (1977) *Disabling Professions*; *Magic Carpet* for 'To deny or not to deny disability' by Vic Finkelstein, New Year 1975, *xxvii*(1); International Association for the Scientific Study of Mental Deficiency and the authors for extracts from 'The Mentally Retarded – Valuable Individuals or Superfluous Population?' from *Research to Practice in Mental Retardation* (1977), edited by P. Mittler, University Park Press; Frances Pinter (Publishers) Ltd for an extract from *The Use of Technology in the Care of the Elderly and the Disabled* (1980) edited by J. Bray and S. Wright; Michael Oliver for his paper presented at the Second European Conference of Rehabilitation International, September 18–21, 1978; United Nations for extracts from *Social Barriers to the Integration of Disabled Persons into Community Life* (1977); Scottish Council for Spastics for extracts from *You Tell Me* (1977) by M. B. Davidson; The Southern and Western Regional Association for the Blind for 'Relationship and sexual problems of the visually handicapped' by Susan Hicks from *Regional Review*, Spring 1979, No. 65; Yale University Press and the author for extracts from '"The ordinary devoted mother" and her blind baby' from *The Psychoanalytic Study of the Child*, 1979, *34*; The Editor of *Hearing* for extracts from 'Using two aids' by Peter O'Neil, 1979, *34*, No. 2; Souvenir Press for extracts from *Kith and Kids* (1976) by M. and D. Collins; The National Fund for Research into Crippling Diseases for extracts from *Integrating the Disabled* (1980); Richard Gormley and Larry Walters for their paper presented at the Second European Conference of Rehabilitation International, September 18–21, 1978; Spastics International Medical Publications for extracts from M. Oswin (1978) *Children Living in Long-stay Hospitals*. London: SIMP with Heinemann Medical; Philadelphia: Lippincott; Gower Publishing for extracts from 'Power and Inanity' by Mildred Blaxter in *Relationships Between Doctors and Patients* edited by A. Davis; The Chartered Society of Physiotherapy and the authors for extracts from 'Community physiotherapy in a rural area' from *Physiotherapy*, 1980, *66*, No. 1; *Early Childhood* and the authors for an extract from 'The role of a "family group" nursery', 1980,

1(2); Associated Scientific Publishers and the authors for extracts from 'Parents as a Resource in Diagnosis and Assessment' by E. Newson and 'Honeylands – a Family Help Unit in Exeter' by J. Rubissow (now Carlyle) in *Early Management of Handicapping Disorders*, edited by T. E. Oppé and F. P. Woodford; John Wiley and Sons Ltd and the authors for extracts from *Preventing Classroom Failure* (1980) by M. Ainscow and D. A. Tweddle; The author for extracts abstracted from Part II: The Clinical Attitude in Britain, in *The Clinical Attitude in Rehabilitation: A Cross-Cultural View* (in preparation) by Joseph Stubbins; University Center for International Rehabilitation, Michigan State University, and the author for extracts from 'The Movement for Independent Living: Origins, Ideology, and Implications for Disability Research, by Gerben DeJong; The Controller of Her Majesty's Stationery Office for extracts from the Social Services Committee Session 1979/80 *Perinatal and Neonatal Mortality* (HC 590, 493 i, ii,) *Mental Handicap Nursing and Care* (Cmnd 7468–1), and DES: *Special Needs in Education* (White Paper 1980) (crown copyright); Basil Blackwell Publisher and the authors for extracts from *Charter for the Disabled* (1979) by E. Topliss and B. Gould; Michael Bayley for his article in *New Society*, 25 October 1973; Jean Simkins for her paper presented at the Second European Conference of Rehabilitation International, September 18–21, 1978; Macmillan Journals Ltd and the author for 'Volunteer teaching: kith and kids' by Ann Jones from *New Psychiatry*, 14 November, 1974, *1*(5); Rochdale Voluntary Action for extracts from *Housing and Disability* (1978) by Bill Finlay; Ken Davis for his paper presented at the Second European Conference of Rehabilitation International, September 18–21, 1978; National Association of Disablement Information and Advice Services and the authors for extracts from the paper presented by Ken Davis and James I. Woodward at the Fourteenth World Congress of Rehabilitation International, Winnipeg, Canada, 1980.